TAPE RECORDINGS

The authors have recorded on two five-inch tapes ($3\frac{3}{4}$ i.p.s. 9.5 cm.p.s) a representative sample of the material given in Chapters IV and V and the first six dialogues in Chapter VI. To indicate the passages recorded from Chapters IV and V the sign

$$\bullet$$

is placed in the left-hand margin against the relevant verbal contexts. In all cases the *Verbal Context*, as well as the *Drill*, is spoken. The tapes are published by Longman Group Limited and are obtainable direct from the publisher or through any bookseller.

INTONATION OF COLLOQUIAL ENGLISH

Intonation of Colloquial English

A practical handbook

J. D. O'CONNOR, B.A.
and
G. F. ARNOLD, B.A.

Readers in Phonetics
University College London

LONGMAN

Longman Group Ltd.

London

Associated companies, branches, and
representatives throughout the world.

© J. D. O'Connor and G. F. Arnold 1961
Second edition © Longman Group Ltd. 1973

First published 1961
Second edition 1973

ISBN 0 582 52389 3

Printed in Great Britain by
Western Printing Services Ltd.
Bristol

Contents

Contents

Preface

Though we hope that it will appeal to a more diverse circle of readers, this *Intonation of Colloquial English* is intended first and foremost for the foreign learner of English. It is essentially a practical text-book and it is designed to help the foreign learner to a more thorough and, eventually, more instinctive command of the intonation patterns which native Southern British English speakers commonly use in their everyday conversational speech. This general aim we have endeavoured to further in various ways. In the first place we have limited our discussion of intonation theory to an indispensable minimum, so as to be able to include the maximum amount of drill material. Secondly we have restricted this drill material to the kinds of sentences which the foreign learner is likely to find useful, and is certain to meet at some time or another, when conversing with English people. Consequently we have included no narrative or descriptive prose though, of course, the intonation patterns, appropriate for that kind of material, also occur in conversational speech and therefore find a place in this book. Thirdly we have emphasised this exclusively conversational approach to our subject by presenting every drill sentence with some indication of the speech situation in which it might be used. This we believe to be very important since, not only will the foreign student now be able to learn the tunes, he will also be able to learn at the same time *when* to use them.

Notwithstanding this bias towards the needs of the foreign learner, this book will, we hope, also offer something to those whose interest in English intonation is more academic. While the chapter dealing with the anatomy of English intonation will perhaps contain little that is new to readers already familiar with the writings of, for example, Dr. H. E. Palmer, and Mr. R. Kingdon, our treatment of intonation and meaning will, we believe, make some contribution towards the general understanding of the functions of intonation in English. In the past much has been written about English intonation in terms of sentence structure. If, in Chapter II, we appear to have emphasised the relation between intonation and speaker's attitude, it is merely that we have sought to redress the balance and to show that sentence structure and speaker's attitude both play a very important part in determining intonation pattern.

At the same time we freely and gratefully acknowledge the debt we owe to all those who have preceded us in the field of English intonation studies; their names are well-known but too numerous to list here. We must however record our special indebtedness to Mr. R. Kingdon whose system of tone-marks we have in some large measure adopted. There are however certain major differences between his system and the one used in this book. We must therefore emphasise that where we have departed from Mr. Kingdon's system we have done so on our own responsibility and that such changes as we have made should in no way be construed as representing Mr. Kingdon's views.

J. D. O'CONNOR
G. F. ARNOLD

University College London
   October, 1959

Preface to the Second Edition

In the thirteen years since we finished writing the first edition of this book a good deal of water has flowed under the intonation bridge; the importance of the published work in the field and the friendly criticism we have had from our colleagues and students have convinced us that changes are called for. Two of these changes are of some importance, the remainder are matters of re-ordering and notation.

The major changes are that we have introduced the idea of emphasis as a tone group feature and we have loosened the tie between accent and pitch change. Consequently we now consider that accent in the head of an unemphatic tone group is achieved by stress alone, without the help of pitch change; and that stress and pitch change, when they co-occur in the head of a tone group, not only accent the stress-bearing words but also confer emphasis on the tone group as a whole. For unemphatic tone groups we now establish four heads: Low, High, Falling and Rising. In the first edition the Low Head had two complementary forms: a rising form before the High Fall and a low-pitched level form before the Low Fall and the Low Rise. These two forms we now regard as two entirely separate features: the Low Head [ˌ], which is always low, and the Rising Head [ˌ], which has an emphatic form called the Climbing Head. The unemphatic High and Falling Heads are new, but they have a link with the first edition in that their respective emphatic forms are the old Stepping and Sliding Heads.

These changes have entailed the introduction of some new symbols, [ₒ], [°] and [ˌ], the redefinition of the scope of others, [ˈ], [ˈ] and [ˌ], and the disappearance of both [ˈ] and [ˌ]. These are fully explained in the text. Also, we have now overtly recognised a Mid-Level nuclear tone, which is marked by the new symbol [ʔ].

We still deal with ten tone groups, but their pitch features and the attitudes which we associate with them do not correspond exactly with those of the original ten. For this reason and also because we have found that numbers as labels are not easily remembered, we have given the tone groups names. It may be helpful to set out the correspondences between the new and old tone groups here.

The new Jackknife, Take-Off, Low Bounce, High Bounce and Switchback correspond exactly to the old Tone Groups 5, 6, 7, 8 and 9 respectively. The new Low Drop includes most elements of both the old Tone Groups 1 and 2: only the combination Low Head plus Low Fall of Tone Group 1 has been omitted on the grounds that it is not very useful to the foreign learner. Similarly, the High Drop has all the elements of old Tone Groups 3 and 4 except the combination Low Head (rising variant) plus High Fall of Tone Group 3. This combination, with the head renamed Rising, is the main constituent of the new Long Jump. The High Dive corresponds to old Tone Group 10, minus certain forms which we think it more helpful to regard as sequences of tone groups. Finally the Terrace, with its Mid-Level nuclear tone, is new as an independent tone group.

The order in which the tone groups are presented has been somewhat modified. It is our experience that the new order in Chapters II and IV is a more valid list of priorities for the foreign learner.

We have also introduced a new section on tone group sequences, together with associated drills for them.

We hope that these changes will make the book more comprehensive and no less useful for both the beginner and the advanced student; and we would like to thank all those who, by their writings or in discussion, have helped us so greatly in re-formulating our ideas.

J. D. O'C.
G. F. A.

University College London
April, 1972

I The Anatomy of English Intonation

No language that we know of is spoken on a monotone; in all languages there are variations of pitch, though not all languages use these pitch variations in the same way. When we talk about English intonation we mean the pitch patterns of spoken English, the speech tunes or melodies, the musical features of English. All that is written here in this book—as indeed in any other book on intonation—is based on three major premises:

1. *Intonation is significant.* Utterances which are different only in respect of intonation may, as a result, differ from each other in meaning. The same phrase may be said in a downright, or a reserved, or a questioning tone of voice, amongst others.

2. *Intonation is systematic.* We do not invent the words that we use in speaking, nor do we invent the sounds of which they are composed; we learn them, mainly in childhood, and spend the rest of our lives using the same words and the same sounds. Similarly we do not invent tunes as we go along; we use tunes which we originally learned as children, and we do not choose them or use them at random. There is a limited number of pitch patterns in any one language, and we use them to produce definite meaningful effects. It is therefore possible to describe frequently recurring patterns of pitch and to give rules for their use.

3. *Intonation is characteristic.* The pitch patterns or tunes of English are not necessarily the same in form as those of other languages, nor do they necessarily produce the same effect as they would in other languages, though there may be resemblances here and there. This being so, the pitch patterns of any other language may, and very often do, sound wrong if they are applied to English, and give rise to difficulties in communication. In the first place, the use of a tune which is not normally used in English will give a foreign accent to the speech and may make understanding difficult; secondly, and

more serious, the use of a tune which *is* used in English but in different circumstances will lead to misunderstandings and possible embarrassment. As an example of this latter type of danger, the phrase *Thank you* may be said with one tune which makes it sound genuinely grateful, and with a different tune which makes it sound rather casual. Now if the foreign learner unintentionally uses the casual form when an English listener feels entitled to the other one, then the listener may get a very bad impression, since he will probably assume that the casual effect given by the tune was the one which the speaker deliberately set out to give. This is very important— English speakers are able to make a good deal of allowance for imperfect sound-making, but being for the most part unaware of the far-reaching effects of intonation in their own language, they are much less able to make the same allowance for mistakenly used tunes. The result is that they may hold the foreigner responsible for what his intonation *seems* to say—as they would rightly hold an Englishman responsible in a similar case—even though the tune does not faithfully reflect his intention.

WORD GROUPS   In the sentence *Even if he does come he won't be able to stay very long* there is a clear grammatical division between the two clauses *Even if he does come* and *he won't be able to stay very long*, even though the division is not marked in any way in the writing. In speech, however, the grammatical division *is* marked, and it is marked by intonation. The pattern of pitch which accompanies the first clause will be recognised by an English listener as in some way complete and it will hold the clause together as a unit and separate it from the following clause, which will also be held together by intonation. But it is not always a matter of clauses. In *That extraordinary-looking woman by the door is John's aunt* the whole subject of the sentence *That extraordinary-looking woman by the door* would normally be presented as a unit by means of intonation, with the predicate *is John's aunt* treated as a separate unit. And in *As a matter of fact, I hardly know him* the opening phrase will most often be divided from the main clause, again through the intonation. We need some neutral term to refer to these groups of words which are grammatically relevant—they are not always clauses or subjects or phrases—and the term we shall use in this book is simply *word groups*. So *Even if he does come* is a word group, and so are *he won't be able to stay very long* and *That extraordinary-looking woman by the door* and so on.

Sometimes the number of word groups we choose to use may be important for the meaning. For example, *My sister who lives in Edinburgh has just had twins* may mean two different things. In writing the difference would be marked by punctuation; in speech it is marked by using either two or three word groups. If the meaning is: 'My only sister, who happens to live in Edinburgh . . .', then the division would be into three word groups:

My sister, | *who lives in Edinburgh,* | *has just had twins.* ‖

On the other hand, if the meaning is: 'That one of my several sisters who lives in Edinburgh . . .', the division is into only two word groups:

My sister who lives in Edinburgh | *has just had twins.* ‖

Similarly in *She dressed and fed the baby.* As one word group, it is the baby which is both dressed and fed; in two word groups:

She dressed, | *and fed the baby.* ‖

the word group *She dressed* is equivalent to 'She dressed herself'.

There is often some choice in how we divide up utterances into word groups. In *My father was born in Manchester* the subject *My father* may or may not form a separate word group, and similarly in *If you like I'll tell him* the two clauses may be separated or not. *April, June, September and November all have thirty days* may be

April | *June* | *September* | *and November* | *. . .* or
April June September and November | *. . .*

This kind of division into word groups by means of intonation occurs in all languages and there is nothing difficult about either the principle or practice of it, even in those cases where a choice is possible.

In our examples we use the single bar [|] to separate word groups which have a very close grammatical connection, and the double bar [‖] at the end of utterances which are not closely connected to what follows. For example:

When I got there | the bus had left. ‖ I was furious. ‖

The single bar separates the two connected clauses, and the double bar separates the two sentences, as well as marking the end of the whole utterance. The single bar may correspond to a slight pause, but more often there is no actual silence between the two word groups it separates. The double bar indicates a definite pause.

THE ROLES OF
INTONATION

The division of longer utterances into grammatically relevant word groups is one of the roles of intonation. A second is the use of different tunes, different patterns of pitch, for grammatical purposes. For example:

You can have beans | or cabbage ‖

may mean: 'There are beans and cabbage and nothing else; you must choose between them'. Or it may be that the beans and cabbage are simply examples and there may be other vegetables too. In the first case the voice rises on *beans* and falls on *cabbage,* and this is marked as a limited choice. In the second, the voice rises on both *beans* and *cabbage* and it is then clear that these are simply examples. In *Didn't you enjoy it?* if the voice rises at the end it is a simple question; but if it falls at the end the sentence is an exclamation, meaning 'You enjoyed it enormously, didn't you?'

Apart from these two clearly grammatical roles of intonation there is also a third and very important one, that of expressing *the speaker's attitude, at the moment of speaking, to the situation in which he is placed.* Our example of *Thank you* illustrates this: if the voice falls we express genuine gratitude,

diff. attit. of Speaker

inton. → add. inform.

but if it rises we sound rather casual. This is not a grammatical difference; it is a difference in the attitude of the speaker, and every utterance we make contains, in its intonation, some indication of this attitude. Clearly the speaker's words and grammatical structures are also used with the intention of expressing his attitude; but intonation gives additional information; that is why different actors can give such widely varying interpretations of the same role in a play. We may regard the words as a rough guide to the meaning, and the intonation as giving greater precision and point, but this is not to say that intonation makes a greater contribution to the whole than does the verbal structure; indeed the intonation without words would give a very vague impression of the total meaning. Nevertheless, it does provide important information which is not contained in any of the other features of utterances, and without this additional information there would be many more imprecisions and ambiguities in English speech than in fact there are.

To describe exactly the attitude which a given pitch pattern expresses is not always easy, for the very good reason that such attitudes are more often conveyed in tunes than in words, so that the words are not readily available. It is this difficulty that writers are constantly facing, and one measure of a writer's success is his ability to solve the problem of suggesting the exact meaning he has in mind even though he has no direct method of conveying intonation. The English speaker learns by experience from earliest childhood what attitudes are linked with the various tunes he hears and uses, but he would be hard put to it to explain them. Our attempt to explain the attitudes, the meanings which the English tunes convey, will be found in Chapter II, but first we must show how the tunes of English are constructed and a method of symbolising the pitch treatment of English utterances.

ACCENT

The words in a word group do not necessarily all contribute an equal amount of information, some are more important to the meaning than others; and this largely depends on the context or situation in which the word group is said.

Consider the sentence *It was an unusually dark night*. As the beginning of, say, a story told on the radio the last three words would all be particularly important. It is easy to show that the first three words play a minor part; suppose that the first three words were drowned by some outside noise and the last three heard clearly, '. . . unusually dark night'. Then the listener would still get a pretty clear picture of the story's setting. But suppose the reverse were the case and only the first three words were heard clearly and the remainder lost, 'It was an . . .'. In this case there would be virtually no information gained at all. So in the situation we have imagined the last three words all help to paint a picture and to this extent they are important.

But if the same sentence were said in response to the question *What sort of night was it?* the word *night* in the reply would lose some of its force because the questioner is already in possession of the information that it might otherwise have given him. In this situation there are only two important words—*unusually dark*—and they could be used alone as a complete answer to the question. Going further still, in reply to the question *Was it dark last night?* the single word *unusually* would bear the major part of the information, and would in this sense be more important than all the others. Any word in any word group may be important to the meaning if the context makes it so. The word *was* has had little value in our examples, but if the sentence were said as a contradiction, in reply to *It wasn't unusually dark last night, was it?* then *was* would be the most important word of all, and indeed the reply might simply be *It was*, omitting the following words as no longer worth saying.

And it is not only verbal contexts which alter the values of words; if both the speaker and the listener know something, even if it has not been said, then it is not necessary to underline their knowledge. For example, John lives in Oxford and says to Tim *Come and stay with me*. Tim might then reply *I'd love to come to Oxford*, and the word *Oxford* would not be important because both of them already know where John lives. Similarly, if both of them know that Harry was going to take a driving test on Monday, John might say on Tuesday *Did Harry pass his driving test?* In these circumstances *pass* would be important, but *his driving test* would not, because it is common knowledge between them.

In the written language the reader is generally left to make up his mind which are the important words, helped to a greater or lesser extent by the style of the author and by such devices as italicisation, spacing and the like; but in speech these words are specifically pointed out so that the listener shall be left in no doubt. Words are pointed out by means of what we shall call *accent*. The workings of accent, what it is and how it makes words stand out, will become clearer as we go on to analyse tunes.

THE TUNES OF SINGLE-SYLLABLE WORD GROUPS

Up to this point we have used the term *tune* in a very general way; we shall now define it as the complete pitch treatment of a word group. Tunes, like word groups, may therefore be long or short, but we shall start by dealing with the shortest possible tunes, those found in word groups consisting of a single, monosyllabic word. Below are seven examples showing different tunes for the word *Two* in different contexts. The changes of pitch are shown graphically between two horizontal lines representing the normal high and low limits of the voice.

1. PETER: Would you like one packet, or two?
   JOHN: Two. ‖

2. PETER: How many shoes in a pair?
   JOHN: Two. ‖

3. PETER: Did you know Richard has two wives?
   JOHN: Two! ‖

4. PETER: How many cigarettes have you got?
   JOHN: Two. ‖

5. PETER: I've only got two pounds.
   JOHN: Two? ‖

6. PETER: You've got one brother, haven't you?
   JOHN: Two. ‖

7. PETER: Can you let me have two pounds?
   JOHN: Two │ (or three, │ or four. ‖)

The seven tunes are:

Low Fall: the voice falls during the word from a medium to a very low pitch.

High Fall: the voice falls during the word from a high to a very low pitch.

Rise-Fall: the voice first rises from a fairly low to a high pitch, and then quickly falls to a very low pitch.

Low Rise: the voice rises during the word from a low to a medium pitch or a little above.

High Rise: the voice rises during the word from a medium to a high pitch.

Fall-Rise: the voice first falls from a fairly high to a rather low pitch, and then, still within the word, rises to a medium pitch.

Mid-Level: the voice maintains a level pitch between high and low, neither rising nor falling.

THE TUNES OF LONGER WORD GROUPS CONTAINING ONLY ONE IMPORTANT WORD

In the examples above, the word *Two*, being the only word in the word group, must naturally be important (otherwise there would be no point in saying it) and therefore accented. Now suppose that John's response was not *Two* but *Twenty*. This is still a word group of a single accented word, but there are now two syllables instead of one. The first of these syllables is stressed, i.e. said with a greater general effort than the second, which is unstressed. Our seven tunes will now be as follows (and here we use large dots to represent the stressed syllable and smaller dots to represent the unstressed syllable):

Low Fall: Twenty. ‖

High Fall: Twenty. ‖

Rise-Fall: Twenty. ‖   Twenty. ‖

Low Rise: Twenty. ‖

High Rise: Twenty. ‖

Fall-Rise: Twenty. ‖

Mid-Level: Twenty │ (or thirty │ or forty. ‖)

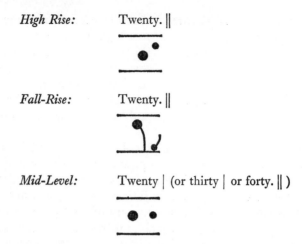

The similarities with the treatment of *Two* are obvious, but there are some differences which must be noticed. In the two rising tunes the stressed syllable is level in pitch and there is no upward glide as there was in *Two*, but rather a jump from the pitch of the stressed to that of the unstressed syllable; in other words the rise is not complete before the end of the word group. In the same way the Fall-Rise is spread over the two syllables and not completed on the first. Whether or not, in the falling tunes, the fall is completed within the stressed syllable depends on the structure of that syllable: if the stressed vowel is short and followed by a voiceless sound (having no vocal cord vibration and therefore no pitch) there is often not time to complete the fall within the stressed syllable, and the effect is of a jump from the higher to the lower pitch level. For example:

Fifty. ‖   Sixty. ‖

If, on the other hand, the stressed syllable contains a long vowel or diphthong, or a short vowel followed by a voiced sound, then the fall is usually completed within that syllable. For example:

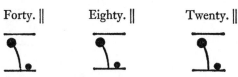

Forty. ‖   Eighty. ‖   Twenty. ‖

The Rise-Fall may be said in either of the two ways shown above.

Below are seven more examples, this time of word groups containing one important word followed by other words which are not important and therefore *not accented*:

1. PETER: Will you have one packet, or two?
   JOHN: Two, Peter. ‖

2. PETER: How many shoes in a pair?
   JOHN: Two, you silly fool. ‖

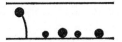

3. PETER: Did you know Richard has two wives?
   JOHN: Two, indeed! ‖   Two, indeed! ‖

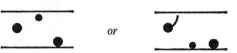

or

4. PETER: How many cigarettes have you got?
   JOHN: Two, I think. ‖

5. PETER: I've only got two pounds.
   JOHN: Two, did you say? ‖

6. PETER: You've got one brother, haven't you?
   JOHN: Two, you mean. ‖

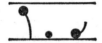

7. PETER: How many tickets would you like?
   JOHN: Two, perhaps. ‖

These examples show that when the single accented word is followed by other words which are not accented, the pitch patterns remain very similar to the patterns in the examples *Two* and *Twenty*. In the Low Fall and High Fall the fall of the voice to the lowest pitch level takes place during the stressed syllable of the accented word or from that syllable to the next, whether in the same word or not, and any subsequent syllables are all on the same low level. The Rise-Fall is spread over either two or three syllables, as shown above, both patterns being commonly heard; once the voice has reached the low pitch, on either the second or third syllable, it continues on this pitch during any other following syllables. In the Low Rise and High Rise the stressed syllable of the accented word does not itself rise in pitch, but each of the following syllables is a step higher than the previous one, and the final pitch, medium in the case of the Low Rise and high in the case of the High Rise, is reached on the last syllable of the word group. So whereas in the Low and High Fall the fall must be completed not later than the syllable immediately following the stressed syllable of the accented word, in the Low and High Rise the rise is not complete until the end of the word group. It may be noticed too that in the rising tunes, when the final syllable of the word group is stressed (and only then), there is a tendency to slide upwards in pitch during the syllable, whereas there is no parallel tendency in the falling tunes. In the Fall-Rise the fall takes place during the stressed syllable of the accented word (or from that syllable to the next) and the rise takes place on or from the last stressed syllable of the word group. For example:

I don't want it. ||

If there is no stressed syllable following the fall, then the rise takes place between the last two syllables. For example:

Fortunately. ||

NUCLEUS AND TAIL The cases we have just been discussing are important because *all* tunes, and not merely those with a single accented word, must *end* in one of the ways described above. No matter how long or how short the word group is, no matter how many or how few accented words it contains, the pattern of its tune from the stressed syllable of the last accented word onwards will correspond to one or other of the seven general patterns. In the examples below all the accented words are italicised and it can be seen that, although the tunes differ in various ways, the endings conform to the patterns already laid down.

Low Fall ending: I *want* to be *absolutely sure* about it. ||

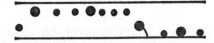

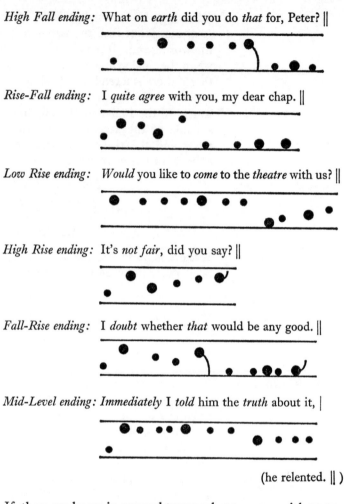

High Fall ending: What on *earth* did you do *that* for, Peter? ‖

Rise-Fall ending: I *quite agree* with you, my dear chap. ‖

Low Rise ending: *Would* you like to *come* to the *theatre* with us? ‖

High Rise ending: It's *not fair*, did you say? ‖

Fall-Rise ending: I *doubt* whether *that* would be any good. ‖

Mid-Level ending: *Immediately* I *told* him the *truth* about it, |

(he relented. ‖)

If, then, we know in general terms what tune we wish to use in saying any word group, and if we can identify the stressed syllable of the last accented word, we now know the exact pattern of the tune's ending. Clearly the stressed syllable of the last accented word is a landmark of the highest importance, and it is on this syllable that the whole tune centres. This syllable is called the *nucleus* of the tune, and all syllables following the nucleus are called the *tail*. In our last example above the nucleus is *truth* and the tail consists of the words *about it*.

The rising, falling or level tune endings which take place on the nucleus or start from it are known as *nuclear tones*; there are seven of these nuclear tones corresponding to the seven tune endings already described. The last accented word is made to stand out by a combination of stress and the pitch features of the nuclear tones. By definition there can be no accented word in the tail, though there may be *stressed* words in it, as the last seven examples show.

So far, in order to give a fairly complete picture of the intonation of our examples, we have used a graphic method of large and small dots. It is more convenient in practice to use a shorter and more economical method of marking the intonation. This consists of placing a single symbol immediately before the nucleus to indicate the nuclear tone; this symbol tells us, by its position and its shape, which syllable is the nucleus of the tune and which of the seven main endings is to be used.

Low Fall:	ˏTwo.	ˏTwenty.	ˏSeventy.
High Fall:	ˋTwo.	ˋTwenty.	ˋSeventy.
Rise-Fall:	^Two.	^Twenty.	^Seventy.
Low Rise:	ˎTwo.	ˎTwenty.	ˎSeventy.

High Rise:	'Two.	'Twenty.	'Seventy.

Fall-Rise:	ˇTwo.	ˇTwenty.	ˇSeventy.

Mid-Level:	>Two.	>Twenty.	>Seventy.

These examples show that unstressed syllables in the tail have no separate symbol. However, as we have already explained, the tail can include stressed syllables occurring in words which are not accented; and the rhythm of English speech, which is a characteristic and important part of it, depends on *all* the stressed syllables in the word group, not just those in the accented words, being made to occur at approximately equal intervals of time. So it is necessary for the student to know all of the syllables which are stressed, and not just those which occur in accented words. To mark the stressed syllables in the tail the degree sign is used. Placed low [ₒ] it indicates that the following stressed syllable has, or begins on, the lowest pitch level. Placed high [°] it indicates any stressed syllable of the tail which is higher than the lowest pitch.

Low Fall: ˎTwo, ₒPeter.

High Fall: ˋTwo, you ₒsilly ₒfool.

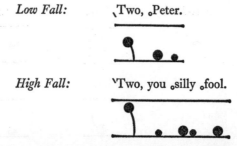

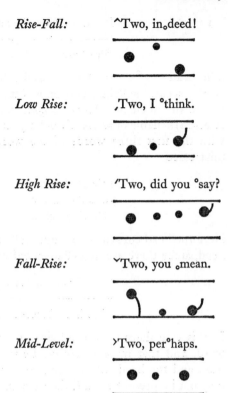

Rise-Fall: ⌃Two, in₀deed!

Low Rise: ‚Two, I °think.

High Rise: ′Two, did you °say?

Fall-Rise: ˅Two, you ₀mean.

Mid-Level: ˃Two, per°haps.

PRE-NUCLEAR PATTERNS

We know the seven main endings that tunes may have, but up to now we have considered only word groups with a single accented word right at the beginning of the group. Now we must consider word groups containing words and syllables before the nucleus. It is convenient to divide the pre-nuclear pattern (i.e. that part of the tune preceding the nucleus) into two parts, the *head* and the *pre-head*. The head begins with the stressed syllable of the first accented word (before the nucleus) and ends with the syllable immediately preceding the nucleus; the pre-head consists of any syllables before the stressed syllable of the first accented word. In the examples below, accented words are again italicised.

1.   It was an *unusually dark night.*

                      Pre-head   Head   Nucleus

The head begins with the stressed syllable of *unusually*, that is, the second syllable, and ends with *dark*, the last syllable before the nucleus, which is *night*. Notice that the first (unstressed) syllable of *unusually* belongs to the pre-head, together with the first three words of the word group which are all unstressed.

2.   *Where's John?*

                      Head Nucleus

Here the head consists of a single syllable and there is no pre-head, since there are no syllables before the head.

3.   I could have *kicked* myself.

                      Pre-head Nucleus Tail

In this case there is no head since there is only one accented word, and that must of course be the nucleus. So the pre-head and the head may occur together or separately, or they may not be present at all if the nucleus is the first syllable of a word group; but the nucleus is always present in every complete tune.

HEADS

There are four different types of head, the *low head*, the *high head*, the *falling head* and the *rising head*.

THE LOW HEAD

In the low head, which in this book occurs only before the Low Rise nuclear tone, all the syllables are said on the same low pitch as the beginning of the Low Rise. For example:

Someone's bound to *come along soon.*

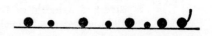

The important (italicised) words are accented by means of stress alone, with no help from pitch features of the kind mentioned in dealing with the accentuation of the nuclear word (p. 15). Words which are not accented do not bear stress. For example:

Don't upset yourself about *that.*

In this example the stresses which might be heard in other circumstances on the second syllables of *yourself* and *about* are suppressed, and the four consecutive unstressed syllables are all said more quickly as a result.

The low head is symbolised by placing the mark [ˌ] before it, that is, before the first stressed syllable of the head. In some word groups there is only one accented word in the head, and so this is the only mark used. For example:

ˌ*Don't* be ˌ*silly.*

However, if there are other accented words within the head, their stressed syllables are preceded by [ₒ], the low placing of this sign showing very low pitch. Unstressed syllables are left unmarked. So the other two examples above read as follows:

ˌSomeone's ₒbound to ₒcome aₒlong ˌsoon.
ˌDon't upₒset yourself about ˌthat.

THE HIGH HEAD

In the high head all the syllables are said on the same rather high pitch. For example:

Why did you *tell* me you *couldn't come?*

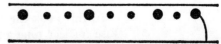

Accent is again indicated by stress alone, and words which are not accented do not bear stress. For example:

Plenty of people *don't* really *care.*

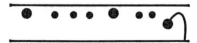

In this example, the words *people* and *really* are not felt to be important, so no syllable in either word bears a stress because such a stress would indicate accent.

The high head is symbolised by placing the mark ['] before it. In a sentence like the following there is only one accented word in the head and this is the only mark used:

'*What* a ˎ*pity!*

If there are other accented words in the head they have [°] before their stressed syllable. The other two examples above read as follows:

'Why did you °tell me you °couldn't ˋcome?
'Plenty of people °don't really ˆcare.

In this book the high head occurs before all nuclear tones except the Fall-Rise tone.

THE FALLING HEAD

The first syllable of the falling head is rather high in pitch and any following syllables gradually carry the pitch lower. For example:

Everyone's bound to *see* it *sometime.*

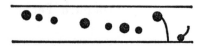

In this book the falling head occurs only before the Fall-Rise nuclear tone and the last syllable of the head is always lower than the beginning of the Fall-Rise. If there is only one syllable in the head, that syllable is high and level. For example:

Don't fall.

The symbol for the falling head is ['] placed before the stressed syllable of the first accented word in the head. If there is only one accented word in the head, then that is the only symbol used; but if there are other accented words, the mark [°] is placed before the stressed syllables of each of them. The examples above read as follows:

ˋEveryone's °bound to °see it ˇsometime.
ˋDon't ˇfall.

THE RISING HEAD

The rising head is the opposite of the falling head: its first syllable is low in pitch and any following syllables gradually carry the pitch higher. For example:

How did you *manage* to do *that?*

In this book the rising head occurs only before the High Fall nuclear tone, and the last syllable of the head is lower than the beginning of the High Fall. If there is only one syllable in the head, that syllable is low and level. For example:

Don't pay him.

The symbol for the rising head is [ˌ] placed before the stressed syllable of the first accented word in the head. The stressed syllable of any other accented word in the head is marked with [°]. So the examples above read as follows:

,How did you °manage to do 'that?
,Don't 'pay him.

PRE-HEADS

The pre-head of a tune consists of all the syllables which precede the stressed syllable of the first accented word, whether the latter syllable is the nucleus or the beginning of the head. There are two types of pre-head, the *low pre-head* and the *high pre-head*.

THE LOW PRE-HEAD

All the syllables in the low pre-head are said on the same rather low pitch. For example:

It was an *unusually dark night.*

This pitch is not usually so low as that of a final falling nuclear tone, but it must never be higher than the starting pitch of the stressed syllable of the first accented word. Before the Low Fall, the High Fall, the Rise-Fall, the High Rise, the Fall-Rise and the Mid-Level tones it must be lower than the starting pitch of the nucleus; and before the high head and the falling head it must be lower than the initial pitch of the head. For example:

Low Fall: You're a *fool.*

High Fall: I was at *school.*

Rise-Fall: Oh, *do* you, indeed?

High Rise: Did you *see* him?

Fall-Rise: You'll be *late.*

Mid-Level: And when I *tried* | ...

High Head: He can be *absolutely infuriating.*

Falling Head: It was an *expensive oversight.*

Before the Low Rise, the low head and the rising head, the low pre-head is on the same pitch level as the start of the rise or the head. For example:

Low Rise: You could have *tried.*

Low Head: You're looking *very smart.*

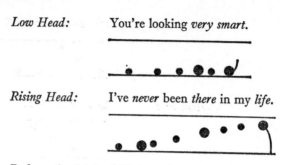

Rising Head: I've *never* been *there* in my *life.*

Before the high, falling and rising heads the low pre-head may contain stressed syllables, but these are not to be considered accented. For example:

High Head: The man was *perfectly right.*

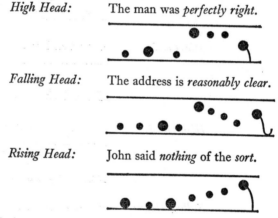

Falling Head: The address is *reasonably clear.*

Rising Head: John said *nothing* of the *sort.*

It is usual for such stresses to be weakened if not wholly suppressed.

Unstressed syllables in the low pre-head are not marked at all; any unmarked syllables at the beginning of a word group are therefore taken to belong to the low pre-head. Stressed syllables in the low pre-head, if they occur, are marked by placing the symbol [ₒ] immediately before them. The following examples are thus completely marked:

I was at ˋschool.
It was an exˎpensive ˇoverₒsight.
The ₒman was ˈperfectly ˎright.

THE HIGH PRE-HEAD

In the high pre-head all the syllables are said on the same relatively high pitch. For example:

But you *can't* do *that*.

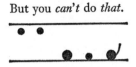

The high pre-head is never very long, rarely containing more than two or three syllables. It is also very much less common than the low pre-head. The high pre-head before a High Fall is said on the same pitch as the beginning of the fall. For example:

You *didn't*!   It was *amazing*!

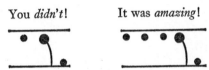

Before any other nuclear tone or any head the high pre-head is said on a pitch higher than the beginning of the stressed syllable of the following accented word. For example:

Low Fall: The *brute*!

Rise-Fall: It was *amazing*!

Low Rise: *Hullo*.

High Rise: At *eleven*?

Fall-Rise: It *wasn't.*

Mid-Level: At *times.*

Low Head: It's an *extraordinary thing.*

High Head: I *can't* be *bothered.*

Falling Head: He's the *queerest chap.*

Rising Head: But you *intended* to *go* there *anyway.*

Stressed syllables may occur in high pre-heads before the low, falling and rising heads. For example:

Low Head: John was *perfectly willing* to *compromise.*

Falling Head: The house is *very expensive.*

Rising Head: The train was *absolutely packed.*

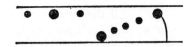

As is the case with the low pre-head, these stresses are usually suppressed.

If the first syllable of a high pre-head is stressed, as in the first example, the mark [°] is placed before it:

°John was ˌperfectly ₒwilling to ˌcompromise.

Any following unmarked syllables are to be said on the same high level pitch.

If the first syllable of a high pre-head is unstressed, as in the other two examples above, the symbol [⁻] is placed before it, and any following stressed syllable in the pre-head is marked with [°]:

⁻The °house is ˇvery exˇpensive.
⁻The °train was ˌabsolutely ˋpacked.

If there is no stressed syllable in the high pre-head, the symbol [⁻] before the first syllable indicates that all syllables between this mark and the following tone mark belong to the high pre-head. Other examples given above are completely marked as follows:

⁻But you ˌcan't do ˌthat.
⁻You ˋdidn't!
⁻It was aˋmazing!
⁻The ˌbrute!
⁻It was aˆmazing!
⁻Hulˌlo.
⁻At eˊleven?
⁻It ˇwasn't.

⁻At ˎtimes.
⁻It's an ex˒traordinary ˏthing.
⁻I 'can't be ˎbothered.
⁻He's the ˠqueerest ˅chap.
⁻But you in˷tended to °go there ˎanyway.

SIMPLE AND COMPOUND TUNES

All the tunes we have dealt with up to now have contained only one nuclear tone; these are called *simple tunes*, and the majority of tunes in English are of this kind. However, there is one very important tune which contains two nuclear tones, and this is called a *compound tune*. It consists basically of a High Fall followed by a Low Rise. For example:

I ˋlike ˏchocolate.
We were ˋsorry you ₒcouldn't ˏcome.
ˋNo-one ₒlikes to be ₒtaken for ˏgranted.

The High Fall may be preceded by a high head if there are important, accented words before it. For example:

I 'rather ˋlike ˏchocolate.
'Everybody °said they were ˋsorry you ₒcouldn't ˏcome.
'Absolutely ˋno-one ₒlikes to be ₒtaken for ˏgranted.

Every syllable between the High Fall and the Low Rise is on a low pitch. If one of these low syllables is stressed, the word in which it occurs is recognised as being accented and important to the meaning.

This compound Fall plus Rise tune may be very similar to some forms of the simple tune containing the Fall-Rise nuclear tone; but, as we shall see in Chapter II, the two tunes are very different in their meanings. So it is necessary to keep them separate. The first example above *I ˋlike ˏchocolate* represents a pattern like this:

I like chocolate.

But so too does the notation *I ˅like ₒchocolate*. So there may
be no difference of pattern between the two tunes. Yet there
may be certain differences between them which it is worth
while pointing out. Notice in the first place that, if the fall and
rise in pitch both occur on the same word, then we are dealing
with the simple Fall-Rise tune. The Fall and the Rise of the
compound tune are always on different words. Also, if the rise
in pitch takes place on an unstressed syllable, we are again
dealing with the simple tune, since the Rise in the compound
tune is always attached to a stressed syllable. So the form

I like it.

must represent *I ˅like it* because *it* is unstressed.

The more troublesome cases are those in which the fall and
the rise take place on different words and the rise is attached
to a stressed syllable. For example:

My mother was born in Sheffield.

But even in these cases there *may* be some indications as to
whether we are dealing with a simple or compound tune:

1. In the compound tune the fall on *mother* often has a
wider range than in the simple tune: it starts on a higher pitch
than the simple Fall-Rise and falls to a lower one.

2. In the simple tune the syllables after the fall often
gradually rise one after the other; in the compound tune they
always remain at the lowest level until the final rise.

3. In the simple tune all the stresses after the fall may be
weakened or indeed suppressed altogether; in the compound
tune this does not happen.

If all three of these differences are operating, the patterns of
the simple and compound tunes will look like this:

My ˇmother was born in Sheffield | (but not my father.)

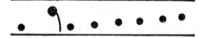

My ˋmother was ₒborn in ˏSheffield | (Isn't that interesting?)

But these differences are not always operating; the stresses after the fall may be present in both tunes; the syllables after the fall in the simple tune may not start rising immediately; and it may not be possible to tell whether the range of the fall is wider or not so wide. Yet because of the different attitudes that the two tunes convey it is helpful to distinguish them in notation. For example:

ˇTry not to be ₒlate, | (even if it's difficult.)
ˋTry not to be ˏlate, | (please!)

I ˇhope you'll be ₒable to ₒcome, | (even if it's doubtful.)
I ˋhope you'll be ₒable to ˏcome, | (I really do.)

If the Fall-Rise or the compound Fall plus Rise are preceded by a head, the difference between the two tunes is made clear, because in this book the Fall-Rise always has the falling head before it, and the Fall plus Rise always has the high head before it. For example:

My ˎfather and ˇmother were ₒborn in ₒSheffield.

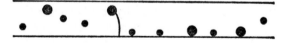

My ˈfather and ˋmother were ₒborn in ˏSheffield.

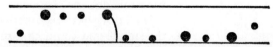

STRESS AND ACCENT

It may be useful at this point to consider afresh the relation between stress and accent and the way in which our notation shows these features.

We have seen (p. 5) that words are accented when they are important to the meaning in a particular situation and not accented when they are not especially important. All the tone marks which indicate the four types of head and the seven nuclear tones show that the word to which any one of them is attached is accented. So in the examples

It was a re'markable ˋeffort.
ˉIt was ˌperfectly ˌnatural.
₀Andrew ˅certainly ˇtried.
It was a riˆdiculous ₀thing to ₀do.

the words *remarkable, effort, perfectly, natural, certainly, tried* and *ridiculous* are all accented, as the tone marks show. But how do we recognise that they are accented when we hear them? Firstly, each of them contains a stressed syllable, and that is always so: every accented word must carry a stress. But stress alone does not necessarily imply accent; in the last two examples, *Andrew* is stressed but not accented, forming the low pre-head, and *thing* and *do* are stressed too, but not accented, being in the tail of the tune. Pitch as well as stress is involved in the recognition of accent. All the nuclear tones have a *movement* of pitch except [ˀ], which has a *sustention* of pitch; and this movement or sustention, combined with the stress, makes us recognise them as accented. As for the heads, it is their general pitch shape, combined with stress, which indicates accent. In

'What's ˋthat?

we know that *What* is accented because it is stressed and high in pitch before the High Fall. In

ˌDon't ˌworry.

we recognise *Don't* as accented because of its low pitch and stress. In

ˌSend it to his ˋhome ad₀dress.

the stress on *Send* at the beginning of the rising sequence marks it as accented; and in

ˈNo-one will ˇknow.

the high-pitched stress at the beginning of the falling sequence marks *No-one* as accented.

Sometimes a jump in pitch to the beginning of the head helps us to identify accent. For example, in

ˉYou ˌmustn't ˌworry.

there is a jump down in pitch from the high, unstressed (and therefore very short) *You* to the low, stressed *mustn't*; this jump in pitch reinforces our recognition of the accent on *mustn't*. Similarly in

You could have ˈheard him in ˋLondon.

the jump from the low pitch of the pre-head to the stressed syllable at the beginning of the head makes *heard* stand out as accented. But this does not always happen, and it is the general shape of the head, High or Low, Rising or Falling, and the stresses associated with it, which mainly enable us to recognise accent.

This is true of accents within the head as well as at the beginning of it. For example, in

ˈPeter °wanted to °make them ˇpay for it.

all three of the stresses in the high head mark accented words; and this applies to the other three heads as well. For example:

You were ˌonly ˳trying to ˳help him ˌout.
ˌWhy on °earth did you °want to do ˋthat?
ˈPlenty of °people would be pre°pared to ˇhelp.

In these examples all the stresses of the heads show accent, and all the stressed words are therefore recognised as important parts of each message.

In the compound Fall plus Rise tune, stressed syllables between the Fall and the Rise also mark accented words. For example, in

I ˈlike the ₀colour of the ₀paint you've ₀used in the ˌkitchen.

the words *like* and *kitchen* are accented by their stress and their nuclear pitch movement, whilst *colour*, *paint* and *used* are accented by stress alone.

We can sum up the situation with regard to accent as follows:

1. Any stressed syllable associated with a nuclear tone shows accent.
2. Any stressed syllable in any head shows accent.
3. Any stressed syllable between the two nuclear tones in a compound Fall plus Rise tune shows accent.

As we have seen, the general shape of the head is shown by the symbol placed at its beginning, namely ['], [ˌ], [ˈ] or [ˌ]. Other accents in the head are marked by [₀] if their pitch is low, as in the low head; and by [°] if it is *not* low, as in the other three heads. In the compound Fall plus Rise tune, the accents between the Fall and the Rise are on a low pitch, and [₀] is therefore used to mark them.

When stresses occur in positions other than the three mentioned above, that is, when they occur in pre-heads and tails, they do not indicate accents. So in the four examples

I've ₀taught him 'everything I ˌknow.
°People ˌwon't eat ˌthat.
ˇPeter ₀won't ₀mind.
'Blow your ˌnose, °darling.

[₀] and [°] do *not* mark accent, because they appear only in pre-head or tail. There is no difficulty about stresses in tails, since by definition the nuclear tone occurs on the last important word in the word group; that is therefore the last accented word and any following stresses cannot indicate accent. Once the nucleus has been identified by its pitch behaviour, any following stresses can be ignored for accent purposes, though not for rhythmical purposes of course (see p. 16).

However, we must look a little more closely at stresses in pre-heads. In the example above

I've ₒtaught him 'everything I ˎknow.

the first three syllables are on a low pitch and *taught* is stressed. If we consider only those three syllables

I've taught him

this could be the beginning of a low head, in which case the stress on *taught* would give it accent. What tells us that it is not part of a low head is what happens afterwards. A low head would continue on a low pitch right up to the nuclear tone, but in our example *everything I* is said on a high pitch, and *everything* has a stress. This can only be a high head and therefore what comes before it must be a low pre-head. In other words, before we can decide whether the pre-nuclear pattern of a word group—*I've taught him everything I* in our example—consists of head alone, or pre-head alone, or, as in this case, both pre-head and head, we must consider the pre-nuclear pattern as a whole. If the pre-nuclear pattern contains no stresses, there is of course no problem: it consists of pre-head only, since a head means at least one pre-nuclear stress. Similarly, when the pre-nuclear pattern shows only one stress, the decision is simple: the single stress marks the beginning of a head and shows accent; and any unstressed syllables before that stress will of course be a pre-head. But when, as in the above example, the pre-nuclear pattern includes more than one stress, it must be viewed as a whole. Only then can we decide whether all the pre-nuclear stresses fall within the head and are therefore all accents; or whether, like that of *taught* above, the first of the pre-nuclear stresses—a pre-head rarely contains more than one stress—forms part of a pre-head and so is not to be considered an accent.

The other example above

°People ˌwon't eat ˏthat.

has two stresses in its pre-nuclear pattern and shows exactly
the same process. *People* is stressed and on a high pitch; it
might, therefore, be the beginning of a high head; but the
low-pitched syllables which follow and the stress on *won't*
make this impossible, and we are forced to interpret *People*
as a high pre-head containing a stress and what follows as a
low head.

Finally, consider the following example:

ₒAndrew was ˏquite °sure he'd ˋlost it.

The low pitch of the first four syllables and the two stresses
could quite well be the beginning of a low head; but after
quite the syllables do not stay low, as they would in a low head:
on the contrary, they rise. So the stressed *quite* must be the
beginning of a rising head; all before it must be a low pre-head
and the stressed *Andrew* is not an accent. Notice the difference
from

ˏAndrew was °quite °sure he'd ˋlost it.

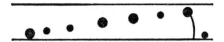

In this case the gradual rise in pitch starts right at the beginning of the tune; so the rising head starts with *Andrew*, the
stress on *Andrew* indicates accent, and there is no pre-head.

In pre-heads and tails we use [ₒ] and [°] again, but now they
mark stressed syllables and do not indicate accents. Once more
[ₒ] is used when the pitch is low, that is, in the low pre-head
and in tails after falling nuclear tones; and [°] is used when the
pitch is *not* low, that is, in the high pre-head and in tails
following the Low Rise and High Rise nuclear tones. In the
tail of a Fall-Rise nuclear tone, as for example in

ᵛPeter ₒwon't ₒmind.

ᵛPeter ₒwon't ₒcarry it.

we use [ₒ] to mark the stresses, on the understanding that the final rise takes place on, or begins from, the last [ₒ] mark.

EMPHASIS

There are various ways in which a whole word group can be made to sound more lively, more emotional, more *emphatic* by means of pitch. Compare for instance

The ˎfool.   with   ⁻*The ˎfool*!

The use of the high pre-head in the second example gives a liveliness to the whole word group which is far greater than that shown by the first example, with the low pre-head. This is not a question of accent, which affects single words, but rather of *emphasis*, which affects whole word groups; in both examples *The* is unstressed and *fool* is accented, and the high pre-head does not make *The* stand out as an important word. What it does, in combination with the Low Fall, is to make the whole utterance more exclamatory, more emphatic, as the exclamation mark suggests. The more the high pitch of the high pre-head contrasts with what follows, the more emphasis is given; so ⁻*The ˎfool* sounds quite emphatic because of the contrast between the high pitch of *The* and the much lower pitch at the beginning of *fool*. On the other hand ⁻*The* ᵛ*fool* does not sound so emphatic, because of the lack of contrast between the high-pitched *The* and the high pitch at the beginning of *fool*. Other examples showing considerable emphasis because of this contrast are:

⁻You ˏcan't do ˏthat.
⁻I ˏsimply °don't beˎlieve it.

Another common way of adding emphasis is by modifying the shape of the head. For instance, the high head can be modified for emphasis by making the stressed syllable of each accented word a step lower in pitch than the previous one. For example:

I simply don't know what to do.

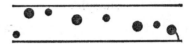

This series of downward steps makes the whole word group sound weightier than the normal high head does. We show this emphatic treatment of the high head by repeating the head mark ['] at each stress:

I 'simply 'don't know 'what to ˏdo.

This may be referred to as either the emphatic high head or the *Stepping Head*.

The falling head is modified for emphasis by having a series of falls, one from each stressed syllable, instead of the single fall of the normal falling head. For example:

You can't expect me to hold your hand.

If there are no unstressed syllables to carry the falls, the stressed syllables do so themselves. For example:

I don't really believe that.

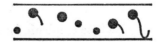

We indicate this emphatic treatment of the falling head by again repeating the head mark [ˋ] before each stressed syllable; so our two examples are marked as follows:

You ˇcan't exˇpect me to ˇhold your ˇhand.
I ˇdon't ˇreally beˇlieve ˇthat.

This may be referred to as the emphatic falling head or the *Sliding Head*.

The rising head is emphasised similarly: there is a series of rises, one from each stress, instead of the single rise. For example:

Why on earth did you want to do that?

If there are no unstressed syllables to carry the rises, the stressed syllables do so themselves. For example:

John simply can't bear it.

Again this treatment is shown by repeating the head mark [ˏ] at each stress; so our examples read as follows:

ˏWhy on ˏearth did you ˏwant to do ˇthat?
ˏJohn ˏsimply ˏcan't ˋbear it.

This may be referred to as the emphatic rising head or the *Climbing Head*.

Even greater emphasis can be added by having a High Fall tone at each stressed syllable in the head. This occurs before a final High Fall or Fall-Rise nuclear tone. For example:

ˋFancy ˋanyone ˋwanting to do ˋthat!
It was an ˋabsoˋlutely ˋterrible ˇparty.

These emphatic forms will all find their place in the following chapters. There are others, such as changes of pitch range and the use of different voice-qualities, which are beyond the scope of this book; but their existence should be borne in mind and listened for.

A simple tune may have a low pre-head, a high pre-head or no pre-head at all; it may have one of the four different kinds of head or no head at all; and it will have one of the seven nuclear tones (with or without the appropriate tail). If every one of these parts of a tune can be combined with every other part, the total number of basic pitch patterns will be 105, without even considering compound tunes. But it is not necessary to deal with 105 or more different units for two reasons:

1. Some of the patterns occur very much more frequently and with a much wider usefulness than others; attention must be concentrated, at least for a time, on the commonest ones.

2. Some patterns which are different have differences of meaning so slight that they would be very difficult to define in any very helpful way. Indeed some patterns which are different have exactly the *same* meaning, so far as the intonation is concerned. This is the case with the two examples below:

'John was 'late.
But 'John was 'late.

The difference between the two tunes is certainly very slight —a low pitched unstressed syllable at the beginning of the second example which is absent in the first—but even so the actual patterns of pitch are not identical. Yet the meaning, or at any rate that part of it which the intonation gives, is exactly the same in both cases; and as it is meaning which is the really important factor, we can usefully group together any tunes which mean substantially the same. Such a grouping of tunes all conveying the same attitude on the part of the speaker is called a *Tone Group*. Besides expressing the same attitude, the tunes in a tone group also have one or more pitch features in common, as the following specification makes clear. So a tone group is unified and distinguished from all other tone groups both by the attitude it conveys and by the pitch features of its tunes.

In this book ten tone groups are described and practised.

Each has been given a mnemonic, a name which will serve to remind the learner of some or all of the pitch features in the tone group by evoking for him some commonplace situation:

1 *The Low Drop*: imagine a small child, standing on the bottom stair and then jumping down to the foot of the staircase: *Low Fall*.

2 *The High Drop*: now imagine a parachutist descending from a great height and finally landing: *High Fall*.

3 *The Take-Off*: your plane taxis along the runway at speed: *Low Pre-head* and *Low Head*. Then finally it begins to rise into the air: *Low Rise*.

4 *The Low Bounce*: first you hold a ball at arm's length high in the air: *High Head*. Then, when you have thrown it to the ground, it rebounds into the air: *Low Rise*.

5 *The Switchback*: now you are enjoying a ride on the switchback at a fair. It takes you down: *Falling Head*. Then up and down and up again: *Fall-Rise*.

6 *The Long Jump*: imagine you are at the Olympic Games. You watch the long jumper running along the track: *Low Prehead*. He then hits the board and his leap carries him forwards and upwards: *Rising Head*. And finally he falls into the sand pit: *High Fall*.

7 *The High Bounce*: you are about to make a winning smash at table-tennis. You hit the ball hard, shoulder-high: *High Head*. Then the ball bounces up from the surface of the table, some feet above the floor: *High Rise*.

8 *The Jackknife*: at the swimming-pool you catch sight of a spring-board diver in the middle of his jackknife dive. He is bent double, head and feet both pointing to the water: *Rise-Fall*.

9 *The High Dive*: then you watch the swimmer make his dive from the high board. He plunges in: *High Fall*. He disappears for a second and then rises to the surface again further down the pool: *Low Rise*.

10 *The Terrace*: now back at your hotel, you see a fellow visitor walk across the terrace: *High Head*. He then descends to the rose-garden overlooking the river: *Mid-Level*.

Now follows the specification of all the pitch features found in the tunes of each of these tone groups. Items enclosed in brackets may be present or absent; unbracketed items must be present. Tails are not mentioned since their presence or absence never affects the intonation meaning. Emphatic forms of the tone groups are listed separately. This is merely to make the presentation clearer. It does not imply any difference of attitude between the emphatic and unemphatic tunes of any one tone group; and the attitudes described in Chapter II apply whether tunes are emphatic or not.

THE TEN TONE GROUPS: UNEMPHATIC

1 THE LOW DROP   (Low Pre-head+) (High Head+) Low Fall

E.g. ˏNo. ˏNobody. Imˏpossible. It's ˏArthur's ₒturn.
'Sit ˏdown. I 'don't beˏlieve it.
'Why don't you °look where you're ˏgoing?

2 THE HIGH DROP   (Low Pre-head+) (High Head+) High Fall

E.g. ˋNo. ˋSplendid! It's aˋmazing. 'What's ˋthat?
I 'liked it imˋmensely. He 'doesn't °really ˋknow the ₒanswer.

3 THE TAKE-OFF   (Low Pre-head+) (Low Head+) Low Rise

E.g. ˏNo. ˏSometimes. I ˏthink so.
ˏDon't ˏworry a°bout it. It's ˏnot so ˏbad.
ˌNobody's going to ₒtake it aˏway from you.

4 THE LOW BOUNCE   (Low Pre-head+) High Head+ Low Rise
or
High Pre-head+Low Rise

E.g. 'What's ˏthat? 'Try not to be ˏlate.
'Will you be °staying to ˏlunch, °Tony?
⁻Is ˏJohn °going to °be there? ⁻Hulˏlo.

5 THE SWITCHBACK   (Low Pre-head +) (Falling Head +)
                             Fall-Rise

E.g.   ˇNo. ˇPossibly. ˇSome people can ₒdo it.
           You can ˇtry. ˋNo-one °wants to ˇforce you to ₒplay.
           It ˋisn't °only a °question of ˇmoney, you ₒknow.

6 THE LONG JUMP   (Low Pre-head +) Rising Head +
                             High Fall

E.g.   ˌTry it aˋgain. You ˌdidn't ˋask me to.
           ˌHow on °earth did they °manage to ˋget there?
           Well, ˌcan you re°turn it toˋmorrow, ₒthen?

7 THE HIGH BOUNCE   (Low Pre-head +) (High Head +)
                             High Rise

E.g.   ′Sugar? Is ′this the °one you °mean?
           You ′think I'd en′joy it?
           ′Why don't I °write to the ′secretary, did you °say?

8 THE JACKKNIFE   (Low Pre-head +) (High Head +)
                             Rise-Fall

E.g.   ^No. ^Certainly. ^Lots of ₒpeople ₒdo it.
           It's ri^diculous. I can i^magine how ₒtired you ₒwere.
           I can ′hardly °wait to ^hear about it.

9 THE HIGH DIVE   (Low Pre-head +) (High Head +)
                             High Fall +(Low Accents +) Low
                             Rise

E.g.   ˋAndrew was the ˌwinner. ˋMost people ₒtell me ˌthat.
           Yes, I ˋthought his ₒface was faˌmiliar.
           ′Going by ˋunderground would be the ˌquickest.
           The ′little old °man in the ˋcorner's been ₒwaiting ˌlongest.

| 10 THE TERRACE | (Low Pre-head +) (High Head +) Mid-Level |

E.g. ˃Then | (I went out for a walk.)
ˊAir °travel | (I find so frightening.)
Oc˃casionally | (I meet him on the train.)
Well, 'since you in˃sist, | (I will have a drink.)
'When did you °see your ˃brother | (to ask him about it?)

THE TEN TONE
GROUPS: EMPHATIC

| 1 THE LOW DROP | High Pre-head + (High Head +) Low Fall
or
(Pre-head +) Stepping Head + Low Fall |

E.g. ⁻The ˏfool! ⁻I said 'no such ˏthing.
I 'can't 'hear what you're ˏsaying.
⁻It 'isn't like 'that at ˏall.

| 2 THE HIGH DROP | High Pre-head + (High Head +) High Fall
or
(Pre-head +) Stepping Head + High Fall
or
(Pre-head +) High Fall(s) + High Fall |

E.g. ⁻I'm not ˋsure. ⁻They 'don't °really ˋlike it.
They 'simply 'don't know 'what to ˋdo.
ˋFancy ˋanyone ˋwanting to do ˋthat.

| 3 THE TAKE-OFF | High Pre-head + Low Head + Low Rise |

E.g. ⁻Well, ˏdon't make ₒso much ˏfuss about it.
⁻But you ˏdidn't ₒhave to wait ˏlong.
⁻It's got ˏnothing to ₒdo with ˏyou.

4 THE LOW BOUNCE   High Pre-head+High Head+Low
Rise
or
(Pre-head+) Stepping Head+
Low Rise

E.g.   ⌐I 'promise I won't ‚tell °anyone.
'Oughtn't we to 'book in ad‚vance?
⌐Come when'ever you 'feel you'd ‚like to.

5 THE SWITCHBACK   High Pre-head+ (Falling Head+)
Fall-Rise
or
(Pre-head+) Sliding Head+Fall-
Rise
or
(Pre-head+) High Fall(s)+Fall-
Rise

E.g.   ⌐We shall be ˇlate. ⌐It'll ˇdo for the °time ˇbeing.
You'll ˇnever be ˇable to ˇkeep it ˇup.
It was an ˋabsoˇlutely ˋterrible ˇparty.

6 THE LONG JUMP   High Pre-head + Rising Head +
High Fall
or
(Pre-head+) Climbing Head+
High Fall

E.g.   ⌐But it'll ‚do you a °lot of ˋgood.
‚Why on ‚earth did you ‚say you ˋcouldn't?
⌐Pa‚tricia ‚simply ‚can't ˋbear it.

7 THE HIGH BOUNCE   High Pre-head + (High Head+)
High Rise
or
(Pre-head+) Stepping Head+
High Rise

E.g.   ⁻D'you ′mean it? ⁻You 'haven't °seen it ′anywhere?
⁻Would you 'mind if he 'comes on ′later?

8 THE JACKKNIFE   High Pre-head + (High Head+)
Rise-Fall
or
(Pre-head+) Stepping Head+
Rise-Fall

E.g.   ⁻Of ^course! ⁻But 'will it °really ^help?
Is there 'any 'reason to be^lieve that?
⁻Well, pre'tend you 'don't ^know him.

9 THE HIGH DIVE   High Pre-head + (High Head+)
High Fall+ (Low Accents+) Low
Rise
or
(Pre-head+) Stepping Head+
High Fall+ (Low Accents+) Low
Rise

E.g.   ⁻I was ˅sure I could re₀ly on ,you.
⁻My 'father and ˅mother ₀came from ,Bristol.
Well, 'Joan and 'Tim ˅Bennett are the ₀most ,likely to
°help.

10 THE TERRACE   High Pre-head + (High Head+)
Mid-Level
or
(Pre-head+) Stepping Head+
Mid-Level

E.g.   ⁻Un˃fortunately, | (I can't.)
⁻No matter 'what he ˃says, | (just carry on with it.)
For the 'sake of 'peace and ˃quiet | (ignore her bad be-
haviour.)

II Intonation and Meaning

It has often been pointed out, and rightly, that no tone group is used exclusively with this or that sentence type—question, statement and the like—and also that no sentence type always requires the use of one and only one tone group. As a concrete example it would be quite untrue to say that sentences having the form of a question are always said with the Low Bounce. What is true, though, is that some sentence types are more likely to be said with one tone group than with any other: more Yes-No questions, for instance, are said with the Low Bounce than with any other tone group. In this sense one can speak of a 'normal' tone group for a particular structure, and whenever this applies we will mention it in the following pages. Broadly speaking however any sentence type can be linked with any tone group.

In this chapter we shall consider the effect of our ten tone groups in association with each of five main sentence types, *statement*, *wh-question* (containing interrogative words such as *why*, *when*, *where*, *who*, etc.), *yes-no question* (to be answered by *yes* or *no*), *command* and *interjection*; and we shall try to explain at every step the contribution which the tone group makes to the total meaning of the word group. The five sentence types are, and are meant to be, very wide and at times overlapping categories, and we shall not try to define or limit them. They will simply provide examples of the working of intonation in very different sentence structures.

This implied separation of intonation and sentence structure is an analytical procedure which is thoroughly justifiable as an aid to teaching and learning, but it should be remembered that in reality that part of the speaker's meaning which is assumed to be carried by the structure of the sentence—words and word order—and that part attributed to intonation are welded together to form the total meaning of the utterance at a particular time and in a particular context. However, the student using this book undoubtedly understands the basic meaning of English words, though not the role of intonation; so the separation can and does exist for him, and it is convenient to make use of this in what follows.

So this chapter provides a description of the attitudes conveyed by the different tone groups in association with the various sentence types. This description is a difficult business because it involves using words to suggest effects which are usually achieved by intonation. This means that words alone do not always give a very accurate impression of the attitude conveyed, yet enough can be done to produce a basis for the further development of the student's comprehension which will be tackled in Chapters III, IV and V.

The Ten Tone Groups
I *The Low Drop*

STATEMENTS

All statements associated with tone groups containing falling nuclear tones (the Low Drop, the High Drop, the Long Jump and the Jackknife) sound *definite* and *complete* in the sense that the speaker wishes them to be regarded as separate items of interest. For example, if we say

He was ˎtall, | ˎdark | and ˎhandsome. ‖

we are treating each of these three attributes as being a complete and separately interesting feature of the man; but if we say

He was ˊtall, | ˊdark | and ˎhandsome. ‖

we are linking the three together into a single, composite picture. In the same way the final item in a list which is taken to be complete is normally said with the Low Drop, the other items in the list having a tone group with a rising nuclear tone.

Examples
You can have ˊtea, | or ˊcoffee | or ˎmilk. ‖
You can 'send it ˏhome, | or 'leave it ˏhere | or 'take it ˏwith you. ‖

The use of the Low Drop for the last word group in each of these examples implies that the list is really complete, that there are no other possibilities.

If the Low Drop has no head, it typically conveys *detachment*, a *lack of involvement* in the situation. This may be variously interpreted as *coolness, dispassionateness, reserve, dullness*, and possibly *grimness* or *surliness*, on the part of the speaker.

Examples

(i) *Answers to questions*

What's your name?	ˏJohnson.
How old are you?	ˏTwenty.
Occupation?	I'm a ˏshop asₒsistant.
D'you work in London?	ˏYes, | I ˏdo.
D'you take sugar?	I ˏdon't, | ˏno.

(ii) *Announcements*

You've got ˏpaint on your ₒjacket.
You're a ˏfool.
I must ˏgo.

(iii) *Comments*

I've got the sack.	I can beˏlieve it.
I promised him nothing.	I should ˏhope not, inₒdeed.
You can go to blazes.	So ˏthat's how you ₒfeel about it.

If the High Drop were used instead of the Low Drop for these examples, with the High Fall nuclear tone rather than the Low Fall, the speaker would sound much less detached, much more involved in the situation.

In examples containing a head, the effect of the Low Drop is of very considerable *power* and *strength*, in addition to the definiteness and completeness mentioned before. This power may lend itself to utterances of a *categoric, weighty, judicial, considered* kind.

Examples

(i) *Answers to questions*

Are you sure?	'Abso°lutely ˎcertain.
What shall I do?	I 'simply °can't iˌmagine.
Can't we do something?	You 'must be ˌpatient.

(ii) *Announcements*

He's the 'stupidest °man I ˎknow.
I en'tirely aˎgree with you.
I 'hope it'll be a ˎlesson to you.

This tone group is commonly used to give weight to expressions of both approval and disapproval, of both enthusiasm and impatience.

Examples

Why did he do it?	I ₒhaven't the 'slightest iˌdea.
What was it like?	It was 'simply ˎterrible.
Was it nice?	It was 'perfectly ˎwonderful.
How do I look?	'Absolutely ˎravishing.

WH-QUESTIONS

With the Low Drop these questions sound *searching, serious, intense, urgent*, because of the power that the tone group carries. This power may again be used to reinforce both approval and disapproval.

Examples

Now 'where did I °put my ˌpipe?
'Why did you ˎdo such a ₒstupid ₒthing?
'How can I ˎthank you?
'What can I °get you to ˎdrink?
'Why don't you °look where you're ˌgoing?

Extra power can be conveyed by these questions if the special finite is accented, rather than the interrogative word.

Examples

How 'could you be so ˎstupid?
How 'can I ˎthank you?

The general effect is to lend such questions an exclamatory air, as if the speaker were saying that he could not begin to think how to answer his own question.

If the Low Fall occurs on the *wh*-word, as in single-word questions or in longer questions with only the *wh*-word accented, the attitude is again one of *detachment* and they often sound *flat* or *unsympathetic*, even *hostile*.

Examples

Got any cigarettes?	ˎWhy?
I've found a way to do it.	ˎHow?
Someone told me to tell you.	ˎWho told you to ₒtell me?
I've been there often.	ˎWhen have you ₒbeen there?

The use of the High Fall instead of the Low Fall in such examples makes the questions sound altogether more interested and more concerned.

YES-NO QUESTIONS   As we have already said, the most common way of asking yes-no questions is with the Low Bounce. When the Low Drop is used, the question is put forward as a *serious* suggestion or as a subject for *urgent* discussion.

Examples

Well 'couldn't we ˎborrow some ₒmoney?
'Would you pre°fer ˎthis ₒchair?
'Shall we post°pone it till ˎTuesday?

The Low Drop is also used when we are trying to keep someone to the point, to make him give a straight answer to a straight question.

Examples

But 'did you °see him on ˎSunday?
'Will you be °there by ˎsix?

Questions beginning with 'Will you . . .' are more often than not imperatives, and very strong ones at that.

Examples

'Will you be ˌquiet!
'Will you °stop ˌpestering me!

It would be a bold child who would dare to answer either question!

With negative questions of this kind the Low Drop gives **a** purely exclamatory effect.

Examples

'Isn't it ˌwonderful!
'Haven't they °made a ˌmess of it!
'Wouldn't you °think they'd ˌdo something aₒbout it!

Similarly, '*Would you beˌlieve it*! is entirely exclamatory. Extra exclamatory force can be obtained by placing the nuclear tone on the special finite.

Examples

ˌIsn't it ₒwonderful!
ˌAren't you a ₒlovely ₒcat!
ˌDidn't they ₒmake a ₒmess of it!

In alternative questions the Low Drop is used to mark the last of the possibilities, the previous ones having tone groups with a rising nuclear tone.

Examples

'Would you like ˌtea | or ˌcoffee? ‖
'Have you seen ˌJohn | or 'is he °still aˌway? ‖

The fall in the last word group implies that these are the *only* possibilities.

For question tags—*isn't it?*, *won't there?*, *oughtn't you?* in the examples below—the Low Drop is used when the preceding word group also ends with a Low Fall nuclear tone and when the speaker is *demanding agreement* from the listener.

Examples

What a 'beautiful ˎday, | ˏisn't it?
There'll be ˎseven of us, | ˏwon't there?
You 'ought to be aˎshamed of yourₒself, | ˏoughtn't you?

Question tags are also used independently as comments on statements made by other speakers. If the Low Drop is used in these circumstances it conveys either *lack of interest* or *hostility*.

Examples

I've just come back from Paris.   ˎHave you?
John damaged your car today.   ˎDid he?

If the High Fall is used for such comments, the speaker sounds interested and not hostile at all.

COMMANDS

The power of the Low Drop is very evident with commands. They sound *very serious* and *very strong*. The speaker appears to take it for granted that his words will be heeded, that he will be obeyed.

Examples

'Come and have ˎdinner with us.
'Try the ˎother ₒkey.
Now 'take it ˎslowly.
For 'heaven's °sake be ˎcareful.
'Don't be riˎdiculous.

This tone group is particularly common with commands containing *do* and *please*; these emphatic words combine with the Low Drop to produce a very powerful effect.

Examples

'Do stop ˎtickling.
'Please be ˎquiet.

Sometimes the Low Drop, with a Low Fall nuclear tone

alone and no head, is used for short commands. These sound *unemotional, calm, controlled,* often *cold.*

Examples

ˌDon't. ˌTake it. ˌSit, ˳Fido.
ˌGently, you ˳clumsy ˳man.

INTERJECTIONS

The power of the Low Drop makes it a very suitable tone group for interjections. This power is at its greatest in interjections where a head is present, and for these the Low Drop is commonly used.

Examples

'Oh ˌgood! 'How riˌdiculous!
How 'very peˌculiar! 'What ˌnonsense!
What a 'lovely ˳day for a ˌpicnic!
You 'lazy ˳good for nothing ˌwretch!

In shorter interjections, when the Low Drop has no head and there is only the one accent, the power of this tone group is somewhat less in evidence; and the interjections sound *calm, unsurprised, self-possessed, reserved.*

Examples

ˌGood. ˌRight. ˌOh. ˌNonsense.
Good ˌmorning. Good ˌevening.

Greetings like the last two examples can also be said with *Good* accented; in this case the power of the Low Drop is underlined and they sound rather ponderous. Notice, finally, that ˌ*Thank you* and ˌ*Thanks* express genuine, though unexcited, gratitude.

2 *The High Drop*

STATEMENTS

Statements sound as complete and definite with the High Drop as they do with the Low Drop, but they no longer sound reserved or detached. On the contrary, they give the impression of *involvement in the situation*, of *participation*, and of a *lightness* and *airiness* which is in contrast to the weight and power of the Low Drop.

Examples

What time is it?	It's 'half past ˅twelve. ‖ I 'didn't °realise how ˅late it was.
How did the game go?	'Very ˅well. ‖ We ˳won sur'prisingly ˅easily.
Is Mike still doing well?	˅Yes, │ ˅splendidly. ‖ I can 'hardly be˅lieve it.

This lightness of the High Drop is often an indication of *warmth*, of a desire not to appear cool towards the listener; and because of this the High Drop is very frequently used in everyday conversation.

Examples

| Can you come and see me? | I'm a'fraid I ˅can't. ‖ I've 'got to °catch a ˅train. |
| What's the time? | I 'don't ˅know. ‖ I sup'pose it's about ˅twelve. |

Consider *It was a 'very °dark ˎnight*, said with the Low Drop: this would be appropriate as the opening of a story, where the narrator wishes to keep aloof from the proceedings; but in conversation, for instance as an answer to the question *How did you manage to lose yourself?* it would usually be more suitable to use the High Drop, *It was a 'very °dark ˅night*, since it is lighter in tone and less solemn-sounding.

WH-QUESTIONS

The High Drop is probably the most common way of asking these questions. It avoids the seriousness and urgency of the Low Drop, and such questions sound *brisk, businesslike, considerate, not unfriendly.*

Examples

'What's the ˅time?
'When did you ar˅rive?
'How °long did it °take you to ˅get here?
'Where on °earth have you ˅been all this ₒtime?

An even more friendly way of asking these questions is with the Low Bounce; the business-like attitude of the High Drop is then replaced by interest in the other person and friendliness towards him.

If there is no head and the High Fall nuclear tone occurs on the *wh*-word, there is no detachment or flatness as with the Low Drop. On the contrary, the questions sound *bright* and *interested*.

Examples

I saw the Queen today.	˅Where?
I know an easy way to do it.	But ˅how?
We'll meet tomorrow.	Well ˅when shall we ₒmeet?

YES-NO QUESTIONS

As with the Low Drop, yes-no questions asked with the High Drop are put forward as suggestions or as subjects for discussion and decision. The difference is that the Low Drop sounds more serious, whereas the High Drop sounds *lighter* and *less urgent*. Often enough the speaker puts the question so that he may answer it himself negatively; he may therefore sound *sceptical* about the result.

Examples

John says he's got an alibi.	'Can he ˅prove it? ‖ (I doubt it.)
Shall we tell Frank about it?	'Dare we ˅risk it?
Shall we try again?	Well 'would it be °any ˅use?
I can't get comfortable.	'Would you pre°fer ˅this ₒchair?
I don't know what to do.	'Can I ˅help you at ₒall?

Question tags have the High Fall nuclear tone on the special finite when the preceding word group ends either with a High Fall or with a rising nuclear tone of some kind. In either case, as with the Low Drop, the speaker is *demanding agreement*.

Examples

It's ri`diculous, | `isn't it?
You're ˏnot ˏfrightened, | `are you?
It's ˇnot im`possible, | `is it?
`John could do ˏthat, | `couldn't he?

Used as independent comments, these phrases express *mild surprise but acceptance of the listener's statement.*

Examples

I like it here.	`Do you? ‖ (I'm glad of that. I thought you mightn't.)
She's thirty-five.	`Is she? ‖ (I thought she was younger.)
They won't help us.	`Won't they? ‖ (That's interesting.)

With a dissenting word the question demands scrutiny of something which the listener appears to be assuming.

Examples

I'm glad the car's all right again.	But `is it? ‖ (That's the whole point.)
It'll be easy if John helps.	`Will he, ˏthough? ‖ (We're not sure.)

COMMANDS

With the High Drop, commands seem to *suggest a course of action* rather than to give an order, as they do with the Low Drop; and even if the intention is to give an order, the speaker does not seem to be worrying whether he will be obeyed or not.

Examples

What shall I do with this rubbish?	`Burn it.
How much d'you want for it?	'Make me an `offer.
This tea's too hot.	'Put some more `milk in it.
But the lid doesn't fit.	'Try °turning it the °other way `round.

INTERJECTIONS

The High Drop here expresses *mild surprise*, with very much less power and impact than the Low Drop; and the speaker sounds *less reserved, less self-possessed*.

Examples

Good morning, Jack.	Good ˋmorning, ₒFred. ‖ (I didn't expect to see you here.)
Here's your pen.	ˋOh, │ ˋthank you. ‖ (I thought I'd lost it.)
It's six o'clock.	ˋHeavens! ‖ (I'm late.)
I must stay in and work.	How 'very ˋnoble of you!
We've sold our house.	What an exˈtraordinary °thing to ˋdo!
Look, it's snowing.	ˋOh, │ ˋyes. ‖ 'So it ˋis.

3 *The Take-Off*

STATEMENTS

Statements with the Take-Off invite a further contribution to the conversation from the listener.

Examples

Good morning, Mr. Thomson.	(Good morning.) ‖ It's a ˎnice ˎday.
Hullo, Frank.	(Hullo, Jimmy.) ‖ You're ˎlooking ₒvery ˎsmart. ‖ (Going to a wedding?)
Come in and sit down.	It's ˎvery ˎnice of you.
Have you heard about Max?	ˎNo.

Usually the speaker gives (and wishes to give) the impression that he is *reserving judgment* until he has heard more from the listener.

Examples

Have you any money on you?	ˎYes.
D'you go to the theatre?	ˎSometimes.
Shall we be in time?	I ˎthink °so.
Can I have your autograph?	ˎIf you ˎlike.

Going on from this *guarded* attitude, the Take-Off is often used to *appeal* to the listener to change his attitude, which the speaker considers wrong.

Examples

I shall have to sack him.	You ˌcan't do ˌthat. ‖ (He's too useful.)
What a terrible play!	It ˌwasn't as ₒbad as ₒall ˌthat.
You said we could come on Tuesday.	It's ˌnot ₒTuesday to ˌday.
Must I do it now?	ˌNot if you ₒdon't ˌwant to.
I'm most grateful to you.	ˌThat's all °right. ‖ (It was nothing at all.)

Very common is the use of this tone group in *resentful contradictions*.

Examples

You haven't written that letter.	ˌYes I ˌhave. ‖ (I wrote it this morning.)
There's our train.	ˌNo it's ˌnot. ‖ (It's the next one.)

Notice that the implied criticism of the listener may be because he is blaming himself too much or praising the speaker too much, when the statement sounds *deprecatory*.

Examples

You've done a fine job.	I ˌdon't ˌknow. ‖ ˌYou could have ₒdone it ₒjust as ˌwell.
I feel terrible about it.	You've ˌnothing to re ˌproach yourself °with. ‖ It ˌwasn't ˌyour °fault.

This tone group is also used for *continuative* purposes, to show that there is more to be said, as, for example, in enumerations:

ˌOne, │ ˌtwo, │ ˌthree, │ ˌfour, │ ˌfive, │

If the enumeration is completed the last item has a falling tone:

You can have ,coffee, | or ,tea, | or ˅cocoa. ‖

In the examples below, where the tone group is again used to express non-finality, the *deprecatory* attitude, absent in the simple enumeration, is present, as though the speaker were denying that his utterance contained anything very new or interesting.

Examples

And ˌwhen I ˌgot °there | he ˅gave it me.
I ˌwent ˌup to him | and he ˅snubbed me.

WH-QUESTIONS

When the nucleus is the interrogative word the effect may be either of repeating the listener's question or of asking for information to be repeated. In both cases the questioner's tone is *wondering*, as though he was mildly puzzled that such a question should have been asked or that he should have been given the information he was given.

Examples

The meeting's at five.	,When? ‖ (I thought it was six.)
How did he do it?	,How did he °do it? ‖ (Perfectly obvious.)
His name was Scroggs.	,What was °that? ‖ ,Scroggs?

It is fairly rare to ask any but the above repeated type of *wh*-question with the Take-Off; any other sounds very calm but very *disapproving* and *resentful*.

Examples

| You shouldn't have done it. | And ˌwhat's it ₀got to ₀do with ,you, may I °ask? |
| Please don't do that. | And ˌwhy ,shouldn't I? ‖ (It's a free country.) |

YES-NO QUESTIONS

Such questions almost invariably express *disapproval* or *scepticism* and should only be used where this is appropriate.

Examples

You mean to say you're getting married?	ˌIs it so ₀very surˏprising?
I'm sorry now that I did it.	ˌAre you ˏreally °sorry?

When used as independent comments, question tags said with the Take-Off show exactly the same disapproval and scepticism.

Examples

I saw you on Wednesday.	ˏDid you? ‖ (I thought it was Thursday.)
He's only thirty-five.	ˏIs he? ‖ (He looks about fifty.)

On the other hand, when they are used in conjunction with a preceding statement, question tags having this tone group do *not* express this disapproving, sceptical attitude. Nor do they demand confirmation of the speaker's view, as with the Low Drop and the High Drop. Rather they leave the listener free to answer either *Yes* or *No*, though it is very clear that the speaker inclines to one view rather than the other and that the listener's agreement with that view is *expected*.

Examples

It's about 'ten oˋclock, | ˏisn't it?
You 'didn't feel °very ˋwell, | ˏdid you?
I 'don't think you could have ˎdone it, | ˏcould you?

Notice that when a speaker says:

She's a ˋnice ₀girl, | ˏisn't she?

he has probably not met the girl concerned, or at any rate not completely made up his mind about her niceness, since he is genuinely concerned to have the listener's view; whereas when he says:

She's a ˋnice ₀girl, | ˋisn't she?

he almost certainly has met the girl and formed an opinion

about her niceness, and is *demanding* confirmation of that opinion by the listener.

The question tags *will you?*, *won't you?*, *would you?* are commonly used after imperative forms in order to make it plain that the command is in fact a form of invitation.

Examples

'Come and sit ˎdown, | ˏwon't you?
'Come over ˎhere a ₒminute, | ˏwill you?
'Make mine a ˎsherry, | ˏwould you?

Contrast this with the use of a falling tone on *will you!*, which strengthens and emphasises the command.

Example

'Stand ˎstill, | ˎwill you!

Direct question tags, i.e. those which are in the negative when the preceding statement is in the negative, or in the affirmative when the statement is in the affirmative, *always* have the Take-Off. Such utterances are used to acknowledge something which has previously been stated, to refer back to something already established and accepted by both parties.

Examples

What a lovely dress!   You ˋlike it, | ˏdo you?
I slapped John's face today. You've ˋquarrelled with him, |
                             ˏhave you?

COMMANDS

The Take-Off is not widely used with commands except those beginning with *Don't*, when the effect is of *appealing to the listener*, exactly as with statements.

Examples

I'm going to sack him.   ˏDon't do ˏthat. ‖ (He's not a bad chap.)
I'm afraid I've broken it.   ˏDon't ₒworry about ˏthat.

This tone group is also commonly heard with a few short commands, when they are intended as a rather *calm warning* or *exhortation.*

Examples
,Careful. ,Steady. ,Watch. A,gain.

With either the Low Drop or the High Drop all these examples would sound much more like orders and less like appeals.

INTERJECTIONS

Most interjections are rarely said in this way, but some—usually short—quite commonly have this tone group; some seem to imply *reserved judgment* and to require more explanation from the hearer.

Examples

John says he can't come.	,Oh. ‖ (Why not?)
It's half past ten.	,Well. ‖ (We're not in a hurry.)

Others imply *calm, casual acknowledgment* of a not unexpected matter.

Examples

The car's here.	,Good. ‖ (We're just about ready.)
Your change, sir.	,Thank you.
I can't help you.	‚Very ,well. ‖ (We'll do it alone.)

4 *The Low Bounce*

STATEMENTS

Such statements tend to sound *soothing, reassuring*; they offer the information as a means of setting the listener's mind at rest; no criticism is implied such as is found with the Take-Off, but there is a *hint of great self-confidence* or *self-reliance* on the part of the speaker.

Examples

Where are you going?	'Just to °post a ˌletter.
I've no head for heights.	It's 'all ˌright. ‖ You 'won't ˌfall.
Are you ready to go?	I 'shan't be a ˌmoment.

In *echoed* statements, i.e. those which repeat more or less what has just been said by the other person, this tone group turns the statement into a *surprised and disbelieving question*.

Examples

I said he was a liar.	You 'actually °called him a ˌliar?
He's broken his leg.	'Broken his ˌleg?

The same attitude is present in other statements which are not obviously echoes.

Examples

I won the first prize.	And you 'didn't ˌtell us?
You mustn't drive that car.	You 'mean it's ˌdangerous?

This tone group is frequently used with non-final groups, when the speaker is leading up to something more.

Examples

'When I arˌrived │ there was 'nobody at ˋhome. ‖
I 'opened the °door ˌquietly │ and 'looked ˌin. ‖
As 'soon as you ˌsee him │ 'tell him I'm ˋhere. ‖
⁻At ˌOxford │ he was 'very ˋlazy. ‖

The effect of the Low Bounce here is to create *expectancy* regarding whatever is to follow: the listener is led to believe that it will be something very interesting.

WH-QUESTIONS

By using the Low Bounce with *wh*-questions the speaker seeks to establish a bond with the listener, to show interest not only in receiving the information asked for but also in the listener himself. Since this tone group avoids the possible sternness of the Low Drop and the brisk, businesslike attitude of the High Drop, it is a very common way of asking these questions of young children. Among adults too it is often used for an opening question, when the speaker wants to make it absolutely clear that his enquiry is a friendly one, not an attempt to pry or to criticise. Once this friendliness has been established he may then revert, in subsequent *wh*-questions, to the High Drop as being more businesslike.

Examples
> (Hullo, darling.) ‖ 'What have you °got ‚there?
> 'What ‚train are you °thinking of °catching?
> 'Why did you °let him °think we °didn't ‚know?

Note that when the nucleus is the interrogative word, the effect of repetition and the puzzlement of the Take-Off returns.

Examples

I saw him at Wembley.	You 'saw him ‚where?
They did it last week.	They 'did it ‚when?

In *echoed questions* this tone group shows *disapproval* of the questions being asked.

Examples

When are you going home?	'When am I °going ‚home? ‖ (How dare you!)
How long will you be?	'How ‚long? ‖ (How on earth should I know?)

YES-NO QUESTIONS

This is by far the most common way of asking yes-no questions; it should be regarded as the normal way, with the speaker displaying *genuine interest* in obtaining the information requested. Any other tone group should be used only in the special circumstances outlined in the appropriate place in this chapter.

Examples

'Are you °coming ˏwith us?
'Did you en°joy the ˏplay last °night?
'Would you mind °moving aˏlong a bit?
'Seen the °Times ˏleader to°day?

When there is no accent before the nucleus, that is, when there is no head, the High Pre-head is used to avoid the scepticism of the Take-Off.

Examples

⁻Is ˏthis the °one?
⁻Can ˏI °help at °all?

COMMANDS

Commands with the Low Bounce have the *soothing* effect of statements with this tone group. They imply that the speaker is somehow, perhaps only temporarily, in a superior position to the listener, with the result that the speaker sounds *encouraging* and perhaps *calmly patronising*. For this reason these commands are frequently used to children but less commonly to adults who may find the soothing effect overdone and irritating.

Examples

'Come to ˏDaddy.   'Blow your ˏnose, °dear.
'Don't ˏworry.   'Move aˏlong, °please.

With either the Low Fall or the High Fall nuclear tones of the Low Drop and the High Drop, commands such as these would sound much more purposeful and insistent.

INTERJECTIONS

This tone group is rather commonly used with a few interjections. The effect is rather brighter than with the Take-Off, not so reserved, but still quite *airy* and *casual* and with the *encouraging* effect mentioned above.

Examples

I'll see you tomorrow.   'Right you ˏare.

I've managed it at last.	'Well ˏdone!
It's my exam tomorrow.	'Good ˏluck!
There's no escaping it.	'Ah ˏwell! ‖ (I don't suppose it'll kill us.)
More tea?	'No, ˏthank you. ‖ (That was very nice.)
Shall I stand over here?	'Yes, ˏplease.

Greetings very frequently employ this tone group, when they sound *bright* and *friendly*. If the syllable before the nuclear syllable is accented the effect is rather ponderous; so most often it is unstressed though high in pitch, a High Prehead being used.

Examples

⁻Good ˏmorning.   ⁻Hulˏlo, °there.

Leave-takings are almost invariably in this form since any tone group with a falling nuclear tone sounds too brusque and final, and the Take-Off sounds too reserved. The Low Bounce, however, sounds *bright* and *friendly*.

Examples

⁻Good ˏmorning.   ⁻Good͵bye.   ⁻Good ˏnight, °dear.

5   *The Switchback*

The simplest case is that of *non-final* word groups, where the Fall-Rise draws particular attention to one element for the purpose of contrast, and at the same time shows an intention to continue the utterance. In the example

On ˇweekdays | I ˋwork, ‖ but on ˇSaturdays | I ˋdon't. ‖

there is an obvious contrast between *weekdays* on the one hand and *Saturdays* on the other, and the contrast is under-

lined by the use of the Fall-Rise nuclear tone on both words;
it is clearly *weekdays* as opposed to *Saturdays*, and *Saturdays*
as opposed to *weekdays*. What are the oppositions in the
following?

Examples
'We all ˋlike it, ‖ but 'Mr. ˇSmith | ˋdoesn't. ‖
I ˋtravel a ₒgreat ₒdeal, ‖ so whenˋever I'm at ˇhome | I 'make the
ˋmost of it. ‖
I ˋknow his ˇface, | but I 'can't re˚call his ˋname. ‖

In these examples the oppositions can be found in the text:
they are, of course, *We—Mr Smith*; *travel—home*; *face—
name*. But in other cases the opposition must be imagined.
Consider this example:

In ˇmy oₒpinion | he's a ˋfool. ‖

What is opposed here to *my*? There is nothing in the rest of
the sentence which could conceivably contrast with it. So we
must look outside the sentence and ask ourselves what is
likely to be contrasted with *my*. And obviously it is words like
your, or *his*, or *their* which spring to mind. So what the speaker
is saying in effect is: 'I'm giving *my* opinion, and it isn't
necessarily the opinion of anyone else.' What are the unex-
pressed contrasts in the following?

Examples
ˋIf I could have ˇseen the ₒactors | I'd have enˋjoyed it. ‖
Whenˋever I ˚see him in the ˇevening | he's ˋdrunk. ‖
In the ˇlater ₒstages | it was ˋmarvellous. ‖
Acˋcording to ˇJohn | it 'cost a ˋfortune. ‖

In all these and most other examples, the appropriate contrast, whether expressed in the text or not, is very clearly
brought out by the use of the Fall-Rise nuclear tone in the
non-final group. When however the Fall-Rise is the only
accent in the non-final word group, the contrasting power of
the Fall-Rise is much less apparent.

Examples

ˇSometimes | he ˈirritates me ˋterribly. ‖
He ˇtold me | she'd ˈgone aˋway. ‖
In ˇthat ˳case | we'd ˈbetter °leave ˋnow. ‖

In these cases we quite often use the Fall-Rise in the non-final group, not so much to mark a contrast, but to avoid the dull, deprecatory effect of the Low Rise in the Take-Off and the tentative, somewhat casual effect of the High Rise in the High Bounce.

The pointing of contrasts by the use of the Fall-Rise nuclear tone is not restricted to non-final word groups. It is also apparent in final word groups, where this tone group does not serve an introductory purpose. Consider the following:

Did you play cricket at the weekend?   I ˈdid on ˇSaturday.

Here *Saturday* is being singled out for contrast, since it bears the Fall-Rise, and the implied contrast is with the rest of the weekend, namely, Sunday. So it is clear that the speaker did *not* play cricket on Sunday, and he does not need to put it into words. What are the unspoken contrasts in the following?

Examples

I didn't know you drank coffee.   I ˈdo ˇsometimes.
Will you have dinner with us?   I ˈwill if I ˇcan.
Is it going to keep fine?   I ˇthink ˳so.
Why did you go there?   ˈNone of us °really ˇwanted to.

This distinguishing of two conflicting factors within the immediate situation is particularly useful in the field of *concession*. The example

She has a ˈlovely ˇvoice.

can be found in two quite different types of context:

1. What a lovely voice!   ˋYes, | she has a ˈlovely ˇvoice. ‖
(But I don't think much of her as an actress.)

In this situation the speaker explicitly, though *grudgingly*, concedes that the lady sings very well; at the same time he implies reservations about other aspects of her professional talents, about her acting ability as the extended context shows. When a speaker makes an explicit concession to his listener about part of the subject but implies reservations on the remainder, we call this situation *grudging admission*.

Examples

I'd like it as soon as possible.	You could ˈhave it by ˅dinner ˌtime. ‖ (But no earlier.)
Can I take this one?	You ˈcan if you ˅like. ‖ (But the other one's better.)
Is it raining?	It ˈis at the ˅moment. ‖ (But it may clear up later.)
What was the film like?	Well it ˈwasn't the °worst I've °ever ˅seen. ‖ (But it was far from the best.)
2. I don't think much of her as an actress.	She has a ˈlovely ˅voice. ‖ (Even if she can't act.)

In this second situation the speaker explicitly asks the listener to concede that the voice is good; at the same time, as the extended context makes clear, he implicitly leaves the way open for agreement on the listener's criticism of the lady's acting talents. In this situation the speaker sounds *reluctant, defensive*. So, when a speaker explicitly requires a concession from his listener about part of the subject but implies agreement on the remainder, we call this *reluctant* or *defensive dissent*.

Examples

I'd like it by tomorrow.	I ˈdoubt whether I can °do it by ˅then. ‖ (But it won't be much later.)
You look cold.	I'm ˈnot e°xactly ˅cold. ‖ (Just a bit shivery now and then.)
You might win a fortune.	It's ˈnot very ˅likely, I'm aˌfraid. ‖ (But I wouldn't deny the possibility.)

Everyone's gone home.   ˟Not   ˅everyone. ‖ (Most   have,   but John's still here.)

From this point it is only a short step to the expression of explicit *corrections* which, with this tone group, often sound *concerned, reproachful* or *hurt*.

Examples

When's he due? On Monday?	On ˅Tuesday.
It won't take long, will it?	It'll ₒtake at ˟least a ˅week.
How many were there? Sixty?	˅Seventy.
About midnight, was it?	It was ˟earlier than ˅that.
I play golf rather well.	You ˅think you ₒdo.

This same *concerned, reproachful, hurt* attitude is apparent also in *direct contradictions*.

Examples

It didn't take you long.	It ˅did. ‖ (It took ages.)
So you don't like golf.	I ˅do.
John won't be here today.	I ˟think he ˅will.
You're not trying.	I most ˟certainly ˅am.

Compare the following reactions to the statement: *I can do that on Monday.*

High Drop:	You ˎcan't.	(I've just explained you can't.)
Take-Off:	You ˏcan't.	(You ought to know very well you can't.)
Switchback:	You ˅can't.	(And I'm sorry you should think you can.)

The first contradiction sounds lively and dogmatic, the second resentful and the third rather reproachful. Notice, however, that if the original statement were: *I'll do that on Monday*, the only appropriate response would be the one having the High Drop.

This concern or reproach is carried on into other utterances which cannot be regarded as contradictions.

Examples

I've been sacked.	You're ˇnot ˇserious!
Did you catch the train?	ˇOnly by the °skin of my ˇteeth.
I went to London today.	I ˇwish you'd ˇtold me.
Could you call at the post-office?	Well, it's ˇrather a ˇnuisance.
How did it happen?	ˇI ₒdon't ₒknow.

This same attitude of concern or reproach is found in *warnings*.

Examples

You'll ˇfall.
Your ˇchair's ₒslipping.
You'll ˇmiss your ˇtrain.
You'd ˇbetter be °careful with the ˇfragile ₒones.

In *apologies*, where the concern might seem to be appropriate, this tone group tends to suggest reservations on the part of the speaker.

Examples

I'm ˇsorry. ‖ (But I'm afraid it's impossible.)
I ˇbeg your ˇpardon. ‖ (But I'm afraid I must contradict you.)

ˇ*Sorry*, by itself, *is* an apology, but rather a perfunctory one.

One other category in which the Switchback is often used is that of *tentative suggestions*, where the speaker wants to help but not to commit himself too deeply to the course suggested.

Examples

We need another player.	You could ˇask ˇJohn.
When can we meet?	ˇWednesday ₒmight be a possiₒbility.
What will you do?	I could ˇtry ˇphoning him, I supₒpose.

QUESTIONS

In echoed questions, whether of the *wh-* or the yes-no kind, the effect of the Switchback is of *astonishment*, as if the speaker can hardly believe his ears.

Examples

Are you going to the wedding?	Am ˇI ₒgoing?! ‖ (Well, of course I am!)
What's the matter?	ˈWhat's the ˇmatter?! ‖ (Everything's the matter!)

In questions where there is only one word to be accented, the Switchback is used in a way reminiscent of the Take-Off in similar questions.

Examples

I've just seen Pablo Aron.	ˇWho, did you ₒsay?
They must be here, somewhere.	Well, where ˇare they, ₒthen?
It's your turn.	ˇIs it?
John liked it.	ˇDid he?

The possible disapproval of the Take-Off is minimised, and *surprise*, *interest*, and *concern* are dominant.

The Switchback is also used to make corrections to questions, as to statements.

Examples

How will Henry get home?	ˈHow will ˇJane get ₒhome, you ₒmean. ‖ (Henry's journey's simple.)
Is John going to play?	ˈIs he ˇwilling to ₒplay, you ₒmean.

COMMANDS

Commands with the Switchback have a *warning* note, but more *urgency* than with either the Take-Off or the Low Bounce, since the reproach or concern mentioned in relation to statements is also present here.

Examples

ˇSteady! ‖ (You'll have me over.)
ˇMind! ‖ (There's a step here.)
ˈCareful with that ˇglass! ‖ (You'll drop it.)
ˈDon't be any °stupider than you can ˇhelp!
ˈTry and be °there by ˇsix. ‖ (Otherwise it'll be too late.)

INTERJECTIONS

A very few interjections of *scorn* take the Switchback.

Examples

Did you lend him any money?	ˋNot ˇI!
Shall you be going again?	ˋNo ˇfear!
Will you give in?	ˋNot ˇlikely!
He'll probably give you his car.	ˋSome ˇhope!

As with other sentence types, corrections may also be made to interjections by this means.

Example

What a lovely swimsuit!   What a ˋlovely ˇhandkerchief!

6 *The Long Jump*

STATEMENTS

Statements with the Long Jump have the definiteness and completeness of all the falling tone groups; and, as we might expect from the fact that both have the High Fall nuclear tone, it also shares the sense of participation and involvement of the High Drop. In addition the Long Jump, with its rising head, adds an attitude of *protest*, as if the speaker were suffering under a sense of injustice.

Examples

John said you disliked the play.	I ˏliked it imˋmensely.
Haven't you brought the car?	You ˏdidn't ˋask me to.
You ought to have told me.	I ˏdidn't °think it was imˋportant.

If these replies were given with the High Drop they would sound light, airy and relatively mild; but with the Long Jump they are much more emotional and protesting.

WH-QUESTIONS

These give much the same effect as statements; the speaker is asking about something very unexpected to him and perhaps not very pleasing. The *protest* is still very evident.

Examples

I told David about it.	₌Why did you do ˋthat? ‖ (It wasn't necessary.)
I know I brought a knife.	But ₌where in the °world have you ˋput it?
John's here.	How on ₌earth did he °manage to ˋget here? ‖ (The road's flooded.)

YES-NO QUESTIONS

As with the Low Drop and the High Drop, yes-no questions with the Long Jump are offered as subjects for discussion and decision rather than for an immediate answer. In addition, the speaker is suggesting, with the same overtone of *protest*, that the question is crucial, and if it can be decided, then everything will be straightforward.

Examples

I can't think who to turn to.	₌Would it be °any °good °trying ˋJohn?
I doubt whether David'll help.	₌Is it °fair to exˋpect him to?
I can't do it today.	Well ₌can you °do it toˋmorrow, ₀then?

COMMANDS

As with the High Drop, commands with the Long Jump are not so much orders as recommendations for a course of action. At the same time the speaker expresses *surprise*, and some *criticism*, that such an obvious course has not occurred to the listener before.

Examples

What on earth shall I do?	₌Try it aˋgain. ‖ (You've no alternative.)
I wish Ann didn't dislike me so.	Well ₌don't be so ˋrude to her in ₀future.
I wonder who'd repair it.	₌Take it °back to the °shop where you ˋbought it.

INTERJECTIONS

The *protest* associated with the Long Jump in statements is equally present in interjections. The speaker seems to feel that he has been taken, perhaps unfairly, by surprise and that some explanation is due to him.

Examples

John refuses to come.	ˏWhat an ex°traordinary ˋthing!
You've passed your exam.	What ˏwonderful ˋnews! ‖ (It's almost incredible.)
But I really wanted them.	What a ˏpity you °didn't °say so ˋsooner!

7   *The High Bounce*

STATEMENTS

Complete statements said with the High Bounce have the effect of *questions* in most cases, as in so many other European languages.

Examples

You ′like him?	means	′Do you ˏlike him?
′Sugar?	means	′Do you take ˏsugar?
He's ′definitely ′going?	means	′Is he °definitely ˏgoing?

Very often this tone group is used in *echoed* statements to elicit a repetition by the listener of something he has said; it is as if the speaker were saying: 'Did you say . . .?' or 'Did you mean . . .?'.

Examples

It's your fault.	′My °fault?
They were all delighted.	′All of them?
It isn't fair.	′Not ′fair, did you °say?

The difference between this and the Take-Off is that there is no suggestion of the disapproval of the latter. Similarly the puzzlement, often found in echoed statements said with the Low Bounce, is also absent. The effect of the High Bounce is purely questioning.

    The High Bounce is also used in *non-final* word groups to

suggest continuation. It sounds somewhat *casual,* rather more *tentative* than the Take-Off or the Low Bounce in similar circumstances.

Examples

You can have 'milk, | or 'tea, | or ˋcoffee. ‖
I like the 'colour, | the 'shape, | and the ˌpattern. ‖
You can 'stay 'here | or 'come with ˋus. ‖
If 'ever you 'need me | I'll ˋwillingly ˳help. ‖

In cases such as these the use of the Low Bounce in the non-final groups would create an air of expectancy. With the High Bounce there is far less of this expectancy and the effect is much more of pure continuation.

WH-QUESTIONS

When the nuclear tone is on the interrogative word, the High Bounce calls for the *repetition of information already given,* as does the Take-Off, but the wondering, puzzled flavour of the Take-Off is absent.

Examples

'What was his °name again? ‖ (I've forgotten.)
'When did you °say he was °coming?
He's 'coming for 'how long?

When the nuclear tone is not on the interrogative word, the speaker is often *echoing* the listener's question in order to get it clear in his mind before giving an answer; again there is no criticism implied as there is with the Low Bounce.

Examples

When's he arriving?   'When's he ar'riving? ‖ (Is that what you asked?)

How many children has he?   'How 'many?

This might also apply to the case where the nuclear tone is on the interrogative word; then it would be this particular part of the question that the speaker wants to get clear.

Example

When's he arriving?   ′When? ‖ (Or where?)

The High Bounce is also used in straightforward *wh*-questions, that is, not echoes or requests for repetition; and such questions sound rather like those with the Low Bounce, but very much more *tentative* and *casual*, as if to avoid the appearance of prying.

Examples

ˈWho were you ′talking to? ‖ (Anyone I know?)
ˈWhen can we ′meet? ‖ (Sometime on Thursday?)

YES-NO QUESTIONS Yes-no questions with the High Bounce may be *echoed* questions (as with *wh*-questions above) or not. The following are echoes.

Examples

Is it raining?   ˈIs it ′raining, did you °say?
Would you like one?   Would ′I °like one? ‖ (I'd love one.)

Straightforward questions may, however, be asked with this tone group, when they sound *lighter*, *more casual* than with the Take-Off or the Low Bounce.

Examples

Put your mac on.   ˈIs it ′raining?
I don't know what to do. Can ′I °help at °all?

This tone group is particularly common with short comments of the type below, the effect being of a minimum response designed to keep the conversation going. There is no suggestion of the disapproval or scepticism of the Take-Off.

Examples

I've just seen John.   ′Have you?
He said he was tired. ′Did he?

COMMANDS AND
INTERJECTIONS

The High Bounce is used with these almost exclusively to question a part or all of an utterance of the listener and elucidate his exact meaning, with no particular critical intention.

Examples

Take it home.	'Take it ′home? ‖ (Is that what you said?)
Don't!	′Don't? ‖ (Why not?)
What a shame!	'What a ′shame? ‖ (Why?)
The silly young fool!	′Young °fool? ‖ (He's old enough to know better.)

The interjections *Oh* and *Really* are often heard with this tone group, when they are equivalent to the minimum comments, mentioned under yes-no questions above.

Examples

I've just seen John.	′Oh?
He said he was tired.	′Really?

8   *The Jackknife*

STATEMENTS

The Jackknife implies all the definiteness and completeness associated with the other tone groups having falling nuclear tones. It particularly shows that the speaker is greatly *impressed*, perhaps *awed*.

Examples

Have you heard about Pat?	^Yes! ‖ (Isn't it scandalous!)
He's got two wives.	I ^know!

With the High Drop, that is, with the High Fall nuclear tone instead of the Rise-Fall as here, these statements would sound politely interested but not nearly so impressed.

The Jackknife is very often used in *echoing* an immediately prior remark, in order to show how impressed the speaker is, whether favourably or not.

Examples

She was wearing purple tights.	^Purple!
I got two hundred pounds for it.	'Two ^hundred!

The speaker often sounds *complacent, self-satisfied*, even *smug*.

Examples

Are you sure?	^Certain.
It's absolutely ridiculous.	I 'quite a^gree with you.
Is that your last word?	I'm a'fraid it ^is.
John's failed his driving test.	I'm 'not sur^prised.

This tone group lends itself especially well to the expression of a *challenging* or *censorious* attitude.

Examples

I don't like the man.	You've 'never even ^spoken to him.
Why don't you like it?	I ^do.
Jane was terribly upset.	You can 'hardly ^blame her.
He thinks you're afraid.	He can 'think what he ^likes.

This tone group has an *intensifying* function very similar to the use of the word *even*.

Examples

Do you weigh as much as twelve stone?	^More. (=Even more.)
(It doesn't need an expert.)	^I could ₒdo it. (=Even I . . .)
I can't do it.	You 'aren't ^trying. (= . . . even trying.)

Sometimes the speaker gives the impression of *disclaiming responsibility*, of *shrugging aside any involvement*; he emphasises that he is an onlooker rather than a responsible authority.

Examples

May I take this chair?	^Certainly.

Can I have a word with you?   By ^all ₒmeans.
Do you mind if I join you?   'Not in the ^least.

WH-QUESTIONS

The Jackknife gives to these questions a note of *challenge* and *antagonism,* which is usually equivalent to the word *but* placed before the question or the word *though* after it.

Examples

You could surely find some
   money somewhere.   (But) ^where?
I know it for a fact.   ^How do you ₒknow, (though)?
He's rather a nuisance.   'Why not ^tell him ₒso?
I'm worried about the situation.   'What's it °got to °do with ^you?

As with statements, there is often a *disclaiming of responsibility* for the situation.

Examples

I've had this pain for days.   'Why don't you ^do something a₀bout it?

Where's Jane?   How on 'earth should ^I ₒknow?
I can't understand her.   'Who ^can?

YES-NO QUESTIONS

The Jackknife is very commonly found with comments of the type below, where it shows that the speaker *accepts what has been said and is impressed by it, either favourably or unfavourably.*

Examples

He shot an elephant.   ^Did he!
They've nowhere to live.   ^Haven't they!

Quite often such comments sound *challenging.*

Examples

You can't do that.   ^Can't I! ‖ (We'll see about that!)
I'll punch your head.   ^Will you!
You'd better mind your
   manners.   ^Had I!

Negative question forms used exclamatorily again show that the speaker is *vastly impressed, favourably or unfavourably.*

Examples

What do you think of my roses?   ^Aren't they ₀lovely!
And this is Charles, the eldest.   'Hasn't he ^grown!

Maximum exclamatory effect is gained if the Rise-Fall is placed on the special finite, as in the first example above.

This tone group is used with question tags when the preceding word group also has the Rise-Fall as its nuclear tone and the speaker wishes to *compel agreement.*

Examples

It's ^terrible, | ^isn't it?
You can 'hardly ^blame her, | ^can you?

With fuller questions the Jackknife puts the matter forward for discussion, with the same *challenging,* rather *antagonistic* note as with *wh-*questions.

Examples

Can we afford to buy it?   'Can we af°ford ^not to?
It's a faster car.   But 'is it °any ^safer?
You certainly ought to sit for   But 'have I °any °chance of
  the exam.   ^passing?
They're not much good now.   'Were they ^ever any ₀good?

COMMANDS   The main contribution of the Jackknife with commands is again a matter of *shrugging off responsibility,* of *refusing to be embroiled.*

Examples

Which of these hats shall I buy?   'Please your^self.
My doctor's useless.   'Try a ^different one.
I hate it, but what can I do?   ^Tell them you ₀hate it.
Could you help?   'You °fight your ^own
                                      ₀battles.

The intention of the speaker is not necessarily hostile (though it obviously may be so), and sometimes he is concerned to refuse credit for his acts.

Examples

Thank you very much.	'Don't ^mention it.
May I take this newspaper?	^Do.

INTERJECTIONS

When the speaker uses the Jackknife with interjections he sounds *greatly impressed by something not entirely expected.*

Examples

You can borrow my Jaguar.	^Thank you.
I've got a knighthood.	^Splendid!
Had your twenty-first yet?	^Heavens, ₒyes!
Sally's just had triplets.	'My ^goodness!

The same is true of greetings, and there may also be a *hint of accusation.* For instance, *Good ^morning* suggests in a bantering way that the listener has some explaining to do, perhaps because he is late or because of his conduct the previous night, or for some other reason that his conscience is expected to appreciate.

9   *The High Dive*

STATEMENTS

The example *I ˅like ˏchocolate* has already been given (p. 28) to illustrate the compound Fall plus Rise tune. It also illustrates very clearly one of the ways in which the High Dive tone group is used. Notice first that the example is a plain statement: it conveys none of the reservations which are evident if we use the Fall-Rise in this sentence: *I ˅like ₒchocolate.* Here the Fall-Rise on *like* expresses a clear contrast between *like* and some other idea; so the speaker might continue '. . . *but* it tends to make me fat.' No such reservation is conveyed by the Fall plus Rise of the High Dive; no ifs or buts are associated with it. The difference between the attitudes of the High Dive and the Switchback in this sentence are brought out by the following contexts:

I've got some chocolate here. 'Oh ˎgood. ‖ I ˋlike ˏchocolate. ‖ 'Pass it ˎover. ‖

I've got some chocolate here. 'Oh ˎdear. ‖ I ˇlike ₀chocolate, | but it 'makes me ˋfat.

If *I ˋlike ˏchocolate* is a plain statement with no reservations, why not use the High Drop and say *I 'like ˋchocolate*? The High Drop is commonly used for plain statements. The answer again lies in the differing contexts in which the two are used:

I've got some chocolate here. 'Oh ˎgood. ‖ I ˋlike ˏchocolate. ‖ 'Pass it ˎover. ‖

I've got some toffees here. You can ˋkeep them. ‖ I 'like ˋchocolate.

In the second example *chocolate* is the most important word in the last word group because it is new and contrasts directly with *toffees*; and that is why *chocolate* has the High Fall nuclear tone. In the other context however *chocolate* is not the most important word: it is not new, and what the speaker wants to make clear is mainly his *liking* for it. That is why the High Fall is on *like*. But why the Low Rise on *chocolate*? Why not simply say *I ˋlike ₀chocolate*, leaving *chocolate* unaccented? There seem to be two reasons for this. Firstly the speaker wants to give some importance to *chocolate*, not to lose it altogether: it is as if he were acknowledging the topic of conversation—*chocolate*—but being careful at the same time not to make the word *chocolate* seem as important as *like*. Secondly, by using the High Dive, the speaker is able to avoid creating the impression, as he might if he used the High Drop, that he is bringing the conversation to an end, at least so far as chocolate is concerned; and so, by using the Low Rise, he encourages his listener to feel that the conversation can continue. So in general we can say that, in the High Dive, the Fall is used to mark the most important idea in a plain statement, while the Low Rise indicates some less important but not completely negligible idea that follows the main idea; and in addition we can say that the Low Rise constitutes an *appeal to the listener* and invites him to say something more about the subject of the previous conversation. So in the example

I'm going to Sheffield tomorrow.	′Really? ‖ My ˋmother ₒcame from ˌSheffield.

mother, which is new, is clearly more important than *Sheffield*, which has already been mentioned, and the way is open for the conversation to continue. Contrast this with

You come from Sheffield, don't you?	ˇNo, ‖ my ˇmother ₒcame from ₒSheffield, │ (but ˋnot ˇme. ‖)

Here *Sheffield* is completely unimportant since, with no effect at all on the general meaning of the utterance, the phrase *came from Sheffield* can be replaced by the empty word *did*:

ˇNo, ‖ my ˇmother ₒdid, │ (but ˋnot ˇme. ‖)

Notice also that, as the context shows, there is a reservation here which is entirely absent from the previous example with the High Dive.

Now consider the following:

I'm going to Sheffield tomorrow.	′Really? ‖ ′Sheffield's where my ˋmother ₒcame from.

This last sentence, with its High Drop intonation, says very much the same thing as the High Dive on the sentence *My mother came from Sheffield*: in both the High Fall is on *mother*, marking it as the most important word; and *Sheffield* is accented (and therefore not negligible) by the Low Rise of the High Dive and by its position at the beginning of the High Head in the High Drop. So the relative importance of the two words is the same in both sentences. By contrast the balance is different in

So yours is a Leeds family.	ˋNot enˇtirely. ‖ My ′mother °came from ˋSheffield.

Here *Sheffield* is entirely new and the most important word, as the High Fall nuclear tone points out.

We use the High Dive then whenever the first part of a word group contains the most important idea, and the second part an idea of subsidiary importance. Often the High Fall occurs on the last important word of the subject of the sentence and the Low Rise on the last important word of the predicate.

Examples

Who could help me?	ˋJohn would be the ˏbest °chap.
Is this mine?	ˋNo, | the ˈsmall ˋred one's ˏyours.
Who's next?	The ˈlittle old °man in the ˋcorner's been ₒwaiting ˏlongest.

On the other hand the main verb may be the most important feature, with the complement less so.

Examples

Turn it clockwise.	I've ˋtried ₒdoing it ˏthat °way.
D'you like my hat?	ˋLovely. || I've ˈalways ˋwanted one like ˏthat.
I won't eat it.	ˈPlenty of °little °boys would ˋlove a ₒnice ₒrice ˏpudding.
It was a marvellous play.	I ˈdidn't ˋknow you were ₒgoing to the ˏtheatre.

An interesting case is the following:

She's wearing a wedding ring.   I ˋthought she was ˏmarried.

Wedding ring implies *marriage*, so *married* here is less important than *thought*; and the High Fall on *thought* implies that the speaker's opinion was correct. But notice what happens when his opinion turns out to be wrong:

She's wearing an engagement ring.   I ˈthought she was ˋmarried.

Now the High Fall is on *married*, the really important word because of the difference between being engaged and being married; and the clear indication is that the speaker was wrong.

In the following examples, the speaker's judgment is confirmed correct:

Examples

He's gone bankrupt.	I ˈheard he was in ˌtrouble.
I can't understand it.	I ˈtold you you'd ₒfind it ˌdifficult.
I entirely agree.	I 'rather ˈhoped you ˌwould.
He's going to resign.	I've 'always been aˈfraid he ₒwouldn't acˌcept it.

The same reasoning applies to *knowing*, where the speaker's certainty, expressed by the verb, is underlined by the intonation.

Examples

It won't work.	I ˈknew it ₒwouldn't be ₒany ˌgood.
They went bankrupt.	I 'somehow ˈknew they'd ₒburn their ˌfingers.

Expressions of *gladness*, *regret* and *surprise* usually have the High Dive, with the High Fall on the appropriate emotive word, provided that the subject of the emotion is obvious to both the speaker and the listener.

Examples

John's arrived.	I'm ˈglad he was ₒable to ˌcome.
We must go.	I'm ˈsorry you ₒcan't stay ˌlonger.
The phone was out of order.	He was 'rather surˈprised you ₒdidn't ˌring him.

If there is an extra intensifying word, like *so*, *very*, *extremely*, the High Fall takes place on that.

Examples

I'm ˈso ₒglad you could ˌcome.
I'm ˈawfully ₒsorry you ₒcan't stay ˌlonger.
I'm ˈso ˌsorry.

The last example is a really heartfelt expression of regret. The intensifying use of *do* and other special finites is treated in the same way.

Examples

He's a fool.   I ˈdo think you're ₒbeing unˌkind.
The car broke down.   We ˈwere ₒsorry ₒnot to ˌsee you.

QUESTIONS

The use of the High Dive with questions of any kind is unusual. When it occurs, the High Fall is normally placed on the *wh*-word or the special finite, and the effect is of considerable emotion. This emotion may take the form of *plaintiveness, despair* or the like.

Examples

Oh, no!   ˈWhat have you ₒdone ˌnow?
Shut up!   ˈHave you ₒquite ˌfinished?

Or it may be a matter of *gushing warmth.*

Examples

Mummy! Mummy!   ˈWhat's the ˌmatter, °darling?
What's up, John?   ˈCould you ₒpossibly ˌhelp me?

This use is perhaps better avoided by the foreign learner.

COMMANDS

For commands, unlike questions, the High Dive is quite common. The High Fall takes place on the main verb in affirmative commands, on *don't* in negative commands, and on *do* or *please* used as intensifiers. The effect is of *pleading* or *persuading* rather than ordering.

Examples

I'll be back by midnight.   ˈTry ₒnot to be ₒany ˌlater.
But you were wrong.   Now ˈdon't ₒstart ₒall ˌthat a°gain.
I'm going to see John.   ˈDo try and perₒsuade him to ˌcome.
Will you be all right?   ˈPlease don't ₒworry about ˌme.

All commands with the High Dive are much more like requests than orders; this is no doubt why commands occur quite commonly with the High Dive.

INTERJECTIONS

The High Dive is used with the same kind of interjections as the Low Bounce (p. 65); and its effect is similar to that of the Low Bounce, but much more *intense*.

Examples

I'll see you tomorrow.	ˋRight you ˏare.
I've managed it at last.	ˋWell ˏdone.
That's the path we should take.	ˋHalf a ˏminute. ‖ (You just said it was the other one.)
Do make up the fire.	ˋAll ˏright. ‖ (Don't go on about it. I was just going.)

The intensity expressed by the High Dive here may be used for extra encouragement, as in the first two examples; or it may be a form of protest, as in the last two examples. It is probably preferable for the foreign learner to use this intensity sparingly and to stick to the Low Bounce for such expressions.

10   *The Terrace*

The only common use for the Terrace is for *non-final* word groups; and, as the following examples make clear, this tone group is readily used to show non-finality with all five sentence types.

STATEMENTS

ˑSoon | it'll be ˋSpring aˑgain. ‖
If you 'don't ˑwant it | I should 'just ˋleave it. ‖
I 'found the ˑbottle, | 'took out the ˑcork | and 'poured a ˏdrink. ‖
I 'went aˑcross the ˑroad | with ˋmurder in my ˑheart. ‖
ˑSix, | ˑseven, | ˑeight, | ˑnine, | ˏten. ‖

WH-QUESTIONS

'When did you ˑsee ˑJohn | to 'ask him about ˋmoney? ‖
'How can we deˑcide | if we 'haven't ˑgot the ˋfacts? ‖

'Why did you ›act | so 'very im͵pulsively? ‖
'Where were °John and ›Ann °going | be'fore they °came to ͵us? ‖

YES-NO QUESTIONS

Is 'that the °best you can ›do | to 'patch it ͵up? ‖
'Are you ›ready | to ₒmake a 'real ͵effort? ‖
'Did ›John | 'ever °give you that ͵money °back? ‖
'Isn't it a ›shame | that we so 'rarely ͵see them! ‖

COMMANDS

'Come over ›here | and 'tell me °all a͵bout it. ‖
'Don't make accu›sations | with'out ͵evidence. ‖
'Let me have a ›look | and I'll ˎtell you. ‖
'Send them °down to ›Brighton | in 'charge of the ˎguard. ‖
›Play | as if your 'life de͵pended on it. ‖

INTERJECTIONS

'What a ›pity | you 'just °couldn't ͵manage it! ‖
'How ›strange | that they 'never °really ͵tried! ‖
'Good›bye | and 'good ͵riddance! ‖
The 'best of ›luck | and 'take ͵care of your°self. ‖

In all these examples the Terrace shows simply that the word group is introducing something more. It creates none of the expectancy about what follows which we mentioned in connection with the Low Bounce (p. 63) and which even the High Bounce expresses, though to a much smaller extent (p. 76). It is fair to say that the Terrace implies continuation and nothing else in non-final word groups.

With final word groups the Terrace is rare. It is possible with statements and interjections; and then it gives an impression of calling out to someone, as if at a distance.

Examples

Where are you, John?	'Just ›coming.
What did you say?	'Dinner's ›ready.
I've brought your hammer.	'Good ›girl! ‖ 'Thank ›you!
See you soon.	'Bye›bye.

This use is not necessary for foreign learners: the Terrace, with its Mid-Level nuclear tone, can always be replaced by the High Bounce and its High Rise; the result of this is simply the disappearance of the chant-like element which is sometimes conveyed by the Terrace in statements and interjections of this kind.

Tone Group Sequences

In the preceding pages we have been concerned mostly with the uses of the ten tone groups in sentences consisting of a single word group. Here and there however we have discussed their application to sentences comprising two word groups separated by the single bar [|]. We have seen how non-final word groups can be said with the Take-Off (p. 58), the Low Bounce (p. 63), the Switchback (p. 66) and the High Bounce (p. 75), as well as with the Terrace which we have just been considering. Drills for practising sequences arising from the use of these tone groups in non-final word groups, and drills for the sequence *Low Bounce | Low Drop* (p. 51) in alternative Yes-No questions are given in Chapter V, Sections 1–8. The various attitudes expressed in these sequences are described in the earlier parts of this present chapter.

The drills in Sections 9–19 of Chapter V practise sentences in which the second word group is a question tag. The first five of these sections drill question tags which are said with a falling nuclear tone and so demand the listener's agreement (p. 51). In Sections 15–19 on the other hand, the tag is to be said with the Low Rise nuclear tone; the speaker now clearly expects his listener to agree with him, but at the same time the way is left open for disagreement (p. 60). In addition to indicating the degree of certainty of his expectations by means of the falling or rising tag, the speaker is also able to express a wide variety of attitudes depending on the intonation which he chooses for the word group preceding the tag. These attitudes are also described in the earlier parts of this present chapter.

Chapter V ends with the four sections 20–23, which provide practice for four very common tone group sequences:

High Drop | *Take-Off*   *Long Jump* | *Take-Off*
High Drop | *Switchback*   *High Drop* | *High Drop*

HIGH DROP |
TAKE-OFF

When a speaker uses this tone group sequence, he first of all makes a complete, definite assertion which, since it is said with the High Drop, conveys an attitude of *warmth*, of *involvement* (p. 54). Having made his assertion, he then goes on to lessen its impact by the Take-Off in the following word group. This second word group may be merely a comment on his previous assertion; or it may clear up some possible ambiguity in it; or in some other way limit its scope, as if to say that on reflection he felt it a bit too sweeping.

An obvious application of this particular sequence is to statements ending with a politeness phrase, such as *please*, *thanks* or *thank you*.

Examples

Would you like some?   ˋYes, | ˏplease.
More tea?   ˋNo, | ˏthank you.

Here the Take-Off softens the forceful impact of the High Drop; and the speaker is able to show some real consideration for his listener which enhances the formal, conventional politeness of the words.

A similar effect is produced when vocatives follow greetings and farewells.

Examples

Good ˋmorning, | ˏJohn.   ˋGoodbye, | ˏArthur.
ˋHullo, | Mrs. ˏJones.   Good ˈafterˋnoon, | ˏeverybody.

These sound forthcoming and friendly, and contrast sharply with the rather stiff formality of *Good* ˋ*morning*, ₒ*John*, for instance.

Sometimes the second word group with its Take-Off tune is used to amplify the subject in the first word group.

Examples

Why ever go by boat?	Well, it 'rather up'sets me, | ˌgoing by ˌair.
He made me feel so at ease.	Yes, he's a ˋnice chap, | ˌJohn.

Notice in the first example that air-travel is not mentioned by the questioner; and so the speaker makes it absolutely clear what is meant by the vague *it*. Similarly in the second example the Take-Off serves the purpose of identifying *John* with the *he* of the first word group.

Sometimes the second word group is a comment by the speaker on his assertion in the first word group, or on the general situation in which he is talking, or even on his own frame of mind.

Examples

Don't you like it?	I ˋdon't, | ˌfrankly.
What shall I do about them?	ˋSell them, | of ˌcourse.
Where did you last have it?	I 'don't reˋmember, | I'm aˌfraid.
When will Jones get back?	Toˋmorrow, | I ˌthink.

In this last example the speaker is fairly confident that his answer is the correct one, though there remains for him some slight element of doubt. Contrast this with *Toˋmorrow, I ˳think*, where virtual certainty is indicated; so much so that *I ˳think* could be omitted without substantially changing the meaning of the speaker's answer.

Perhaps the most common use of the High Drop | Take-Off sequence is for sentences ending with an adverbial: this may be a single adverb, like *today*, a phrase such as *for the moment*, or a full clause. Consider the following:

How are they going?	They're ˋflying | as ˌfar as New ˌYork.

Here the questioner's enquiry is solely about the means of transport. So in his reply the speaker wants primarily to say that the travellers are going by air. But their ultimate destination is in fact a small country town an hour beyond New York;

so the second part of his reply effectively limits the application of the sweeping assertion in the first part. Contrast this situation with the following:

How far are they flying?   They're 'flying as °far as New `York.

Here the means of transport is actually mentioned in the question; so the speaker, if he chooses, could ignore it altogether and shorten his reply to: *As 'far as New `York.*

Examples

Any news of John?	He's 'coming `home | to‚day.
(It's still confidential.)	So 'keep it °under your `hat | for the ‚moment.
He's just been promoted.	I must con`gratulate him | when I ‚see him.
Whatever shall I do?	'Carry on as `usual | if you ‚possibly ‚can.

Note that the main assertion may be either a statement or a command, but that in all cases the adverbial with the Take-Off limits the application of the assertion with the High Drop.

In some respects this High Drop | Take-Off sequence is very much like the single High Dive tone group. In both, that part of the sentence marked by the Low Rise nuclear tone is felt to be less important than the earlier part with the High Fall tone; and most often the single bar [|] of the sequence has no pause value at all. How then can we decide that a tune, which falls and then rises and which does not belong to the Switchback (p. 82), is this High Drop | Take-Off sequence rather **than** the single High Dive? The answer lies in the grammar. In the sequence the early part of the sentence, marked by the High Fall, is complete in itself; the first word group in all the above examples is grammatically a single unit which could, in the appropriate situation, stand on its own. This is never so with the High Dive. An example like *I `like ‚chocolate*, with the intonation that is marked, is a single, indivisible grammatical unit: *‚chocolate* cannot be omitted since *I `like* cannot stand on its own. Notice too that very often the order of the two word groups of the sequence can be reversed, their wording and intonation can be retained, and the overall meaning remains the same. So instead of the third example above we can say with the same effect: *When I ˏsee him | I must conˋgratulate him.* We have already seen (p. 84) that this reversal of the falling and rising parts of the sentence is sometimes also possible in the case of the single High Dive; but some rephrasing is usually necessary and, if the same overall impression is to be given, the rephrased sentence has to be said with a single High Drop tune. Compare the High Dive in *My ˋmother ₒcame from ˏSheffield* with the High Drop in the rephrased *'Sheffield's where my ˋmother ₒcame from.*

LONG JUMP | This sequence is used in much the same ways as the High
TAKE-OFF   Drop | Take-Off. The difference lies solely in the attitude expressed in the first of the two word groups: *protesting* in the case of the Long Jump, *warm, involved* with the High Drop.

> *Examples*
>
> I thought you went by car.   ˏSo I ˋdo, | ˏnormally.
> Haven't you nearly finished?   I've ˏonly °just beˋgun it, | as a
>   ˎmatter of ˏfact.
>
> You really shouldn't have   But it was so ˏₓterribly ˋchildish, |
>   been so cross with him.   making ˎall that ₒfuss about a
>   ₒbroken ˏwindow.

HIGH DROP | The role of the Switchback here is similar to that of the Take-
SWITCHBACK   Off when following the High Drop: it limits the impact of the High Drop of the preceding word group. The main difference is that the contrast expressed by the Fall-Rise and the attitude of reservation often associated with the Switchback (p. 66) are both very much in evidence in this sequence too. So, for instance, in *Toˋmorrow, | I ˇthink,* the speaker is obviously much less sure of his ground than in either *Toˋmorrow, | I ˏthink* or *Toˋmorrow, I ₒthink,* which were discussed above (p. 92); it is as if he were saying that he is merely giving his opinion and that he could well be wrong.

Examples

Don't you go by underground?	I ˋdo, | ˇnormally. ‖ (But toˎday | they were on ˋstrike.)
How much does George know?	ˋNothing, | his ˇbrother ˳says. ‖ (But 'he's misˋtaken, I ˳think.)
Let's go and see Othello.	'Not a ˋhope, | unˋless you've al˚ready ˇbooked. ‖ (And 'that I ˋdoubt.)

In these examples the full force of the reservation expressed by the Switchback is spelt out in the extended contexts. As with the High Drop \| Take-Off sequence, the order of the two word groups can be reversed without any change in their intonation or phrasing and the overall meaning of the sentence remains the same: compare ˇ*Normally*, \| *I* ˋ*do.*

HIGH DROP \|
HIGH DROP

In the three preceding sequences the rising nuclear tones of the Take-Off and the Switchback contrast sharply with the High Falling nuclear tone of the High Drop and the Long Jump; and it is this contrast which is very largely responsible for the limiting effect of the second word group on the scope or application of the first. In this High Drop \| High Drop sequence, however, the nuclear tones match and so are mutually reinforcing: each reinforces the *warm, involved* attitude which the other expresses in a single word group said with the High Drop, and the general effect is one of emphasis. Sometimes one of the word groups is an emphatic comment on or qualification of the main proposition in the other word group.

Examples

Why are you so late?	I 'had to ˋwork ˳late, | ˋhonestly.
I wonder why Jill didn't come.	You inˋvited her, | of ˋcourse.
What about Alice?	'She'll get a ˋfree ˳copy, | ˋnaturally.

In these examples the comment comes last; but once again the order of the word groups can be reversed: ˋ*Naturally*, \|

'*she'll get a* `free ˳copy*. In other cases the second word group is virtually a repetition, for emphasis, of the proposition in the first word group; and here too reversal of word group order is always possible.

Examples

| May I borrow it? | `Yes, \| `do. `Do, \| `yes. |
| Don't you like it? | `No, \| I `don't. I `don't, \| `no. |

In yet other examples the second word group is an emphatic clarification of the first word group: with the second High Drop the speaker is making much more precise the information which he has just given by the first High Drop.

Examples

| Where does he live? | In `Essex, \| near `Chelmsford. |
| Where's Peter? | He's 'gone to `Manchester, \| on `business. |

All the tone group sequences discussed above and exemplified in Chapter V concern sentences divided into two word groups by the single bar [|]. In extended utterance many other tone group sequences can arise; and the division into word groups then involves the double bar [‖] as well as [|]. These other sequences are too numerous to study here; but in general it can be said that, unless there is an obvious reason for a change, the attitudes expressed by a speaker in a succession of several word groups will either be the same or, if not the same, be consistent with each other. Consider the following situation:

| Well, yes. Nothing else was broken. | ˏWhy did you °make so much `fuss about it? ‖ You can ˏsoon buy aˏnother one. |

This represents a perfectly consistent sequence of attitudes that are not identical: the *reproof* of the Take-Off in the second word group is foreshadowed by the *protest* of the Long Jump in the first. Replace the Long Jump by the Low Bounce and the latter's overt friendliness jars in a most inappropriate way with the reproof that follows. Similarly in

| Oh, I am sorry about that vase. | 'How did it °come to get ˏbroken? ‖ I 'told you °not to ˆtouch it. |

the sequence Low Bounce | Jackknife is most improbable: there is no reason at all for the marked change in attitude after the friendly *Wh*-question. The censorious Jackknife in the second word group is realistic only if some equally strong, critical attitude is given by the first word group. But notice what happens if we change the situation somewhat:

| Oh, I am sorry about that vase. I picked it up to show John. | 'How did it °come to get ˏbroken? I 'told you °not to ˆtouch it. |

Here at the outset the speaker has no quarrel with his listener; and so his question is friendly and invites an answer. This answer however reveals that the listener has blatantly ignored some previous injunction made by the speaker. So the latter's switch from the friendly Low Bounce in the question to the censorious Jackknife in what follows is both reasonable and logical in the circumstances.

III Introduction to the Drills

AIMS OF THE DRILLS There is only one way to master the pronunciation of a foreign language: to repeat the sound features of the language over and over again, *correctly and systematically*, until they can be said without any conscious thought at all, until the learner is incapable of saying them in any other way. This is the drill method, and it has been used for many years in teaching the sounds of English; the major aim of this book is to provide graded material suitable for use in teaching and learning English intonation.

The drills, which follow in Chapters IV and V, have two purposes: first, to help the learner to say the tunes in the English way, to get the notes right, and to provide so much practice in this that he will no longer be tempted to substitute his own native intonation; and secondly, and much more important, to get him to use the tunes appropriately, so that he automatically chooses the tune which will best express his own attitude of mind in any circumstances.

For the first purpose a teacher is almost certainly needed; there are some gifted people who can acquire the tunes of English by simply imitating what they hear around them, but most foreign students cannot do this and would be unwise to think that they can. For these it is essential, particularly in the early stages, to have a teacher to serve as a model and to correct them meticulously whenever they go wrong. It is worse than useless to drill the *wrong* tunes; the teacher must see to it that the tunes are right and stay right.

For the second purpose, that of making the student automatically choose the appropriate tunes, a teacher is perhaps less necessary, and the intelligent student can probably get a good deal of benefit from using the drills on his own. On the other hand, a good teacher will certainly help and enliven the process.

ARRANGEMENT OF The ten tone groups are tackled one by one in the drills in
THE DRILLS Chapter IV. At the beginning of each tone group there is a **brief recapitulation of the attitudes conveyed by the tone**

group in conjunction with the five sentence types, Statement, Wh-Question, Yes-No Question, Command and Interjection. Then follows a reminder of the pitch value of the tone marks used in the drill sentences in the tone group.

Within each tone group the material is presented in sections, the drill sentences in any one section all illustrating one particular pitch feature or combination of pitch features. Thus in the Take-Off, for instance, there are four sections; the first contains sentences said with a Low Rise nuclear tone only; the second, sentences said with a sequence of Low Rise nuclear tone and Tail; the third, sentences said with a sequence of Pre-head and Low Rise nuclear tone with or without a Tail; and the fourth, sentences said with a sequence of Low Head and Low Rise nuclear tone with or without a Tail and with or without a Pre-head. The sections in the ten tone groups have been devised in such a way that, at some stage in the drills in Chapter IV, the student has the opportunity to practise systematically all the important sequences of pitch features as well as all those features which occur on their own.

At the beginning of each section in each tone group a general heading specifies the tune, that is to say, the pitch feature or sequence of features which the drill sentences in that section are designed to illustrate. Note that some features in some headings are enclosed in round brackets. These brackets indicate that not all sentences in the section contain the particular feature which they enclose. Features not enclosed in these brackets are present in all the drill sentences in the section. This general heading is accompanied by one or more schematic interlinear diagrams, designed to show at a glance the overall tune shape. In these diagrams the top horizontal line indicates a very high pitch and the bottom horizontal line a very low pitch. Between these two lines the pitch of the various features in the tune, as well as the pitch relationship between them, is represented by means of thick strokes for *Head* and *Nucleus* and by means of thin strokes for *Pre-head* and *Tail*. When only one thick stroke is shown, this stands for the Nucleus of a tune which consequently has no Head.

Within each tone group the student will, in general, first

deal with the most simply constructed tune and gradually progress to longer and more complicated ones. This is for instance the case with the Take-Off, as can be seen from the list of its sections above. Occasionally, as in the Switchback and the Jackknife, the most simply constructed tune, *Nucleus Only*, presents the student with more difficulties than the somewhat longer tune, *Nucleus + Tail*; in such cases the longer but simpler tune is given first. It is most important that the student should not be allowed to go on to the longer tunes until he is able to cope with the shorter ones satisfactorily. In this the teacher must be merciless—no fault must be allowed to slip by, because the longer tunes are based on the shorter and any fault tolerated at first will recur again and again and become more and more fossilised until it can no longer be dealt with.

In each section there are scores of drill sentences divided amongst Statements, Wh-Questions, Yes-No Questions, Commands and Interjections. Each of these structures must be practised, but whether every structure in every section is to be exhausted is a matter for the teacher's judgment; however, he should always go on *well beyond* the point where the student begins to perform acceptably. Only in this way is mechanisation achieved. Incidentally, each drill sentence is in principle quite unconnected with the preceding or following one. Occasionally, as for instance in the material given under Yes-No Questions in the first section of the Low Bounce, it has been found convenient to connect a number of drill sentences together into a sort of controlled conversation. Generally speaking, however, each drill sentence represents a response to a new situation.

By working steadily under guidance through the material the student should be able to pronounce all the different intonation patterns acceptably; but will he be any more able to choose the right pattern at the right time, which is the real difficulty? The answer is almost certainly yes, because each drill sentence has been regarded not just as an isolated utterance, but as a response to a given situation; this situation is sketched by what we have called the *Verbal Context*, which precedes the drill sentence; it is a very brief, very rudimentary setting of the scene, but it gives the student a peg on which to hang his drill sentence, his response to the situation. In particular the verbal context may account for accentual features in the drill sentence; for example, in the sequence

'What °sort of ˎnight was it?   It was a 'very ˋdark ₒnight.

the accent on *night* in the verbal context question explains the lack of accent on that word in the drill sentence statement. The verbal context may also give some indication of the attitude to be expected from the speaker of the drill sentence; for example, in the sequence

'Why did you ˎdo it, you
    ₒsilly ₒfool?   I ˌdidn't ₒdo it on ˌpurpose.

the use of the words *you silly fool* is deliberately tendentious and helps to highlight the grumbling, defensive note of the response.

Similarly the drill sentence itself may be coloured so as to underline the attitude which it conveys, as, for example, in the sequence

D'you 'think it's ˌtrue?   I'm 'absolutely ˎpositive it's ₒtrue.

The strong expression *absolutely positive* is a pointer to the weight and intensity carried by the tune; this weight and intensity would still be present if the less forceful words *quite sure* had been used, but they might have been less obvious to the student. Such indicative words are not present in every drill sentence, but there are enough examples of this kind to keep the student reminded of the attitude which a tune is meant to express.

There is one other way in which we have tried to help the learner to appreciate intonation attitudes, namely, by sometimes adding a sentence after the drill sentence. These additional sentences are placed between round brackets to show that they are not part of the formal drill, but they should be said by the student so that he may better grasp the full meaning of the drill sentence; for example, the sequence

He's 'over ˋseventy.   ˎWell. ‖ (I'd 'never have beˎlieved it.)

In the classroom the verbal context will usually be spoken by the teacher and the drill sentence by the student, but sometimes it is more useful and natural if the context sentence is said by the student before he says the drill sentence. In these cases the verbal context is placed between round brackets; for example

(That 'you, Mr. °Archer?)   Good 'morning.

Occasionally the context is not verbal at all, but a concrete situation; this is briefly sketched and enclosed in square brackets; for example

[A loud noise]   What on 'earth was ˎthat?

The single vertical bar and the double vertical bar, which are used to separate word groups, sometimes occur in the drills; for example

| 'How much 'holiday will you ₒget? | 'Three 'weeks, \| I ˏhope. |
| 'When'll he °make up his 'mind? | ˏNobody 'knows. \|\| ˏThat's the 'trouble. |

In these and all similar sequences of word groups the bar, whether single or double, implies that the two (or more) word groups are to be said consecutively by the same speaker. This is also true of word group sequences in the verbal contexts.

The absence of the double bar between drill sentences means that they are intended as alternative responses to the same verbal context; for example

'Whose ˎbook is that?   ˎMine. ˎDad's. ˎMum's. ˎJack's.

By means of these devices, added to the explanations in Chapter II, the student is led to use the various intonation patterns in situations which are appropriate to their use, and this comes about to a large extent unconsciously. After a great deal of this kind of practice he will be very much more likely to hit instinctively upon the right tune in everyday conversation than if he had to work it out logically.

The drills will most often be used in the classroom under the
direction of a teacher; experience of using them in this way
enables us to give some advice on how to get the best out of
them.

The Teacher

At the beginning of each section in each tone group the
teacher must explain what the general shape of the tune is,
what tone marks are used to symbolise this shape, and in
general terms what attitude the tone group conveys in relation
to the grammatical structure under consideration; in other
words, a brief résumé of the relevant information in Chapters
I and II.

He must then make sure, with a few isolated examples,
that the students can actually say the tune, and make whatever
corrections are necessary; also that they can hear it accurately, placing the correct tone marks in the appropriate places
in dictated sentences. A certain amount of chorus work may
be useful at this point, to create confidence, but this should
not be the general rule unless it is unavoidable, since it tends
to mask individual errors and therefore to reinforce them.

In beginning the drills, the teacher will say the context
sentence with the intonation given, and one student will give
the drill sentence in reply. At this stage the important thing
is to be sure that the tune is correctly said; if it is not, the
error must be pointed out and eliminated. The teacher re-
peats the context sentence and the same student replies
correctly; if not, more correction, until such time as the
student is able to make the correct response. It is valuable
for a while to make all the students repeat, one by one, the
same response to the same context sentence; this fastens it
rather quickly in their minds. But always the teacher must
say the context sentence, so that the drill sentence comes in
response to a definite situation, never as merely another sentence in the void. Where we have provided a number of drill
sentences in response to a single context, the teacher must

repeat his context sentence before every reply. Once the tune is coming fairly freely and accurately the teacher can concentrate more on the meaning, using all his ability to bring out the basic elements of the rudimentary situations so that the student is brought to realise to what and in what manner he is responding.

As a matter of tactics it is wise to vary the order in which students are called upon to answer; if the same order is used throughout, most students spend their time calculating which is their next sentence and preparing it. This obviously lessens the number of useful examples to which they are exposed and is to this extent a bad thing.

The Student

The student must be sure that he understands at every point what is required of him, what the tone marks mean, what basic attitude the tone group under consideration reflects, and that he keeps this constantly in mind. He should be prepared at the beginning to sound silly or funny to himself, since foreign tunes usually seem even odder than foreign sounds; this is a phase which soon passes if faced firmly. He must make a careful note of his errors in each tune and work to avoid them. He must pay attention to every context sentence as well as to every drill sentence and try to think himself into the kind of situation at which the sentences hint. This creative imagination will not only make the whole process more interesting; it will also speed up the rate at which correct responses in everyday situations come instinctively to his tongue. In private work and revision just as much attention should be paid to the verbal context and the attitude expressed as to the actual speaking of the drill sentence, and repetition should be done *aloud* if at all possible. If the student is working with a teacher he should avoid breaking new ground on his own; the likely result will be to form bad habits rather than good. But once a tune is correctly established, the more thoughtful repetition the better; one useful by-product of the drill method is that some of the examples used—and they are all usable everyday sentences—will stick in the mind and be available for future use.

When all the tunes, illustrated by the various sections of the ten tone groups, have been drilled to the point where a correct intonation pattern is automatically used in the appropriate place, we still cannot say that English intonation has been mastered; there will still be plenty to learn. But hard and intelligent work on the drills, like scale-playing for the pianist, will provide a firm basis for advance.

IV Intonation Drills
THE TEN TONE GROUPS

1 *The Low Drop*

Attitude

In STATEMENTS: with no head, detached, cool, dispassionate, reserved, dull, possibly grim or surly; with a high head, categoric, weighty, judicial, considered.

In WH-QUESTIONS: with no head, detached, flat, unsympathetic, even hostile; with a high head, searching, serious, intense, urgent.

In YES-NO QUESTIONS: with no head (in tags used as independent comments), uninterested, hostile; with a high head, serious, urgent.

In COMMANDS: with no head, unemotional, calm, controlled, cold; with a high head, very serious, very strong.

In INTERJECTIONS: with no head, calm, unsurprised, reserved, self-possessed; with a high head, very strong.

Tone marks used in *LOW DROP* drills

A Stressed, accented syllables (Nucleus, Head)
[ˏ] Medium falling to very low pitch.
['] Relatively high level pitch.
[°] Relatively high level pitch, the same pitch as the *preceding* ['].

B Stressed, unaccented syllables (Tail)
[₀] Very low level pitch, the same pitch as the end of the *preceding* [ˏ].

Tune	⟍	Low Fall only

Verbal context	*Drill*

Statements

● 'Can you °come to ˏmorrow?	ˏYes. ˏNo.
'Whose ˏbook is ₀this?	ˏMine. ˏDad's. ˏMum's. ˏJack's. ˏJohn's. ˏTom's. ˏAnne's.

Verbal context	*Drill*
'When can you ˎdo it?	ˎNow.
'Where does he ˎcome from?	ˎFrance. ˎSpain. ˎWales.
'Which °subject do ˎyou pre°fer?	ˎFrench. ˎMaths.
'What's your ˎname?	ˎSmith. ˎJones. ˎBrown. ˎRees.
'How many ˎcousins have you °got?	ˎOne. ˎTwo. ˎThree. ˎFour. ˎFive. ˎSix. ˎEight. ˎNine. ˎTen.
'What °colour's ˎyour °car?	ˎBlue. ˎGreen. ˎRed. ˎBlack. ˎBrown. ˎBeige. ˎPink. ˎWhite.
'What's in that ˎbottle?	ˎInk. ˎGin. ˎBeer. ˎMilk. ˎOil. ˎWine.
'What d'you °need from the ˎgrocer's?	ˎCheese. ˎHam. ˎEggs. ˎFlour. ˎJam. ˎTea. ˎSoap. ˎSalt.
'What ˎmeat d'you °like °best?	ˎBeef. ˎVeal. ˎPork. ˎLamb.
'What's your °favourite ˎfish?	ˎSole. ˎPlaice. ˎShrimps. ˎHake. ˎCod. ˎTrout. ˎCrab. ˎBream.

WH-Questions

● You must 'ask for them ˎnow.	ˎWhy?
He 'simply °must ˎgo.	ˎWhen?
'Take only ˎone of them.	ˎWhich?
'Just ˎtell him.	ˎWhat?
'Make them at ˎonce.	ˎHow?
I 'saw a ˋfriend of °yours | toˏday.	ˎWho?
'Borrow °someone's ˎdictionary.	ˎWhose?
I've 'just seen ˎJohn.	ˎWhere?

Commands

● I'll ˎsend it °to him.	ˎDon't. ˎDo.
'What d'you ad°vise me to ˎdo?	ˎGo. ˎStay. ˎTry. ˎWait. ˎWrite. ˎPhone. ˎPray.
'Would you mind °calling your ˏdog?	ˎHeel. ˎSit. ˎDown. ˎHere.
'Shall we °have aˏnother °game?	ˎLet's.

Interjections

● He's 'just arˏrived.	ˎOh! ˎRight! ˎGood! ˎFine! ˎGreat!
ˋJohn °says | he ran a 'four minute ˋmile.	ˎRot! ˎBilge! ˎTripe!
'Here's your ˎsweater.	ˎThanks!

Verbal context	Drill
What a 'very pe°culiar ˎhat you've got ₒon!	ˎPlease! ˎJohn!
Your 'very °good ˎhealth.	ˎCheers!
⁻Let's ˎgo, │ ˎshall we?	ˎRight!

Tune ╲‾ Low Fall+Tail

Statements

'How ˎold are you?	ˎSeven. ˎTwenty. ˎThirty. ˎForty.
'Will you ˎsend it °to me?	ˎGladly. ˎYes, sir. ˎNo, ₒJohn. ˎCertainly, ₒmadam.
'Who can ˎsay that?	ˎI can. ˎWe can. ˎAlice ₒcan. ˎMarjorie ₒcan. ˎTimothy ₒcan.
'Who °gave him the ˎbook?	ˎJohn did. ˎFather ₒdid. ˎMother ₒdid. ˎPeggy ₒdid.
'Whose is this ˎbox?	ˎMary's. ˎStephen's. ˎJennifer's. ˎAlison's, I ₒthink.
'Where d'you ˎcome from?	ˎChina. ˎIndia. ˎGermany. ˎPoland. ˎSweden. ˎDenmark. ˎItaly. ˎNorway. ˎHolland. ˎEngland. ˎScotland. ˎIreland. ˎYorkshire. ˎLancashire. ˎGloucestershire. ˎSomerset. ˎDevon. ˎSussex. ˎSurrey. ˎEdinburgh. ˎLeicester. ˎWorcester.
'Which is the °nearest ˎtube ₒstation?	ˎEuston. ˎHighgate. ˎHolborn. ˎAldwych. ˎGoodge ₒStreet. ˎLiverpool ₒStreet. ˎMarylebone. ˎPaddington.
'What's your °favourite ˎsubject?	ˎHistory. ˎLatin. ˎAlgebra. ˎPhysics. ˎBotany. ˎChemistry. ˎEnglish. ˎGerman.
● 'What's your ˎname?	ˎJohnson. ˎRobinson. ˎBuckingham. ˎChapman, sir. ˎFotheringham, sir. ˎJames, ₒmadam.
● 'Who's °running the ˎmusic ₒclub this ₒyear?	ˎPeter. ˎPeter's ₒrunning it. ˎPeter's ₒgoing to ₒrun it. ˎPeter's ₒgoing to ₒtry and ₒrun it. ˎPeter's ₒgoing to have a ₒtry at ₒrunning it.

Verbal context	*Drill*
'Why d'you °want more ˎmoney?	ˎFares are ₒup. ˎFares are ₒgoing ₒup. ˎFares are ₒgoing ₒup aˎgain. ˎRailway ₒfares are ₒgoing ₒup aˎgain. ˎRailway ₒfares are ₒprobably ₒgoing ₒup ₒagain.
'Which firm °painted `John's ₒhouse?	ˎWatson's. ˎWatson and ₒSons. ˎWatson and ₒSons ˎdid it. ˎWatson and ₒSons ˎdid it, I ₒgather. ˎWatson and ₒSons ˎdid it, I ₒunderₒstand.

WH-Questions

'Pass me that ˎbox, ₒJoan.	ˎWhich ₒbox?
He's aˏway quite `often.	ˎHow ₒoften?
She's got 'something in her `eye.	ˎWhich ₒeye? ˎWho ₒhas?
He's 'broken a `window.	ˎWhose ₒwindow? ˎWhose ₒwindow, may I ₒask? ˎWhose ₒwindow has he ₒbroken?
ˏSomeone's `bound to ₒhave one.	ˎWho, eₒxactly?
● She'll 'ring you on ˎSunday.	ˎWhen, preₒcisely?
I've ˏasked him `several ₒtimes.	ˎHow many ₒtimes?
He 'says he's ˎcoming.	ˎWhy's he ₒcoming? ˎWhen, d'you ₒthink?
I'm `sorry to ˏtrouble you a°gain.	ˎNow ₒwhat's the ₒmatter?
We `started `off | at the 'Red `Lion.	ˎThen ₒwhere did you ₒgo?

Yes-No Questions

I 'think you'll `like it.	ˎWill I?
It 'all de°pends on the ˎweather.	ˎDoes it?
I've 'just °mowed my ˎlawn.	ˎHave you?
They ˏwon't °even `try.	ˎWon't they?
You can't `possibly lift `that.	ˎCan't I?
We'd `never be ₒable to afˏford it.	ˎWouldn't we?
He 'says he'll re`paint it.	ˎWill he reₒpaint it?
● It'll `be all °right provided `John can ₒhelp.	ˎCan he, ₒthough?
I'm 'going to `Paris | toˏmorrow.	ˎAre you, inₒdeed?
He's for'gotten to °shut the ˎgate.	ˎIsn't he ₒstupid!
What 'glorious ˏroses!	ˎAren't they a ₒpicture!
Yes, I `saw Pygˎmalion.	ˎWasn't it a ₒsplendid proₒduction!
ˏJohn's been pro`moted.	ˎIsn't it ₒstrange!

Verbal context	Drill
He's going to ˈgive it ₒto us.	ˌWon't that be ₒlovely!
● ˈWhat a °cold ˋday!	ˌIsn't it ₒjust!

Note: Examples of this tune used for question tags in sentences like

ˌYes, │ ˌisn't it?

are given in Chapter V, Section 13, p. 264.

Commands

What ˈshall I ˌdo with this ₒrubbish?	ˌBurn it. ˌBury it. ˌLose it. ˌKeep it. ˌSell it. ˌScrap the ₒwretched ₒstuff.
ˈCall your ˌdog, │ ˌwill you?	ˌDown, ₒFido. ˌHeel, ₒboy. ˌSit, you ₒhorrible ₒanimal.
● ˈLet me °see if I can ˌlift you.	ˌStop it. ˌDon't, you ₒfathead.
ˈHow can I °get in ˋtouch with ₒMiles?	ˌPhone him. ˌWire him. ˌWrite to him. ˌCable him.
ˈWatch me °juggle with these ˋplates.	ˌCareful, you ₒclown. ˌNow ₒlook what you've ₒdone.
What deˈlicious °looking ˌgrapes!	ˌHave a ₒfew. ˌTake one or ₒtwo.
ˌWho's going to °bath the ˋbaby?	ˌYou ₒtry. ˌYou have a ₒgo. ˌYou have a ₒshot at it.

Interjections

ˈWould you °like an ˌapple?	ˌThank you.
Oh I ˋam ₒcold.	ˌNonsense! ˌRubbish! ˌFiddlesticks! ˌPoor old ₒsoul!
He's reˈfused to ˌgo.	ˌPity! ˌIdiot! ˌSilly ₒboy!
He'll be ˈwith you on ˌFriday.	ˌMarvellous! ˌSmashing! ˌSplendid! ˌSuper!
● ˈWill you be °ready by ˌsix?	ˌLord, ₒyes! ˌHeavens, ₒno!

Tune   — \\ __   **Low Pre-Head+Low Fall (+Tail)**

Statements

ˈWhose ˌpen is ₒthis?	Paˌtricia's. Diˌana's. Eˌlizabeth's. It's ˌmine. It's ˌFreddie's. It's ˌChristine's. It's ˌSusan's.

Verbal context	*Drill*
'What are you °studying ˎthis ₒyear?	Geˎography. Psyˎchology. Aˎnatomy. Physiˎology. Zoˎology. Iˎtalian. Matheˎmatics. Ecoˎnomics. Staˎtistics.
'When can you °let me ˎhave them?	Toˎday. Toˎnight. Toˎmorrow. By toˎnight. By this ˎevening. By ˎMonday. On ˎSunday.
'What's he ˎcharging?	A ˎpound, I ₒthink. The ˎsame, I beₒlieve.
'How d'you °go to the ˎoffice?	By ˎbus. By ˎtube. I ˎwalk. In my ˎcar. By ˎUnderground.
I'd `love to ˏhelp.	I ˎknow you ₒwould. ‖ But you ˎcan't.
I ˎdon't be°lieve you `posted it.	I ˎdid ₒpost it.
`John's the ˏwinner.	He ˎwill be surₒprised.
‾D'you 'think he's forˏgotten?	I'm ˎsure he ₒhasn't.
I'll 'fetch you in the `car.	That ˎis ₒgood of you.
It's 'no good at ˎall.	You're ˎalways disₒsatisfied.
He's 'given up `everything.	I ˎdo think it's a ₒpity.
● 'What's your ˎjob?	I'm a ˎshop asₒsistant. I'm a ˎbank ₒclerk. I'm a ˎpainter. I'm a ˎschoolₒteacher. I'm an ˎactor. I'm a ˎtaxiₒdriver.
'Where did you °go to ˎschool?	Well I was at a ˎnumber of ₒschools. At a most exˎtraordinary ₒplace.
I've `finished my eₒxams.	So you can reˎlax at ₒlast. It must be a reˎlief for you.
'Where will you °be at ˎeight, ₒthen?	I shall be at a reˎhearsal. I shall be at the baˎzaar. At a comˎmittee ₒmeeting, unₒfortunately.

WH-Questions

● ˇSomeone'll ₒhave to ₒdo it.	But ˎwho?
You ˇwon't do it ˇthat ₒway.	Well, ˏhow, ₒthen?
You'll 'find it in the ˎdrawer.	In ˎwhich ₒdrawer?
We 'must have a ˎmeeting.	Well ˎwhen, eₒxactly?
'Alec °won't ˎhelp.	And ˎwhy ₒwon't he?
They 'stayed aˊway │ for a ˇvery good ₒreason.	For ˎwhat good ₒreason?
You'll 'have to °make it yourˎself.	Just ˎhow, if I may ₒask?

Verbal context	*Drill*
I'll 'call on them ˌpersonally.	But ˌwhen, for ˌheaven's ˌsake?
He 'still does a ˌfull day's ˌwork.	How ˌdoes he ˌkeep it ˌup?
They 'won't ˌlend it ˌto us.	Why ˌnot, for ˌheaven's ˌsake?
We 'can't ˌplay. ‖ 'Tim's not ˌhere.	What's ˌthat got to ˌdo with it? ‖ (We can play ˌsingles, °can't we?)
I 'haven't °time ˇnow.	When ˌwill you have ˌtime, may I ˌask?
I've ˇsaid I'll ˌmeet you.	Yes but ˌwhere?
No ˇthat's not ˌStephen's house.	Well where ˌdoes he ˌlive, then?
You're 'not getting 'on very ˌfast, │ 'are you?	When are ˌyou going to ˌtake a ˌturn?
ˇI'm quite ˌwilling.	What are we ˌwaiting ˌfor, then?
● ˊWhat did you °say the ad°dress was?	How many ˌmore ˌtimes d'you ˌwant ˌtelling?

Yes-No Questions

They ˇought to be ˌable to afˌford it.	But ˌcan they afˌford it?
I've got 'so many °things to ˌdo.	Can ˌI ˌhelp at ˌall?
I was 'worried a°bout the ˇmoney.	Was ˌthat all?
I 'can't °manage ˌMonday.	Would ˌTuesday be ˌmore conˌvenient?
● 'This °knife's too ˌblunt.	Is this ˌother one ˌany ˌbetter?
ˇThank you │ for your ˌoffer.	Will it ˌhelp, d'you ˌthink?
ˌBother. ‖ I've forˌgotten to °tell ˌFrank.	Does it ˌmatter ˌall that ˌmuch?
ˇThat's ˌnot ˌmuch ˌgood.	Well can ˌyou do ˌany ˌbetter?
Well he ˇsays he ˌneeds it.	Yes but ˌdoes he, in ˌall ˌhonesty?
That's a ˇpossible ˌplan.	Is it ˌwise, I ˌwonder?
ˌWhere will we °find a 'skeleton?	Could we ˌborrow one?
He 'says he's ˌill.	Is he ˌreally ˌill?
I'll reˈturn it this ˌevening.	Can I ˌcount on ˌthat?
I'm at my 'wits' ˌend.	Well has your ˌfather got ˌany iˌdeas?
ˇSad about ˇJames.	Yes ˌwasn't it ˌawful!
'Let me °show you ˌhow.	Now ˌaren't you ˌkind!
They're 'making him ˌcaptain.	Oh ˌwon't he be ˌpleased!
'Look. ‖ It's ˇraining.	Now ˌisn't that inˌfuriating!

'Guess what ˌcolour her ˌnew suit ˌis.	Is it ˌred?
ˌNo.	Is it ˌblue?
ˌNo.	Is it ˌgreen?

Verbal context	Drill
ˏNo.	Is it ˏyellow?
ˏNo.	Is it ˏblack?
Corˏrect. ‖ 'Now °guess where she ˏbought it.	Was it at ˏSelfridge's?
ˏNo.	Was it at ˏGamage's?
ˏNo.	Was it at ˏButler's?
ˏNo.	Was it at ˏOliver and ₒSons?
ˏYes.	Now ˏhaven't I been ₒquick!

Commands

It's ˏmy ₒbook.	Well ˏtake it, ₒthen.
'May I °borrow this ˏpen?	Yes ˏdo.
ˏWhat shall I 'do with these ₒfigures?	Subˏtract them. Diˏvide them. Igˏnore them. Reˏpeat them. Disˏcard them. Reˏmember them. Make a ˏnote of them.
'Johnnie's been °pulling my 'hair.	Now ˏstop it, ₒyou ₒtwo.
'What shall I ˏdo with her ₒletters?	Hang ˏon to them ₒfor her.
● I 'can't tell you ˇnow.	Then ˏphone me aₒbout it.
ˏHurry ˏup, °Molly.	Don't ˏrush me, ₒTom.
What's 'up?	Be ˏquiet for a ₒminute. ‖ (I'm 'listening to the ˏnews.)
You're a 'blithering ˏidiot.	Don't ˏtalk to me like ₒthat.
● It's 'terribly ₒdifficult.	Let ˏme have a ₒshot at it.
ˇThese tunes don't °sound very ˇdifferent.	Well exˏaggerate them.
ˏWhat have I °done wrong 'now?	Go aˏway, ₒBill. ‖ (ˏCan't you ₒsee I'm ˏbusy?)
ˉThey're ˏbound to ₒlose.	Don't you beˏlieve it.
I 'don't want ˇyour ₒhelp.	Do it yourˏself, ₒthen.

Interjections

I be'lieve he's ˏfinished the ₒjob.	At ˏlast!
Did you 'lock the °back ˏdoor?	Of ˏcourse!
He just 'shouted me 'down.	The ˏbrute!
I've ˏgot to 'work on ₒSaturday.	Oh ˏno!
He's 'won.	Fanˏtastic! Good ˏheavens!
They say they 'won't ˏsell.	What ˏnonsense!

Verbal context	*Drill*
I'm a'fraid I've °got a ˏcold.	No ˎwonder!
I 'hit him °over the ˎhead.	You ˎdidn't!
They've 'given me the ˋsack.	They ˎhaven't! Riˎdiculous! Preˎposterous! The ˎfools! At ˎyour ₒtime of ₒlife!
D'you 'still re°quire ˏsix?	Inˎdeed I ˎdo!
They were ˎvery apoloˏgetic.	I should ˎthink so, inˏdeed!
He re'fuses to ˏpay.	The ˎcheek of it!
● ⁻They're ˏnot the °same, | ˋare they?	Of ˎcourse ₒnot! Of ˎcourse they're ₒnot! Of ˎcourse they're ₒnot the ₒsame!
I reˎpeat. || You're a 'stupid ˎfool.	How ˎdare you ₒspeak to me like ₒthat!
I ˋstill can't ₒfind it.	How exˎtraordinary!

Note: All the drills given above with the tune

LOW PRE-HEAD+LOW FALL (+TAIL)

can be said with emphasis if the low pre-head is replaced by the high pre-head (see Chapter I, p. 36). If marked for this emphasis, the last drill in this section would read

⁻How exˎtraordinary!

Tune **High Head+Low Fall (+Tail)**

Statements

I ˋhate ˏcabbage.	'So do ˎI. 'So does ˏPeter. 'So do we ˎall.
I can't ˋbear ˏJulia.	'Nor can ˎBill. 'Neither can ˎI. 'Nor can my ˎmother.
ˏDavid's °grown a ˋbeard.	'So he ˎhas. 'So I ˎsee.
'How much does it ˎcost?	'Almost a ˎpound. 'More than you'd ˎthink. 'More than we can afˎford.
● 'What's the ˎtime, ₒplease?	'Four oˎclock. 'Half past ˎone. 'Five past eˎleven. 'Quarter past ˎsix. 'Quarter to ˎseven. 'Twenty °five to ˎone. 'Ten °minutes to ˎnine.
'What are you ˎdoing ₒthese ₒdays?	'Working ˎhard. 'Earning my ˎliving. 'Still on ˎholiday. 'Going to ˎevening ₒclasses.
'What sort of ˎholiday did you ₒhave?	'Simply ˎwonderful. 'Quite ˎperfect. 'Perfectly ˎhorrid. 'Too bad for ˎwords. 'Couldn't have been ˎbetter.

Verbal context	*Drill*
'Isn't she °very ˏbright?	'Mad as a ˎhatter. 'Dull as ˎditchwater. 'Not a °brain in her ˎhead.
D'you 'come here ˏoften?	'Hardly ˎever. 'Every ˎnight. 'Every °chance I ˎget.
'What did you ˎthink of the ₒplay?	'First ˏrate. 'Utter ˏtripe. 'Very °cleverly conˎstructed. 'Quite the °best thing he's ˎwritten.
‾Is it ˏeasy?	'Pure ˎchild's ₒplay. 'Simple as °A B ˎC. 'Not so °easy as you might ˎthink.
'How was ˎEric ₒlooking?	'Fit as a ˎfiddle. 'Ready to ˎdrop. 'Just the °same as he ˎalways ₒdoes. 'Better than I've °seen him for a ˎlong ₒtime.
'Was the °car ˏdamaged?	'Scarcely ˎmarked. 'Almost °knocked to ˎpieces. 'Not a °scratch ˎanywhere.
● 'When'll it be ˎfinished?	'Next ˎWednesday. 'Not be°fore the weekˎend. 'Sometime °early in ˎJune, I beˎlieve. 'Round about the °middle of the ˎmonth, they ₒsay.
'When are we to exˎpect you?	'Soon after °half past ˎsix. 'Certainly °not ˎthis ₒweek. 'Not until °sometime on ˎFriday. 'Saturday °evening at the ˎearliest.

WH-Questions

I ˇcan't come ˇnow.	'Why ˎnot?
I saw ˋMonty | ˎlast ˏweek.	'How ˎwas the ₒold ₒscoundrel?
ˇHarry's not ₒcoming to ₒtea.	'Who ˎis ₒcoming to ₒtea, then?
ˏTry °using °sticky ˋtape.	'Who asked ˎyour adₒvice?
You ˇcan't have ˇthat ₒbasket.	'Which one ˎcan I ₒhave?
● He 'told me he'd °been in ˋPersia.	'When was ˎthat, I ₒwonder?
We ˎhired a ₒcar.	'Whose ˎwas it, by the ₒway?
The ˏclock's °stopped aˋgain.	'What's ˎwrong with the ₒblessed ₒthing?
He works 'sixteen °hours a ˎday.	'How on °earth does he °keep it ˎup?
'Why not ˇwait a ₒbit?	'What makes you °think ˎwaiting'll ₒmake any ₒdifference?
I must 'go to the ˎbank.	'Which ˎone? 'Why ˎmust you? 'Why not °leave it till toˎmorrow ˏmorning?

Verbal context	*Drill*

'Will you °lend me your ‚pen?

'What ˎfor? 'What d'you ˎwant it ₒfor? 'Why don't you °buy one of your ˎown? 'Where's the one I °bought you for ˎChristmas?

I can't 'possibly ˎdo that.

'What's so ˎdifficult aₒbout it?

The ˎcar's ₒbroken ₒdown.

'What's the ˎmatter with the ₒwretched maₒchine?

I 'gave him a °piece of my ˋmind.

'Why did you ˎdo such a ₒstupid ₒthing?

I ˎthink you ˋought to aₒpologise.

'How d'you make ˎthat out?

ˋSorry I bumped ˏinto you.

'Why don't you °look where you're ˎgoing?

● I'm a'fraid I've up°set the ˋmilk.

'Why can't you °leave things aˎlone?

Oh 'dear, oh ˎdear!

'What's the °matter with you ˎnow?

I'm 'very ˋfond of ₒjellied ˏeel.

'How in the °world can you ˏeat such ₒstuff?

She 'doesn't look a °day over ˋthirty.

'How in °heaven's °name does she ˎdo it?

'Shut ˋup.

'Who the °dickens d'you °think you're ˎtalking to?

'Where's my ˎpenknife?

'What the °deuce d'you °want ˎthat ₒfor?

'Pass the ˎsalt.

'Why the °blazes °don't you say ˎplease?

ˏWhat's he ˋsaying?

'How can I °hear when you're °making °so much ˎnoise?

Yes-No Questions

(ˋNow that I've ˇheard your ₒplans │ there are a 'number of ˎquestions I'd ₒlike to ₒask. ‖ For ˏinstance │)

'Is ˎJohn ₒgoing to coₒoperate? ‖ 'Have we got e°nough ˎmoney in ₒhand? ‖ 'Mightn't it be °wiser to postˏpone ₒmatters a ₒlittle? ‖ 'Shall we be °able to °finish the job on ˏtime?

Well I ˇthink ₒJohn'll ₒhelp.

'Are you ˎsure, ₒthough?

He's a ˏgood ˏchap.

'Are you °certain he'll ˎhelp?

Well ˋno. ‖ ˋNot absoˇlutely.

'Can you find ˎout, d'you ₒthink?

I exˇpect he'll ₒhelp.

'Can you °find ˎout?

He ˋcertainly ˇought ₒto.

'Will you °answer my ˎquestion? ‖ 'Can you find °out whether °John will ˎhelp?

I'll ˇtry. ‖ 'What ˋelse ₒwas there?

'Are you °happy about the fiˎnancial ₒside of it?

Well I'm ˋnot °sure about the ˇdetails.

'Have we °got e°nough ˎmoney?

We'll be ˋgetting °more ˇsoon.

'Have we e°nough ˎnow? ‖ 'Can we reˎly on ₒgetting ₒmore ₒsoon?

Verbal context	Drill
Yes I'm 'sure we ₀can.	'Don't you °think it would be °better to ˎwait a ₀bit?
I ˇthink we can ₀go aˎhead.	'Dare we ˎrisk it?
It's ʹnot ˇmuch of a ₀risk.	'Is it °wise to °take ˎany ₀risk?
● It'll be ʹvery exˇciting.	'Will you °stick to the ˎpoint?

The eˈxams are °over at ˎlast.	'Isn't it ˎwonderful!
You've made the ʹsame mis°take aˎgain.	'Aren't I a ˎfool! 'Would you beˎlieve it!
I've ʹjust °bought a ˎcar.	'Have you ˎreally!
'Look at this ˎcoat.	'Haven't they °made a ˎmess of it!
'Isn't this °path in a ˎstate!	'Wouldn't you °think they'd ˎdo ₀something aˎbout it!
ˎLovely ₀evening, | ˎwasn't it?	'Wasn't it °nice to see ˎMabel a₀gain!
'Larry's °playing ˎRomeo.	'Can you iˎmagine it! 'Can't you °just ˎsee him!
'What d'you °think of their ˎhouse?	'Isn't it ˎshabby! 'Doesn't it °need ˎpainting!
The 'eight °ten's a ˎterrible ₀train.	'Don't I ˎknow it!
The 'jacket's °worn out alˎready.	'Isn't it °absolute ˎnonsense to ₀buy such ₀shoddy ₀clothes!
'How did the ˎpress reports ₀strike you?	'Couldn't you ˎlaugh at ₀all the ₀fuss they ₀make!
We're 'moving on ˎTuesday.	'Won't it be ˎmarvellous to have your ₀own ₀flat!

Commands

It 'can't be ˎdone.	'Look ˎhere. || ('That's ˎnonsense.)
ˎLend me a ˎfiver, | ˎwill you?	'Go to ˎblazes. || 'Use your ˎown ₀money.
I 'didn't °quite ˎcatch that.	'Pay atˎtention, ₀then.
● I'm 'going to reˎsign.	'Don't be riˎdiculous.
But I ˎdon't ˎlike the ₀pudding.	'Eat it ˎup, I ₀say.
ˎWhat do ˎyou ₀want?	'Show me your ˎticket, ₀madam.
Shall I send it to 'you or to ˎArthur?	'Send it to ˎArthur.
Shall I 'pass them to ˎRobert?	'Pass them to ˎme, ₀rather.
'What d'you °think you're ˎdoing?	'Mind your own ˎbusiness.
I've ˎfinished ˎthat.	'Now reˎpeat the ₀process.

Verbal context	*Drill*
I ‚can't un°do the ‛door.	'Try the ‚other ₒkey. 'Try °turning the ‚knob.
I 'shan't stay a °minute ‚longer.	'Don't be so ‚silly. ‖ 'Come °back at ‚once.
'What shall I ‚do with the ₒbox?	'Throw it a‚way. 'Chop it °up for ‚firewood. 'Give it °back to the ‚greengrocer.
'How much °ought they to ‚have?	'Give them a ‚teaspoonful ₒof it. 'Start them °off with °half an ‚ounce.
I've 'brought you a °tonic from the ‛chemist's.	'Drink it your‚self. 'Take the °wretched °stuff a‚way.
'Where shall I put ‛this ₒchair?	'Leave it °where it ‚is. 'Stand it a°gainst the ‚wall. 'Stack it a°way with the ‚others.
I'm ‛so sorry I inter‚rupted.	'Don't give it a°nother ‚thought.
D'you 'think it'll be all ‚right?	'Don't °you ‚worry.
'How many ‚pencils d'you ₒwant?	'Buy me °half a ‚dozen, ₒplease.
The ˅answer to the ˇfirst ₒsum ǀ is ‛six.	'Have a °go at the ‚next one. 'See if you can do the °second one more ‚quickly.
'What shall I °do with my ‚boots?	'Take them °out into the ‚kitchen. 'Put them in the °cupboard under the ‚stairs.
● 'Arthur ‛Thomas is ₒon the ‚phone.	'Ask him to °ring me again ‚later.

Interjections

'Peter ‚Mainwaring'll be ₒsinging the ₒlead.	'Oh ‚good! 'What a disap‚pointment!
● 'What did you ‚think of it?	'Not ‚bad! 'Not at ˅all ‚bad!
He 'says it was ‛your ₒfault.	'How ri‚diculous! 'Stuff and ‚nonsense! 'What ‚rubbish he ₒdoes ₒtalk!
'Michael ‛Robins has ₒjust ₒdied.	'Good ‚heavens! 'What a ‚tragedy! 'What a °happy re‚lease, poor ₒman!
I've ‛got the ₒjob.	'Well ‚done! 'Nice ‚work! 'Good for ‚you!
He's 'not °calling after ‛all.	'What a ‚nuisance he ₒis! 'How an°noying for your ‚mother!
'Ann's °getting ‛better.	'What a re‚lief! 'How ‚wonderful! 'How re‚lieved you ₒall must ₒbe!
Ap˅parently ǀ they've 'buried the ‛hatchet.	'High ‚time! 'How ‚silly it ₒall ₒwas!
He's won a 'gold ‛medal.	'Fancy ‚that! 'How ex‚traordinary! 'Well I °never ‚did!
Some ‛flowers ₒfor you.	'How ‚nice! 'How ‚sweet of you!

Verbal context	*Drill*
● We're 'going 'picnicking. At 'last °French has 'gone.	'What ˎfun! 'What a °good iˏdea! 'What a ˏbore that ₒfellow ₒis! 'How he °does ˏtalk!
I've 'sprained my 'ankle.	'Too ˏbad! 'Bad ˏluck! 'Hard ˏlines! 'You ˏhaven't! 'Poor old ˏDavid!
'That's °Tom 'Mason.	'Never ˏheard of him!
Does the 'noise ˏbother you?	'Not at ˏall! 'Not in the ˏleast! 'Not the °slightest ˏbit!
'This is °Mr. 'Bradshaw.	'How d'you ˏdo! 'Pleased to ˏmeet you!
'Where's 'Liz ₒgot to?	'Goodness °only ˏknows!
'Hullo, | ˏMickey.	'Fancy °meeting ˏyou here, ₒPeter!
I'll 'make you a 'present ₒof it.	'Thanks ˏawfully! 'Thank you °very ˏmuch! 'Thank you ˏvery ₒmuch! 'Thank you °very °much inˏdeed!
'Here I °am at ˏlast.	'Welcome ˏback! 'Welcome to ˏEngland! 'Welcome °back to ˏEngland!
It's my 'birthday.	'Many °happy reˏturns! 'Very °many °happy reˏturns!

Note: All the relevant drills given above with the tune

HIGH HEAD+LOW FALL (+TAIL)

can be said with emphasis if the emphatic form of the high head is used (see Chapter I, p. 37). If marked for this emphasis, the last drill in this section would read

'Very 'many 'happy reˏturns!

Tune ▬▬▬ \\▬ **Low Pre-Head+High Head +Low Fall (+Tail)**

Statements

Have you 'any °news of ˏMalcolm?	He's 'passed his eˏxam. I was 'talking to him ˏyesterday. We 'haven't °heard from him for ˏages.
ˏWhere did you run 'into ₒTony?	In 'Tottenham °Court ˏRoad. At 'Baker °Street ˏstation. In 'Lower ˏRegent ₒStreet. Near the 'Albert Meˏmorial. On my 'way to °King's ˏCross.

Verbal context	*Drill*
'Why did he °run a'way?	I 'don't °think he ˎdid run aₒway. I simply 'can't ˎthink. I haven't the 'slightest iˎdea. He just 'couldn't face °up to his fi°nancial ˎdifficulties.
'What would 'you do?	It's 'up to ˎyou. I 'simply °can't iˎmagine. You must 'make up your ˎown ₒmind. I'm afraid I've 'nothing °more to sugˎgest.
'When can you ˎcome?	This 'afterˎnoon, I ₒthink. I 'don't °think I ˎcan ₒcome. To'morrow °morning at the ˎearliest. When'ever you °care to inˎvite me. I 'think I shall be °free on ˎSunday. As 'soon as the °weather imˎproves. I'm afraid I 'can't °manage it ˎyet aₒwhile.
● 'How about the 'jacket?	It 'won't °do at ˎall. It 'isn't °quite what I ˎwant. It's a 'bit too °small in the ˎwaist. I 'can't quite °make up my ˎmind aₒbout it.
'Where's that ˎbook of ₒmine?	I 'think you °left it in the ˎlounge. I've 'put it °back on the ˎshelves. I 'can't i°magine ˎwhat you've ₒdone with it.
'How did you °spend the 'morning?	I 'stayed in °bed until °nearly ˎlunch time. I 'went to °see my °brother in ˎKensington. Getting 'up to °date with my °corresˎpondence. I 'stayed at °home and ˎworked.
'What's that °tray ˎmade of?	It's 'made of ˎwood. It's 'made of ˎplastic. It's 'made of a °sort of ˎplastic. It's 'made of °some sort of ˎwood, I beₒlieve. I 'think it's °made of °some sort of ˎplastic.
● 'Why have you ˎcome?	I 'want to ˎtalk to you. I 'wanted to °have a ˎchat with you. I 'thought we °ought to °have a ˎtalk.

WH-Questions

I 'shan't be °able to ˎgo.	Why 'ever ˎnot? For 'heaven's °sake °why ˎnot?

Verbal context	*Drill*
It's ˎyour ｡turn to ｡pay.	What on 'earth are you ˎgetting at?
It ˇwasn't a ˇserious ｡error.	Then 'why are you so ˎangry?
He 'slapped her ˎface.	What'ever came ˎover him?
You'll 'have to °keep ˎquiet a｡bout it.	But 'how ˎcan I?
I've 'changed your ˎplans a ｡bit.	By 'whose auˎthority?
● Did you 'see that °pretty ˏgirl?	Now 'which one d'you ˎmean?
'Will you ˏhelp?	How could I 'possibly reˎfuse?
It's the 'absolute ˎtruth, │ I ˎswear it.	But 'who's going to beˎlieve such a fan-｡tastic ｡story?
We ˏsimply ˇmust ｡buy him a ｡present.	Yes but 'where's the ˎmoney ｡coming ｡from?
I 'can't find my °handbag ˇanywhere.	Well 'when did you °have it ˎlast?
I ˇwon that ˏgame.	How'ever did you °pull it ˎoff?
He says ˇyou'll ｡give him the ｡money.	What'ever will he sug°gest ˎnext?
He ˇdidn't let out °anything imˇportant.	But 'why can't he °keep his ˎmouth shut?
You're being 'very unˎfair.	What the 'devil d'you °mean by ˎthat?
I ar'rived on °Tuesday ˏmorning.	At e'xactly °what ˎtime?
I'm 'on my °way to ˎPuddle ｡Duck.	Where in 'heaven's °name is ˎthat?
ˇSorry I ｡wasn't aˏvailable.	Why'ever didn't you °say you were ˎbusy?
'Try °hanging the °door the ˇother ｡way.	What'ever made you °think of ˎthat?
I 'saw you °talking to ˇRosemary.	And 'what d'you °think ˎshe was ｡going ｡on a｡bout?
He's 'pulled up °all the ˎasters.	What 'will he do ˎnext?
I 'don't °care if I ˎdo ｡lose my ｡job.	What 'are you ˎsaying? How 'can you ˎsay such a ｡thing?
I'm a'fraid I for°got to reˎturn it.	What 'were you ˎthinking ｡of?
I've 'missed the °last ˇbus.	How 'are you °going to get ˏhome?
'Mary's put ˏpaint │ 'all °over the ˎcarpet.	When 'is she going to °learn to be °more ˎcareful?
● 'Oh for a °bit of ˇquiet!	When 'will they °stop °making that °dreadful ˎdin?
'Frank reˎfused the ｡chairman's ｡offer.	When'ever will he get a °chance like ˎthat a｡gain?

Yes-No Questions

I 'might be °struck by ˇlightning.	But 'is it ˎlikely? Is 'that ˎlikely?

Verbal context	*Drill*
(I 'think it's °time to adˎjourn.)	Does 'everyone aˎgree? Are there 'any ob-ˎjections? Will you 'all be °back in an ˎhour, ˳please?
● We shall 'have to °take a ˎtaxi.	But 'can we afˎford it?
ˎTom ex˳plained the ˳method ˳to me.	But do you 'really underˎstand it?
'I'm broke ˎtoo. ‖ So we ˎcan't ˳go.	Well 'couldn't we ˎborrow some ˳money?
I ˅won't be °late a˅gain.	But 'can I beˎlieve you when you ˳say that?
It's °quite an ˅interesting i˳dea.	Would you 'say it's a °practical propoˎsition?
Mr. ˎSmith's rather `busy just ˳now.	Can I 'see him if I °come back ˎlater?
It was °certainly an ex˅perience.	But can you 'honestly °say you enˎjoyed it?
I'd 'like to °know who ˎbroke it.	Would it sur'prise you to °know ˎI ˳didn't?
I ˅hope you won't ˅spoil ˳things.	Now have I 'ever °let you ˎdown?
'What shall we °do `now?	Does 'anyone °feel like a ˎwalk?
He's a ˅likeable ˳sort of ˳fellow.	Yes but 'do you °think he's ˎhonest?
You ˎought to `write to them.	Yes but 'need I °write toˎday?
‾I'm ˎlistening.	But 'are you °listening ˎcarefully?
I sup°pose we °could °try the ˅other ˳plan.	But 'would it have °any °chance of sucˎcess?
He was ex˅tremely ˳rude.	Have you 'any i°dea ˎwhy he was so ˳rude?
He 'turned me °down ˎflat.	Would it be 'any °good ˎmy ˳trying to per-˳suade him?
I'm a'fraid I'm `busy ǀ on ˎTuesday.	Then 'could we °meet on ˎWednesday?
I 'don't know `what to ˳tell ˳Jean.	Well 'need we °tell her ˎanything?
I can ˎonly °find `two ˳books.	Well have you 'left °any at ˎhome?
'What about °Muriel `Gray?	D'you 'think she'd ac°cept if we ˎasked her?
I've 'lived here a ˎlong time.	Yes, but 'have you °lived here °all your ˎlife?
We've 'both got the °same `answer.	Now 'isn't °that peˎculiar!
'Harry's won a °fortune on the `pools.	Well 'would you ˎcredit it!
'I thought it was a `huge suc˳cess.	Yes, 'didn't it go ˎwell!
‾Do ˎyou re°member that °party?	Shall I 'ever forˎget it!
It would be `awful ǀ if we ˎfailed.	Wouldn't it be 'simply apˎpalling!
'Bernard's re°fused to ˎhelp, of ˳course.	Isn't it 'just °what you'd exˎpect of him!
Have you 'heard about Diˎana?	Wasn't it 'abso°lutely ˎmarvellous, her ˳passing that e˳xam!
● It's a 'long ˎtime you've ˳been a˳way.	And am 'I °glad to be ˎhome!
It's as 'cold as ˎcharity in ˳here.	Is it 'ever °anything ˎelse!
I'll recomˎmend you for the ˳job.	Can I 'ever °thank you eˎnough!

Verbal context	*Drill*
What an ex'traordinary ˎhat!	Have you 'ever seen °anything ˎlike it!
'All he had to °do was ˎtell us.	Could 'anything have been °simpler than ˎthat!

Commands

We'll be 'there in ˎno time.	Now 'take it ˎslowly.
I ˏthought he °played °rather ˋwell.	Now 'don't enˎcourage him.
I supˏpose I shall ˋhave to ˳help.	Well 'don't be so °disaˎgreeable aˎbout it.
I'm 'going to ˎchance it.	For 'heaven's °sake be ˎcareful.
● ˅That made you ˳jump.	Don't 'ever do °that aˏgain.
The ˅doctor ˳says │ it's ˏnot ˋserious.	Then 'don't °make so much ˎfuss aˎbout it.
'What shall I °do ˎnow?	Go 'right °back to the beˏginning aˎgain.
It's ˏnot ˏmuch of a °risk.	Well 'don't °say I °didn't ˏwarn you.
'Which would ˋyou choose, if ˳you were ˳me?	For 'goodness °sake °make up your ˎown mind.
'How much ˏpractice shall I ˳do?	Do as 'much as ˏpossible.
'What °time shall I ˎjoin you?	Come when'ever you're ˏready.
I'm 'going to °punch him in the ˏnose.	Don't you 'dare °lay a ˏfinger ˳on him.
'How do I °get to ˎWest ˳Street?	Take the 'first °turning on the ˎleft.
● 'How long d'you °want me to ˏstay?	Stay as 'long as you °possibly ˏcan.
D'you 'think °Tom's ˏserious?	Take the 'whole °thing with a °pinch of ˏsalt.
˅Clive's amˏbition │ is to ˏbe Prime ˋMinister.	May I 'never °live to °see the ˎday.
'How ˏtight d'you ˳want the ˳knot?	Make it as 'tight as you ˏcan.
How ˋcritical should I ˳be?	Don't accept 'anything but the ˎbest.
'What shall I ˎwear?	Put on your 'very °best ˎdress.
I'll ˅never °eat all ˅that.	Well eat as 'much as you ˏcan.
'What about the °washing ˋup?	Just leave it 'all to °Peter and ˏme.
'When d'you °want it ˏback?	Return it when'ever it's conˏvenient.
'How °long can I ˏhave it °for?	Keep it for as 'long as you ˎlike.

Interjections

He ˏcharged me a °pound too ˋmuch.	The 'old ˏrogue!
He 'says he'll ˋsue me.	The 'very iˏdea of it!
You've won 'first ˏprize.	Be'ginner's ˎluck! Good 'heavens aˏbove! What an a'stounding °bit of ˎluck!
'Here's ˏto you.	Your 'very good ˎhealth!

Verbal context	*Drill*
I've 'called it Dy°namic Quiˎescence.	Dy'namic ˏfiddlesticks! Pre'tentious ˏnon-sense!
I 'can't find my °purse ˏanywhere.	How 'very peˏculiar!
We've 'just reˏfurnished ₒthis ₒroom.	What 'wonderful ˏcurtains!
She's 'asked us to ˏtea.	How 'perfectly ˏcharming of her!
ˋHullo, | ˏStevens.	Good 'afterˏnoon, Mr. ₒDavis.
'This is from my °Uncle ˋJack.	How 'kind of him to ˏgive you such a mag-ₒnificent ₒpresent!
It's my 'final eˋxam | toˏmorrow.	The 'very °best of ˏluck to you!
It's a 'bit ˋchilly | toˏday, | ˋisn't it?	Yes what 'ghastly °weather for Juˏly!
● I ˏhaven't °even ˋstarted the ₒjob.	You 'lazy °good for nothing ˏwretch!
They're 'making us a ˏpresent ₒof it.	How 'abso°lutely ˏmarvellous!
I'm ˋglad you could ˏcome.	How 'nice of you to °ask me a°gain so ˏsoon!
ˇThis ₒsnapshot | is of 'John and ˋMaud.	What a 'splendid ˏpicture they ₒmake!
I've 'brought you some ˏflowers.	What a de'lightful surˏprise!
'Don't °make such a ˏfuss, ₒFrank.	You un'feeling ˏmonster!
It's 'going to be a ˋscorcher.	What a 'lovely °day for the ˏpicnic!
'Here's the ˋpen you ₒlost.	Thank you 'very °much inˏdeed!
I 'made °rather a ˋmess of it.	I should 'just °think you ˏdid!
● I 'haven't °seen you for ˋages.	And i'magine us °meeting ˏhere of ₒall ₒplaces!
He's 'just made a°nother ap'pointment.	What a 'pity we didn't °ring him ˏyesterday!
'Come and °look out ˋhere.	What a mag'nificent ˏview!
He's 'really ˏcharming, | ˏisn't he?	And what a 'marvellous ˏstory he ₒtells!
'Here's your ˋtea.	What an e'normous °piece of ˏcake you've ₒgiven me!
It's 'John ˋThomson, | ˏisn't it?	Well 'blow me ˏdown! || If it 'isn't °old ˏMurdoch!

Note: All the relevant drills given above with the tune
LOW PRE-HEAD+HIGH HEAD+LOW FALL (+TAIL)
can be said with emphasis if one or both of the following features are used:
(*a*) the emphatic form of the high head (see Chapter I, p. 37);
(*b*) the high pre-head instead of the low pre-head (see Chapter I, p. 36).
With both of these features marked, the last drill in this section would read
‾Well 'blow me ˏdown! \|\| ‾If it 'isn't 'old ˏMurdoch!

2 *The High Drop*

Attitude

In STATEMENTS: conveying a sense of involvement, light, airy.

In WH-QUESTIONS: brisk, businesslike, considerate, not unfriendly, lively, interested.

In YES-NO QUESTIONS: willing to discuss but not urgently, sometimes sceptical; (in question tags used as independent comments) mildly surprised acceptance of the listener's premises.

In COMMANDS: suggesting a course of action and not worrying about being obeyed.

In INTERJECTIONS: mildly surprised, not so reserved or self-possessed as with the Low Drop.

Tone marks used in HIGH DROP drills

A Stressed, accented syllables (Nucleus, Head)
[ˋ] High falling to very low pitch.
['] Relatively high level pitch.
[°] Relatively high level pitch, the same pitch as the *preceding* ['].
B Stressed, unaccented syllables (Tail)
[ₒ] Very low level pitch, the same pitch as the end of the *preceding* [ˋ].

Tune ⟍___ **High Fall (+Tail)**

Verbal context	*Drill*
Statements	
'Do you know °Basil ˏFish?	ˋNo. ‖ (I ˋdon't.) ˋYes. ‖ (I ˋdo.)
● 'How °long'll it ˏtake?	ˋHours. ˋDays. ˋWeeks. ˋYears. ˋAges. ˋNo ₒtime.
● ‾Is that ˏreally the °quickest °way?	ˋMuch. ˋMuch the ₒquickest. ˋMuch the ₒquickest ₒway.
Does 'John ˏalways for°get?	ˋAlways.
'How °often has he ˎvisited you?	ˋNever.
ˋNow ₒwhat have you been ₒup to?	ˋNothing.

Verbal context	*Drill*
'Who's been °eating my ‚grapes?	ˋNo-one. ˋNo-one ‚has. ˋNo-one's been ‚eating your ‚wretched ‚grapes.
'Who on °earth would ‚take such a ‚risk?	ˋI would. ˋWe would. ˋMichael ‚would. ˋAnthony ‚would.
Is there 'any °silly °ass who ˋdoesn't ‚like it?	ˋI don't. ˋWe don't. ˋJohnnie ‚doesn't. ˋPeter ‚doesn't.
And ‚who'll ˋmake me ‚say I'm ‚sorry?	ˋI will. ˋHe will. ˋFather ‚will.
'Which will ˋyou take, ‚Henry?	ˋBoth. ˋThis one. ˋThat one.
Were there 'many ‚people °there?	ˋCrowds. ˋHundreds. ˋThousands. ˋMillions. ˋMasses. ˋCrowds of them. ˋMasses of ‚people.
¯Are you ‚certain he °stole them?	ˋPositive. ˋQuite ‚certain.
'How did you get ˋon?	ˋTerribly. ˋWonderfully ‚well. ˋSplendidly, I'm ‚pleased to ‚say.
'How many of his °books have you ˋread?	ˋAll of them. ˋNone of them.
'Wasn't it ‚cold in the ‚hall!	ˋFreezing. ˋFearfully ‚cold.
‚Why didn't you ˋbuy the ‚picture?	ˋMuch too ex‚pensive.
It'll ˋcost a °lot of ˇmoney.	ˋObviously. ˋNaturally. ˋCertainly. ˋNaturally it ‚will. ˋCertainly it'll ‚cost a ‚lot of ‚money.
● 'What's the ˋnext ‚move?	ˋAnything can ‚happen.
¯Do we ‚have to °pay for it?	ˋCertainly we ‚must.
'Which °time would suit ˋyou?	ˋEither would ‚suit me.
Who on 'earth °gave you per‚mission?	ˋJames ‚said I ‚could.
Where's ˋmy ‚copy?	ˋPeter ‚took it ‚for you.
‚Have I °met him be°fore?	ˋSurely you ‚have.

WH-Questions

I 'saw the ˋQueen ǀ ‚yesterday.	ˋWhere?
● I shall ˋhave to ˇgive it ‚to him.	ˋWhy?
I'm 'going to ˋSwitzerland.	ˋWhen?
You'll ˋnever °guess who's ˇhere.	ˋWho?
You can ‚win ˋeasily.	ˋHow? ˋHow can I ‚win?
I was 'punched in the ˋnose ǀ by a ˋman.	ˋWhat ‚man?
There's 'somebody's ˋbag in the ‚car.	ˋWhose ‚bag?
● I shall be ˋlate, I'm a‚fraid.	ˋHow ‚late?

Verbal context	*Drill*
'May I °bother you a‚gain?	'Now ₒwhat?
I 'haven't °time toˇday.	'When have you ₒtime, then?
It 'certainly isn't ˇmine.	'Whose ₒis it, ₒthen?
He's 'coming to 'stay with us.	'When, may I ₒask?
I 'know ₒTim'll be ₒthere.	'How d'you ₒknow, though?
I was 'told you'd re'signed.	'Who ₒtold you?
It 'says in the °paper you 'won.	'Where does it ₒsay that?
I've 'got a con'fession to ₒmake.	'Now ₒwhat have you been ₒup to?
I 'mustn't ‚take them.	'Why ₒmustn't you ₒtake them?
He's planted 'ten °kinds of ‚apple ₒtree.	'What ₒkinds has he ₒplanted?
The shop 'may be 'shut.	'Then ₒwhat should I ₒdo?
● 'Let's paint °one of the °walls 'pink.	'Which of them, d'you ₒthink?
The 'shop's in a °turning off the 'High Street.	'Which ₒturning ₒis it?
‚Leslie °may not 'want to take ₒpart.	'Then ₒwho could we ₒrope ₒin?

Yes-No Questions

● I 'like it | ‚here.	'Do you? ‖ (I ‚thought you'd 'hate it.)
She's 'thirty‚five.	'Is she? ‖ (I 'didn't 'know that.)
They 'won't ‚help us.	'Won't they? ‖ (We shall 'see.)
It 'doesn't appear ˇregularly.	'Doesn't it? ‖ (You 'do surₒprise me.)
You're 'too 'late.	'Am I?
She ˇcan atₒtend | 'after ₒall.	'Can she?
They don't ˇoften ₒgo there.	'Don't they?
I simply 'daren't ‚think aₒbout it.	'Daren't you?
He 'wouldn't a°gree at 'all.	'Wouldn't he?
I shall be in 'Paris | by ‚tea-time.	'Will you?
I 'can't 'bear ‚cats.	'Can't you?
I 'must be °home by ‚six.	'Must you?
They 'oughtn't to have 'told you.	'Oughtn't they?
I've ‚sold my ₒhouse.	'Have you, ₒnow?
It'll be 'easy | if ‚John °helps.	'Will he, ₒthough? ‖ ('That's °what we're not 'sure of.)
He can 'write what he ‚likes.	'Can he, ₒnow? ‖ (I'm 'not so 'sure about ₒthat.)
They 'wouldn't °let us 'in.	'Wouldn't they, inₒdeed?

Verbal context	_Drill_

We're 'doing it be°cause we 'have to.   'Do you ₒhave to ₒdo it, in ₒfact?
So 'long as we °get there in ˇtime │ it's 'easy.   'Shall we ₒget there in ₒtime, though?
● 'John's gene°rosity's a'mazing.   'Is it geneₒrosity, d'you ₒthink?

Note: Examples of this tune used for question tags in sentences such as
'Pity, │ 'isn't it?
are given in Chapter V, Sections 9–12.

Commands

('Ready °steady . . .)   'Go.
'Watch me 'jump off this ₒwall.   'Don't. ‖ (You'll 'hurt yourₒself.)
ˌWhat's the 'matter?   'Look. ‖ (It's 'snowing.)
ˇCareful. ‖ You'll 'fall.   'Help. ‖ (I 'am ₒfalling.)
'Balance it °on your 'head, │ like 'this.   'Mind. ‖ (You'll 'drop it.)
'May I °borrow your ˌpen?   'Yes. ‖ 'Do.
'Shall we have a °game of ˌbridge?   'Yes. ‖ 'Let's.
D'you 'think this °hat'll ˌfit me?   'Try it.
● He'll be 'terribly ˇangry.   'Let him. 'Let him be ₒterribly ₒangry.
He takes 'no ˌnotice ₒof me.   'Make him. 'Make him take ₒnotice ₒof you.
● A 'letter °won't reach °Ann in 'time.   'Phone her, ₒthen.
'Let's ˌgo.   'Wait a ₒmoment.
I ˌcan't un°tie the 'string.   'Cut it, ₒthen.
I ˌcan't af'ford a ₒnew ₒdress.   'Make yourself ₒone.
Peter 'won't ˌlend me his ₒcase.   'Buy it ₒfrom him, ₒthen.
'Was that your ˌtoe I °trod on?   'Careful, you ₒclumsy ₒelephant.
● I 'love ₒsalted ˌalmonds.   'Take a ₒcouple of ₒhandfuls.
I ˇcan't ₒdrink this ₒhorrid ₒmedicine.   'Force yourₒself to ₒdrink it.
The ˌpaper's too °big for the 'envelope.   'Fold it, ₒthen, you ₒhelpless ₒman.
ˌMike's °pulling my 'hair, ₒMummy.   'Stop it, ₒMike, you ₒbig ₒbully.

Interjections

'Boo.   'Oh! ‖ (You 'did ₒstartle me.)
I'll be 'there by °six at the 'latest.   'Fine! ‖ (I 'thought you'd be 'later than ₒthat.)
He's 'over 'seventy.   'Well! ‖ (I'd 'never have beˌlieved it.)
It's 'eight o'ˇclock.   'Heavens! ‖ (I'm 'late.)

Verbal context	*Drill*
May ˏsaid you'd reˋfused.	ˋNonsense! ‖ (I've done ˏnothing of the ˋsort.)
Tim's 'back alˋready.	ˋGoodness! ‖ (⌐He ˏhas been ₒquick.)
'Alice is °coming as ˋwell.	ˋReally! ‖ (What a 'lovely surˏprise!) ˋSplendid! ‖ (I was a'fraid she °wouldn't be ˋable to.)
'Will you °have a ˏdrink?	ˋThank you. ‖ (I'd ˋlove one.)
● I've 'turned up at ˋlast.	ˋAh! ‖ ˋThere you are, ₒJohnson!
I 'didn't °pull it ˏoff, I'm aₒfraid.	ˋWhat a ₒpity! ˋWhat a ₒshame! ˋWhat a disapₒpointment ₒfor you!
● 'When are you °going to ˏItaly a°gain?	ˋGoodness ₒknows!
Have you 'taken °over your °new ˏhouse?	ˋHeavens ₒyes! ‖ ˋAges aₒgo!
⌐Can I tell ˏMarjorie a°bout it?	ˋGoodness ₒno! ‖ (She'll tell ˋeveryone.)
ˏFancy ˋtrying it ₒthat way!	ˋWasn't it riₒdiculous!
Ann's 'broken her enˋgagement.	ˋFine ₒgoings ₒon! ˋWhat a misₒtake!
⌐He's ˏdropped it aˋgain.	ˋSilly ₒlittle ₒman!
I 'painted it myˋself, ₒDaddy.	ˋThere's a ₒclever ₒboy!
I've been 'helping ˋMummy, ₒDaddy.	ˋThat's a ₒgood ₒgirl!
It's ˋraining aₒgain.	ˋBother the ₒwretched ₒweather!

Tune ⎯⎯⎯⎯╲⎯⎯ **Low Pre-Head+High Fall (+Tail)**

Statements

'When did you ˏsee him?	On ˋThursday. ‖ (I ˏthought you ˋknew.)
● Would you 'like to ˏjoin us?	I'd ˋlove to. With ˋpleasure.
¹Come ˏon. ‖ 'Let's get ˏgoing.	We ˋcan't. ‖ It's ˋraining.
'Can you °lend me a ˏpound?	Why ˋyes. ‖ I'd be ˋglad to.
You °ought to inˋvite him.	I ˋhave. I'm ˋgoing to. I inˋtend to. I ˋhave inₒvited him.
It ˏisn't as °if he were ˋill.	Eˋxactly. ‖ He's got ˋno exₒcuse.
ˏWhere's Miss ˋSmith?	She's ˋill. ‖ Pneuˋmonia, I ₒthink.
I've reˋsigned.	I ˋknow. ‖ The ˋsecretary ₒtold me.
For 'goodness °sake ˏhurry.	I ˋcan't. ‖ My ˋleg's ₒhurting.
'How did you °come to ˋlose it?	I ˋhaven't ₒlost it. ‖ I've just misˋlaid it.

Verbal context	*Drill*
I'd ˈlike aˋnother ˳sweet.	There ˋaren't ˳any. ‖ You've ˋeaten them ˳all.
So you ˈthink he's disˋhonest.	I've ˋalways ˳thought so.
I ˆdon't think ˇthat's ˳right.	It ˋmust be ˳right.
↗What are ˋyou ˳doing here at ˳this hour?	I'm ˋwaiting for ˳somebody.
ˈHave a °good ˏtime.	I'm ˋsure I ˳shall.
ˋHere we ˏare.	So ˋthis is ˳your ˳house.
↗What's the °matter ˋnow?	My ˋshoelace has ˳come un˳done.
ˆNo sign of ˇMichael ˳yet.	He ˋalways ˳keeps us ˳waiting.
She'll be ˈhere at ˎtwelve.	Eˋleven, I ˳thought she ˳said.
He's ˈangling for a ˋloan.	So ˋthat's ˳what he was ˳getting at.
I'd ˋlove to stay ˳up for ˏtelevision.	I ˋknow you ˳would. ‖ But you ˋcan't. ‖ It's ˋbedtime.
ˈI'll take ˋthis book.	You ˋmustn't. ‖ That's ˋMary's.
I'm ˈnot ˎgoing to the ˳wretched ˳party.	You ˋmust turn ˳up. ‖ You ˋpromised you ˳would.
He ↗says he's hard ˋup.	That's abˋsurd. ‖ He's got ˋplenty of ˳money.
The ˈlast °train's ˋgone.	It ˋcan't have ˳done. ‖ We're in ˋloads of ˳time.
He's ˈpromised to aˎpologise.	It's the ˋleast he can ˳do.
ˇThis is the ˳bag you ˳asked for, | ˏisn't it?	No it's ˋthat one I ˳want. ‖ The ˋblue one.
ˈWhat did you °think of the ˎshow?	It was ˋwonderful. ‖ I was aˋmazed how ˳good it ˳was.
You ˇwill ˳stay a bit ˳longer, | ˋwon't you?	But I ˋtold you. ‖ I've got a ˋtrain to ˳catch.
It was ↗all ˋyour ˳fault.	But it ˋwasn't. ‖ And I can ˋprove it.
● ˈDid you ˏlike °Box °Hill?	Imˋmensely. ‖ It's a deˋlightful ˳spot.
● You ˆcan't eat all ˇthat.	Oh but I ˋcan. ‖ I'm ˋstarving.
You ˇwill come ˳next week, | ˋwon't you?	I ˋcan't, I'm a˳fraid. ‖ I shall be in ˋRome.

WH-Questions

● You ˈmust ˎdo it.	But ˋhow?
Is there ˈanyone ˋelse you ˳don't ˳know?	Who's ˋthat?
ˋSorry to ˳be so ˏlate.	What ˋhappened?
I ˈought to ˋwrite to him.	Why ˋbother? ‖ (He ˌnever ˳writes to ˏyou.)
(ˋHullo, | ˏDennis.)	How ˋare you?
(I'm ˆnot °standing for ˇthat.)	Why ˋshould I?

Verbal context	*Drill*
I 'know I ˇbrought an um͜brella.	Where ˋis it, ͛then?
We're ˋstuck. ‖ The ˋcar won't ͜start.	What's ˋwrong with it?
I said 'no such ͵thing.	What ˋdid you ͜say, then?
He's 'just bought a °new ˋcar.	What ˋmake has he ͜got?
I've ˇfound that ͵polish.	Which ˋtin was it ͜in?
I ˋdon't live ˇhere.	Where ˋdo you ͜live, then?
We'll 'meet °sometime toˋmorrow.	Well ˋwhen, e͜xactly?
I ˋhope we ˇwin.	Why ˋshouldn't we ͜win?
● D'you 'think it was ͵Terry?	Who ˋelse ͜could it have ͜been?
It's ˋnot ˇmy ͜coat.	Whose ˋis it, d'you sup͜pose?
Toˇday's im͜possible, │ ˋtoo.	When ˋcan you ͜come, may I ͜ask?
You ͵can't eat ͵that.	But why ˋnot?
● I know 'all a͵bout it.	But how ˋcan you ͜know?
I 'must °find ͵out.	But just ˋhow will you ͜find ͜out?

Yes-No Questions

He ͵says he's al°ready ˋgot one.	Oh ˋhas he?
They ˋboth ͜passed the e͜xam.	Oh ˋdid they?
I'm ˋglad the ˇcar's all ͜right again.	But ˋis it?
I ˇought to ͜go to the ͜lecture.	But ˋwill you ͜go, d'you ͵think?
They 'said they'd ˋsue him.	Well ˋhave they ͜done so?
If we ˋstop ˇsmoking │ we'll 'better ˋoff.	But ˋshall we be ͜any ͜better ͜off?
● She ˋsaid she inˇtended to re͜turn it.	Yes but ˋdid she ͜bring it ͜back, in ͜fact?
ˋNobody seems ͜anxious to ͜do it.	Can ˋI have a ͜try?
I'm afraid ˇten won't ͜do.	Will ˋtwenty be e͜nough?
I'm at the 'end of my ͵tether.	Can't ˋI do ͜something?
ˇThat ͜knife │ ͵won't cut at ˋall.	Is ˋthis one ͜any ͜better?
ˇPeggy ͜doesn't think ͜much of it.	Do ˋyou ͜think it would be ͜useful?
It's ˋhopeless for ˇyou to ͜try.	Would ˋPeter ͜stand a ͜better ͜chance?
ˋNo-one seems ͜very ͜keen.	Can you ˋwonder?
͵How can we get ˋhold of a gui͜tar?	Could we ˋhire one?
I'd ˋlove to ͵help.	Wouldn't we ˋall?
We ˇmay get ͜there in ͵time.	Is it ˋlikely, d'you ͜think?
● We'll ˋnever be ͜ready │ by ͵Monday.	Shall we postˋpone the ͜meeting, ͜then?
͵What shall we ˋdo about that ͜party?	Need we do ˋanything a͜bout it?
It's ˋno good °asking ˇBrown.	Well would Mr. ˋSmith be a ͜better ͜choice?

Verbal context	*Drill*

ˇI can't ˌtell you about it. ‖ I 'wasn't ˎthere. | Well was your ˋwife ˌpresent? ‖ Can ˋshe ˌhelp at ˌall?

Commands

He 'doesn't °want to ˋplay.	Then ˋmake him.
ˌHow can I °make it ˋup with ˌMary?	Aˋpologise ˌto her.
I'm ˋawfully ˌsorry.	Forˋget it.
● He 'can't af°ford to ˋpay.	Well ˋgive it to him, ˌthen.
I just ˋcan't ˌmake this thing ˌwork.	Let ˋme have a ˌgo at it.
I ˋcan't hold this ˇmuch ˌlonger.	Let ˋgo of it, ˌthen.
I've ˌno °real exˋcuse.	Inˋvent one, ˌthen.
'Pat's being °very ˌobstinate.	Then ˋyou be ˌobstinate, ˌMartin.
I'm 'most ˌgrateful ˌto you.	Don't ˋmention it, my ˌdear ˌchap.
'What about ˋButler's ˌoffer?	Reˋfuse it, you ˌsilly ˌfool.
I 'couldn't ˋget them ｜ on the ˌphone.	Well then ˋwrite to them.
What 'can I °say to ˋthank you?	Don't say ˋanything.
ˋGoodness! ‖ This ˌgin ˋis ˌstrong.	Put some ˋtonic ˌin it.
'Peter doesn't ˋwant his ˌcake.	Oh well ˋyou ˌhave it.
I simply ˇcan't manage it aˇlone.	Then let's ˋall get ˌdown to it.
● 'Lots of people °don't ˋlike it.	Well take ˋme, for ˌinstance.
● I 'won't ˌhear of it.	Now be ˋreasonable, ˌFrank.
What exˋcuse shall I ˌgive?	Say your ˋgrandmother's ˌdied.
I ˇcan't af°ford the ˇdecorators.	Get your ˋhusband to ˌdo it.
I'm an inˌtelligent ˌhuman ˌbeing.	Well beˋhave like ˌone, then.
'This °coat doesn't ˋfit me ｜ ˌnow.	Get the ˋtailor to have a ˌlook at it.

Interjections

(⌒That ✓you Mr. °Archer?)	Good ˋmorning. Good ˋmorning ˌto you. Good ˋevening.
He ˌscored a ˋcentury.	Magˋnificent! Coˋlossal!
I'll ˋgive it ˌto you.	How ˋlovely!
He's 'finished the °job alˋready.	Good ˋgracious!
ˌShe says ˋyou're to ˌblame.	What ˋnonsense!
ˋIsn't it a ˌlovely ˌview!	Enˋchanting! Deˋlightful!
He's 'broken the ˋrecord.	Stuˋpendous! Fanˋtastic!
'Thank you °very ˋmuch.	Thank ˋyou.

Verbal context	*Drill*
'Could you °give me a ,light, °please?	With `pleasure!
You're a 'pompous ˎass, ˳David.	Well `really, ˳Peter!
`Hullo, | ,Tom.	Oh `there you ˳are, ˳George!
,Jack says °you're a `bore.	Con`found his ˳impudence!
I'm `sure to ˳pass the eˎxam.	The con`ceit of the ˳man!
‾Do you think ,Don'll °stand °in?	Of `course he'll ˳stand ˳in!
Would you 'like to °go to the ˏopera?	In`deed I ˳would.
'May I °use your ,phone?	By `all means.
I ˎthought they'd °all `gone.	By `no means.
‾D'you play ,tennis?	Of `course I ˳do. || A `silly ˳question!
You `won't ˳give me aˏway, | `will you?	Of `course ˳not.
The ˏapple's `bad.	No `wonder ˳Jim didn't ˳want it!
You ˎsaid she was `beautiful.	Not at `all.
I 'owe you an a`pology.	I should `think so, inˏdeed!
He 'seems °rather a `dull ˳dog.	You'd be sur`prised!

Note: All the drills given above with the tune

LOW PRE-HEAD+HIGH FALL (+TAIL)

can be said with emphasis if the low pre-head is replaced by the high pre-head (see Chapter I, p. 36). With the high pre-head marked the last drill in this section would read

‾You'd be sur`prised!

Tune 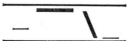 **(Low Pre-Head+) High Head +High Fall (+Tail)**

Statements

'When's the ,concert?	'Next `Sunday. 'Next `Wednesday. 'Tuesday `week.
It's 'going to be a `fine ˳place.	'So it `seems. 'So I've `heard.
'What was the `show like?	'First `rate. 'Simply `splendid.
He ˏought to have °booked in ad`vance.	'That's what `I said.
I feel 'so `sleepy.	'So do `I. 'So does `Timothy.
'Where on °earth are my `slippers?	I 'can't think `what's ˳happened to them.
You're ˏnot ˳eating ,that, | ,are you?	It tastes 'very `nice.

Verbal context	*Drill*
They ˇare ₒtwins, │ ˎaren't they?	Yes but they're 'not a ˋbit aₒlike.
'How did the ˌgame °go?	'Very ˋwell. ‖ 'Four °nil to ˋus.
● 'Which would you ˌlike, │ 'tea or ˌcoffee?	'I'd pre°fer ˋtea. 'I'd like ˋcoffee.
‾Does your ˌleg still °hurt?	'Hardly at ˋall. 'Not in the ˋleast.
He ˋdidn't get ˇmany ₒright, │ ˌdid he?	'More than you'd ˋthink.
Is 'Mike °still doing ˌwell?	'Better than ˋever. ‖ 'Top of his ˋclass.
They 'didn't °care for it at ˋall.	'Nor did my ˋsister. 'Neither did ˋDick. 'Nor did ˋwe.
I'm de'lighted with his ₒwork.	'So am ˋI. 'So's Mr. ˋRobinson.
I ˋcan't ˇgive it ₒto you.	'Nobody ˋasked you to.
ˌWhy don't they °work in the ˋevenings?	'Some of them ˋdo, I beₒlieve.
'How are you °feeling ˋnow?	'Fit as a ˋfiddle, I'm ₒpleased to ₒsay.
'Can you °stay a little ˌlonger?	I'm 'sorry I ˋcan't. ‖ (I've a ˋtrain to ₒcatch.)
I ad'vised him to ˋsell.	That's 'just what he ˋdid do.
Are 'these ˌshop °cakes?	No, I 'made them myˋself.
You've won 'first ˌprize.	I can 'hardly beˋlieve it. ‖ My 'luck's inˋcredible.
ˇI'm ₒgoing to the ₒparty, │ but ˇJane ₒisn't.	We were 'hoping you'd ˋboth be ₒthere.
'How about °asking °Jack and ˋMarion?	'No ˋuse, I'm aₒfraid. ‖ 'Jack's a°way in ˋLondon.
'Would you mind °shutting the ˌdoor?	'Somebody's al'ready ₒshut it.
Oh he's ˌalways ₒmaking exₒcuses.	I 'wonder you put ˋup with it.
'What's the ˌtime, ₒplease?	I 'don't ˋknow. ‖ I sup'pose it's a°bout ˋtwelve.
No, 'I'm a ˋforeigner.	I should 'never have beˋlieved it. ‖ Your 'English is ˋperfect.
'Why did you °lock the ˋdoor?	So that 'no-one should disˋturb us.
'What was it ˌlike in Niₒgeria?	Oh the 'heat was ˋterrible. ‖ I 'thought I should have ˋdied.
Thank you 'very °much inˌdeed.	'Not at ˋall. ‖ 'Glad to have °been of ˋhelp.
Are you 'still in that °dingy little ˌoffice?	It's 'just been done ˋup. ‖ And 'now it's °much more ˋpleasant to ₒwork in.
We're 'quite sold ˋout, I'm aₒfraid.	Then I must 'try °somewhere ˋelse, I supₒpose.
Could you 'tell me where the ˌLuckins °live?	'Just a°cross the ˋroad. ‖ 'Number °twentyˋfour.

Verbal context	*Drill*
That ˅parcel's ar₀rived.	'Better °late than ˋnever.
'Where does ˒Peter °live?	'Next °door to the ˋsweet shop.
What an a'mazing ˎtrick!	'Can't i°magine ˋhow it's ₀done.
'Come ˒on. ‖ ¯Let's 'go for a ˋwalk.	We 'really ˋcan't. ‖ It's 'raining °cats and ˋdogs.
It's ˋAnn's ₀turn, you ₀know.	I 'quite °thought it was ˋmine.
'What a ˋpity you ₀didn't pull it ₀off!	I'd 'like to °try aˋgain. ‖ Per'haps in the ˋspring.
● 'Why didn't ˋyou ₀play?	I 'couldn't °find my ˋracquet.
'Don't °bother to ˒fetch me.	It's 'not the ˋleast ₀trouble. ‖ I'm 'only too ˋhappy to ₀do it.
'Time to get ˒up.	But it's 'only °half past ˋfive.
D'you 'think they'd ˒like to °come?	They'd be 'only °too deˋlighted.
The 'manager was °very ˋnice a₀bout it.	I was a'fraid he °might be ˋdifficult.
D'you 'think it's ˒possible °that way?	'Never been °known to ˋfail.
'When will the °school be ˋready?	'Probably °not for ˋages.
'How are you °finding your °new ˋjob?	'Liking the °work imˋmensely.
'Didn't you °hear any °strange ˒noises?	'Nobody °heard the ˋslightest ₀sound.
˅Terry doesn't ₀seem to be ₀worried.	'He won't °feel the efˋfect of it so ₀much.
I'm 'here at ˎlast.	I'd 'almost °given you ˋup.
¯What ˒time is it?	It's 'half past eˋleven. ‖ I 'didn't °realise how ˋlate it ₀was.
˅He's no ₀chicken!	No he's 'fifty °if he's a ˋday.
Well where ˋis their ₀shop, then?	It's 'right next °door to the ˋstation. ‖ You 'can't °possibly ˋmiss it.
What's ˋyour ₀view on their ₀findings?	I 'haven't had °time to ˋread their re₀port. ‖ I've been 'up to my °eyes in ˋwork.
● You're 'just in ˎtime.	I was a'fraid I should be ˋlate. ‖ I 'missed the ˋbus.
ˎHere. ‖ 'Use ˎmy ₀pen.	'Thank you °very ˋmuch. ‖ 'Mine seems to be °out of ˋink.
˒Where are you °off to ˋnow?	'Going to °look at the ˋtimetable.
'Bill's still ˋvery ₀keen on ₀golf.	'Can't under°stand what he ˋsees in it.
'What was the ˋweather ₀like?	I 'thought it was °going to ˋrain. ‖ But it 'turned out °fine after ˋall.
It's ˒not very ˒valuable, °is it?	It cost over 'three °hundred ˋpounds.

Verbal context	*Drill*
We'll `never ₒget there.	It's 'not as °far as you i`magine.
⁻Was it a ˏrough °crossing °then?	No the 'sea was as °smooth as a `millpond. ‖ But I'm a 'very °poor `sailor. ‖ So I'm 'easily up`set.
'What does he °do for a `living?	He 'was a `bank ₒclerk. ‖ But 'now he's in °business on his `own.
You've ˏonly got to ₒscore fifˏteen.	That 'isn't as °simple as it `sounds.
'What pos`sessed him to beₒhave like ₒthat?	He 'must have been `dreaming. ‖ I've 'always re°garded him as the `sanest of ₒpersons.
What's `Vernon's oₒpinion?	He 'can't °make up his °mind `which he preₒfers.
'How °far is it to ˏChelmsford?	'All depends °which way you `go.
'Which do `you preₒfer, Tom?	I 'rather °fancy that °blue `striped one.
I've 'just been pro`moted.	That's the 'best news I've °heard for a `long time.
'What about `this maₒterial?	I'd have 'liked something of °rather `better ₒquality.
'Can I read that °novel after ˏyou?	'Can't be `done, I'm aₒfraid. ‖ 'One of my `nephews has alₒready ₒspoken for it. ‖ 'Pity you didn't °ask me `earlier.
'How long are °letters to Ja`pan ₒtaking?	You 'ought to allow a °week at `least.
`Here are the ˏtickets.	'These are `singles. ‖ I 'thought we were °taking re`turns.
'When can we °have a ˏtalk?	'Praps you'd °come to °lunch on `Sunday.
I `may be a bit `late.	'That wouldn't °matter in the `least.

'By the `way, ǀ 'where do you `live?	'Not °far from the `office.
'Whereaˏbouts?	'Near °King's Cross `station.
That `is ₒhandy.	'Only about °five minutes' `walk aₒway.
'Aren't you ˏlucky!	'That's what `everybody ₒsays.
It `must save you a °lot of `time.	'More than I'd °ever have `thought.
`How ₒmuch, d'you ₒthink?	'Ten or e°leven hours a `week.
As 'much as `that?	'Maybe °even `more, I shouldn't ₒwonder.
'How does your `wife ₒfind it?	'She likes it as °much as `I do.

Verbal context	*Drill*

WH-Questions

● I've 'just seen that °new `musical.  ·  'What's it `called?

● 'Under°neath the `Arches.  ·  'What did you `think of it?

ˌQuite `good, | ˌreally.  ·  'Who com°posed the `music?

'John `Adams, I ˌthink his ˌname is.  ·  'Which `theatre is it ˌplaying at?

The 'Prince of ˌWales. · 'Which e°xactly `is the ˌPrince of ˌWales?

The 'one near °Piccadilly `Circus.  ·  'How did you `get there?

By a 'fourteen ˌbus. · 'Why didn't you °go by `tube? ‖ (It's `much ˌquicker.)

I 'can't `bear the ˌUnderground.  ·  'How many `acts in the ˌplay?

ˌThree. · 'Which per`formance did you ˌgo to?

Oh the `early one.  ·  'When does that be`gin?

At 'six ˌthirty. · 'When does the `late house ˌstart?

About 'nine oˌclock. · 'When does it `end?

'Usually around e`leven.  ·  'What's the °price of ad`mission?

The ˇcheapest ˌseat | costs a `pound.  ·  'Who did you `go with?

My `cousin.  ·  'What's her `name?

It's `not a ˌshe. ‖ It's a `he. · 'What's `his ˌname, then?

'Peter ˌDrake. · 'Where does he `come from?

From New `York.  ·  'Where's he °living over `here?

'Just outside `Colchester | at the ˌmoment.  ·  'When did he ar°rive in `England?

A 'couple of ˌmonths aˌgo. · 'When did he °come to `London?

'Nearly a `week ago | ˌnow.  ·  'How long is he °staying `up ˌhere?

He's 'not `sure | ˌyet.  ·  'What was his `reason for ˌcoming to ˌTown?

To 'be with his `mother.  ·  'What's `she ˌhere for?

'Looking for a `flat, I ˌgather.

● ˌWhat was °that you °said? · 'Where did you °go for your °summer `holiday?

'First to ˃London | and 'then to ˌCornwall. · 'How long did you °have in `London?

'Just a ˌweek. · 'Which part of your °holiday did you pre-`fer?

Oh, our 'fortnight in `Cornwall.  ·  'Where did you `stay while you were ˌdown there?

In a 'little °village near Penˌzance. · 'What sort of °weather did you °have in `London?

Verbal context	*Drill*
'Really ˏexcellent ˳weather.	'What did you ˋdo there?
ˋSight seeing | ˏmostly.	'Where are you °thinking of °spending your ˋChristmas ˳holidays?
With my ˋfather. || At ˋIpswich.	'When are you °coming to see ˋus aˏgain?
'Just as °soon as my ˏwork alˏlows.	'When d'you °think ˋthat'll ˳be?
'Sometime towards the °end of the ˏmonth, I iˏmagine.	'Why not come °down for a week ˋend ˳while you're aˏbout it?
I'd ˋlove to.	

I 'shan't be ˋseeing you, I'm aˏfraid.	Why 'ever ˋnot?
I've reˋsigned.	What'ever °made you do ˋthat?
There's been some 'jiggery ˋpokery.	How on 'earth do you °make ˋthat out?
'Somebody's been °telling ˋlies.	Who on 'earth would do ˋthat?
'Mark ˋSmith, for ˳instance.	Well 'when did you °find ˋthis out?
'Just to ˋday.	And who 'else have you ˋtold aˏbout it?
ˏOnly ˏThomson.	Now 'which °Thomson d'you ˋmean?
ˋNorman.	And 'whose °side was ˋhe on?
I 'didn't ˋask the ˳silly ˳fool.	What 'earthly °good's ˋthat sort of ˳talk?
I've 'no ˏpatience with him.	Why 'must you °be so ˋheadstrong?
Are 'you °talking to ˏme?	Well who the 'devil d'you ˋthink I'm ˳talking to?
You'll 'hear from my soˏlicitors.	But for 'heaven's °sake ˋwhy?

Yes-No Questions

'John °says he has an ˋalibi.	'Can he ˋprove it?
● 'Shall we tell ˏFrank a°bout it?	'Dare we ˋrisk ˳that?
He ˇsays he'll ˳play.	'Will he ˋreally ˳play?
Father'll be ˇvery upˇset.	'Must we ˋtell him aˏbout it?
'How about °visiting St. ˋPaul's?	'Have we ˋtime this ˳afterˏnoon?
We must 'find °someone ˋelse. || 'Andrew's ˋhopeless.	'Mightn't ˋChristopher be ˳worth conˏsidering?
'Could she ˋcome, d'you ˳think?	And 'does she ˋwant to?
She'll be 'very upˋset by that ˳news.	Well 'shall we ˋkeep it ˳from her?
ˇTony ˳won't be ˳there.	D'you 'think the ˋothers ˳will?
Shall we 'try aˏgain?	Would it be 'any ˋuse, d'you ˳think?
I've 'drawn out °six ˏpounds.	Will 'six be sufˋficient?

Verbal context	*Drill*
I ˇcould let him ˎtry on his ˎown.	But 'would that be ˋwise, I ˎwonder?
We could ˆoffer him °five ˇpounds.	Will 'that be the ˋend of it, ˎthough?
Can 'David °borrow your ˏpenknife?	Did he 'say what he ˋwanted it ˎfor?
ˋThank you | for ˏall you've ˏdone.	Is there 'anything ˋelse I can ˎdo to ˎhelp?
I 'wonder if we could ˋborrow the ˎmoney.	Ought we 'even to conˋsider such a ˎthing?
'William exˋplained it ˎto me.	Yes but 'did you underˋstand his explaˎnation?
We 'ought to have °taken the ˋother ˎfootpath.	Isn't that eˋxactly what I ˋtold you?
I shall 'give her a °good ˋtalking to.	Wouldn't it be 'better to igˋnore her ˎbad beˎhaviour?
'What a ˋnuisance! || The 'Watford °road's °blocked by ˋsnow.	Can we 'get °there by any ˋother ˏroute?
The ˏlawn's in a ˋterrible ˎstate.	Have you 'tried °using ˋweed ˎkiller?
She inˋsists on °going aˋlone.	'Does she °know the ˋway?
ˋSorry I ˎcan't come this ˏevening.	'Are you °free toˋmorrow ˎnight?
We 'ought to ˋsack him.	'Can we °do withˋout him, ˎthough?
He's 'promised to °stop ˏsmoking.	'Does he °really ˋmean what he ˎsays?
David's ˋnot at his ˇoffice.	'Should we °try his ˋhome, d'you ˎthink?
I'm afraid 'six is imˋpossible.	'Would a °little ˋlater ˎsuit you ˎbetter?
● This 'pen of °mine's ˋuseless.	Would you 'like to °borrow ˋmine?
I can't ˏhelp being °right, | ˏcan I?	But must you 'always °be so ˋsmug aˎbout it?
Well I'll have ˋthis ˎpair.	'Is it the °pair you °really ˋwant?
He ˏsaid he ˋdidn't ˎbreak the ˎwindow.	'Was he °telling the ˋtruth, d'you ˎthink?
He ˋwon't take ˇmy adˎvice.	'Would he °listen to ˋme, d'you supˎpose?
He's 'on his °way ˏback.	But 'will he be °back in ˋtime?
I 'don't think we ˋcan comˎplete it | toˏday.	'Couldn't we °leave it till ˋFriday?
They ˋwon't take ˇmoney.	'Could they be reˋpaid some ˋother ˎway?
But he has ˋplenty of ˎspare ˎcopies.	'Will he be °willing to ˋlend them, ˎthough?
● D'you 'think I should ˏring him?	'Mightn't it be °better to ˋwait?
I ˋhate the ˎthought of ˏspring°cleaning.	'Ought we to de°lay it any ˋlonger, ˎthough?
I don't ˇreally ˎwant to ˎmeet them.	Will you be 'able to get ˋout of it?
I'm ˇsorry, | but I ˋhate ˏcocoa.	Would you 'like a °cup of ˋtea, ˎthen?
They 'sent me the °wrong ˋkind.	Does it 'really make °very much ˋdifference?
She ˋplays a ˇfair ˎgame.	Is she 'worth a °place in the ˋteam?
I ˏcan't think ˋwhat to ˎgive him.	Has he 'got an e°lectric ˋrailway?

Verbal context	*Drill*

I ˏcan't find my °hat ˋanywhere.

Could you 'possibly have °left it at the ˋoffice?

We're ˋnot making °much ˇprogress.

Don't you 'think it would be as °well to give ˋup the iˏdea?

Commands

My ˋpencil's ˏbroken.
'Use ˋmine. 'Try ˋthis one.

It was 'most ˋkind of you.
'Don't ˋmention it.

I ˏcan't make °head or ˋtail of it.
'Let ˋJohnson have a ˏlook at it.

I ˋshan't be ˏlate.
'Mind you're ˋnot, then.

What deˈlicious °cheese ˏstraws!
'Take a ˋhandful of them.

● I ˋhate ˏquarrelling with ˏClare.
Then 'make it ˋup with her.

'How °much d'you ˋwant for it?
'Make me an ˋoffer.

I ˋshan't be °able to ˇphone you.
'Drop me a ˋline, then.

This 'tea's too ˋhot.
'Put some more ˋmilk in it.

'Can't we be ˏfriends aˋgain?
Ad'mit you were ˋwrong, then.

Jane just 'won't °make a deˋcision.
Well 'you de°cide ˋfor her, ˏthen.

Bob ˋdoesn't °frighten ˇme.
Then 'don't let him ˋbully you ˏso.

'Why not °wear a ˋwig?
I'magine how ˋsilly I'd ˏlook.

ˋSorry I forˏgot to ˏchange my ˏshoes.
Just 'look at the ˋmud you've ˏbrought in ˏhere.

We must 'just °hope for the ˋbest.
And pre'pare for the ˋworst.

I ˋhope I'm not disˇturbing you.
'Come ˋin. ‖ 'Sit ˋdown. ‖ 'Have a ciˋgar. ‖ 'Make yourself at ˋhome.

She 'didn't reˋply.
'Write to her aˋgain, then.

I 'don't ˋlike ˏgin ˏneat.
'Have a °drop of ˋtonic ˏwith it.

'Can I °take a ˏcouple?
Take as 'many as you ˋlike.

'Which ˏquality should I ˏbuy?
Buy the 'best you can afˋford.

'What shall I ˋtell her?
Tell her 'no °more than is ˋnecessary.

I 'can't think °what to ˋsay.
Don't say 'anything at ˋall. ‖ Leave it en-'tirely to ˋme.

'When shall I ˏcome?
Come as 'soon as you ˋcan.

My ˋhair ˏgets so ˏwet.
'Buy yourself an umˋbrella.

'What shall I °do with ˋthis?
'Put it in the °waste ˋpaper ˏbasket.

I'm aˈfraid I've °made a misˋtake.
Well 'copy it °out aˋgain, ˏthen.

Sup'pose I °have no ˋmoney.
Then for 'goodness °sake ˋsay so.

Verbal context	*Drill*

'What does a ˏJaguar ˳look like?

'Have a °look at ˋmy car. ‖ ('Then you'll ˋknow.)

I'm un'lucky. ‖ The 'shop's ˋshut.
'Try the °nearest ˋpub, then.

This 'bulb's ˋuseless.
'Take it °back and ˋchange it.

Shall we 'play °safe and °turn ˏback?
'Let's go °on and ˋchance the ˳tyre ˳bursting.

I'm pro'posing to put ˋHamlet ˳on.
But 'think of °all the ˋdifficulties.

'Must we be °very ˏquiet?
Make as 'much °noise as you ˋwant.

'What about this ˏmoney?
'Lock it °up in the ˋsafe.

He's ˋruined my ˳shoes.
'Make him °buy you a ˋnew pair.

I've 'no ciga'rettes.
'Send °Clare round to the ˋshop for ˳some.

'When shall I °cut the ˏgrass?
Cut it when'ever the °spirit ˋmoves you.

● This ˇcocoa's ˳not very ˳sweet.
Have a'nother °lump of ˋsugar.

Oh I ˋcouldn't be ˳rude to him.
'Don't be ˋsilly. ‖ 'Show him he °can't get a'way with it.

I 'think I'm °going to ˋfaint.
Then for 'heaven's °sake °go and lie ˋdown.

ˇTom ˳tells me | the 'Smiths' °car's not a'vailable.
'Tell him to °get one from °someone ˋelse.

● The ˏlid doesn't ˋfit.
'Try °turning it the °other way ˋround.

'What's the °car ˋworth, d'you ˳think?
Offer him 'three °hundred and °fifty ˋpounds.

Interjections

● 'Thank you °very ˋmuch.
'Not at ˋall! ‖ 'Thank ˋyou.

I 'now find I ˋcan ˳manage ˳Friday.
'Oh ˋgood! 'Braˋvo.

He 'won't be °back till ˋten.
'How ˋawkward!

'Look out of the ˋwindow.
'Good ˋheavens! ‖ (It's 'simply ˋteeming ˳down.)

He 'won't °give us per'mission.
So 'that's ˋthat. ‖ (We must a'bandon the iˏdea.)

ˋLook. ‖ It's ˏstopped ˋraining.
'Oh ˋyes. ‖ 'So it ˋhas.

I 'had to wait °three ˋhours.
'Bad ˋluck! 'What a ˋshame!

I 'gave him a °piece of my ˋmind.
'Well ˋdone! 'Good for ˋyou!

'Smith's °sprained his ˋankle.
'Poor old ˋchap!

'Praps I'll °take a °week ˋoff.
'Good iˋdea!

I lost ˏten ˋpounds.
'Well I ˋnever! 'Well I °never ˋdid!

D'you 'mind if I ˏsmoke?
Good 'heavens ˋno!

'Tom has ˋpassed his eˏxam.
Well 'fancy ˋthat!

Verbal context	*Drill*
He's ˈsending you a ͺcopy.	How ˈvery ˋnice of him!
Can ˈwe come ͵too?	The ˈmore the ˋmerrier!
I must ˈstay in and °do some ˋwork.	How ˈvery ˋnoble of you!
I've ˈjust be°come a ˋfather.	Conˈgratuˋlations, my ͺdear ͺchap!
ˈWould you like a °glass of ͵beer?	I should ˈthink I ˋwould!
I've ˈgot a ˋboxing ͺmatch │ to ͵night.	And the ˈbest of ˋluck to you!
I forgot ˈevery °word aͺbout it.	What a ˈfine mess ˋyou've made of ͺthings!
⌐D'you ˈthink I should ͵fight him?	ˈHeaven forˋbid! ˈGood °lord ˋno!
I ˈhear you're °being proˋmoted.	ˈAbsolute ˋnonsense!
ˈJock's let us °down aˋgain.	ˈWould you beˋlieve it!
We'll ˈgo there on ͵Friday.	The ˈsooner the ˋbetter!
He ˈwanted me to °do it for ˋnothing.	The ˈvery iˋdea of it!
He's been ˈmissing for °ten ˋdays │ ͵now.	How ˈvery peˋculiar!
ˈWhy not dis°cuss it with ˋBrian?	A ˈlot of °good ˋthat would ͺdo!
I've ˈcome to aˋpologise.	I should ˈjolly well ˋthink so!
She's ˈonly °got a ˋsmall part │ ͵this time.	But what a ˈterrible ˋcomedown ͺfor her!
I was ˈtold you were ˋIrish.	ˈNothing of the ˋsort!
We've ˈsold our ˋhouse.	What an exˈtraordinary °thing to ˋdo!
I was ˋsorry to ͺhave to ͺvote a͵gainst you.	A ˈfine °friend ˋyou turned ͺout to ͺbe!
I ˈhad to give ˋup. ‖ I ˈtwisted my ˋknee.	ˈBetter °luck °next ˋtime!
⌐Peter won't apͺprove.	I ˈcouldn't °care ˋless!
I've ˈgot °hold of a ˋcrib.	ˈMuch °good may it ˋdo you!
It's ˈall °very ˋpuzzling.	I ˈcouldn't a°gree ˋmore.
I'm ˋnot taking it °lying ˇdown.	ˈMore °power to your ˋelbow!
ˋHullo, │ ͵Fred.	Well if it ˈisn't °old ˋTom!

Note: All the relevant drills given above with the tune
> (LOW PRE-HEAD+) HIGH HEAD+HIGH FALL (+TAIL)

can be said with emphasis if one or more of the following features are used:

(a) the high pre-head instead of the low pre-head (see Chapter I, p. 36);

(b) the emphatic form of the high head (see Chapter I, p. 37);

(c) a high fall tone for each accent in the head (see Chapter I, p. 38).

The following drills are marked to show these features:

> ⌐Well if it ˈisn't °old ˋTom!
>
> ˈBetter ˈluck ˈnext ˋtime!
>
> I ˋcouldn't ˋcare ˋless!

3 *The Take-Off*

Attitude

In STATEMENTS: encouraging further conversation, guarded, reserving judgment, appealing to the listener to change his mind, deprecatory, (in contradictions) resentful; in non-final word groups, deprecatory.

In WH-QUESTIONS: with the nuclear tone on the interrogative word, wondering, mildly puzzled; otherwise, very calm but very disapproving and resentful.

In YES-NO QUESTIONS: disapproving, sceptical.

In COMMANDS: (beginning with *Don't*) appealing to the listener to change his mind; (in a few short commands) calmly warning, exhortative.

In INTERJECTIONS: sometimes reserving judgment, sometimes calm, casual acknowledgment.

Tone marks used in TAKE-OFF drills

A Stressed, accented syllables (Nucleus, Head)
[ˌ] (i) without Tail: very low rising to medium pitch.
   (ii) with Tail: very low level pitch; the rise is completed by the tail syllable(s).
[ˌ] Very low level pitch.
[₀] Very low level pitch, the same pitch as the *preceding* [ˌ] and the beginning of the *following* [ˌ].

B Stressed, unaccented syllables (Tail)
[°] Level pitch, higher than the lowest possible and always higher than the *preceding* [ˌ] or [°].

Tune   **/**   **Low Rise only**

Verbal context	*Drill*

Statements

● Have you 'heard about ˌMax?	ˌNo.
You 'know where ˌJohn °lives?	ˌYes.
'Whose ˌbook is ₀this?	ˌMine. ˌJack's. ˌJoan's. ˌTom's. ˌJohn's.
	ˌJean's. ˌAnn's.

Verbal context	*Drill*
'How many ciga͵rettes have you ₒgot?	͵One. ͵Two. ͵Three. ͵Four. ͵Five. ͵Six. ͵None.
'How many °times did you ͵go ₒthere?	͵Once. ͵Twice.
'When may he ͵have them?	͵Now. ͵Soon.
'Where does she ˋcome from?	͵Bath. ͵York. ͵Leeds. ͵Kent. ͵Wales. ͵France. ͵Spain.
'When will it be ˋfinished?	͵March. ͵May. ͵June.
'Where did ˋyou ₒcome?	͵First. ͵Last. ͵Third. ͵Fourth.
'Was it a ͵good °game?	͵Fair. ͵Quite.
Did you 'catch the °last ͵train?	͵Just.
What on 'earth d'you °want at the ˋgrocer's?	͵Tea. ͵Rice. ͵Flour. ͵Cheese.
'What's ˋthat stuff you're ₒdrinking?	͵Beer. ͵Gin. ͵Scotch. ͵Wine.
'What d'you at°tribute your suc͵cess to?	͵Luck. ͵Work.

WH-Questions

● 'When's the °meeting °due to take ˋplace?   ͵When? ‖ (Why, at ˋfive.)
● The 'meeting's at ˋfive.   ͵When? ‖ (I ͵thought it was at ˋsix.)
  'How must I ͵do it?   ͵How? ‖ (͵Perfectly ˋobvious.)
  You must 'do it ˋthis way.   ͵How? ‖ (I thought ˋJohn's ₒmethod was the ₒbest.)

  'Which is ˋWilliam's ₒbook?   ͵Which? ‖ (The ˋred one, | of ͵course.)
  ˇWilliam's | is the ˋblue ₒbook.   ͵Which? ‖ (I ͵thought it was the ˋred one.)
  'Who's coming ˋthis ₒFriday?   ͵Who? ‖ (Why, ˋMary, | of ͵course.)
  ˋMary's ₒcoming | on ͵Friday.   ͵Who? ‖ (I ͵thought it was ˋJack.)
  'Where shall we °go for ͵lunch?   ͵Where? ‖ (It's ͵up to ˋyou.)
  'See you at °Charing ͵Cross.   ͵Where? ‖ (I ͵thought it was Vicˋtoria we ₒwent from.)

  Why on 'earth did you °ask ˋhim?   ͵Why? ‖ (Because I ˋwanted to.)
  ˋYou must ₒsend them an invi͵tation.   ͵Why? ‖ (I thought ͵that was ˋPeter's ₒjob.)
  'Whose ͵coat is ₒthis?   ͵Whose? ‖ (ˋMine, | of ͵course.)
  'This is Eˋlizabeth's ₒcoat.   ͵Whose? ‖ (I ͵thought it was her ˋsister's.)
  I'm a'fraid I shall be ˋlate.   ͵What? ‖ (You ͵promised you'd be ˋearly.)

Commands

● ‾But ͵how do you ˋdo it?   ͵Watch. ‖ (Like ˋthat.)
  [Batsman at cricket]   ͵Wait.

Verbal context	*Drill*
[To someone in the way]	ˏMind.
[Photographer to sitter]	ˏStill. ˏSmile.
[Teacher to class]	ˏStart. ˏStop. ˏGo.
[Driving-instructor to learner]	ˏBack. ˏHalt. ˏBrake. ˏClutch. ˏSlow.
[Tennis coach to pupil]	ˏServe. ˏDrive. ˏSmash. ˏLob.
[P.T. instructor to class]	ˏUp. ˏDown. ˏBend. ˏStretch. ˏRest.

Note: The contexts given in square brackets are *situational* and not verbal; these short commands, said with this tune, are rarely preceded by a verbal context.

Interjections

I've ˈleft my umˋbrella beₒhind.	ˏFool! ˏDolt! ˏClot!
● ˈJohn says he °can't ˎcome.	ˏOh! ‖ (ˏWhy ˋnot?)
It's ˋhalf past ˇten.	ˏWell! ‖ (We're ˌnot in a ˏhurry.)
You're ˌlooking ₒrather ˏold.	ˏNow! ‖ (ˈDon't be ˎcheeky.)
The ˇcar's ₒhere.	ˏGood! ‖ (We're ˈjust about ˎready.)
Your ˇbook's arₒrived, sir.	ˏRight! ‖ (I'll call ˋin for it.)
I shall have ˋfinished | by ˏFriday.	ˏFine! ‖ (ˈThat'll be ˋplenty ₒsoon enough.)
ˈHere's your ˋhat, ₒdear.	ˏThanks! ‖ (I ˈhadn't forˏgotten it.)
ˈShall I °ring the ˏbell?	ˏPlease!

Tune 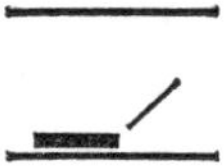 Low Rise+Tail

Statements

● D'you ˈever °go to the ˏclub?	ˏSometimes.
ˈWhat's his nationˎality?	ˏRussian. ˏSwedish. ˏDanish.
ˈWhere did he °go ˋthen?	ˏSalisbury. ˏDurham. ˏNorwich.
Who on ˈearth °wants a ˋfire?	ˏMichael. ˏPeter. ˏWinter°bottom.
Is ˈeverything all ˏright?	ˏSo °far. ˏMostly, I °think.
ˈHow many ˎstudents has he ₒgot?	ˏTwenty. ˏThirty. ˏForty. ˏFifty. ˏNinety, I should i°magine.
ˈWhen did you °last ˋsee him?	ˏYesterday. ˏMonday. ˏWednesday. ˏThursday.
What's ˋyour ₒhobby?	ˏFishing. ˏGardening. ˏStamp col°lecting. ˏWine °making.

Verbal context	*Drill*
D'you 'mean you °actually ˌliked it?	ˌCertainly. ˌNaturally. ˌParts of it. ˌParts of it I °did.
'Aren't they °rather exˌpensive?	ˌSome of them °are.
Can 'Tommy come to ˌtea to°morrow?	ˌMaybe he °can.
I'm 'going to °use my ˋold one.	ˌThat should be all °right.
'Will you be °able to ˌfetch them?	ˌProbably I °shall.
He's ˋlate aˌgain.	ˌThat's all °right. ˌThat doesn't °matter.
Oh I ˋdo wish I could ˌgo.	ˌI'm not °stopping you.
They're ˌall ˋhopeless.	ˌAndrew °isn't too °bad.
I ˋdon't think ˇwe ought to ˌtell him.	ˌSomeone's °got to °do it.
'This car's ˋalways ˌbreaking ˌdown.	ˌUsually it's all °right.
There 'aren't e°nough ˋchairs.	ˌTwenty should be e°nough.
We must 'win at ˋall ˌcosts.	ˌWinning isn't °everything.
'Dare we ˌrisk °hitch hiking?	ˌSomeone'll °give us a °lift.
'What about °asking ˋAlfred?	ˌHe won't be °able to °help us.
Your ˌcar's too ˋslow.	ˌYours isn't °very much °faster.
'Isn't °fruit a ˋprice!	ˌApples °aren't °all that ex°pensive.
What a 'wretched ˌweek it's ˌbeen!	ˌYesterday °wasn't a °bad day.
It's ˋno good °asking °either of ˇthem.	ˌOne of them must °know the °answer.
It was ˋterribly ˌdifficult.	ˌPeter didn't °find it °difficult.
What a con'founded ˌnuisance it ˌis!	ˌGrumbling won't °make it any °better.
ˌWhy didn't you disˋcuss the ˌmatter?	ˌTalking wouldn't have °been any °good.
ˋNo-one can ˌgo in ˌthere.	ˌI °can. ˌMembers °can.
ˇNo house was °ever as °dear as ˇthat.	ˌMine °was. ˌRichardson's °was.
ˌNo-one ˋever ˌgoes to ˌsee him.	ˌMother °does. ˌSome of us °do.
ˋNone of them is ˌany ˌgood.	ˌThis one °is. ˌJennifer's is all °right.
ˋPity they ˌall disˌliked it.	ˌJohn °liked it. ˌI °didn't dis°like it.
I'm 'glad I was °able to ˋhelp.	ˌYou didn't °help.
'Everyone was ˋsure he'd ˌmanage it.	ˌI didn't °think so.
● You 'said you'd ˋgive me ˌone.	ˌThat's not °what I °said.
'How about postˌponing the ˌgame?	ˌThat's no °good, you °chump.
ˌTony's ˋalways ˌlate.	ˌLast °week he was on °time.
I've brought ˋsix ˌcopies.	ˌSix °won't be suf°ficient.
'What are you °going to ˌdo aˌbout it?	ˌI'm not re°sponsible.
I'm 'taking my °half day on ˋMonday.	ˌMonday's °not your °half °day.
I ˇhope he °won't blame ˇus.	ˌWe didn't °let him °down.

Verbal context	*Drill*
What a 'terrible °waste of ˏmoney!	ˏYou didn't °lose by it.
ˋThere you ˏare. ‖ Your ˋlibrary ₒbook.	ˏThis isn't the °one I °asked for.

WH-Questions

No, ˇthat one's ₒyours.	ˏWhich one? ‖ (I ˏthought it was the ˋgreen one.)
I 'sold the ˋcarpet │ toˏday.	ˏWhat, °dear?
His 'name was ˏScroggs.	ˏWhat was °that?
Richard's 'due at e°leven oˋclock.	ˏWhen is he °due? ‖ (I ˏthought it was ˋten.)
I 'won't allow °any such ˏthing.	ˏWhat did you °say?
He 'lives in ˋGlasgow.	ˏWhere does he °live? ‖ (¯In ˏGlasgow?)
She's 'thirty ˏsix.	ˏHow old °is she?
I'm 'fed ˏup with you.	ˏWhy, may I °ask?
He's 'gone to °see his ˏfather.	ˏWho's he °gone to °see?
They 'used their ˋfather's ₒcar.	ˏWhose °car did they °use?
She 'gave up for ˋhealth ₒreasons.	ˏWhy did she give °up?
You should 'write to the ˋsecretary.	ˏWho should I °write to?
● That's 'two °pounds eˏxactly.	ˏHow much d'you °make it?
ˋLook. ‖ 'There's the °Prime ˋMinister.	ˏWho d'you °say it is?
'Come °round at ˏfive.	ˏWhat time d'you °want me?
He must take it 'three °times a ˏday.	ˏHow often must he °take it?
He's alˋready °called there ˇten ₒtimes.	ˏHow many °times has he °called there?
Can I 'have it for a °couple of ˏweeks?	ˏHow long d'you °want to °keep it?
'When are you ˋfree?	ˏWhen am I °free? ‖ (ˋAny ₒday │ after ˏsix.)
● 'How did he ˏdo it?	ˏHow did he °do it? ‖ (ˏPerfectly ˋobvious.)
'Who ˏgave it ₒto you?	ˏWho °gave it °to me? ‖ (Why, ˋAndrew, │ of ˏcourse.)
'Where did you °find your ˏgloves?	ˏWhere did I °find them? ‖ (In ˏJohn's ˋsuitcase.)
'What can I ˏdo for you?	ˏWhat can you °do for me? ‖ (ˋNothing. ‖ I've ˋfinished.)

Yes-No Questions

● ˏMary said ˋMaisie was ₒgoing to ₒplay.	ˏDid she °play, in °fact?
We ˇought to ₒfollow his adₒvice.	ˏMust we, d'you °think?
He'd alˏready ˋposted it, │ ˏso he ˏsaid.	ˏHad he °sent it °off?

Verbal context	*Drill*
They ˅might fall ₒin with our ₒwishes.	ˏWould they a°ˏgree to it?
Mike ˅may be ₒable to ₒhelp us.	ˏHas he °anything to °offer?
I 'said I'd ˇcall for him.	ˏAre you °going to °call for him?
We ˅ought perₒhaps | to have 'tried some ˇother ₒroute.	ˏCould we have °got there any °other way?
They're sup'posed to be ˇdifferent.	ˏIs there any °difference be°ˏtween them?
'Let's °keep it for a ˎfortnight.	ˏDare we °keep it as °long as °that?
They're ar'riving ˎnext ₒweek.	ˏAre they? || (I ˏthought it was ˇthis ₒweek.)
● It's 'very imˎportant.	ˏIs it?
You were 'quite ˎwrong aₒbout it.	ˏWas I?
The 'Smiths weren't inˇvited.	ˏWeren't they?
He just 'won't ˎlisten.	ˏWon't he?
They'd 'give it to you ˇwillingly.	ˏWould they?
You 'shouldn't °eat so ˇquickly.	ˏShouldn't I?
He 'comes from the U°nited ˇStates.	ˏDoes he?
You ˇnever ₒcome.	ˏDon't I?
I 'thought she was ˇpretty.	ˏDid you?
You can 'leave at ˎonce.	ˏCan I?
He must 'never °try that aˎgain.	ˏMustn't he?
He'd 'bought it be°fore I could ˇstop him.	ˏHad he?
I'll 'sing you my ˎsong.	ˏMust you?

Note: Examples of this tune used for question tags in sentences like

ˇTom's \| ˏisn't it?

are given in Chapter V, Sections 15–19.

Commands

[Mother to small daughter who is over-excited]	ˏSteady.
[Father to small son who is riding his bicycle a little too fast]	ˏSlowly.
[Mother to small son who is teasing a puppy]	ˏGently. ˏCareful.
[Starter to sprinter who has beaten the gun]	ˏWait °for it.

Note: The contexts given in square brackets are *situational* and not verbal; these short commands said with this tune are rarely preceded by a verbal context.

Verbal context	*Drill*

Interjections

They've 'sold ˏout.	ˏReally! ‖ (I 'thought they had ˋplenty.)
I've 'broken a ˋcup.	ˏStupid! ˏIdiot! ˏClumsy!
'Michael's ˋhurting me.	ˏMichael!
I'll 'tell ˋMummy.	ˏTell°tale! ˏCoward! ˏBaby!
● Your ˋchange, sir.	ˏThank you!
I've ˋfinished my ˏwork.	ˏSplendid!
'Let ˏme ₒcarry your ₒbag.	ˏBless you!
● You're 'on my ˋtoe.	ˏSorry!
Good ˋmorning, sir.	ˏMorning!
ˋEverything's °all right ˇso ˏfar.	ˏExcellent!

Tune ‾‾‾‾ / **Low Pre-Head+Low Rise (+Tail)**

or

‾‾‾ ▬ /

Statements

'Have you ˏbeen °there?	I ˏhave.
'Do you °sell ˏstamps?	We ˏdo.
'Can he °play the piˏano?	He ˏcan.
Did 'Mary ˏpost that °letter?	She ˏdid.
'How many ˏshirts have you ₒgot?	A ˏfew. Eˏleven.
'Will he °buy aˏnother °one?	Perˏhaps. He ˏmay. He ˏmight.
'Shall we be in ˏtime?	I ˏthink °so. I iˏmagine °so. I exˏpect °so. I ˏhope °so.
'When did he °last ˋwrite?	A ˏweek a°go. A ˏfortnight a°go. About a ˏmonth a°go.
What's ˋyour oₒpinion of ₒDan's ₒtale?	It ˏmay be a °true °story.
'How about °asking ˋMax to ₒjoin us?	He ˏought to be °able to °get a°way.
'Can you turn °up at ˏnine on °Tuesdays?	As a ˏrule I °can.
● D'you 'think his pro°posal's ˋreasonable?	On the ˏwhole it's °quite °fair.

Verbal context	*Drill*
˅Martin ₒsays | the 'answer's ˎsix.	I supˏpose °that's the °right °answer.
It's ˏno ˎuse ₒbuying ₒthat ₒclock.	It ˏworks. || (So ˏwhy ˎshouldn't I?)
Why 'ever didn't you ˎwrite to me?	I'm ˏsorry. || (I ˏthought I ˋhad.)
What'ever made you °recommend ˋprawns?	They're ˏusually all °right here.
The 'party'll be an °absolute ˅failure.	If ˏPaul °comes it'll °go °well.
ˏWhy didn't you °talk them ˋout of it?	We ˏtried to °make them see °reason.
ˋNo | ˏthanks. || I 'don't ˋsmoke.	But you ˏused to.
I 'wonder if they °sell ˋsocks.	You could enˏquire.
You 'can't ˎhave one.	I ˏcan. || (ˏWho's to ˋstop me?)
You 'haven't ˎwritten to them.	I ˏhave. || (I ˏwrote this ˋmorning.)
She'll 'get aˋway with it.	She ˏwon't. || (ˋI'll see to ˅that.)
˅Mine's the ˅biggest.	It's ˏnot. || (ˋChristopher's ₒis.)
'Tom says °you've been ˋcheating.	I have ˏnot been °cheating.
Adˋmit it. || You forˏgot to ˋtell him.	I did ˏnot for°get to °tell him.
You 'promised to ˋsell it ₒto me.	I did ˏnot °promise to °sell it °to you.
● ˋThank you | for your ˏhelp.	You're ˏwelcome. It was ˏnothing.

WH-Questions

● I 'went with °Mr. ˋSpang.	With ˏwho?
I comˋmuted | in New ˏYork.	You ˏwhat?
I 'won by a ˋmile.	By ˏhow °much?
'I live in ˋthat house.	In ˏwhich °house?
I 'lost by °three ˎpoints.	By ˏhow °many?
Your 'train goes from °Waterˋloo.	From ˏwhich °station?
The 'bus °leaves at ˋseven.	At ˏwhat time, did you °say?
There's 'someone to ˋsee you.	Who ˏis it?
He ˅wasn't at ˅home.	Where ˏwas he, °then?
I 'shan't be ˋcoming.	Why ˏnot, may I °ask?
I ˅didn't °leave it in the ˅kitchen.	Where ˏdid you °leave it, °then?
It ˅wasn't °made with ˅flour.	How ˏdid you °make it, °then?
● I'm afraid ˅I can't ₒmeet them.	Who ˏis °going to °meet them, °then?

Yes-No Questions

You 'daren't ˋdo it.	Dare ˏyou?
● He 'says they'll ˋboth ₒcome.	Can ˏJohn °come?
I said I ˅might have ₒtime to ₒmake some.	But ˏhave you °time, in °fact?

Verbal context	*Drill*
I got 'three °out of ˎten.	Is ˎthat the °best you can °do?
He 'gave me ˋthese.	Was ˎthat °all he ˋwanted you °for?
ˏWhy didn't you °have a °set of ˋtennis?	Can ˎyou play °tennis on your °own?
'Charles didn't °pass his ˋdriving ˎtest, I ˎhear.	Does ˎanyone get °through the °first time?
'Stop ˎgrumbling aˎbout it.	Would ˎyou like your °garden °trampled over?
He deˈserves to be ˋsacked.	Will ˎsacking him im°prove the situ°ation?
You've 'done it the °wrong ˋway.	Does it ˎmatter?
It's 'going to ˋsnow.	D'you ˎthink so?
Yes I 'had a °letter from him ˋages aˎgo.	Have you ˎanswered it?
'How about °six o'clock?	Can you ˎget here by °then?
I 'wonder what ˋAubrey will ˎthink of it.	Does it ˎmatter what he °thinks?
'Why d'you °give me °extra ˎhomework?	Is it ˎmy fault you're °stupid?
You 'haven't °told me the ˋanswer.	Must I ˎalways °spoonfeed you?
● Oh ˋgood! ‖ 'Breakfast in ˋbed!	D'you ˎlike °breakfast in °bed?
We 'turn down ˋhere, I ˎthink.	Are you ˎsure °this is the °right °road?
He says his 'mind's °quite made ˋup.	Does he ˎreally °mean what he °says?
I ˋhaven't told my ˇfather.	Was it ˎwise to °keep it °from him?

Commands

I've a conˋfession to ˎmake.	Go ˎon. Conˎtinue.
I've a ˋbone to ˎpick ‖ with ˎyou.	Go aˎhead.
● ˋThank you.	Don't ˎmention it.
'Come ˎon. ‖ 'Let's get ˎgoing.	Now ˎwait a °minute. ‖ (We 'haven't ˋpaid ˎyet.)
[Response to a knock at the door]	Come ˎin.
[Teacher to student practising pronunciation]	Aˎgain. Once ˎmore.
[Doctor to patient]	Reˎlax. ‖ Inˎhale. ‖ And ˎout a°gain.
[To someone who has almost dropped a glass]	Be ˎcareful.
[Immigration officer to traveller]	Your ˎpassport, °please.

Note: The contexts given in square brackets are *situational* and not verbal; these short commands said with this tune are rarely preceded by a verbal context.

Verbal context	*Drill*

Interjections

You must 'give it to me `now.	In͵deed! ‖ (͵What's the `hurry?)
I 'won't `hear of it.	Oh ͵really! ‖ (͵What have you a`gainst it?)
● 'Is that °really ͵yours?	Of ͵course!
● 'Shall we °meet at ͵ten?	All ͵right! O͵K!
I 'took your °suit to the `cleaners.	Oh ͵good!
Good `morning, sir!	Good ͵morning!
So you 'think I'm `wrong.	E͵xactly!
Your um`brella, ₒJoyce.	Oh ͵thank you!
I'll 'bring it to`morrow.	Many ͵thanks!

Tune

(Low Pre-Head+) Low Head +Low Rise (+Tail)

or

Statements

(⌐That ͵you, °Timothy?)	You're ͵home ͵early to°day. ‖ ('Didn't you ͵play?)
'Let me °get you some more `tea.	You're ͵very ͵kind.
Have 'this one on `me.	It's ͵very ͵nice of you.
(⌐Hul͵lo, you old °rascal!)	͵Nice looking ͵girl I °saw you with °yesterday.
(⌐Hul͵lo, °Jimmy!)	You're ͵looking ₒvery ͵smart. ‖ ('Going to a ⌐wedding?)
I'm 'just back from °seeing my `mother.	I ͵trust you ₒfound her ͵well.
(͵What have you been `up to, ₒFred?)	You're ͵looking ₒrather ͵seedy.
(Good `morning, Mrs. ₒJones.)	It's a ͵nice ͵day. It's ͵turned out ͵nice a°gain. ͵Rather ₒchilly for ͵June.
What a 'glorious `day!	You ͵sound re₀markably ͵cheerful.
(Why, it's ͵Bill `Jameson!)	It's ͵good to ͵see you a°gain. I ͵didn't ex₀pect to see ͵you °here.

Verbal context	*Drill*
I've 'just been °playing ˋbadminton.	I ˌhope you had a ₒgood ˌgame.
'How °long have you been ˋback?	ˌNot ˌlong. ˌNot very ˌlong.
'Could you °send him aˌnother °copy?	ˌMay₋be. I ˌdare ˌsay.
● I 'can't find your °book ˋanywhere.	ˌThat's ˌfunny. ‖ (Where on ˌearth did I ˋput it?)
What's ˋyour oₒpinion of his ₒwork?	It's ˌnot ˌbad.
I'm 'told you reˋfused his ₒoffer.	That's ˌquite ˌright.
'Will you be °calling aˌgain?	It's ˌquite ˌpossible.
● 'Can I have a°nother ˌapple?	I ˌdon't ₒsee ₒwhy ˌnot. ‖ We've ˌplenty ˌleft.
He's ˋnice, │ ˋisn't he?	ˌSo they ˌsay.
'How're you ˋkeeping?	ˌFair to ˌmoderate.
What a 'charming ˌperson she ₒis!	She's ˌquite good ˌlooking.
'Can I °have your ˌautograph?	ˌIf you ˌlike. ˌIf you inˌsist. If you ˌreally ˌwant it.
'How much did you ˋwin?	About a ˌthousand ˌpounds.
D'you 'like ˌprunes?	ˌNot very ˌmuch.
Is he 'putting up aˌgain?	As ˌfar as I ˌknow he °is.
And 'whose °photo d'you think ˋthis is?	I ˌdon't seem to ˌrecognise it.
Can 'Tom have the °afternoon ˌoff?	I supˌpose I can ˌspare him.
'Will he come ˌback?	I ˌshouldn't be surˌprised.
'What was ˋyour ₒholiday ₒlike?	ˌNothing to ₒwrite ˌhome aˋbout.
Would you like a 'black one or a ˌblue one?	It's ˌall the ₒsame to ˌme.
'How much ˋsugar have they ₒsent?	The ˌsame aₒmount as beˌfore.
'How much ˋpolish have we ₒgot?	Eˌnough to be ₒgoing ˌon with.
'When did you °last ˋsee him?	A ˌfortnight aₒgo last ˌSaturday.
It was her 'fortieth ˌbirthday.	('Good ˌlord!) ‖ I ˌshouldn't have ₒthought she was ˌforty.
Can I 'come a°gain on ˌMonday?	There's ˌno ₒreason ₒwhy you ˌshouldn't.
He 'gets his to°bacco at ˋMilton's.	ˌNot ˌalways.
I ˋshan't sucˇceed.	But you ˌmight ˌtry.
You're ˋalways ₒmaking misₒtakes.	ˌSo are ˌyou.
'Send it imˋmediately.	ˌIf you ˌsay so.
I shall 'have to ˌsack him.	You ˌcan't do ˌthat.
Oh I've ˋleft ˌthat job.	You ˌnever ˌtold me.
It's so ˋshoddy, ₒthat ₒsuit.	It'll ˌdo for ˌme.
I shall ˌgive them ˋall to ₒMary.	That's ˌvery unˌfair.

Verbal context	*Drill*
'How ⌄funny, your ₒslipping on the ₒice!	It was ˌnothing to ˌlaugh at.
'That's the 'second ₒcup I've ₒbroken.	It's ˌnothing to ˌbrag aᵒbout.
What'ever ᵒmade you 'pay him?	It ˌcouldn't be aˌvoided.
I 'am ₒmiserable.	You were ˌhappy enough ˌyesterday.
He 'really ᵒis the ⌄limit.	You ˌshouldn't ₒsay ˌthat.
'Must I ᵒeat it ˌnow?	ˌNot if you ₒdon't ˌwant to.
You must a'pologise at ⌄once.	I ˌdon't see ₒwhy I ˌshould.
What a 'horrid ᵒcup of ⌄coffee!	It ˌseems all ₒright to ˌme.
You ⌄said we could ₒcome on ₒTuesday.	It's ˌnot ₒTuesday toˌday.
Oh 'come ˌon. ‖ 'Let's get 'out of ₒhere.	We ˌcan't ₒleave without ˌpaying.
I've 'lost my 'handkerchief.	You ˌneedn't ₒbe so ˌproud of it.
'Where on ᵒearth's ⌄Joan ₒgot to?	She'll be ˌcoming aₒlong ˌpresently.
The a'mount of 'time one ₒwastes there.	You ˌdidn't ₒhave to wait ˌlong.
ˌWhat made you 'do such a ₒstupid ₒthing?	It's ˌnothing to ₒdo with ˌyou.
Oh you 'clumsy ₒthing, ₒbreaking that ₒwindow!	I ˌdidn't ₒdo it on ˌpurpose.
I 'don't ᵒthink he can ˌmanage it.	He ˌcan if he ₒputs his ˌmind to it.
They 'haven't ᵒtime to ⌄finish the ₒjob.	That's ˌno ₒreason for not ˌstarting it.
You 'haven't ᵒbrought e'nough of them.	I shall be ˌbringing some ₒmore toˌmorrow.
'Have some 'sugar.	I ˌnever take ₒsugar in ˌcoffee.
'Why haven't you ᵒmended my ˌshoes?	I'll atˌtend to them as ₒsoon as I ˌcan.
You'd 'better ᵒtake your 'mac.	It ˌisn't ₒraining as ₒmuch as all ˌthat.
I'm 'awfully ˌsorry.	It's ˌno ₒgood aₒpologising ˌnow.
Where 'have you ⌄been?	We've ˌonly ₒbeen for a ₒride in the ˌcar.
You 'haven't ᵒfixed it as I ⌄told you.	ˌYes, I ˌhave.
He can 'use what he ⌄likes.	ˌNo, he ˌcan't.
● You've 'made a mis'take.	ˌNo, I ˌhaven't.
'Go at ⌄once.	Inˌdeed I ˌwon't.
You 'said you'd al'ready 'got one.	I said ˌno such ˌthing.
He can 'drive 'your ₒcar.	ˌOh no he ˌcan't.
'I'll ask him 'for you.	I'll ˌask him myˌself.
He 'gave it ₒto you, │ ˌdidn't he?	He did ˌnothing of the ˌsort.
'Hand it ⌄over.	I most ˌcertainly ₒwill ˌnot.
'How did you get ⌄on?	ˌNot too ˌbadly.
'Nice of you to in'vite me.	You're ˌvery ˌwelcome.
‾How ⌄generous you've ₒbeen!	Oh but it's ˌnothing ˌmuch.

Verbal context	*Drill*
ˈThank you | for your ˌhelp.	You've ˌoften helped ˌme.
What a 'fine piece of ˎwork you've pro-ₒduced!	It's ˌnot as ₒgood as all ˌthat.
‾How ˎbrave to ₒdive in ₒafter him!	ˌAnyone ₒelse would have ₒdone the ˌsame.
You've done a 'fine ˎjob.	Oh I ˌdon't ˌknow. || ˌYou could have ₒdone it ₒjust as ˌwell.
I'm ˈterribly ˌsorry.	You've ˌno ˌreason to be. || It ˌwasn't ˌyour °fault.
ˈSorry to ₒmake you go ₒout aˌgain.	I ˌdon't ˌmind. || It's ˌno ˌtrouble.
It was 'really °very 'clumsy of me.	It ˌdoesn't ˌmatter. || There's ˌno great ˌharm done.
How'ever did I °come to 'drop such a ₒbrick?	I ˌshouldn't ˌworry a°bout it.
I've got 'odd 'socks on.	ˌNo-one'll ˌnotice.
I feel ˈterrible aₒbout it.	You've ˌnothing to reˌproach yourself a°bout.
What 'will they ˎthink of me?	You ˌmustn't ₒtake it to ˌheart.
I 'wish I were ˎdead.	It's ˌnot a ₒmatter of ₒlife and ˌdeath.
But I ˌshan't °finish it in ˈtime.	There's ˌno ₒneed to upₒset yourself on ˌthat ac°count.

WH-Questions

● I 'don't aˌgree.	ˌWhy ˌnot?
You were ˈrather ˇharsh with him.	Well ˌwhat ˌof it?
I'll 'give you a °jolly good ˈhiding.	And ˌwho'll ˌhelp you?
'Please don't ˎdo that.	And ˌwhy ˌshouldn't I?
'Fetch me my ˎgloves, ₒplease.	ˌWhy can't ˌyou °fetch them?
I ˈdon't think °much of ˇthat ₒcolour.	ˌWhich do ˌyou pre°fer, then?
I ˈdidn't °take his remark ˇthat ₒway.	ˌWhich way ˌdid you °take it, °then?
ˈSorry I'm ˌlate.	ˌWhere have you ˌbeen all this °time?
I 'think you °looked ˈterrible.	And ˌwho asked for ˌyour o°pinion?
ˈHarry's ₒjust arₒrived.	Who on ˌearth told ˌhim to °come?
I'd 'like a °new ˈhat.	ˌWho's ₒgoing to ˌpay for it?
I 'thought she was in ˈFrance.	ˌWhere did you ₒget ˌthat i°dea from?
'Let's °talk to him on the ˈphone.	ˌWhat makes you ₒthink ˌthat will °do any °good?
It's ˈyour ₒturn to ₒdo the ₒwashing ₒup.	And ˌhow d'you ₒmake ˌthat out?

Verbal context	*Drill*

'Tommy's °broken a ˅window.
Oh 'dear oh ˏdear!
I'm a'fraid she's ˅lost your ˏtrowel.
'Shut the ˏdoor, for ˳heaven's ˳sake.
● I've got a con˅fession to ˳make.
There are ˅no ˳trains │ on ˏSundays. ‖ I've
'just rung ˅up.
You 'shouldn't have ˏdone it.

ˏHow did he ˳manage ˏthat?
Now ˏwhat's the ˳matter with ˏyou?
ˏWhat's she ˳going to ˏdo a°bout it?
Just ˏwho do you ˳think you're ˏtalking to?
And ˏwhat have you been ˳up to ˏnow?

ˏWhy didn't you ˳find out ˏsooner?
And ˏwhat's it ˳got to ˳do with ˏyou, may I
    °ask?

Yes-No Questions

I'm ˅so ˏsorry, °Mummy.
I shall 'give them °all to ˅Edward.
● You must re˅turn it.
I'd 'no i°dea ˅how to ˳get there.
We must ˅send ˳John his ˳ticket.

ˏAre you ˏreally °sorry?
D'you ˏthink that's ˏfair?
D'you ˏmean that ˏseriously?
ˏCouldn't you have ˏasked?
Is there ˏreally any ˏneed to? ‖ (We're ˅see-
ing him │ this ˏevening.)

Yet a˅gain he's ˳broken a ˳promise.
The 'bus is at ˅five, I'm ˳told.
'Ivan °said it was a ˅stupid ˳question.
But ˏwhat'll your ˅uncle ˳say?
He's not ˅good enough, I ˳tell you.
Your ˅cabbage, ˳madam.
'What about ˅Marjorie?
● You 'mean to °say you're getting ˏmarried?
The 'answer's ˅no.
Oh 'let's °go to the ˏpictures.
We must get 'on with it ˅now.
'Let's use it ˅now.
'Here's an ˅apple ˳for you.
I'll 'bring them °round on ˅Saturday.
The 'coach °goes at ˅three, I ˳think.

Are you ˏletting him get aˏway with it?
ˏHave you ˳made ˏsure?
Could ˏhe have ˳thought of a ˏbetter °one?
D'you ˏthink I ˳care what ˏhe °says?
ˏMayn't you ˳be misˏtaken?
Is ˏthis the ˳best you can ˏoffer me?
Would it be ˏany ˳good bringing ˏher into it?
ˏIs it so ˳very surˏprising?
ˏAm I to ˳take that as ˏfinal?
ˏOughtn't you to ˳ask your ˏmother °first?
ˏCouldn't it be ˳left till this ˏevening?
ˏWouldn't it be ˳better to ˳wait till it's ˏcold?
ˏCan't you ˳give me ˳more than ˏone?
ˏCan't you let me ˳have them ˳rather ˏsooner?
ˏHadn't we ˳better ˳phone and ˳find out for
    ˏcertain?

Commands

‾Hold ˏon a °minute.

ˏCome ˏon. ‖ (We ˏhaven't ˳all ˏday.)

Verbal context	*Drill*
ˋLook. ‖ A ˋspider.	ˌDon't ˌhurt it.
I'm 'not °sure whether I ˋought to.	ˌBe a ˌsport.
ˋGracious. ‖ I ˌnearly ˋdropped it.	ˌHold it ˌcarefully.
● I ˇdon't think I can °dive from ˇthat ₒheight.	ˌHave a ˌshot at it. ‖ (ˌPeter's ₒdone it.)
ˋSorry I ₒhave to ˌdash.	ˌDon't let ˌme de°tain you.
I 'won't have °anything to ˌdo with him.	ˌDon't be so ˌsilly.
He's 'going to °pay at the °end of the ˋmonth.	ˌDon't you beˌlieve it. ‖ (ˌThat's what he ˋalways ₒsays.)
'Hang ˌon a °second.	Oh ˌdo hurry ˌup. ‖ (I've been ˌwaiting °ages alˋready.)
I'm 'going to ˌsack him.	ˌDon't ₒdo ˌthat. ‖ (He's ˌnot such a ˌbad °chap.)
He'll 'let me °have it by ˌMonday.	ˌDon't be ₒtoo ˌsure. ‖ (He's ˋvery unre-ₒliable.)
I shall ˋnever ₒget it ₒright.	ˌDon't desₒpair ˌyet. ‖ (It's ˋmuch too ₒearly to exₒpect perₒfection.)
ˋDad'll ₒpay for me.	ˌDon't you ₒtake so ₒmuch for ˌgranted.
She's so ˌterribly ˋrude.	ˌDon't take ₒany ₒnotice of ˌher. ‖ (She was ˋborn ₒrude.)
'Do it aˌgain.	ˌHave a ˌheart. ‖ (I'm ˌtired ˋout.)
I must deˋcline your ₒoffer.	ˌPlease your ˌself.
I 'shan't be °coming after ˌall.	Well ˌmake up your ˌmind.
'How °much did he ˋlend you?	ˌMind your ₒown ˌbusiness!
I ˋknow I'm ₒright.	ˌHave it your ₒown ˌway, °then.
● I'm ˋsorry.	Well ˌsay it as ₒif you ˌmeant it.
'Shall I °buy you a reˌplacement?	ˌDon't ˌtrouble. ‖ (I ˌshan't be ˌneeding it a°gain.)
'Thanks ˋawfully.	ˌDon't ˌmention it. ‖ (It was a ˋpleasure.)
I'm ˋterribly ˌsorry.	ˌDon't aˌpologise. ‖ (It could ˌhappen to ˋanybody.)
ˋThank you | for ˌfetching my ˌparcel.	Think ˌnothing ˌof it. ‖ (I was ˌgoing to the °station ˋanyway.)
I'm aˋfraid I've ˋbroken it.	ˌDon't ₒworry about ˌthat. ‖ (I can ˋsoon buy aˌnother.)
But we've ˋlost.	ˌDon't take it ₒtoo much to ˌheart. ‖ (It's ₒonly a ˌgame.)

Verbal context	*Drill*

Interjections

I ’can’t make ˇsix o₀clock.

We ’pulled it ˇoff.

I 'lent him °five ‛pounds.

● 'Let’s do it ‛my way for a ₀change.

I 'can’t ˎhelp you.

'Let me have ‛six of them.

⁻Goodˌbye, Sir °Roger.

You can ‛have it | if you ˌlike.

● We had 'no °sunshine at ‛all.

ˌAll ˌright. ‖ (ˌCome when°ever you ‛can.)

ˌGood ˌshow! ˌNice ˌwork! ˌGood for ˌyou!

ˌMore fool ˌyou! ‖ (You’ll ‛never get it ₀back.)

ˌAs you ˌwish.

ˌVery ˌwell. ‖ (We’ll ˏdo it a‛lone.)

ˌVery ˌgood, sir.

Good ˌafterˌnoon.

ˌThanks very ˌmuch.

I ˌbeg your ˌpardon. ‖ (It was ˏsunny °all the ‛morning.)

Note: All the relevant drills given above with the tune

$$\text{(LOW PRE-HEAD}+\text{) LOW HEAD}+\text{LOW RISE (}+\text{TAIL)}$$

can be said with emphasis if the high pre-head is used instead of the low pre-head (see Chapter I, p. 36). With this feature indicated the last drill in this section would read

⁻I ˌbeg your ˌpardon.

4 *The Low Bounce*

Attitude

In STATEMENTS: soothing, reassuring, hint of great self-confidence and self-reliance; (in echoes) questioning with a tone of surprise and disbelief; (in non-final word groups) creating expectancy about what is to follow.

In WH-QUESTIONS: with the nuclear tone on the interrogative word, puzzled; (in echoes) disapproving; otherwise, sympathetically interested.

In YES-NO QUESTIONS: genuinely interested.

In COMMANDS: soothing, encouraging, calmly patronising.

In INTERJECTIONS: airy, casual yet encouraging, often friendly, brighter than when said with the Take-Off.

Tone marks used in LOW BOUNCE drills

A Stressed, accented syllables (Nucleus, Head)

[ˌ] (i) without Tail: very low rising to medium pitch.

(ii) with Tail: very low level pitch; the rise is completed by the tail syllable(s).

['] Relatively high level pitch.

[°] Relatively high level pitch, the same pitch as the *preceding* ['].

B Stressed, unaccented syllables (Tail)

[°] Level pitch, higher than the lowest possible and always higher than the *preceding* [ˌ] or [°].

C Unstressed, unaccented syllables (Pre-head)

[⁻] High level pitch, higher than a *following* ['] and very much higher than the *following* [ˌ].

Tune

(Low Pre-Head+) High Head + Low Rise (+Tail)

or

Verbal context	*Drill*

Statements

'Have you °posted those ˌletters?	'Not ˌyet.
'Can we °go to the ˌcircus, °Daddy?	'I'll ˌsee.
● I ˋhate ₒclimbing ˌladders.	It's 'all ˌright. ‖ You 'won't ˌfall.
I just 'daren't °pick it ˌup.	You 'won't ˌbreak it.
ˋQuick. ‖ The ˋkettle's ₒboiling ₒover.	I'm 'just ˌcoming.
I'm ˋsorry to ˌtrouble you │ but 'could I °borrow your ˌspade?	It's 'no ˌtrouble. ‖ I'm 'not ˌusing it at the °moment.
It's 'going to be ˋpainful, │ ˋisn't it?	No, I 'shan't ˌhurt you.
I ˇhope he doesn't ˇhurt himₒself.	No, he's 'quite ˌused to °motor°bikes.
'Who's ˋthere?	It's 'only ˌme. ‖ (Paˋtricia.)
These ˌbus journeys ˋalways upₒset me.	It's 'not much ˌfurther.
She 'hasn't forˌgotten, °has she?	I 'shouldn't ˌthink °so.

Verbal context	*Drill*
You ˏdo beˑ°lieve me, │ ˏdon't you?	Yes, 'I beˏlieve you.
I 'don't °want them to °go at ˋall.	But they'll be 'back by ˏlunch time.
'Who were you ˋtalking to?	'Only the ˏmilkman.
'Aren't you °ready to ˏstart?	I 'shan't be a ˏminute.
'Can I °have an ice ˏcream, °Daddy?	'Later ˏon. ‖ When 'Mummy and ˏJoyce come °back.
'Where are you ˋgoing?	'Just to °post a ˏletter.
● I must 'pay you what I ˋowe you.	There's 'no ˏhurry. ‖ When'ever it's conˏvenient.
Now I ˋhave let the ˳cat out of the ˳bag.	I 'promise I won't ˏtell anyone.
'Can't we ˏdo °something aˑ°bout it?	'All in °good ˏtime.
● ˋTell me, ˳doctor. ‖ 'Is he ˏbadly °hurt?	'Nothing at °all ˏserious. ‖ 'Just a °few ˏbruises.
I ˋam sorry I ˳gave the ˏgame aˑ°way.	It 'doesn't ˏmatter, °dear. ‖ We 'all make misˑ°takes ˏsometime.
'Oh ˋdear! ‖ I ˋhave made a ˳mess of it.	There's 'nothing to °get up ˏset aˑ°bout.
I 'don't think I'll ˋever ˳do it.	'You ˏwill. ‖ It's 'just a °matter of ˏpractice.
‾Do you ˏhave to °leave us?	Yes but I'll 'see you aˑ°gain on ˏMonday.
You 'said you'd have °finished it by this ˋmorning.	It'll be 'quite °ready by toˏmorrow °morning.
Now 'what about my ˎshoes?	I'll reˑ'pair them as °soon as I ˏcan.
I'm ˋsure I shall ˳fall.	You'll be 'safe enough if you °don't look ˏdown.
It'll ˋhurt, │ ˋwon't it?	Yes but it'll be 'over in a °couple of ˏseconds.
● Well 'when shall we ˋstart?	'Any time that °suits ˏyou.
'Aren't you °nearly ˏready?	I've 'only got my °hat and ˏcoat to put °on.
'Shall we go °out for a ˏwalk, °Mummy?	When I've 'cleared aˑ°way and washed ˏup, we °will.
'How °much did you ˎtell him, ˳then?	'Only e°nough to °keep him ˏquiet.
Where 'have you ˎbeen?	'Only °down to the °village with ˏTony.
What 'will he ˎdo, ˳all on his ˳own?	'No °need to feel ˏanxious aˑ°bout him. ‖ He's 'perfectly °capable of looking °after himˏself.
'Isn't it °nearly ˏmy °turn?	I 'shan't keep you °waiting °much ˏlonger.
Well when ˋcan you ˳let me ˳have it ˳back?	I'll reˑ'turn it without °fail at the week ˏend.

Verbal context	*Drill*

WH-Questions

I 'don't think I'll ˏgo.	'Why ˏnot?
'Look at this ˏpainting.	'Whose ˏis it?
Oh this 'wretched ˋclock!	'What's ˏwrong with it?
● I 'leave to°morrow ˏmorning.	'What ˏtrain are you °thinking of °catching?
(⌐Hulˏlo, little °girl.)	'What's your ˏname?
Oh 'dear oh ˏdear!	'What's the ˏmatter?
I saw ˋMary | at the ˏparty.	'Who was she ˏthere with?
'Agnes °likes the ˋgreen ₒwallpaper.	'Which one do ˏyou pre°fer?
We had a ˋvery ₒpleasant ₒwalk.	'How °far did you ˏget?
I ˋhaven't in°cluded ˊRobert.	'Why have you °left ˏhim out?
ˋThere's ˏMarjorie, | 'over ˋthere.	'Who is it she's ˏtalking °to?
I 'used to °live in ˋAndover.	And 'where d'you °live ˏnow?
Oh I'll ˋnever ₒfinish ₒcutting the ₒlawn.	'Why don't you °let ˏme take a °turn with the °mower?
I'm a'fraid they've gone ˋout.	'How °soon will they be ˏback?
('Glad to ˋsee you, ₒArthur.)	'What'll you °have to ˏdrink?
'Have you any ˏsealing °wax?	'How °much would you ˏwant?
You're 'just the °person I've been ˋlooking ₒfor.	And 'what can I °do for ˏyou?
● ˋAlice is ₒon the ₒphone.	'Who does she °want to ˏspeak to?
I'm 'just °off for a °few days' ˋholiday.	'When will you be re°turning to ˏwork?
'That was my °cousin ˋJack.	'What does he °do for a ˏliving?
'Stevens is °going to reˋtire.	'Who d'you °think will take ˏover °from him?
I've 'got a °bit of a ˋcold.	'How did you °manage to get ˏthat?
I'm 'off to ˋParis | to ˏmorrow.	'How long d'you in°tend to ˏstay there?
I've 'given °Peter ˋtwo ₒsweets.	'How many shall we °give to ˏMichael?
● We 'ought to °go and see ˋJones ₒsometime.	'When's the °best °time to ˏcatch him, d'you sup°pose?
My 'nephew re°turned to °London this ˋmorning.	'When's he °coming °down aˏgain?
'Go and °stand in the ˏcorner, ₒDaddy.	'What have I °done to de°serve ˏthat?
I 'saw him a °few ˋmoments aₒgo.	You 'saw him ˏwhen?
I've 'put your °stud on the ˋdressing ₒtable.	You've 'put it ˏwhere?
I was 'just °doing my ˋfootball ₒpools.	You were 'doing ˏwhat?
They 'charged me °three ˋpounds.	They 'charged you ˏhow much?

Verbal context	Drill
I must 'get my `hair ₒcut.	You must 'get your ‚what °cut?
I've 'lent him ˏyour ₒnewspaper.	You've 'lent him ‚whose °paper?
He 'went to Bar°bados °ten `years aₒgo.	He 'went there ‚how long a°go?
● She's 'waiting for my `brother.	She's 'waiting for ‚who?
They've 'given me a °couple of ˏdozen.	They've 'given you ‚how °many?
● She's 'knitting a ma°genta ˏpullover.	She's 'knitting a ‚what colour °pullover?
He's 'sitting on the `carver.	He's 'sitting on the ‚what?
He 'can't °come before °eight ˏthirty.	He 'can't °come before ‚what °time?
I've 'just been °talking to `Albert | in the `bathroom.	You've 'just been °talking to him ‚where?

Yes-No Questions

● I'm 'going to °do some `shopping.	Can 'I come ‚too?
● I'd `love you to ₒcome.	Are you 'taking the ‚car?
● I sup'pose I'll `have to.	'Would you like ‚me to °drive?
● 'Thank you °very `much.	'Have you seen ‚Tom °lately?
● 'Not since °last °Wednesday `week.	'Wasn't that your °mother's ‚birthday?
● 'Yes it `was.	'Did he °bring her a ‚present?
● `No. || He 'said he for`got.	Was 'that the ‚real °reason?
● `No. || He's 'probably °very hard `up just ₒnow.	'May we go and ‚call on your °mother?
● We 'really °haven't `time | this ‚morning.	Have the 'Smiths in°vited you for ‚Sunday?
Yes they 'rang us °up this `morning.	'Will you ‚go, d'you sup°pose?
I 'haven't °made up my ˏmind ₒyet.	'Did you go ‚last year?
ˏYes. || We 'got home °just in ˏtime for it.	'Hadn't you °been in A‚merica?
No, ˇCanada.	'Was it a ‚good party °last time?
Tre`mendous ₒfun.	Were 'any of ‚our friends °there?
'Only °Bill and his ˏwife.	Will you be 'off to °Canada ‚this °summer?
I'm 'not at °all `sure.	'Hard up for ‚money?
'Yes I `am, | ‚rather.	'Is it your ‚brother who °lives out °there?
ˏYes.	Does he 'ever °come to ‚England?
'Only °very oc‚casionally.	'Is he too ‚busy to come °often?
ˏYes. || And he 'hates °travelling `anyway.	'Is he the ‚youngest of the °family?
ˏNo. || `Frank ₒis.	Is he 'younger than ‚you?
ˏYes. || 'Nine ˏyears ₒyounger.	'Did you say ‚five °years?
No, `nine.	

Verbal context	*Drill*
Good ˋmorning.	'Haven't we met °somewhere be‚fore?
At the ˋRobinsons', | last ˋFriday.	'Aren't you °Paul °Jones, the ‚author?
'Yes, in‚deed.	Are 'you going to °Edinburgh ‚too?
ˎYes. || I'm 'going to °stay with my ˎbrother.	Is 'he a °writer ‚also?
He's a uni'versity ˋlecturer.	Does he 'actually ‚live in °Edinburgh?
He has a 'small °house on the ˎoutskirts.	'Hasn't he °written a °book on ‚physics?
'Yes he ‚has.	Can you 'tell me the ‚title of the °book?
'Physics and the °Man in the ˎStreet.	Would you 'say it was a ‚good °book?
'Abso°lutely °first ˋclass.	Are you 'travelling on your ‚own?
ˎNo. || My ˋson's ₒwith me.	Was 'he that young °fellow I °passed in the ‚corridor?
Yes, 'that's ‚right.	Does he 'go to ‚school °yet?
'Oh ˋyes. || He's 'nearly ˋseven.	'Isn't he °rather ‚small for °seven?
He ˋis, | ‚rather.	'Can you recom°mend a °good ho‚tel in °Edinburgh?
I should 'try the °North ˋScottish.	'Will you be °staying there ‚long?
Until the 'end of the °week at ˋleast.	D'you 'know when the °Festival ‚ends?
A 'week next ˎSaturday.	'Ought I to °book for the °ballet in ad‚vance?
ˋDefinitely. || But I 'think you'll be °too ˋlate.	Is it as 'popular as °all ‚that?
It's 'usually exˋtremely ₒcrowded.	Would I be 'able to get °in to a ‚matinee, d'you °think?
You ˇmight.	May I 'come and °call on you to‚morrow?
Yes ˋdo.	Have you 'any en°gagements for °Saturday ‚evening?
I'm ˇsorry. || I'm 'quite booked ˋup.	Well 'are you °free on the ‚following °evening?
‚Yes.	Would you 'care to °come and have ‚dinner °with me?
ˋThank you. || I'd ˋlove to.	
Hul‚lo.	Is 'that the ‚Browns' °house?
‚No. || 'This is the °Town ˋHall.	'Are you °quite ‚sure?
ˋPositive.	Could you 'ring that °number a‚gain, °operator?

Verbal context	*Drill*
‘Certainly, ₒmadam. ‖ 'Hold the ˎline.	Is 'that the °Browns' house ˎthis time?
ˎYes.	'May I °speak to ˎJimmy, °please? ‖ (It's ‘Simon.)
‘Hullo, │ ˎSimon. ‖ He's not ‘in, I'm, aₒfraid.	'Has he been °gone ˎlong?
'Ten ‘minutes or ₒmore.	'Could I °leave a ˎmessage °for him?
‘Certainly.	'Would he give me a °ring at the ˎoffice?
'All ˎright. ‖ But ‘when?	'Could he ring as °soon as he gets ˎback?
'Righˎto. ‖ I'll ‘tell him ₒthat.	'Did he say °anything about a ˎparcel °for me?
Yes it's ‘here, │ on the 'hall ‘table.	'May I °come and ˎfetch it?
ˇSorry. ‖ I'm 'just off ‘out.	Well 'would this °afterˎnoon be °possible?
ˎYes. ‖ I shall be 'back by ˎlunch time.	Well 'can I call °round at ˎtwo?
‘Surely. ‖ 'See you ˎthen.	

Commands

I'm a'fraid I'm °in your ‘way.	'Don't ˎmove. ‖ (There's 'plenty of ˎroom.)
'Can you °give me his ˎphone °number?	'Hang ˎon. ‖ (I'll ‘find it ₒfor you.)
Oh I ‘am ₒmiserable.	'Cheer ˎup. ‖ (You're ‘more °fortunate than ˇmost ₒpeople.)
'What shall I °do ‘now?	'Carry ˎon.
● ˎWhat a ‘nuisance it ₒall ₒis!	'Don't ˎworry. ‖ (It's 'not for much ˎlonger.)
● I 'just °can't °quite ‘manage it.	Well 'keep ˎtrying.
I'm 'going for a ˎwalk.	'Don't be ˎlong. ‖ (We're 'due at the ‘Smiths' │ after ˎtea.)
I've 'broken that °nice ‘vase.	'Never ˎmind. ‖ (It was 'cracked ‘anyway.)
'What can I °do for ˎyou, sir?	'Twenty ˎPlayers, °please.
‘Daddy. ‖ ˎJohnnie's °fallen ‘over.	'Come to ˎDaddy, °Johnnie.
The ‘clock's ₒstopped.	Well 'wind it ₒup, then.
I'll 'give him a °piece of my ‘mind.	Now 'don't disˎcourage him. ‖ (He's 'only a beˎginner.)
● 'Am I disˎturbing you?	No 'sit ˎdown. No 'come ˎin. No but 'shut the ˎdoor.
● I'm 'just ˎgoing.	'Have a °good ˎtime.
‘Mummy. ‖ ˎJohnnie's °eating a °lump of ‘coal.	'Give it to ˎMummy, °Johnnie.
'What d'you ‘want me ₒfor?	'Come over ˎhere a °minute.

Verbal context	*Drill*
I'm 'going round to ˎJohn's.	Now 'don't stay too ˎlate.
● I 'really °must be ˎoff.	'Don't let °me deˎtain you, °then.
'Where shall I °put my ˋboots?	'Put them in the ˎcloakroom, °silly.
What a 'scrumptious ˎpudding!	'Save °some of it for ˎme.
'Which is ˋmy ˳place?	'Go and °sit beside ˎTommie.
What a deˈlightful ˎcake!	'Let me °give you aˎnother °piece.
I ˋcan't carry ˇall of it.	Well then 'carry as °much as you ˎcan.
I aˋdore ˎchocolate.	'Don't °eat it °all at ˎonce.
ˋPeter's ˳staying with us │ ˎnext ˎweek.	'Bring him °round to ˎsee us.
'Goodˎbye. ‖ I've enˈjoyed myself eˋnormously.	'Come and °stay with us aˎgain ˎsoon.
I ˋcan't col°lect the °parcel toˇday.	Well 'fetch it as °soon as you ˎcan.
I'm 'off to Jaˋmaica │ toˎmorrow.	'Send me a °line when you ˎget there.

Interjections

At 'last I've °got it ˎright.	'Well ˎdone!
There's 'no esˋcaping it.	'Ah ˎwell! ‖ (I 'don't sup°pose it'll ˎkill us.)
I've ˋpassed my ˳driving test.	'Good ˎshow!
● 'Have a °good ˎholiday.	'And ˎyou!
It's 'abso°lutely ˎmonstrous.	'Now ˎnow! ‖ ('Don't get exˎcited.)
And ˋstill you've ˳got it ˳wrong.	'Oh ˎdear! ‖ (And I 'thought I'd °been so ˋclever │ ˎthis time.)
I've 'been to ˋBrighton for a ˳week.	'Oh ˎyes. ‖ (Did you 'have a °good ˎtime?)
Would you 'like a °cup of ˎcoffee?	'Yes, ˎplease.
● 'More ˎtea?	'No ˎthanks. 'No ˎthank you.
I 'take my e°xam toˋmorrow.	'Good ˎluck.
I'll 'see you on ˎTuesday.	'Right you ˎare!
(⌐Goodˎnight, °dear.)	'Pleasant ˎdreams!
⌐Goodˎbye, Mr. °Smith.	Good 'afterˎnoon.
I'll 'let you have it °back toˋnight.	'Righˎto! 'Very ˎwell.
● 'My °name's ˋLumpkin.	I 'beg your ˎpardon. ‖ ('Would you mind °saying that aˎgain?)
I'll be 'back ˎlater.	Good'bye for the ˎpresent. ‖ 'See you ˎthen.
● You've 'got the °wrong ˋnumber.	'Sorry you've been ˎtroubled.

Verbal context	*Drill*

I 'almost `did it | ,then. 'Hard ,luck. 'Better °luck °next ,time.
'John will be °home at `seven, Mrs. ₒRead. 'Thank you for °letting me ,know, °Cyril.

Note: All the relevant drills given above with the tune

(LOW PRE-HEAD+) HIGH HEAD+LOW RISE (+TAIL)

can be said with emphasis if one or both of the following features are used:
(*a*) the high pre-head instead of the low pre-head (see Chapter I, p. 36);
(*b*) the emphatic form of the high head (see Chapter I, p. 37).
The two drills below show how these features are marked:

⁻Good'bye for the ,present.
'Thank you for 'letting me ,know, °Cyril.

Tune High Pre-Head+Low Rise (+Tail)

or

Verbal context	*Drill*

Statements

'Will you ,sell me a °couple? ⁻I ,will.
ˠTime to ˇgo. ⁻I ,know.
⁻Is ,that °right? ⁻I ,think °so.
⁻Did he ,check the re°sult? ⁻He ,did.
⁻Any 'other °jobs to be °done? ⁻That's ,all.
'What will you °make the `handle ₒof? ⁻Of ,wood.
Is 'that ,your °notebook? ⁻It ,is.
'Have you any ciga,rettes °left? ⁻A ,few.
I `do hope he °won't let us ˇdown.  ⁻He ,won't. ‖ (He's `very reₒliable.)
I'm a'fraid I'm °rather `late. ⁻As ,usual.
● ,Do hurry ,up. ⁻I'm ,coming.
,Where's `Billie? ⁻In ,bed, I °hope.

Verbal context	*Drill*
'Will he say ˏyes, d'you °think?	⁻Perˏhaps he °will.
'Can you °let me know ˏsoon?	⁻On ˏSaturday, with °any °luck.
⁻Can I have aˏnother go, °Daddy?	⁻When ˏJoan's had a °turn, you °can.
'Can I have a°nother ˏtoffee?	⁻If you ˏlike.
'Shall we °call in at ˏPeter's?	⁻If there's ˏtime.
'When can I °see you aˏlone?	⁻After ˏtea.
'Where shall we ˎmeet you?	⁻At the ˏtheatre.
'How °long can you ˋstay?	⁻For a ˏminute or °two.
'Shall we °play aˏnother °round?	⁻If it aˏmuses you.
But I may ˋspill ˳some.	⁻If you go ˏcarefully you °won't.

WH-Questions

I 'wouldn't ˎdream of going ˳in for it.	⁻Why ˏnot? ‖ (It would be ˋfun.)
(⁻Hulˏlo, °Leslie. ‖ 'Good to ˋsee you.)	⁻How ˏare you?
You've 'had an ˋaccident.	⁻Where ˏam I?
What an ex'traordinary ˎhandbag!	⁻Whose ˏis it?
I 'see you're °playing ˋRobinson.	⁻How ˏgood is he?
Are 'these ˏgloves any °good to you?	⁻What ˏsize °are they?
● I said 'nothing of the ˎkind.	⁻What ˏdid you °say, then?
ˇThat's not ˳why I've ˳come.	⁻Why ˏhave you °come?
I 'liked the Im°pressionists a ˋlot.	⁻Which ˏothers did you °like?
You ˋwon't catch ˇme ˳going by ˳air.	⁻Why ˏdon't you °like °flying?
I'm a'fraid he's °not ˋfree │ at the ˏmoment.	⁻When ˏis he °likely to be °free?
'These are ˋour two ˳rooms.	⁻Which is ˏmine?
I saw ˋGrace │ at the ˏTaylors' ˏparty.	(ˏOh.) ‖ ⁻And who ˏelse was °there?
He ˋdidn't make it ˇthat ˳way.	⁻Which way ˏdid he °make it, °then?
Can you 'lend me a °couple of ˏpounds?	⁻What d'you ˏwant it °for?
He's 'married at ˎlast.	⁻He's ˏwhat?
I've 'got to °go to ˋGoole.	⁻To ˏwhere?
He 'gives me the ˎwillies.	⁻The ˏwhat?
I 'write with my ˋleft ˳hand.	⁻With ˏwhich °hand?
● He was 'treated by an ˋosteopath.	⁻By ˏwho, did you °say?
'Seven °days out of ˋeight it ˳rained.	⁻On ˏhow many °days?
I've 'got a ˋjob. ‖ As 'Myrtle's ˋsecretary.	⁻As ˏwhose °secretary?
There'll be ˋno °bridge if °Tom has to work ˇlate.	⁻If ˏwho has to °work late?

Verbal context	*Drill*

You 'ought to °use a ˋchinagraph ˳pencil. ⌐A ˏwhat sort of °pencil?
You're a 'blithering ˎidiot. ⌐I'm a ˏwhat?
You must ˋcauterise the ˳wound. ⌐I must do ˏwhat to the °wound?

Yes-No Questions

(ˇI'm not ˳ready.) ⌐Are ˏyou?
Have you 'seen my ˏpen? ⌐Is ˏthis it?
Perhaps ˋAndrew would ˳give you a ˳game. ⌐Does ˏhe play °chess?
Now 'write °down your ˏanswers. ⌐Will ˏpencil °do?
⌐Hul˳lo, °Ian. ‖ 'What can I °do for ˋyou? ⌐Is ˏAngus °in?
● 'When can I ˎcall for it? ⌐Would ˏFriday °suit you?
Are you 'going to °Ann's twenty ˏfirst? ⌐Are ˏyou °going to be °there?
'Anybody for °more ˏtea? ⌐May ˏI have a°nother cup?
'This ˋis ˳difficult. ⌐Can I ˏhelp?
I 'gave them ˋback to you. ⌐Are you ˏsure?
I've 'made myself a ˋwireless ˳set. ⌐Does it ˏwork?
I 'hear her ˋhusband's ˳died. ⌐Did you ˏknow him?
'Take a °couple of ˋpounds. ⌐Can you ˏspare °that much?
'Will you be °coming ˏround this °evening? ⌐Do you ˏwant me °to?
● We had a ˋsplendid ˳game. ⌐Did you ˏwin, by the °way?
'What about a °game of ˋbilliards? ⌐Have we ˏtime, d'you °think?
The 'third is a ˋhopeless ˳day for me. ⌐Is the ˏtenth any °better?
I 'thought we were °going to the ˋcinema. ⌐Do you ˏreally °want to °go?
She 'says she ˋwill ˳buy it. ⌐Does she ˏmean it, would you °say?
Your 'sister °wants her ˋshoes ˳cleaned. ⌐Do I ˏhave to °clean them °for her?
You 'say the °answer's ʹsix? ⌐Am I misˏtaken, °then?
I'm 'going to °get a ˋprogramme. ⌐Will you bring ˏme one, °please?
'How much do I ˎowe you? ⌐Shall we forˏget a°bout it?

Commands

What a 'miserable ˎday! ⌐Cheer ˏup. ‖ (⌐It'll ˏsoon stop °raining.)
⌐Let ˎme ˳carry it ˳for you. ⌐Look ˏout. ‖ (You ˏalmost ˋdropped it.)
'What shall I do ˋnow, sir? ⌐Con˳tinue. ⌐Go ˏon.
ˋSorry to disˏturb you. ⌐Come ˏin. ⌐Sit ˏdown.
'What do you °think of my °new ˋdress? ⌐Turn ˏround. ‖ ('Very ˋnice, ˳dear.)

Verbal context	*Drill*
What‿ever shall we ˋdo?	‾Don't ˏpanic. ‖ (⌐We'll ˏthink of °something.)
ˏWhat's all the ˋfuss a₀bout?	‾Be ˏcareful. ‖ (⌐You ‿trod on my ˋtoe.)
'Race you to the ˎlamp post.	‾Come ˏon, °then.
'Aren't you ˏready °yet?	‾Don't ˏwait for us. ‖ (We'll 'see you at the ˋtheatre.)
ˇThank you for the ˇparcel.	‾Un₀do it, °then.
'Shall I °press the ˏstarter?	‾Hold ˏhard a °second. ‖ (She's ˏstill in ˋgear.)
The ˇbig key ₀doesn't ₀fit.	‾Try ˏthis one, °then.
● Good'bye for ˏnow.	‾Look ˏafter your°self.
ˏWhat's the ˋmatter?	‾Keep ˏstill a °minute. ‖ (Your 'coat's °caught in the ˋdoor.)
(You're 'standing on my ˋpaper.)	‾Get ₀off it a °minute.
I 'think I'll °have some ˋchocolate.	‾Give ˏme a °bit, °will you?
What ˋhappened?	‾Take it ˏeasy, old °chap. ‖ (You've 'had an ˋaccident.)

Interjections

I've lost 'half a ˋstone.	‾In₀deed! ‖ (ˏWhat's caused ˋthat?)
'Would you °like an ˏorange?	‾Yes, ˏplease. ‾No, ˏthank you.
● Good ˋmorning, ₀David.	‾Hul₀lo, °there. ‖ ('Nice to ˋsee you.)
I'm 'off to ˎbed.	‾Good ˏnight, °dear. ‖ ('Sleep ˏwell.)
● 'You ˎare an ₀idiot.	‾I'm ˏsorry.
I'm ˋleaving │ ˏnow. ‖ ‾Good₀bye.	‾Good ˏday to you.
'See you ˎpresently.	‾So ˏlong, old °chap.
You're an 'old ˎfool.	‾I ˏbeg your °pardon. ‖ (⌐How ˎdare you ₀say ₀that?)
Why, it's Mr. ˋHarris. ‖ How ˋare you?	‾Good ˏevening, Mr. °Howells. ‖ ('Fine, │ ˏthank you.)
That's ˋall │ for to₀day. ‖ 'Call a°gain to₀morrow.	‾Very ˏgood, °madam. ‖ ‾Good ˏmorning.

5 *The Switchback*

Attitude

In STATEMENTS: grudgingly admitting, reluctantly or defensively dissenting, concerned, reproachful, hurt, reserved, tentatively suggesting; (in echoes) greatly astonished.

In QUESTIONS: (in echoes) greatly astonished; otherwise, interested and concerned as well as surprised.

In COMMANDS: urgently warning with a note of reproach or concern.

In INTERJECTIONS: scornful.

Tone marks used in SWITCHBACK drills

A Stressed, accented syllables (Nucleus, Head)
['ˇ'] (i) without Tail: moderately high falling to low and then rising to medium.
     (ii) with Tail: moderately high falling to low pitch; the fall-rise is completed by the tail syllable(s).
['ˈ'] Relatively high level pitch, with any following head syllables forming a descending pitch scale.
[°] Level pitch, varying from medium-high to relatively low and always lower than the *preceding* ['ˈ'] or [°].

B Stressed, unaccented syllables (Tail)
[ₒ] (i) on last syllable: very low rising to medium pitch.
    (ii) otherwise: very low level pitch; the fall-rise is completed by the following unstressed tail syllable(s).

Tune		Fall-Rise+Tail of one syllable

Verbal context	*Drill*

Statements

● I ˌthought they ˈall took ₒone.	ˇAnn ₒdid. ‖ (But the ˇothers ₒdidn't.)
'Didn't °Smith and ˌJones °go?	ˇSmith ₒwent. ‖ (But ˇJones ₒdidn't.)
Can 'Jack and °Bill come to ˌtea?	ˇBill ₒcan. ‖ (But ˇJack ₒcan't.)
Have 'Bob and ˌJane ar°rived?	ˇJane's ₒhere. ‖ (But ˇBob ₒisn't.)
‾D'you ˌboth play °tennis?	ˇI ₒdo. ‖ (But my ˇhusband ₒdoesn't.)

Verbal context	_Drill_
We were 'both on ˎtime, | 'surely.	ˇYou ˳were. || (But your ˇwife ˳wasn't.)
'Blue and °green are 'primary ˳colours, | ˏaren't they?	ˇBlue ˳is. || (But ˇgreen ˳isn't.)
'Don't °books or ˏpictures °interest her?	ˇBooks ˳don't. || (But ˇpictures ˳do.)
'Are things °getting ˏdearer?	ˇSome ˳things. || (But not ˇall.)
D'you 'ever °go to the ˏtheatre?	ˇSometimes. || (But not ˇoften.)
I ˇhave ˳finished, | 'haven't I?	ˇAlmost. || (But not ˇquite.)
But he ˏgot it 'right.	ˇHe ˳did. || (But ˇyou ˳didn't.)
ˇMy as˳sistant | is 'first 'class.	ˇYours ˳is. || (But ˇmine ˳isn't.)
I 'like ˏoysters.	ˇYou ˳may. || (But ˇI ˳certainly ˳don't.)
'Who d'you °think'll conˏtribute?	ˇJane ˳might. ˇJack ˳will. ˇMike ˳should.
'Fruit's quite 'cheap | at the ˏmoment.	ˇPears ˳are. ˇPlums ˳are.
‾Haven't you ˏgot that °paper?	ˇSomewhere.
‾D'you aˏgree with him?	ˇPartly.
'Was the °play ˏgood?	ˇFairly.
Can 'anyone ˏlend me a °copy?	ˇI ˳can't.
ˏThese °matches °won't 'strike.	ˇMine ˳will. ˇMine ˳strike.
I ˇdoubt whether °prices are ˇfalling.	ˇSome ˳are.
Not a 'single °fine 'month | ˏthis °year.	ˇMay ˳was. ˇJune ˳was.
I 'don't think she's at 'all ˳nice.	ˇI ˳do. ˇJohn ˳does. ˇTim ˳does.
I 'think it's a dis'grace.	ˇI ˳don't. ˇWe ˳don't.
I 'wonder why °nobody ˏcalled on them.	ˇWatts ˳did. ˇCook ˳did. ˇTed ˳called. ˇBill ˳called.
'Can you °finish it toˏday?	ˇHardly. ˇScarcely.
You 'promised it for 'Saturday.	ˇMonday. ˇThursday. ˇSunday. ˇTuesday.
He 'comes from 'Liverpool.	ˇNorwich. ˇCambridge. ˇSheffield. ˇBristol. ˇReading.
'What's in the ˏbag? || ˊPlums?	ˇCherries. ˇApples. ˇPeaches.
● His 'name's 'John.	ˇHarry. ˇGordon. ˇDesmond.
Her 'name's 'Ann, | ˏisn't it?	ˇMargaret. ˇMabel. ˇKitty.
'Nobody can ˳come.	ˇJohn ˳can. ˇI ˳can.
'Nobody's ˳going.	ˇJones ˳might. ˇWe ˳might.
'Nobody at˳tended the ˳meeting.	ˇSmith ˳went. ˇMax ˳did.
'Don't °tread on °Mummy's 'flowers.	ˇYou ˳did.
‾Hulˏlo, °everyone.	ˇYou're ˳late. || (ˏWhere have you 'been?)
'Shall I °go or ˏshan't I?	ˇI ˳would. ˇI ˳should. ˇI'd ˳go.

Verbal context	*Drill*
('Are you ˌthere, °Peter?)	ˇJohn's ₀here.
('Hurry ˌup, °there.)	ˇBell's ₀gone.
('Can you ˌhear me, °dear?)	ˇTea ₀time.
[Attracting someone's attention]	ˇArchie. ˇLeslie. ˇJulia.
'Can you °sell me aˌnother °copy?	ˇSorry. ‖ (They've 'all ˋgone.)
● He's ˋnever been ₀late.	ˇNever? ‖ (⌐Are you ˌsure?)
She 'only °gave me ˋseven.	ˇSeven? ‖ (I ˌthought it was ˋten, │ at ˋleast.)
They're 'very ˌsorry aˌbout it.	ˇSorry? ‖ (Is ˇthat ₀all?)
It's ˋPeter's ₀fault.	ˇPeter's? ‖ (ˌHow's ˋthat?)
They ˋlost it, I'm aˌfraid.	ˇLost it? ‖ (ˋHow?)
ˋMake him ₀pay.	ˇMake him? ‖ (ˌYou tell me ˋhow.)
ˋYou must ₀pay for it.	ˇI ₀must? ‖ (ˌWhat ˋwith?)
He's 'coming °next ˋweek.	ˇNext ₀week? ‖ ('Not the week ˌafter °next?)

WH-Questions

● 'Which one's ˋmine?	ˇWhich one? ‖ (That ˋblue one, │ ˋsurely.)
● ˇThat's ₀yours, │ 'over ˋthere.	ˇWhich one? ‖ (ˇNot that ˇblue ₀horror?)
'Who °paid for the ˋbeer?	ˇWho ₀paid? ‖ (ˋI did, │ of ˌcourse.)
ˋPeter ₀paid for the ₀beer.	ˇWho ₀paid? ‖ (ˇSurely not ˇPeter?)
'Which °route d'you sugˋgest?	ˇWhich ₀route? ‖ (The 'A ˋ5, │ ˋnaturally.)
'Take the °A ˋ5.	ˇWhich ₀route? ‖ (ˇNot the °A ˇ5?)
It cost 'over °ten ˋpounds.	ˇHow ₀much? ‖ (As 'much as ˌthat?)
She's been 'gone an ˋhour or ₀more.	ˇHow ₀long? ‖ ('Over an ˌhour?)
About 'three ˌmiles it ₀was.	ˇHow ₀far? ‖ (ˌMore than ˌthat, │ ˌwasn't it?)
ˋJane ₀made them.	ˇWho ₀did? ‖ ('Don't you mean ˌJill?)
That's ˋTony's ₀painting.	ˇWho's ₀painting? ‖ (ˇTony's? ‖ ˋSurely ₀not!)

Yes-No Questions

● ⌐Is it ˌdifficult?	ˇIs it? ‖ (ˇNot ˇhalf!)
● It's toˋmorrow he ₀leaves.	ˇIs it? ‖ (⌐Are you ˌsure?)
'Can she °speak ˌFrench?	ˇCan she? ‖ (ˇI'll ₀say!)
She can 'play ˋany ₀day.	ˇCan she? ‖ (⌐Isn't she ˌworking at °all °now?)

Verbal context	*Drill*
Did 'John 'like it?	ˇDid he? ‖ (He was 'mad a₀bout it.)
'John 'loved it.	ˇDid he? ‖ (I ˏthought he'd 'hate it.)
I ˇthink I shall be ₀free.	ˇWill you? ‖ (‾No com∕mittee °meeting?)
'I'd 'certainly a₀gree.	ˇWould you? ‖ (What on ˏearth 'for?)
I 'can't under'stand it.	ˇCan't you? ‖ (It's ˇsimple, │ ˇreally.)
They 'aren't 'members any ₀more.	ˇAren't they? ‖ (Since 'when?)

Commands

ˇCatch me, ₀Daddy.	ˇSteady. ‖ (You'll ˏhave me 'over.)
'I'll take ˏthis ₀pile of ₀plates.	ˇCareful. ‖ (They're ˎrather ˇheavy.)
'Daddy. ‖ 'Daddy. ‖ 'What d'you think's 'happened?	ˇSlowly.
(We'll 'cross the °road ˏhere.)	ˇQuickly.
(I 'can't °hear what he's 'saying.)	ˇQuiet.
● I'll 'dump the °suitcases ˏhere.	ˇGently. ‖ (They're ˎnot made of ˇiron.)
(You'll 'miss your 'train.)	ˇHurry.
(That ˇmilk's nearly ₀boiling.)	ˇWatch it.
(You're 'driving on a °flat 'tyre.)	ˇHold it.
(I've 'got my 'hands ₀full.)	ˇHelp me.
You're 'due in at 'ten, │ ˏaren't you?	ˇMeet me. ‖ ('There's a ₀good ˏchap.)
(The 'dog's ₀running a₀way.)	ˇCatch him. ˇStop him.
I 'don't °like the 'look of them.	ˇTry them. ‖ (It's the 'least you can ₀do.)
● I've found a 'four °leafed 'clover.	ˇShow me.
('That's your 'bus.)	ˇRun, ₀John.

Tune **Fall-Rise+Tail of more than one syllable**

Statements

'Can you °play ˏchess?	ˇOnce I ₀could. ‖ (But I 'haven't °played for 'ages.)
I 'think they'd 'all a₀gree.	ˇStephen ₀would. ‖ (But the ˇothers, │ 'no.)
● 'Have you ˏfinished?	ˇPractically.
But you ˏaren't 'free on ₀Sundays.	ˇUsually I'm ₀not. ‖ (But ˇthis ₀week, │ I 'am.)

Verbal context	*Drill*
˅You can ₀manage ₀Fridays, ǀ ˏcan't you?	˅Normally I ₀can. ǁ (But 'this °week's ˋhopeless.)
⁻D'you 'change your °book ˏevery °week?	˅Generally I ₀do.
Do 'you and °Mary like ˏgin?	˅I ₀like it. ǁ (But I ˋcan't °answer for ˅Mary.)
I ˋhope you °haven't ˅paid ₀for them.	˅I ₀haven't. ǁ (But my ˅wife ₀may have.)
It's a ˅good ₀plan, ǀ ˏisn't it?	˅We ₀think so.
⁻Will you ˏboth °see him to°morrow?	˅I might ₀see him. ǁ (But ˅John ₀certainly ₀won't.)
Then 'do we °all aˏgree to the °scheme?	˅I've got ₀nothing a₀gainst it.
What de'pressing ˎcities we ₀saw!	˅Manchester was ₀pretty ₀miserable. ǁ (But ˅London ₀wasn't ₀bad.)
What a 'fine ˎbook it ₀was!	˅Parts of it were ₀fairly ₀interesting. ǁ (But it was 'too ˋlong.)
Do 'you write ˏnovels?	˅Part of the ₀time I do.
What a 'lovely week˷end it ₀was!	˅Saturday was ₀all ₀right.
'What sort of ˎholiday did you ₀have?	˅Some of it ₀wasn't ₀bad.
⁻Doesn't ˏanyone °want to do the °crossword?	˅I wouldn't ₀mind having a ₀try.
● ˅I didn't ₀say you were ₀wrong.	˅You ₀didn't. ǁ ˅Tom did ₀though.
But ˏPeter's ˋquite ₀satisfied.	˅Peter's ₀satisfied. ǁ ˅I'm not ₀though.
'Could we ˋborrow a ₀typewriter?	˅That's a ₀possi₀bility.
'Who d'you °think'll con°tribute?	˅Harry ₀might give us ₀something.
What a 'foul °cup of ˎcoffee!	˅Mine's all ₀right.
I ˏthought you °didn't °drink at ˋall.	˅Sometimes I ₀do.
ˋNone of them was ₀any ₀good.	˅John's ₀wasn't too ₀bad.
'Don't be so ˎnervous.	˅You're a ₀fine one to ₀talk.
So you ˏall °thought him ˋguilty.	˅I didn't ₀think he was.
I'm ˋsorry about the ˏmess.	˅You ₀couldn't ₀help it.
'Let's ask that °fellow over ˋthere.	˅He won't ₀know what's ₀happened.
We saw some deˋlightful ₀places.	˅Bradford was ₀pretty ₀terrible.
What a 'dull ˎbook!	˅Parts of it were ₀fairly ₀interesting.
You ˋmust be ₀able to ₀see through it. ǁ It's ˋglass.	˅All ₀glass ₀isn't trans₀parent.
He's from ˋBath.	˅Coventry. ˅Devonport. ˅Newcastle.
She ar'rived to`day.	˅Yesterday. ˅Saturday.
ˏNobody ˋever ₀writes to her.	˅Bobby ₀does.

Verbal context	*Drill*
● ˋJack was ₒfirst.	˅George, you ₒmean.
Only a ˋfew are ₒgoing, │ ˏaren't they?	˅Everybody. ˋAll of them.
So you're ˏsaying he's disˋhonest.	˅That's not ₒwhat I ₒmean.
I 'can't find a °carpet I ˋlike.	˅Here's one that ₒmight ₒdo.
'Aren't these °apples ˏsour!	˅Some of them are ₒall ₒright.
ˏWhy didn't you disˋcuss the ₒmatter?	˅Talking wouldn't have ₒbeen any ₒgood.
ˋNobody ₒlikes my ₒcakes.	˅I ₒlike them.
It 'can't be ˏdone.	˅Frank might ₒmanage it.
That's 'just what ˋJones ₒsaid.	˅Robinson ₒsaid it.
But there'll be 'no-one to ˋmeet him.	˅I shall ₒbe at the ₒstation.
We made an ˋexcellent ₒjob of it, │ ˋdidn't we?	˅You ₒdidn't do ₒmuch toₒwards it.
What a 'terrible ˏpainting!	˅Adrian ₒdoesn't ₒthink it's ₒterrible.
'When will °Tom be ˋback?	˅I don't ₒknow. ‖ (ˏWhy not °ask ˋTom?)
'Why not °try ˋvarnishing it?	˅That's ₒno ₒgood.
'Where on °earth does he ˋlive?	˅You ₒought to ₒknow.
ˋIsn't he a ₒnice ₒfellow!	˅You may ₒthink he's ₒall ₒright.
I shall have a 'good ˏrow with him.	˅That won't ₒget you ₒvery ₒfar.
He's an 'old ˏfool.	˅That's not a ₒvery ₒnice thing to ₒsay.
¯I ˏdidn't ˋdo it.	˅Lying won't ₒget you ₒanywhere.
The 'whole thing's °quite a ˋmystery.	˅Somebody must ₒknow who ₒdid it.
'Guess ˋwhat. ‖ I 'scored a ˋgoal.	˅One goal's ₒnothing to get exₒcited about.
(There's 'still this °problem of the ˋmoney.)	˅Something's ₒgot to be ₒdone about it.
ˏDon't just ˏstand there. ‖ ˋHelp me.	˅I ₒcan't do ₒanything aₒbout it.
'What ˏsalary d'you exₒpect to ₒget?	˅Money isn't the ₒonly considerₒation.
('Will you be ˏlong °dear?)	˅Tom's arₒrived.
(Are you 'sure you can afˏford it?)	˅Pay day's a ₒlong way ₒoff.
('Have you °started ˏsaving °yet?)	˅Christmas'll ₒsoon be ₒhere.
(Have you 'said anything to ˏTed °yet?)	˅Someone'll ₒhave to ₒbreak it to him.
('Are your ˏhands °clean, °Johnnie?)	˅Dinner's ₒready.
('Look ˏout.)	˅Teacher's ₒcoming.
'Just °my ˏluck!	˅Moaning ₒisn't going to ₒhelp matters.
'Could you °sell me aˏnother °pineapple?	˅Sorry, sir. ‖ (They've 'all ˋgone.)
'How much ˏlonger are you ₒgoing to ₒbe?	˅Coming, ₒdear.
'Isn't it ˏwonderful!	˅Wonderful? ‖ (ˏWhat's ˋwonderful aₒbout it?)

Verbal context	*Drill*
'See you on ˎSaturday.	˅Saturday? ‖ (˅Friday, you ˳mean, │ ˏdon't you?)
They 'live in ˋManchester.	˅Manchester? ‖ (You mean ˅Liverpool, │ ˏdon't you?)
She 'went home ˋyesterday.	˅Yesterday? ‖ (‾Not on ˏTuesday?)
The 'Browns were ˋvery ˳good at it.	˅Both ˳of them? ‖ (ˋOnly ˅Fred, │ ˋsurely!)
I was ˏonly ˳two hours ˏlate.	˅Two hours ˳late? ‖ (ˋNearly ˅three, it ˳was.)
● She's ˏonly ˳twenty ˏseven.	˅Twenty ˳seven? ‖ (˅Thirty ˳seven, more ˳likely.)
'Alison's ˋvery ˳keen on it.	˅Alison ˳is? ‖ (Are you 'sure it's not ˏAlice?)

WH-Questions

'Why d'you put ˋup with it?	˅Why ˳do I? ‖ (I ˏhaven't much ˋchoice.)
'How's ˋArthur?	˅How ˳is he? ‖ (As ˏtiresome as ˋever.)
'Where did he ˋbuy them?	˅Where did he ˳buy them? ‖ (At the ˋsuper-market, │ of ˏcourse.)
I've 'just seen ˋMarjorie.	˅Who, did you ˳say? ‖ (˅Marjorie?)
She goes 'twice a ˎweek.	˅How ˳often? ‖ (˅Twice, did you ˳say?)
He 'asked for ˋtwenty.	˅How ˳many? ‖ (ˋNot ˅twenty, │ ˋsurely!)
That's ˋPeter's ˳programme.	˅Whose ˳programme? ‖ (ˋNot old °Peter ˅Harrison's?)
I 'come from ˋExeter.	˅Where d'you ˳come from? ‖ (˅Exeter?)
ˋRubbish!	˅What did you ˳say! ‖ (˅Rubbish?)
He 'called me a ˋliar.	˅What did he ˳call you? ‖ (‾A ˏliar?)
ˋJohn's the ˳culprit.	˅Who did you ˳say was to ˳blame? ‖ (ˋSurely not ˅John?)
● They 'said they °sent it last ˋMonday.	˅When did they ˳say they ˳sent it? ‖ (Last ˅Monday?)

Yes-No Questions

● He 'couldn't ˎhelp them.	˅Couldn't he? ‖ (Why ˏever ˋnot?)
They 'needn't ˋpay, │ ˏthis °time.	˅Needn't they? ‖ (ˏWho ˋsaid so?)
I 'didn't °get there in ˋtime.	˅Didn't you? ‖ (Well ˏwhat °kept you to-ˋday?)
You ˳mustn't say 'anything a ˎbout it.	˅Mustn't I? ‖ (ˏWhat's so ˋsecret a˳bout it?)

Verbal context	*Drill*

He'd ˇlike to ₒplay. | ˇWill he, ₒthough?
He was aˈfraid he'd °fall ˋdown. | ˇDid he fall ₒdown?
She's alˈready ˋgot one, she ₒsaid. | ˇHad she ₒgot one, in fact?
We ˈthought they'd °given ˋup. | ˇHad they ₒgiven ₒup, in fact?

Commands

(ˈDaddy's aˋsleep.) | ˇQuietly.
● I ˈfeel I could ˋscream. | ˇSteady, ₒthere.
ˌAll ˌright. ‖ I'm ˌjust ˌgoing. | ˇMove yourₒself.
(You're in ˈtoo much of a ˋhurry.) | ˇWait ₒfor it.
● I ˇhope I don't ˇbreak ₒanything. | ˇTry ₒnot to.
(ˈThat °vase is ˋvaluable.) | ˇCareful ₒwith it.
ˈGo and °boil your ˌhead. | ˇGently, ₒMary.
(It's ˇyour ₒturn.) | ˇHurry, ₒPeter.

Tune **Fall-Rise only**

Statements

Do ˈyou aˌgree with him? | ˇYes. ‖ (ˇUp to a ˇpoint.)
● You ˇwon't ₒtell him, | ˋwill you? | ˇNo. ‖ (But ˇvery reˇluctantly.)
You ˇwill ₒplay, | ˋwon't you? | ˇWell. ‖ (I must ˋthink aₒbout it.)
But you ˋpromised me a ₒpair. | ˇTrue. ‖ (But I ˇdidn't say ˇwhen.)
ˈAre there any ˌnails in the °box? | ˇSome. ‖ (If ˈnot very ˋmany.)
ˈWhen are you °moving ˋin? | ˇSoon. ‖ (Though I ˈcan't °name the ˌday.)
Was it ˈtwins | or ˌtriplets? | ˇTwins. ‖ (We ˇmustn't exˇaggerate.)
ˈIs your °new dress ˌred | or ˋblue? | ˇRed. ‖ (I ˌthought you ˋknew.)
ˈIsn't °Ann ^plain! | ˇPlain. ‖ (But ˇvery ˇlively.)
That was a ˈvery °neat ˌplan. | ˇNeat. ‖ (But ˇquite unˇscrupulous.)
It's ˋhot, | ˋisn't it? | ˇHot. ‖ (But ˋpleasant.)
I ˈthought this was ˋwood. ‖ What ˋis it? | ˇWood. ‖ (But ˋcovered with ˋplastic.)
He's a Conˋservative, | ˋisn't he? | ˇNo.
ˈYou weren't ˋthere, | ˌwere you? | ˇYes.
● It's ˋblack. | ˇWhite. ˇPink. ˇGreen. ˇMauve.
There were ˋseven ₒboys ₒthere. | ˇSix. ˇEight. ˇNine. ˇTen.

Verbal context	*Drill*
'This is ˋHilda's ₒbook.	ˇMine. ˇFrank's. ˇJack's. ˇTom's.
[Attracting attention]	ˇJohn. ˇTom. ˇMark. ˇAnn. ˇPat. ˇMax. ˇFred.
ˋYou must deₒcide.	ˇMe? ‖ (ˏWhy not ˋAlbert?)
It's ˋblue, I ₒthink.	ˇBlue? ‖ (It ˋcan't be, ǀ ˏcan it?)
You 'ought to leave ˋnow.	ˇNow? ‖ (ˇSo ₒsoon?)
They've 'just had ˋtwins.	ˇTwins? ‖ (ˇReally? ‖ You're ˇnot ˇjoking?)
The 'play's quite ˋfun.	ˇFun? ‖ (ˉIt's an ˌabsolute ˋriot.)
'Rather ˋwarm, don't you ₒthink?	ˇWarm? ‖ (It's ˋboiling.)
● They're ˋvery ˏnice.	ˇNice? ‖ (You're ^joking!)

WH-Questions

'Who'll play the ˋcello ₒpart?	ˇWho? ‖ (ˋAndrew, you ₒidiot!)
I've 'just seen °Pablo ˋAron.	ˇWho? ‖ (The ˇcellist?)
'Where's he arˏriving?	ˇWhere? ‖ (ˋTilbury, ǀ of ˏcourse.)
● He's arˋriving at ˏDover.	ˇWhere? ‖ (ˋDon't you mean ˏNew°haven?)
'When's the °next ˋconcert?	ˇWhen? ‖ (On ˋThursday, ǀ ˋsurely!)
The 'concert's on ˋFriday.	ˇWhen? ‖ (ˇFriday? ‖ D'you ˇmean ₒthat?)

Commands

● What's ˋup, ₒTom?	ˇMind. ‖ (There's a ˋstep ǀ ˏhere.)
(You'll 'miss the ˋbus.)	ˇRun.
(ˋHold my ˏparcel ₒfor me.)	ˇQuick.
I 'don't think I can ˋdo it.	ˇTry.
'Can I °give you a ˏhand?	ˇPlease.
('Say good°bye to ˏGranny.)	ˇWave.

Tune   **Low Pre-Head+Fall-Rise (+Tail)**

or

Verbal context	*Drill*

Statements

I sup'pose you're °working ˋall the ₒtime. | On ˇweek ₒdays. ‖ (But on ˇSundays, │ I'm ˋfree.)

● 'Is it °going to keep ˏfine? | I ˇthink ₒso. ‖ (But I'm 'not ˋcertain.)

I 'thought you °played ˋfootball. | I ˇused ₒto. ‖ (But aˇlas, │ no ˋlonger.)

'Will he reˏcover, d'you °think? | I ˇhope ₒso. ‖ (But he's ˇvery ˇill.)

But ˇsurely the °house is ˇlarge eₒnough. | It's ˇlarge eₒnough. ‖ (But ˇterribly negˇlected.)

'What d'you °think of my ˋsuit? | The ˇcolour's all ₒright. ‖ (But the 'fit's aˋtrocious.)

It's ˋdifficult, │ ˋisn't it? | It's ˇdifficult all ₒright. ‖ (But we'll ˇmanage ˇsomehow.)

Is 'this the °best you've ˏgot? | There ˇmight be a ₒbetter one ₒsomewhere. ‖ But I ˇdoubt it.

‾Do ˏyou a°gree, °Mitchell? | I ˇthink the ₒcourse you sugₒgest would be ₒbest. ‖ (But I'd 'like to ˇthink about it.)

Can I 'come and °see him toˏmorrow? | You can ˇcome. ‖ (But you ˇwon't ˇsee him. ‖ He'll be ˋout.)

'Can I °help with those ˏletters? | You can ˇtype them if you ₒlike.

You ˇwill ₒstay, │ ˋwon't you? | If you inˇsist, I ₒwill.

'Can I have the °afternoon ˏoff? | As far as ˇI'm conₒcerned you ₒcan.

Can you de'lay it a °bit ˏlonger? | Well ˇyes. ‖ (If it's ˇreally ˇnecessary.)

‾Is this ˏyour °copy? ‖ ‾Can I ˏborrow it? | It ˇis ₒmine. ‖ (But I 'still ˋneed it, I'm aₒfraid.)

He 'doesn't ˋwant it, │ ˋdoes he? | No ˇhe ₒdoesn't. ‖ But his ˇbrother ₒmay.

I'm ˇpositive he'll ₒturn ₒup. | Well ˇmaybe you're ₒright.

‾Can't ˏanyone °meet the °train? | Well ˇI might ₒmanage it.

'Couldn't you take the °day ˏoff? | It ˇmight be ₒpossible.

'Aren't these °apples ˏterrible! | The ˇbig ones ₒaren't much ₒgood.

‾You ˏcan play on °Saturday, │ ˏcan't you? | I ˇthink that perₒhaps I ₒcan.

'What a ˏnuisance he ₒwas, ₒbeing so ₒlate! | He was ˇlate. ‖ (But it ˇdidn't ˇmatter ₒvery ₒmuch.)

● 'Is he °tall and ˏdark? | Well he's ˇtall. ‖ (But I ˇshouldn't °call him ˇdark.)

ˏMust I °go by °train? | You don't ˇhave ₒto. ‖ (But it's ˇmuch ˇquicker.)

Verbal context	*Drill*
ˇI ͺsay | the 'scheme's °much too amˋbi-tious.	Well that's ˇone way of ͺlooking at it.
What ˋelse could he have ͺdone?	I supˇpose he ͺhad no ͺother ͺchoice.
I'm ˋsure he ͺwon't apͺply for the ͺjob.	It's not very ˇprobable. || (But it's ˈjust ˇpossible.)
You 'don't look ˋwell.	I ˇfeel ͺwell.
ˋPlease don't ͵go yet.	I ˇought ͺto. I really ˇought ͺto.
ˉShe ͵doesn't ͵mean it, | ͵does she?	She ˇmay ͺdo. She ˇmight.
But you ˋnever ͺlose your ͺtemper.	Ocˇcasionally I ͺdo.
The 'tarts have °all ˋgone, | ͵haven't they?	There ˇmight be ͺone more ͺleft.
'Shall I come °in by the ͵front °door?	Your ˇshoes aren't ͺvery ͺclean.
'Nothing °went at ˋall ͺright.	The ˇweather ͺmight have been ͺworse.
ˋWhat a ͺmiserable ͺcrowd they ͺwere!	Your ˇsister ͺseemed quite ͺcheerful.
We're ˋbound to ͺwin.	Your ˇpartner's ͺnot so ͺconfident.
But ˇJack'll ͺhelp, | ͵won't he?	It's unˇlikely.
ˇYou can ͺplay, | ˋcan't you, ͺJohn?	I don't ˇthink ͺso.
'Are you °spending the ͵night °there?	I hadn't ˇthought of ͺdoing so.
And 'now he °wants the °day ˋoff.	It seems a ˇreasonable reͺquest.
He's a 'good Prime ˋMinister.	The Oppoˇsition don't ͺthink so.
I can 'do it on ˋMonday.	You ˇcan't. No you ˇcan't, ͺJohn.
● It ͵didn't ͺtake you ͵long.	It ˇdid. It ˇdid, you ͺknow.
Is your 'birthday on the ͵fourth?	The ˇfifth. The ˇsixth.
'Fred's in the ˋgarden.	He ˇisn't. || (I've ˋlooked.)
You ˇhaven't ˇtold him, | ˋhave you?	I ˇhave, you ͺknow.
I 'play °golf °rather ˋwell.	You ˇthink you ͺdo.
That's ˋJohn's ͺbook.	It's ˇAntony's.
You 'promised it for this ˋmorning.	Toˇmorrow ͺmorning. For ˇWednesday ͺmorning.
You 'said you °wanted a ˋpostal ͺorder.	A ˇmoney ͺorder. Some ˇstamps.
But he ͵wasn't at ˋhome.	He ˇwas at ͺhome, you know.
͵You had ͵all of it.	A ˇpart of it, you ͺmean.
You're ͵not going to ͵buy him one, | ˋsurely.	I'd ˇthought of ͺdoing so.
'Jill came ˋearly | toͺday.	She was ˇlate.
She's 'emigrating to ˋCanada.	To Ausˇtralia. To South ˇAfrica. To the ˇStates.
The 'meeting's in ˋhere, | ͵isn't it?	In the ˇCouncil ͺRoom, sir.

Verbal context	Drill
He rang 'promptly at ˌten.	It was ˇpast ˳ten oˈclock.
She 'keeps it in the ˋgarden ˳shed.	In the ˇgreenhouse, I ˳think you'll ˳find.
'Going by ʹbus?	No I'm ˇwalking ˳there toˈmorrow.
You 'said he was °coming this ˋmorning.	I said toˇnight. I said this ˇevening.
He 'lives in ˌBirmingham.	You mean in ˇNottingham.
What a 'pretty °blue ˌdress she was ˳wearing!	It was a ˇblack ˳dress she had ˳on.
ˇI ˳won't ˳do it. ‖ 'Nor will ˋBill.	Well ˇone of you will ˳have to ˳do it.
I'll 'let you °have a ˌdozen.	A ˇdozen ˳isn't ˳very ˳many.
I ˌjust °don't ˈwant to ˳sing.	But you ˇpromised you ˳would.
I 'couldn't be °more ˌcross.	Getting ˇangry won't ˳help matters.
This piˈano's out of ˋtune.	The piˇano's ˳all ˳right.
'Let's °form a comˌmittee.	A comˇmittee's ˳no ˳good.
'Liz says she °can't ˋdo it.	If she ˇwanted to, she ˳could.
I'll 'ask the proˋfessor.	The proˇfessor's ˳not the ˳man to ˳ask.
(I ˇcan't put my ˇfinger on the ˳trouble.)	But there's ˇsomething that's ˳not ˳quite ˳right.
How ˋcould he ˳let you ˳know? ‖ Your ˋphone wasn't ˳working.	He could have ˇwritten. He could have ˇwired.
‾Did you ˌmind him °coming to °tea?	You might have ˇwarned me.
'What can I °do to ˈmend ˳matters?	You could aˇpologise.
I'm 'going on the °greasy ˋpole.	You'll ˇfall.
(ˇCareful.)	Your ˇchair's ˳slipping.
('Hurry ˌup, °dear.)	Your ˇtoast's getting ˳cold.
ˌWhat did you °say, °Muriel?	Your ˇtaxi's ˳waiting.
I ˌgave him a ˈpound to ˳pay the ˳bill.	A ˇpound ˳won't be eˌnough.
I ˌdon't need a ˌjacket, ǀ ˌdo I?	You'll catch ˇcold.
[Attracting attention]	Mrs. Barˇtholomew. I say, ˇJoan.
● 'Should I or ˌshouldn't I ˳play?	You'd enˇjoy the ˳game.
We simply 'must conˋvince him.	It'll be ˇdifficult, you ˳know.
Can I 'finish °reading the ˌpaper?	We shall be ˇlate.
'Let me °carry your ˌsuitcase °for you.	You'll find it ˇheavy.
I'm ˋsorry I ˳broke the ˌwindow.	You'll have to ˇpay ˳for it.
I'm 'taking ˋJoy ˳out ǀ toˌnight.	She's an exˇtravagant ˳little ˳minx.
● 'Give me aˌnother one, ˳please.	I'm ˇsorry. ‖ (But 'that's imˈpossible.)
'Will you ˌjoin us?	I'd ˇlike ˳to. ‖ (But I'm aˈfraid I ˋcan't.)
'Must you ˌgo?	I'm aˇfraid ˳so.

Verbal context	*Drill*
You ˇwill ˳stay, │ ˋwon't you?	Well we'd ˇlike to ˳stay. ‖ (But we ˋcan't.)
⁻Did you aˎgree?	Aˇgree? ‖ (ˎWhat do ˋyou ˳think?)
I 'put it up'stairs.	Upˇstairs? ‖ (Why ˋthere, of ˳all ˳places?)
It's im'possible.	Imˇpossible? ‖ (ˎHow d'you ˋmean?)
You must a'pologise.	Aˇpologise? ‖ (What on ˎearth ˋfor?)
'I'll go if ˎyou go.	If ˇI ˳go? ‖ (But ˎhow ˋcan I?)
With ˇJack's ˳help │ we could ˋmanage it.	With ˇJack's ˳help? ‖ (But he ˋwon't ˳help. ‖ I've alˎready ˋasked him.)
It 'must be ˳right.	It ˇmust be? ‖ (ˎHow d'you ˋknow?)
● 'Ring me to°morrow afterˎnoon.	Toˇmorrow ˳afterˎnoon? ‖ (ˎWhy to-ˋmorrow?)

WH-Questions

'How °far to 'Ipswich?	How ˇfar? ‖ (Oh, 'twenty °miles at ˋleast.)
'How °many d'you ˋneed?	How ˇmany? ‖ (As 'many as I can °lay my ˋhands on.)
What ˋis it?	What ˇis it? ‖ ('Don't you ˎknow?)
Well, where ˋwere your ˳boots?	Where ˇwere they? ‖ (In the ˋbathroom, of ˳all ˳places.)
● 'Why °wouldn't he ˋbuy it?	Why ˇwouldn't he? ‖ ('No ^money!)
You can 'stay till ˎFriday.	Till ˇwhen? ‖ (You mean ˇSaturday, ˳don't you?)
'Let's ˋwalk ˳there.	How ˇfar ˳is it? ‖ (Not ˇtoo ˳far, I ˳hope.)
They ˋmust be ˳here, │ ˇsomewhere.	Well, where ˇare they, ˳then?
She 'wants some ˋchalk.	How ˇmuch does she ˳want? ‖ (We ˋhaven't much ˇleft.)
ˇWait ˳for me, │ ˋwon't you?	How ˇlong'll you ˳be? ‖ (I'm 'meeting ˋJoan │ at ˎsix.)
'Seen my ˎhat °anywhere? ‖ I've ˋlost it.	What ˇcolour ˳is it?
He's an 'utter ˎliar.	On what ˇgrounds d'you ˳say that? ‖ (Re-'markably ˋtruthful, │ ˇI've always ˳found him.)
He's 'come about the ˋcensus.	About ˇwhat, did you ˳say? ‖ (⁻The ˎcen-sus? ‖ ˋWhat ˳census?)
He'll be 'here by ˎsix, he ˳said.	By ˇwhat time, did you ˳say? ‖ (ˇSix? ‖ ˋNot before ˇthat?)

Verbal context	*Drill*
You ˏhave got a °Johnson °working here, | ˏhaven't you?	In which deˇpartment d'you ₒthink he ₒworks?
'What made you °try at the ˋstationer's?	Well, where ˇelse could I have ₒfound one?
You 'say you don't ˏknow any °Smiths in the °road?	Well, what ˇnumber are you °wanting?

Yes-No Questions

'Has she ˏtold them?	Has she ˇtold them? || (ˋCourse not. || It was ˏconfiˋdential.)
⎺Were you surˏprised?	Was ˇI surₒprised? || (ˋNot ˇhalf!)
Is it 'possible?	Is it ˇpossible? || (It's 'got to be.)
'Only a ˏdozen he ₒwanted.	Is that ˇall? || (ˏNot °worth the ˋtrouble.)
'Let's °use ˏEric's.	Does it ˇwork ₒnow? || (It 'didn't the ˇlast time we ₒtried it.)
But he's alˏready ˋgone.	Are you ˇsure? || (He'd 'wait for me, he ₒsaid.)
⎺Can I ˏlend you a °copy?	Have you ˇgot one? || (You 'hadn't when I °wanted one beˇfore.)
But I ˏhaven't ˋgot a ₒdinner ₒjacket.	Couldn't you ˇhire one?
Of ˋcourse it's ₒgood enough.	D'you ˇthink ₒso? || (ˇReally?)
I'll ˋgive it ₒto you.	D'you ˇmean ₒthat? || (ˇSeriously?)
I don't ˇwant to ₒask them.	Well, d'you ˇhave to? || (We can ˏmanage on our ˏown, °can't we?)
Oh, ˏthis one'll ˏdo.	Is it ˇlarge eₒnough? || (I 'wouldn't have ˇthought ₒso.)
He's 'said he's ˇsorry.	Does he ˇmean it, ₒthough? || (He a'polo-gises very ˇreadily.)
'Let's °sit ˏhere.	Shall we ˇsee from ₒhere? || (I 'rather ˇdoubt it.)
She 'said she'd °vote for ˋJohn.	Yes, but ˇwill she, in ₒfact? || (It 'seems un-ˇlikely.)
We 'haven't re°minded ˇJames.	Does it ˇmatter about ₒthat? || (We 'don't ˇneed him toₒday.)
'How about °six o'ˋclock?	Can you ˇget here by ₒthen? || (You're ˋworking, | ˏaren't you, | till ˏfive?)
'What about °giving it to ˋFrank?	Does he ˇneed it, d'you ₒthink? || ('Hasn't he ˏgot °several?)

Verbal context	*Drill*

Commands

I ˅shan't ˅manage it.
Well, ˅try.

I'm 'going to get ˅rid of it.
Oh, ˅don't. ‖ (You may ˅need it a₀gain.)

˅You have a ₀go at it.
Well, ˅mind. ‖ (You're ˏstanding °in the ˅way.)

I 'can't ac˟cept your ₀invi₀tation.
Oh, ˅do. ‖ (˅Please.)

I'm going 'right to the ˏtop.
Be ˅careful.

● ⌐May I 'just °finish my ˏletter?
Be ˅quick, ₀then.

'Come ˏon. ‖ 'Let's be ˅off.
Hold ˅hard a ₀second. ‖ (ˏWhere's ˅Francis?)

'May I °use the ˏcar?
Well, take ˅care. ‖ (The ˅roads are °terribly ˅icy.)

(He's 'tried that °trick be˅fore.)
So be˅ware.

What'ever made me ˅do such a ₀thing?
Oh, don't ˅worry a₀bout it. ‖ (It could ˏhappen to ˅anyone.)

(You 'must °call at ˏHeal's.)
Now re˅member.

I 'don't think we ˏought to.
Oh, yes, ˅let's.

Don't 'ever °ask me a₀gain.
Now be ˅reasonable.

● ⌐May I ˏhold it for a °minute?
Well, be ˅careful ₀with it.

(That's 'all the °sugar we've ˅got.)
So go ˅easy ₀with it.

(He's ˅not very ˅bright.)
So be ˅patient ₀with him.

Note: All the drills given above with the tune

LOW PRE-HEAD+FALL–RISE (+TAIL)

can be said with emphasis if the low pre-head is replaced by the high pre-head (see Chapter I, p. 36. With this feature marked, the last drill in this section would read

⌐So be ˅patient ₀with him.

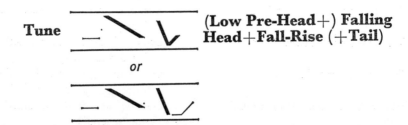

Tune   **(Low Pre-Head+) Falling Head+Fall-Rise (+Tail)**

or

Verbal context	*Drill*
Statements	
● D'you 'smoke?	I ˅do ˅sometimes. ‖ But ˅never before ˅lunch.
Can we 'smoke during ˏlectures?	It's ˅not for˅bidden. ‖ But we ˅don't ˅usually.
‾She ˎis a ₒpretty ₒgirl, │ ˏisn't she?	She has a ˅lovely ˅face. ‖ (But her 'figure's ˅terrible.)
'Are you °using the ˏruler?	˅Not at the ˅moment. ‖ But I ˅may want it °later ˅on.
ˎWhy did you ˅go there?	˅None of us ˅wanted ₒto. ‖ (But we 'felt we ˅had to.)
'Will you °come to ˏdinner this °evening?	I ˅will if I ˅can. ‖ (But I 'may be °working ˅late │ toˏnight.)
What a 'horrid °little ˎflat!	It ˅isn't a ˅house. ‖ (But it's ˅pleasant eₒnough.)
What a 'nasty °cold ˎday!	It's ˅bitterly ˅cold. ‖ But it's 'not ˅nasty.
'Can we ˏsmoke?	˅Only in the ˅Common ₒRoom. ‖ ˅Not in ˅here, I'm aₒfraid.
'Everyone °said she was ˅ugly. ‖ 'I think she's ˅beautiful.	She's ˅prettier than I ex˅pected. ‖ But I ˅wouldn't call her ˅beautiful.
'Would he °lend me his ˏgramophone?	He ˅might if you °talked ˅nicely ₒto him.
˅That ₒchair would ₒdo, │ ˏwouldn't it?	It would ˅do for the °time ˅being.
● But I ˎthought you °didn't ˅take ₒsugar.	I ˅don't take it in °coffee or ˅cocoa. ‖ (But in ˅tea, │ I ˅do.)
˅You ₒbroke the ₒwindow, │ ˅didn't you?	Yes, but ˅not on ˅purpose.
What a 'lovely ˎvoice!	She has a ˅lovely ˅voice. ‖ But she's ˅no ˅actress.
In ˅my oₒpinion │ it's ˎtoo ˅cheap.	That's ˅all very ˅well. ‖ (But I ˎcan't af˅ford a more exₒpensive one.)
‾Is it ˏraining?	It ˅is at the ˅moment. ‖ (But it'll 'soon clear ˅up, I ₒthink.)
What a 'poky °little ˎhouse!	It ˅isn't a ˅large one. ‖ But it's ˅quite ˅nice.
She ˎdidn't °mean to ˅say that.	She ˅may not have ˅meant to ₒsay it. ‖ (But she ˅did ₒsay it.)
I 'don't sup°pose it ˅troubled you ₒmuch.	It ˅wasn't a ˅great deal of ₒtrouble. ‖ But it ˅wasn't alto°gether ˅easy.

Verbal context	*Drill*
˅That won't ₒdo. ‖ The ˋcolour's ₒnot ₒright.	It ˊisn't ex˅actly the ₒshade I ₒwant. ‖ (But it's ˏnear eˏnough.)
I'd 'like it as °soon as ˏpossible.	You could ˊhave it by ˅dinner ₒtime. ‖ But ˊno ˅earlier.
'Can I take ˏthis one?	You ˊcan if you in˅sist. ‖ But the ˊother one's ˅better.
You're ˏnot going to ₒstart that ˏnow, ǀ ˋsurely.	I ˊshan't be °able to ˅finish it. ‖ (But I ˏmay as ₒwell ˏstart.)
Why'ever did you °lose your ˋtemper? ‖ You ˋnever ₒdo.	It's ˊnot what I'm in the ˅habit of ₒdoing. ‖ But there ˊare ˅times!
You'll ˋnever ₒfind that ₒbook.	It's ˊno use °looking for it ˅here. ‖ But it ˊmust be ˅somewhere aₒbout.
'Everyone's °gone ˏhome.	ˊNot ˅everyone.
● You ˅will ₒplay, ǀ ˋwon't you?	I'd ˊrather ˅not.
'Can you ˏspare me a °minute?	Well I'm ˊrather ˅busy.
He's ˋobviously ₒguilty.	It'll be ˊhard to ˅prove.
Now 'what have you to ˏsay for yourₒself?	It ˊwasn't ˅me who ₒbroke the ₒwindow, sir.
What a 'nice ˏplace they've ₒgot!	It ˊisn't a ˅house.
'Can I °borrow your ˏpenknife?	It's ˊnot very ˅sharp.
I'll come 'every ˋday ₒnext ₒweek.	You ˊcan't come on ˅Monday.
What a 'nice ˏhouse!	It ˊisn't a ˅large one.
I'll 'get a °bit ˋcloser.	I ˊshouldn't stand ˅too ₒnear.
You 'might °win a ˋfortune.	It's ˊnot very ˅likely, I'm aₒfraid.
I shall ex'pect you °every ˏmorning.	I ˊcan't come to˅morrow ₒmorning.
Well ˏwhat about ˋthis ₒcolour?	It ˊisn't ex˅actly the ₒshade I ₒwant.
She'll ˋnever ₒdo any ₒbetter.	I've got a ˊfeeling she ˅will.
You 'gave me the im°pression he'd aˋgree.	That ˊisn't what I ˅meant.
‾Well ˏsend ˋJohn to ₒmeet them.	He ˊwon't be °very ˅pleased aₒbout it.
What a 'ghastly ˏwoman!	She's ˊprettier than I ex˅pected.
You 'look ˋcold.	I'm ˊnot ex°actly ˅cold.
'Type out this °letter at ˋonce.	I ˊcan't °possibly ˅finish it.
I 'want those shoes °mended ˏquickly.	I ˊcan't get them °done to˅day.
I supˏpose I must ˋwrite to him, ₒthen.	It would be ˊbetter to °go and ˅see him.
He ˏwon't ˋcome, I ₒtell you.	He ˊhasn't °definitely re˅fused.
‾Will ˏthis com°partment °do?	It ˊisn't par°ticularly ˅clean.

Verbal context	Drill
'Let me °know to͵morrow.	I 'doubt whether I can °give you an °answer by ˇthen.
He 'came at °quarter past ͵two.	ˋHalf past ˇthree it ₒwas.
John 'won't be °here to͵day.	He ˈjolly well ˇwill.
It was ͵quite ˋgood.	It was ˈvery ˇbad.
He 'came °home before eˋleven.	It was ˈafter ˇmidnight.
It 'shouldn't take ͵long.	It'll take at ˈleast a ˇweek.
I ͵gave you a °list of ˋall the ₒcolours.	You ˈdidn't say ˇblue.
What a 'shocking ͵answer!	It ˈwasn't all ˇthat ₒbad.
You're ͵not ˋtrying.	I most ˈcertainly ˇam.
What a 'mild ͵day it ₒwas!	It was ˈbitterly ˇcold.
'Nobody °wants to ͵buy them.	ˈNobody can afˇford to ₒbuy them, you ₒmean.
What a 'lovely °red ͵dress she's ₒwearing!	You ˈmustn't °call it ˇred. ‖ (It's ceˆrise.)
● We 'got here about ˋmidnight.	It was ˈearlier than ˇthat.
The clock's 'twelve °minutes ͵fast.	I'm ˈquite sure it's °not ˇthat much ₒout.
Are you 'coming for a ͵swim?	ˈNot ˇme. ˈNot ˇlikely.
'How am I ˋdoing?	You ˈare ˇslow.
I've been ˋsacked.	You're ˈnot ˇserious.
I could ˈnever say ˇthat ₒword.	You could at ˈleast ˇtry.
I've arˇrived.	You're ˈrather ˇlate.
͵Why bring me ˋthat ₒfile?	It's the ˈone you ˇasked ₒfor.
But I ͵haven't had ˋtime to ₒwrite to them.	You might at ˈleast have ˇphoned them.
͵Alan's for°gotten his umˋbrella.	He ˈalways °leaves ˇsomething beₒhind.
͵How ˋfunny! ‖ I've ͵got it °wrong aˋgain.	It's ˈnothing to be ˇproud ₒof.
Oh I ˈcan't do ˇthat.	You ˈought to have a ˇshot at it.
I'm ˈsure he ˇdoes ₒlike your ₒcooking.	He ˈdoesn't seem to ˇeat very ₒmuch of it.
'These °sweets are deˋlicious.	There's ˈno need to °take them ˇall.
‾Did you ͵mind my in°viting °Eve?	You ˈmight have °asked me ˇfirst.
‾Hang ͵on a °second.	I ˈcan't wait °here all ˇday.
I'm afraid I 'can't ˋmake it | to͵night.	I ˈwish you'd °told me ˇearlier.
‾Could you 'call at the ͵post °office?	Well it's ˈrather °out of my ˇway.
I'll ˈcome ˇnext ₒweek, | ˋhonest I ₒwill.	It's ˈall very °well to make ˇpromises.
It's ͵not ˋfair. ‖ I ˋlost.	You ˈmustn't ex°pect to win ˇall the ₒtime.
Oh 'dry ͵up, you ₒidiot!	It's ˈno use °trying to °shout me ˇdown.

Verbal context	*Drill*
'Come ‚on. ‖ 'Let's get 'out of ₒhere.	But we 'can't °leave without °paying the ˇbill.
⸜One more °game?	You'll 'miss your ˇtrain.
'Let's have a 'shot at it.	It's 'awfully ˇdangerous.
'May I °come to your ‚lecture?	There'll be 'nothing ˇnew in it ₒfor you.
Let 'me have a ₒshot at it.	I 'don't think you'll ˇmanage it.
My 'car ₒlights have ₒfailed.	You'll 'have the poˇlice ₒafter you.
'Let's 'send it ₒto him ǀ by 'post.	He 'won't °get it in ˇtime.
The ˇrecipe ₒsays ǀ a 'pound of °dried ‚fruit.	I 'doubt whether a ˇpound'll be eₒnough.
I'd ˇlike to ₒgo. ‖ But it's ‚such an ex°pensive 'journey.	You 'shouldn't let the ˇcost of it deₒter you from ₒgoing.
It's ‚not very ‚difficult, ǀ ‚is it?	I'm a'fraid you'll °find it ˇrather ₒdifficult.
'Let's °go and see 'Jean.	We'd 'better °not do ˇthat. ‖ (The 'children have got 'mumps.)
I ‚don't think I'll ₒtake a ‚mac.	The 'forecast is °rain ˇlater.
I'm 'thinking of having °central 'heating.	It's 'terribly ex°pensive to inˇstall.
I 'haven't °smoked for °ten 'days.	You'll 'never be °able to °keep it ˇup, you ₒknow.
'When I reˇtire ǀ I'd 'like to °live in the 'Highlands.	You'd 'find it °rather °lonely in the ˇwinter ₒtime, I'm aₒfraid.
I've ordered 'two pints of ‚undercoat ǀ and 'one of ‚top.	You'll need 'more than °two pints of ˇundercoat.
He's 'staying for °ten 'days.	Ex'cuse ˇme. ‖ (It's a 'fortnight.)
'Let me °have them by toₒnight.	I 'beg your ˇpardon. ‖ (That's 'out of the 'question.)
I've 'called for my 'overcoat.	I'm 'awfully ˇsorry. ‖ (It 'isn't °quite 'finished.)
'Have you °any obₒjection?	Well I 'don't °want to be ˇawkward. ‖ (But 'where's the 'money ₒcoming ₒfrom?)
Where 'has he ‚been ₒall this ₒtime?	He's 'sorry to be so ˇlate. ‖ (He was de'layed at the 'office.)
'What d'you °think of my ‚painting?	I 'don't °want to be unˇkind. ‖ (But what 'is it?)
But you 'promised me one.	I'm 'sorry to °have to contraˇdict you. ‖ (But I 'didn't.)
'What's worrying 'you, ₒPeter?	I 'hope you don't °think I'm interˇfering. ‖ (But 'is it ‚wise to °spend so °much?)

Verbal context	*Drill*
Oh, they're ˏnot ˏbad.	ˋNot ˇbad? ‖ (They're ˆhorrible.)
It's ˏnot much ˏfurther.	ˋNot much ˇfurther? ‖ (You've been ˏsaying that for an ˋhour or ˳more.)
He ˋis rather ˇtaciturn.	ˋRather ˇtaciturn? ‖ (He's ˏdownright ˋrude.)
‾Oh, you're a ˏnuisance!	ˋI'm a ˇnuisance? ‖ (‾Just ˏwhat d'you ˳mean by ˏthat?)
It's 'up to ˏyou.	It's 'up to ˇme? ‖ (ˏHow ˋcome?)
Take it 'every °four ˏhours.	ˋEvery °four ˇhours? ‖ (At 'night as ˏwell?)
'Do it when°ever it's conˏvenient.	When°ever it's conˇvenient? ‖ (ˏWho says it'll ˋever be conˏvenient?)
● I need 'two °hundred ˋpounds.	ˋTwo °hundred ˇpounds? ‖ (But ˏthat's a °small ˋfortune!)
I 'haven't °even ˋstarted.	You ˋhaven't °even ˇstarted? ‖ (‾But why ˏever ˋnot?)
WH-Questions	
But ˏwhat could I ˋdo to ˳help?	ˋWhat could ˇyou ˳do? ‖ (Oh, ˋlots, │ if you ˏreally ˏwanted to.)
● 'Where did you ˋmeet him?	ˋWhere did I ˇmeet him? ‖ (ˏWhere d'you ˋthink?)
'What °more d'you exˋpect?	ˋWhat more do ˇI ex˳pect? ‖ (From ˇhim, │ ˋnothing.)
'How °far to ˋLuton?	ˋHow °far to ˇLuton? ‖ (What's ˋLuton got to ˳do with it?)
ˏWhy not °write and ˋwarn him?	ˋWhy not °write and ˇwarn him? ‖ (ˏWhat good would ˋthat do?)
Yes-No Questions	
'Is it a °fair propoˏsition?	ˋIs it ˇfair? ‖ (ˏI'll say it's ˳not!)
● 'Are you ˏsure?	ˋAm I ˇsure? ‖ (I'm 'abso°lutely ˆpositive.)
'Are they °any ˏgood?	ˋAre they °any ˇgood? ‖ (No, they're 'utter ˆrubbish.)
'Have you °had eˏnough?	ˋHave I °had eˇnough? ‖ (I've had ˆmore than eˏnough.)
'Couldn't you °try aˏgain?	ˋCouldn't I °try aˇgain? ‖ (What ˏever ˋfor?)

Verbal context	*Drill*

Commands

● She's an 'absolute ˏfailure. — Now ˈbe ˇfair.

You're a 'clumsy ˏoaf. — ˈSteady ˇon.

We'll 'leave beˈfore ˏdawn. — ˈHave a ˇheart. ˈHave a °bit of ˇsense.

What a deˈlicious ˏwine this °is! — ˈMake the ˇmost of it. ‖ (It's the ˈlast ˇbottle.)

I feel ˈcertain he'll ₒbuy it. — ˈDon't be ˇtoo ₒsure.

I 'think it's °going to ˈrain. — Oh ˈdon't say ˇthat.

ˈLook, ₒMummy. ‖ I'm 'right at the ˈtop. — ˈMind you don't ˇfall.

I'll have ˈthis one. ‖ ˈNo, │ ˈthis. — Well ˈmake up your ˇmind.

And you've a 'date for °lunch next ˈFriday. — ˈDon't for°get to reˇmind me aₒbout it.

I'm 'quite deˏtermined to ₒgo. — Well ˈdon't say I °didn't ˇwarn you.

● I'm ˏsorry. — Well ˈsay it as °if you ˇmeant it.

I shall be a ˈlittle ˇlate. — ˈTry and be °there by ˇsix.

'Can I come °home by myˏself, °Mummy? — Well be ˈcareful when you °cross the °main ˇroad.

Interjections

'Going for a ˈswim to°day? — ˈNot ˇme! ‖ (It's ˈfreezing.)

● 'Why not °take up ˈsquash? — ˈNo ˇfear! ‖ (ˈMuch too ₒenerₒgetic.)

But you ˏmight ˈwin. — ˈSome ˇhope! ‖ (I'm a ˈborn ₒloser.)

'Aren't you going to °give him aˏnother °game? — ˈNot ˇlikely! ‖ (He ^cheats.)

You ˏwill °stay, │ ˏwon't you? — ˈNot on your ˇlife I ₒwon't! ‖ (⌐I've ˏnever been so in°sulted in my ˈlife.)

'One more °game, °George? — ˈNot Pyg°malion ˇlikely! ‖ (⌐I'm ˏon my °knees alˈready!)

Note: All the relevant drills given above with the tune
    (LOW PRE-HEAD+) FALLING HEAD+FALL–RISE (+TAIL)
can be said with emphasis if one or more of the following features are used:
(*a*) the high pre-head instead of the low pre-head (see Chapter I, p. 36);
(*b*) the emphatic form of the falling head (see Chapter I, p. 37);
(*c*) a high fall tone for each accent in the head (see Chapter I, p. 38).
The following drills are marked to show these features:
        ⌐Well ˈsay it as °if you ˇmeant it.
        Well be ˈcareful when you ˈcross the ˈmain ˇroad.
        ˈTry to be ˈthere by ˇsix.

6 *The Long Jump*

Attitude

In STATEMENTS: protesting, as if suffering under a sense of injustice.

In WH-QUESTIONS: protesting, somewhat unpleasantly surprised.

In YES-NO QUESTIONS: willing to discuss but protesting the need for settling a crucial point.

In COMMANDS: recommending a course of action but with a note of critical surprise.

In INTERJECTIONS: protesting, surprised.

Tone marks used in LONG JUMP drills

A Stressed, accented syllables (Nucleus, Head)
[ˋ] High falling to very low pitch.
[ˌ] Very low level pitch, with any following head syllable(s) forming an ascending pitch scale.
[°] Level pitch, varying from relatively low to medium-high, always higher than the *preceding* [ˌ] or [°] and lower than the beginning of [ˋ].

B Stressed, unaccented syllables (Tail)
[₀] Very low level pitch, the same pitch as the end of the *preceding* [ˋ].

Tune		(Low Pre-Head+) Rising Head+High Fall (+Tail)

Verbal context	*Drill*

Statements

Well 'when can you ˋgo?	ˌNext ˋweek. ˌStraight aˋway.
'Aren't these °apples ˋhorrible!	ˌMine's ˋfine.
ˌWho's ˋgot it, ₀then?	ˌJohn ˋBrown. ˌFrank ˋJenkins.
● ˇMay ₀likes it.	Yes but ˌI ˋdon't.
You ˇcan come on ₀Friday, ‖ ˌcan't you?	ˌNo I ˋcan't. ‖ It's ˌmy day ˋoff.
'Peter came ˋearly.	Well ˌso did ˋI.

Verbal context	*Drill*
ˏWhy not wear ˋthis pair?	They're ˏmuch too ˋsmall. ‖ They ˏhurt my ˋfeet.
I 'must °see Mr. ˎRoberts.	I'm aˏfraid you ˋcan't. ‖ He's ˏjust gone ˋout.
It's an ˋoutrage, | ˋisn't it?	ˏYes it ˋis. ˎNo it ˋisn't.
'How °much does it ˋcost?	ˏTwenty ˋpounds. ‖ I ˏthought you ˋknew.
ˏWhy aˋgree to ₒsuch a ₒsilly ₒscheme?	Beˏcause I ˋhad to.
'What did ˋyou ₒthink of the ₒhouse?	I ˏrather ˋliked it. ‖ And it was ˏquite a ˋbargain.
● ˇI'm not ₒgoing to ₒhelp.	ˏNo-one's ˋasked you to.
(ˏWhy not °get them at ˋFowler's?)	ˏTheirs are ˋvery ₒgood.
ˋNow ₒwhat d'you ₒwant?	I ˏdon't want ˋanything.
'What was the °party ˋlike?	The ˏfood was ˋterrible.
I ˏtell you I °won't ˋdrink it.	But it'll ˏdo you ˋgood, ₒStephen.
I just 'don't beˎlieve it.	ˏNor do ˋI. ˏNor do ˋany of us.
‾Didn't they ˏplay very °well?	ˏPeter's ˋhopeless at the ₒgame.
‾Didn't he ˏgive you °any?	ˏNone at ˋall, the ₒold ₒskinflint.
(ˏWhy take a ˋcoat?)	ˏSomeone's ˋbound to ₒgive us a ₒlift ₒhome.
'When'll he °make up his ˋmind?	ˏNobody ˋknows. ‖ ˏThat's the ˋtrouble.
He's ˋfull of aˇpologies.	ˏNo doubt he ˋis. ‖ (But ˏwhat's the °good of ˋthat?)
He's left ˋsix ₒboxes.	ˏThat's not eˋnough.
Well ˏask ˋRobert.	ˎRobert's gone ˋhome.
He 'said he knew °nothing aˎbout it.	But I ˏtold him myˋself.
You ˏsaid they were ˋripe.	ˏMost of them ˋare ₒripe.
'John °said you disˋliked the ₒplay.	That's ˏnot ˋtrue. ‖ I ˏliked it imˋmensely.
Have you 'been here ˏlong?	We've been ˏwaiting for ˋages.
They've 'sent us ˋfifty.	But I ˏordered a ˋhundred.
'How about ˋSaturday?	ˏSaturday's ˋmuch too ₒlate.
ˏWhy didn't they igˋnore it?	ˏSome of them ˋdid, I beˎlieve.
ˏHow many has ˋAndrew ₒgot?	I ˏhaven't the ˋfoggiest ₒnotion.
(ˏGive her some ˋflowers.)	ˏFlowers are ˋalways acₒceptable.
'Did the °job take ˏlong?	ˏAlmost °two ˋyears.
'Have you been °waiting ˏlong?	ˏAll °blinking ˋday.
'What was the °play ˋlike?	It was an ˏabsoˋlute ˋflop.

Verbal context	*Drill*
ˏWhy don't you ˋbuy one?	I ˏcan't afˋford to. ‖ They ˏcost °too much ˋmoney.
He'll ˏhave to °use his ˋown ˳car.	I ˏdon't °think he ˋcan. ‖ It's ˏgone °in for ˋservicing.
You ˏsaid you'd ˋgive it ˳to me.	I said ˏnothing of the ˋsort.
'Haven't you °brought the ˏcar?	You ˏdidn't ˋask me to. ‖ ˏOtherwise I ˋwould have.
'How ˋwas the ˳interview?	('Terrible!) ‖ ˏNothing went at ˋall ˳right.
So he ˏcame ˋlate.	And ˏthat's not ˋall. ‖ He ˏwanted to leave ˋearly.
I must 'go on a ˋdiet.	ˏThat's not a °bad iˋdea.
So you 'want it for ˋnothing.	It's ˏnot like °that at ˋall.
⁻Won't you ˏhave some °gooseberries?	('No, │ ˏthank you.) ‖ Gooseberries ˏalways °make me ˋill.
'How about ˋJane?	ˏJane's aˋway in ˋParis. ‖ I ˏthought you ˋknew.
'What about some ˋbrandy?	ˏBrandy's °so exˋpensive.
'Haven't you ˏfinished that °book?	I've ˳only °just beˋgun it.
● 'When does he ˋget here?	I've ˏjust this °minute ˋtold you. ‖ At a ˏquarter °past ˋsix.
They were 'all ˋterrible.	ˏJohn's was °pretty ˋgood, I ˳thought.
ˏWhy not adˋmit you'd ˳lost it?	I ˏdidn't °know I ˋhad. ‖ It's ˏall °very myˋsterious.
We must ˋgive it ˳to him.	Well I ˏdon't aˋgree. ‖ He ˏnever gives °us ˋanything.
I'm aˏfraid I ˋfailed my eˏxam.	I'm ˏnot at °all surˋprised. ‖ You did ˏhardly °any ˋwork ˳for it.
● What on 'earth's °happened to ˋMarjorie?	I ˏcan't underˋstand it. ‖ She ˏshould have °been here ˋages a˳go.
ˏWhy didn't you ˋmeet them?	We ˏdidn't °know what ˋtrain they'd be ˳on.
'Hasn't he ˏbeen there °often?	ˏOnce or °twice at the ˋmost.
We'll ˏhave to make °do with ˋtwo, ˳then.	That's ˏeasier °said than ˋdone.
'Weren't you surˏprised to °see her?	I could ˏhardly be°lieve my ˋeyes.
(Is 'that °all you've ˏdone?)	ˏFrancis has °nearly ˋfinished.
(⁻For ˏheaven's °sake stop ˋshouting.)	ˏShouting'll °get you ˋnowhere.

Verbal context	_Drill_
'Can I °have an ‚apple?	I'm a‚fraid you ˋcan't. ‖ You ‚ate the °last one this ˋmorning.
You ‚don't still ‚need it, │ ‚do you?	‚More than °ever be'fore, you ₒfool.
What'ever was he ˎthinking ₒof?	I ‚can't i'magine. ‖ He's ‚usually °so re-ˋliable.
‚What made you ˋtake it?	For the ‚simple °reason I ˋwanted to.
You're from ˋMargate, │ ˋaren't you?	I've ‚never been °there in my ˋlife.
'Jackson was ˋuseless.	(ˋRubbish!) ‖ ‚Jackson was ex°tremely ˋhelpful.
'Bill's cried ˋoff, I'm a‚fraid.	It's ‚just the °sort of °thing he ˋwould do.
'Didn't they °make a ˋmess!	There was ciga‚rette ash °even in the ˋbath-room.
'Fancy °liking °rice ˋpudding!	I ‚can't i°magine what he ˋsees in it.
'Any °chance of some ˊtea?	‚Tea was °cleared away an ˋhour a₀go.
‚Why didn't you ˋphone me, ₒthen?	I've been ‚trying to °get you °all ˋday. ‖ But I ‚kept on °getting the en'gaged ₀tone.
● 'How many °days in a ˋyear?	‚Three °hundred and °sixty ˋfive, you ₀idiot.
'Come ‚on. ‖ 'Let's ˋgo.	‚Surely we must °wait for the ˋothers.
Can I 'have my ‚typewriter °back?	I ‚sent it to you °three or four ˋdays a₀go.
● You ‚ought to have °told me at ˋonce.	I ‚didn't °realise it was °that im'portant.
● He 'swears he °didn't ˋknow.	That's ‚downright ˋnonsense. ‖ I dis‚tinctly re°member °telling him my'self.

WH-Questions

'Take a‚nother ₒpiece.	‚What ˋfor?
● You 'mustn't ˎmention it.	‚Why ˋnot?
'Open that ˎtin, ₒplease.	‚What ˋwith?
(I'm ˀnot standing for ˇthat.)	‚Why ˋshould I?
You're ˀnot buying ˇthat one, │ ‚are you?	‚What's ˋwrong with it? ‖ (It ‚seems all ₒright to ‚me.)
I've 'just seen °Pat in 'Oxford ₀Street.	‚What's ˋshe ₒdoing in ₒTown?
I ˀcan't spare the °time ˇnow.	Well ‚when ˋcan you ₀spare the ₒtime?
I've bought 'ten °gallons of ˋink.	‚What's ˋthat for, for ₀heaven's ₀sake?
'Send them at ‚once.	‚Where ˋto? ‚Why at ˋonce?

Verbal context	*Drill*
‾Will ˎyou °talk to her?	ˏWhy don't ‵you? ‖ (ˎYou're her ˏcousin.)
It was ‵Derek's ₒfault.	ˏHow d'you ‵know?
It's so ‵tiring | by ˏtrain.	Well ˏwhy not ‵fly?
● You'll 'have to aˋpologise.	What ˏdo you ‵mean? ‖ Why on ˏearth ‵should I?
I 'wonder what ‵Gordon ₒthinks.	ˏWhy not ‵ask him?
I'll reˋturn it to you ˅soon.	ˏWhen will ‵that ₒbe?
I 'sent the °coat ‵back.	ˏWhat was ‵wrong with it?
(What 'awful ˎhats she ₒwears!)	Where ˏdoes she ‵get them ₒfrom?
˅This isn't the ₒpaper I ˎmeant.	ˏWhich one ‵did you ₒmean, then?
You can ‵easily ₒmend it.	ˏWhat d'you ‵mean, ₒeasily?
● We 'ought to °buy a ‵couple.	ˏWhere's the ‵money ₒcoming ₒfrom?
‾I was ˎflabbergasted.	What on ˏearth does ‵flabbergasted ₒmean?
(ˎGet a ‵move on, | ˎdo.)	ˏHow much ‵longer are you ₒgoing to ₒbe?
I'm 'going to °have a ‵word with him.	ˏWhat good'll ‵that ₒdo?
It's ‵your ₒturn to ₒpay.	ˏHow d'you make ‵that out?
(‾You ˎare in a ₒmess, ₒPeter.)	What ˏhave you been ‵up to?
I 'can't find the °file ‵anywhere.	ˏWhat have you ‵done with it?
ˏWhat's that you °say?	ˏWhy don't you ‵listen, you ₒidiot?
I 'laughed and ˎlaughed.	ˏWhat was so ‵funny aₒbout it?
(He ˎlives in ‵Leicester. ‖ ‵Leicester!)	ˏHow many 'more ₒtimes d'you ₒwant ₒtelling?
She's ‵positive it ₒwon't ₒwork.	But ˏwhat are her ‵reasons for ₒthinking ₒthat?
Exˇcuse me.	ˏWhat d'you °want ‵now?
I ˎtold ‵David aₒbout it.	ˏWhy did you do ‵that?
'Which shall I ˎbuy?	ˏWhich would you pre‵fer?
No you ˋhaven't °left it ˇhere.	Well wherˏever can it ‵be?
‵Sorry I'm so ˎlate, °Arthur.	Wherˏever have you ‵been, ₒFrank?
I 'think he 'ought to be ₒpaid.	Well then ˏhow much shall I ‵offer him?
We 'need a ‵skeleton.	Yes but ˏwhere can we get ‵hold of one?
Oh I ˋknow he °couldn't ˇhelp it.	Then ˏwhy are you so ‵angry ₒwith him?
‵Bother! ‖ It's ‵raining.	Well ˏwhy don't you hang ‵on a ₒminute or ₒtwo?
He's been 'ill for ‵months.	ˏWhen did you °find ‵out?
'Which one °can I ˎhave?	ˏWhich one °would you ‵like?

Verbal context	*Drill*
'John says we ˎmustn't.	ˏWho °cares about ˎJohn?
It's 'all ˎoff. ‖ 'Tim's ˎill.	ˏWhat will °you do ˎnow?
I shall ˎsue him.	ˏWhat's the °good of ˎthat?
ˏHow much °can I ˎhave?	ˏHow much °do you ˎwant?
I 'told him he was a ˏfool.	ˏWhat did you °say ˎthat ˎfor?
They ˏsay it's ˎdangerous.	ˏWhat's a °bit of ˎdanger ˎmatter?
ˏHow many d'you ˎneed?	ˏHow °many can you ˎspare?
'Lend me your ˏpen, °will you?	ˏWhy don't you °use your ˎown?
Of ˎcourse he ˎknows.	ˏHow can you °be so ˎsure?
Well he 'left a ˎweek aˎgo.	ˏWhen d'you ex°pect him ˎback?
I ˎdidn't mind him ˇusing it.	Then ˏwhy were you °so upˎset?
He's ˏtaken °all the ˎwheels ˎoff.	Whatˏever's he °up to ˎnow?
So you ˎasked him aˎbout it.	And ˏwhat d'you °think he reˎplied?
'Look at °all these ˎstamps.	ˏHow °many have you ˎgot, ˎpray?
There's ˎno sign of ˇJack.	ˏWhere on °earth has he ˎgot to?
‾He reˏfused the ˎoffer.	How ˏcould he have °been so ˎfoolish?
I 'bet he °rings you ˏup.	ˏWhat makes you °think he's ˎnear a ˎtelephone?
I'm 'going to ˎemigrate.	ˏWhen did you de°cide to do ˎthat?
The ˎdoor won't ˎopen.	ˏWhy not try °turning the ˎkey?
● I ˎknow I ˇbrought a ˎknife.	But ˏwhere in the °world have you ˎput it?
'How much ˎmoney have you ˎgot?	ˏWhat's that °got to °do with ˎyou?
You ˎmust let me ˎin. ‖ I'm a ˎmember.	ˏWhy didn't you °say so beˎfore?
ˎStill no °word from ˇHenry.	Oh ˏwhy doesn't he °make up his ˎmind?
Oh ˇsorry.	Why the ˏdevil don't you °look where you're ˎgoing?
'Tom's got a °new ˎcar.	How on ˏearth did he °manage to afˎford it?
I shall 'give him a °piece of my ˏmind.	Whatˏever d'you °hope to °gain by ˎthat?
● I was 'too ˎlate. ‖ They'd ˎsold it.	Whyˏever didn't you °buy it when you °had the ˎchance?

Yes-No Questions

ˇI can't ˎplay.	ˏCan 'Frank ˎplay, then?
ˎJack's ˎgot it.	ˏAre you ˎsure?
● But ˏJohn's reˎfused.	ˏDoes that ˎmatter?
I'll ˎgive it to you, │ I ˎpromise.	ˏDo you ˎmean that?

Verbal context	*Drill*
'Can I ‚have it?	‚Do you `need it?
'Let's borrow `Frank's ‚barrow.	‚Has he `got one?
He's 'going to re'sign.	‚Can you `blame him!
You've got a 'flat `tyre.	‚Don't I `know it!
I'll 'come °home `early.	D'you ‚really `mean that?
'Let's °go to the `pictures.	D'you ‚think we `ought to?
● It's ˅always ˅possible.	‚Is it `likely, ‚though?
I've ˅said I'm ˅sorry.	‚Are you `really ‚sorry?
'Come at `seven, ‚then.	But will ‚that be `soon enough ‚for you?
I've for‚gotten to °buy the bal`loons.	Well ‚need we `bother about ‚having ‚any?
But I'm ‚such a `hopeless ‚player.	Does it ‚matter `what sort of ‚player you ‚are?
‚Why not °ask `Robert?	But would ‚he be `interested in ‚such a ‚little ‚job?
The ‚last °bus has `gone.	‚Would you be`lieve it!
'Do you re°member ‚Mary?	Shall I ‚ever for`get her!
I've 'left you `six.	But will ‚six be suf`ficient?
I've ac'cepted the invi‚tation.	‚Will you be `free then, ‚though?
● ‚Fancy °Jack `leaving!	‚Wasn't it ex`traordinary!
‚Praps we could °send `Fred.	‚Would that be `possible?
He re‚fused °point `blank.	Isn't that ‚just what I `said he'd ‚do?
It's ˅only a ˅pound he ‚wants to ‚borrow.	Will ‚that be the `end of it, ‚though?
Well he ˅paid ˅this ‚week.	‚Will he pay `regularly, ‚though?
'Next °Saturday's `difficult.	Will the ‚Saturday `after ‚suit you ‚better?
‾But I'm ‚almost `broke.	‚Couldn't you `borrow a ‚couple of ‚pounds?
They ˅come quite ˅often.	‚Were they °here `yesterday?
So he's 'charging you °ten `pounds.	D'you ‚think °that's un`reasonable?
Have you 'heard about ‚Alec?	‚Isn't it in`credible!
˅That's not ‚very con‚vincing.	Well can ‚you think of a `better ‚argument?
‾I'll ‚ask him ‚sometime.	‚Will you °ask him `now?
'Praps to'morrow I'll ‚write to him.	‚Can't you °write to`day?
Well it's a ˅possible so‚lution.	But ‚dare we °take the `chance?
˅That's not ‚very ‚good.	Could ‚you do °any `better?
I ˅don't know what ˅Joe'll ‚say.	‚Does it °matter `what he ‚says?
Well it's ˅raining.	Yes but ‚is it °raining `heavily?

Verbal context	*Drill*

ˇSo ˏfar | we're a 'man ˋshort. → Is there ˏany °chance of ˋAlbert ˏturning ˏout?

They 'leave us a °paper ˇmost ˏdays. → Yes but ˏdid they °leave one toˋday?
It's 'quite a ˇgood one. → ˏIs it the °best you've ˋgot, though?
It's a 'bit ˋstuffy | in ˏhere. → ˏShall I °open the ˋwindow?
I 'just can't ˋshift this ˏstain. → Have you ˏtried using °soap and ˋwater?
● I ˇdoubt whether ˇDavid'll subˏscribe. → ˏIs it °fair to exˋpect him ˏto?
Oh but ˏThursdays are ˋhopeless. → ˏCould we °make it a ˋFriday, ˏthen?
He ˏcame ˏlast °week. → Yes but ˏought we °really to ˋcount on him?
● You're ˏnot very ˋgood at it, | ˋare you? → Have I ˏever preˋtended ˋotherwise?
ˏWhat did you °say? → ˏWould you mind °shutting the ˋdoor?
'Let's ˋtry it ˏthat way. → But ˏwould it °really be °any adˋvantage?
We ˇcan't go to the °Albert °Hall toˇnight. → ˏCouldn't we °go there on ˋSaturday ˏevening, ˏthen?

It's 'quite ˇlegal. → But ˏis it °absoˋlutely ˋfair?
She's 'only °working °half ˇtime. → Yes but ˏneed she °go to °work at ˋall?
I 'can't find my °keys ˋanywhere. → Are you ˏsure you didn't °leave them at ˋhome?

But he'd alˏready ˋgone. → ˏWere you °there at the °time he ˋsaid?
ˉWould ˏJohn °take it, d'you °think? → ˏIs it °worth the °trouble of ˋasking him?
The ˇshop's open ˇnow. → But ˏwill it be °open this °afterˋnoon?

Commands

● ˇTen's not eˏnough. → ˏTake ˋtwenty, ˏthen.
I 'can't °get it to ˋwork. → ˏLet ˋme have a ˏgo at it.
What 'shall I ˏdo? → ˏTry aˋgain. || (That's ˏall you ˋcan do.)
The 'bus doesn't ˋrun | on ˏSundays. → ˏCome by ˋtrain, ˏthen.
But it's ˋcold outˏside. → ˏStay inˋdoors, ˏthen.
'What shall I ˏdo about that ˏletter? → ˏJust igˋnore it.
● My ˇfeet ˏhurt. → Well ˏtake your ˋshoes ˏoff.
This ˇpaint's very ˏthick. → ˏMix some ˋturps with it.
'What shall I ˋsay? → ˏDon't say ˋanything.
I 'can't ˋhear you. → Well then ˏturn the ˋwireless ˏoff.
I feel ˋvery ˏtired. → ˏGo to ˋbed, in ˏthat case.
I ˏhaven't got a ˋspoon. → ˏGo and ˋget one, ˏthen, ˏstupid.
ˉBut I ˏhaven't °got a ˋracquet. → ˏBorrow ˋFrank's for a ˏday or two.

Verbal context	*Drill*
It's a 'bit ˅cold in ₒhere.	ˏShut the ˅window, ₒthen, you ₒsilly ₒass.
'What °time'll suit ˋyou?	Come whenˏever you're ˋfree.
'How °much d'you ˋwant for it?	ˏMake me an ˋoffer.
ˏAnn doesn't ˋwant it.	ˏGive it to ˋme, ₒthen.
(ˋI'm ₒboss | ˏhere.)	So ˏplease don't ˋargue.
I ˋcan't eat all ˅that.	Eat as ˏmuch as you ˋcan, ₒthen.
'When shall I ˏleave?	Leave whenˏever you're ˋready.
He ˏwon't ˏcome, | ˋanyway.	Well then ˏdon't let's inˋvite him.
'When shall we ˏsend it?	Send it as ˏsoon as you ˋcan.
It's ˏtoo ˋbig.	ˏCut a bit ˋoff it, ₒthen.
We ˋoughtn't to °go a˅lone.	Let's ˏwait for the ˋothers, ₒthen.
D'you 'mind if I °have the ˏradio °on?	(ˏNot a ˋbit.) || ˏTurn it on when°ever you ˋfeel ₒlike it.
'Aren't these °apples ˋsour!	ˏHave some more ˋsugar ₒwith them.
It ˋcan't be °done ˅quickly.	Take as ˏlong as you ˋlike ₒover it.
ˏWhat if he ˋmentions the ₒmatter?	ˏTell him the ˋtruth, for ₒheaven's ₒsake.
It's 'raining ˋharder | ˏnow.	Well hang ₒon a bit ˋlonger, in ₒthat case.
I ˋwish Ann ₒdidn't disˏlike me ˋso.	Then ˏdon't be so ˋrude to her in ₒfuture.
Of ˋcourse he'll aₒgree.	ˏDon't be °too ˋsure.
Bill's ˏturned me ˋdown.	Well then ˏask °someone ˋelse.
'How °much did they ˋgive you?	ˏMind your °own ˋbusiness.
'What shall I ˋtell him?	Tell him eˏxactly what you ˋthink.
'May I °take ˏtwo?	Take as ˏmany as you ˋlike.
Oh I ˋdo feel ₒpoorly.	Well ˏtake a °couple of ˋaspirins.
I 'won't stay a°nother ˋminute.	For ˏgoodness °sake sit ˋdown.
I 'don't feel °very ˋwell.	ˏGo and °see the ˋdoctor.
● I ˋdon't want to °go a˅lone.	ˏCome a°long with ˋus, ₒthen.
ˏHurry ˋup.	ˏDon't be °so imˋpatient, ₒTom.
I'll ˏgive him a °piece of my ˋmind.	Now don't say ˏanything you'll be ˋsorry ₒfor.
ˏWhat's the ˋmatter?	ˏShut the °perishing ˋdoor.
I 'shan't °bother you much ˏlonger.	ˏStay as °long as you ˋlike.
ˋSorry I ₒhaven't ₒfinished ˏreading it.	Well ˏtake it ˋwith you. || And ˏfinish it °on the ˋtrain.
'Dad's ˋsure to aₒgree.	ˏDon't take °so much for ˋgranted.
I ˋcan't manage ˅all of it.	Well ˏeat as °much as you ˋcan, ₒthen.
'What about the ˋtennis ₒballs?	ˏPut them °back in the ˋbox, ₒsilly.

Verbal context	*Drill*
‚What shall I ‛say to him?	‚Tell him it °isn't ‛good enough.
'How many ‚sandwiches shall I °make?	Make as ‚many as you °think we'll ‛eat.
(‚How many ‛more ₒtimes d'you ₒwant ₒtelling?)	
‾But ‚what about my ‛suitcase?	‚Don't put your °feet on the set‛tee.
● 'This room's ‛freezing, │ ‛isn't it?	‚Leave it in the °cloakroom at ‛Euston.
	Well ‚go down°stairs where it's a bit ‛warmer.
'Which do ‛you think I ₒought to ₒbuy?	Buy which‚ever you can °reasonably af‛ford.
● ‾But I've ‚lost my invi‛tation.	Then ‚write and °ask them to °send you a‛nother.

Interjections

She's 'coming °home for ‛Christmas.	‚How ‛nice!
'Didn't he ‚treat you?	‚Some ‛hopes! ‚Lord ‛no!
● ‛Nobody ₒturned ₒup.	‚How ‛strange!
He ‚hadn't got a ‛licence.	‚Good ‛gracious! ‖ ‚How ‛silly!
I 'did it in °half an ‛hour.	‚My ‛goodness! ‖ (‚That's a ‛record.)
I 'gave him °five ‛pounds.	‚No ‛wonder you're ₒpoor!
I ‚told him to °mind his own ‛business.	‚Good for ‛you!
● ‾But you ‚said I ‛could ₒhave it.	‚Not at ‛all!
‚Did you °call him a °liar?	Good ‚heavens ‛no!
He's 'just re‛turned it.	A‚bout time ‛too!
He ‚asked me for a ‛reference.	What‚ever ‛next!
Joan com'pletely ig‛nored us.	How ‚very ‛rude!
'Tom's got ‛married.	Well ‚blow me ‛down!
I 'want them ‚now.	‚Do you ‛really!
Jill ‚can't be ‛there.	‚What a ‛nuisance!
He's ‚brought a ‛dozen.	‚How ri‛diculous!
She's 'passed her e‛xam.	‚Oh how ‛marvellous!
● ‛Look. ‖ It ‛works.	‚Well I ‛never! ‖ ‚How ex‛traordinary!
I 'left it °too ‛late.	A ‚fine mess ‛you've made of ₒthings!
He 'won't ac‛cept it.	‚More °fool ‛him, ₒthen.
Well he's a‛pologised.	‚So I should ‛think!
‾Will you ‚ask her?	‚Certainly ‛not!
You ‛will ₒgo, │ ‛won't you?	‚Not on your ‛life, I ₒwon't.
I 'given ‛up ₒsmoking.	‚Sensible ‛chap!

Verbal context	*Drill*
You're a 'bit ˋgrumpy | to˒day.	˒Not in the ˋleast!
˒Andy's °passed his ˋfinals.	What ˏwonderful ˋnews! ‖ (It's ˏalmost °unbeˋlievable.)
'Malcolm °won't aˋgree.	What an exˏtraordinary ˋthing!
ˎFred ˳says | it's ˋhis ˳turn.	˒Absolute ˋrubbish!
He's ˏactually enˋgaged.	˒Would you beˋlieve it!
He's been made 'managing diˋrector.	A ˏchance of a ˋlifetime!
She ˏdidn't °say a ˋword.	How ˏvery unˋtypical!
ˏSue didn't ˋlike being ˳jilted.	˒Naturally eˋnough!
'Gerry's °being proˋmoted.	What a ˏwonderful surˋprise!
'Two °solid ˋhours to ˳wait!	How ˏterribly anˋnoying!
They've inˋvited us for ˋWhitsun.	How ˏabsolutely ˋmarvellous!
● 'What was the ˋshow like?	ˏVery °good inˋdeed!
'How about a ˋtheatre to˳night?	If ˏonly you'd °asked me ˋearlier!
He 'says he's reˋsigning.	ˏWhat a °stupid iˋdea!
You've won ˏfirst ˋprize.	What an inˏcredible °bit of ˋluck!
I ˋhope we're not °barging ˇin.	ˏGlad you were °able to ˋmake it!
I'm aˋfraid we've ˋfinished your ˳whisky.	ˏSorry I °haven't any ˋmore!
● But I ˏreally ˋwanted them.	What a ˏpity you °didn't °say so ˋsooner!

Note: All the relevant drills in this tone group having the tune

(LOW PRE-HEAD+) RISING HEAD+HIGH FALL (+TAIL)

can be said with emphasis if one or both of the following features are used:

(*a*) the high pre-head instead of the low pre-head (see Chapter I, p. 36);

(*b*) the emphatic form of the rising head (see Chapter I, p. 38).

With both of these features indicated the last drill in this tone group would read

ˉWhat a ˏpity you ˏdidn't ˏsay so ˋsooner!

7   *The High Bounce*

Attitude

In STATEMENTS: questioning, trying to elicit a repetition, but lacking any suggestion of disapproval or puzzlement; (in non-final word groups) casual, tentative.

In WH-QUESTIONS: with the nuclear tone on the interrogative word, calling for a repetition of the information already given; with the nuclear tone following the interrogative word, *either* echoing the listener's question before going on to answer it *or* (in straightforward, non-echo questions) tentative, casual.

In YES-NO QUESTIONS: *either* echoing the listener's question or (in straightforward, non-echo questions) light and casual.

In COMMANDS and INTERJECTIONS: querying all or part of the listener's command or interjection, but with no critical intention.

Tone marks used in HIGH BOUNCE drills

A Stressed, accented syllables (Nucleus, Head)
['] (i) without Tail: medium rising to high pitch.
   (ii) with Tail: medium level pitch; the rise is completed by the following tail syllable(s).
['] Relatively high level pitch, higher than the beginning of the *following* ['].
[°] Relatively high level pitch, the same pitch as the *preceding* ['].

B Stressed, unaccented syllables (Tail)
[°] High level pitch, higher than the *preceding* ['] or [°].

Tune ⟋ *or* ⎯⟋ **High Rise (+Tail)**

Verbal context	*Drill*
Statements	
I 'want you a ₒminute.	'Yes?
I should 'phone him aₒbout it.	'Now?
● It's 'snowing.	'Much?
'What d'you °think of my 'dress?	'New?
He's al'ready 'got one.	'Sure? 'Think so?
Can I 'have some °more ‚tea?	'Milk? 'Sugar? 'China?
I ‚write to him.	'Often? 'Regularly?
'Mavis has °cut her 'finger.	'Badly?
'I must be 'off.	'So °soon?
I 'saw 'Eileen | to‚day.	'Really?
The 'digging's 'finished.	'All of it?
But I've 'been to the ₒdentist.	'Recently?
I've 'just read that °new 'travel ₒbook.	'Interesting?

Verbal context	*Drill*
('What was the ˋweather ₒlike?)	ˊChangeable? ˊRainy?
I'm 'told they're ˋill.	ˊBoth of them? ˊAll the °family?
('Who's the °tall ˋdark ₒman?)	ˊAntony? ˊPeter?
● I've 'just °seen the ˋEdwards ₒgirl.	ˊJoan °Edwards?
He's reˏsigning.	ˊDefinitely?
The 'game's been postˋponed.	ˊSaturday's °game?
It's ˋyour turn to ₒshuffle the ₒcards.	ˊMine? ˊMy °turn?
There were 'fourteen ˏnames on the ₒlist.	ˊForty?
'Five ˋpounds I ₒpaid.	ˊNine °pounds?
● 'Can I °borrow some ˏmatches?	ˊMatches? ‖ (By ˋall ₒmeans.)
We 'never have °coffee after ˏlunch.	ˊNever?
It was ˋyour ₒfault.	ˊMy °fault? ˊMy fault, you °say?
He 'always °writes on ˏSundays.	ˊAlways?
You're 'wanted on the ˋphone, ₒRoger.	ˊI am?
They were 'all deˋlighted.	ˊAll of them?
He's 'been on °holiday in ˋSwitzerland.	ˊSwitzerland? ˊHoliday?
I listened to 'every °word he ˏsaid.	ˊEvery °word?
It's so ˋdangerous.	ˊDangerous? ˊDangerous, did you °say?
They're 'going on the °five o'clock ˏtrain.	ˊNine o'clock °train?
I call 'every ˏMonday.	ˊEvery °Monday?
'Everybody °thinks it's magˋnificent.	ˊEverybody?
● I've 'got to °go to ˋLeeds.	ˊYou've got to °go?
You ˏtold me │ he ˏdidn't in°tend to ˋcome.	ˊI told you he °didn't in°tend to °come?

WH-Questions

I 'think this is ˋJoan's um₀brella.	ˊWhose?
That ˋbig one's ₒmine.	ˊWhich one?
It's 'ten feet ˏlong.	ˊHow °long?
I shall need a ˋdozen, │ at ˋleast.	ˊHow °many?
ˇMy ₒcoat │ is the ˋgreen one.	ˊWhich is °yours?
They 'lunch there °twice a ˏweek.	ˊHow °often?
● 'That was °Arthur ˋThompson.	ˊWhat was his °name? ‖ (I 'didn't quite ˋcatch it.)
'These °flowers are for ˋyou.	ˊWho are they °for?
You can 'phone me to°night.	ˊWhen can I °phone you?
'Sit by the ˋwindow.	ˊWhere must I °sit?

Verbal context	*Drill*

He 'broke his ˇarm. ‖ So he ˇcouldn't ˏplay.　　ˊWhy couldn't he °play?

He 'sails on the °twenty ˇfirst.　　ˊWhat °date does he °sail?

ˇFather'd ˏtake it ˏround for you.　　ˊWho'd take it °round for me?

'All ˏtold │ that makes 'nine ˏpounds, ˏmadam.　　ˊHow much d'you °make it?

I ˇlike my ˏtea │ at 'five ˇsharp.　　ˊWhen d'you °like your °tea?

Tom 'brought her some ˇchocolates.　　ˊWho °brought her some °chocolates?

I collected 'almost °ten ˇpounds.　　ˊHow much did you col°lect?

'That's ˇAlec's ˏfriend.　　ˊWhose °friend did you °say that was?

He'll be here 'soon after °six oˏclock.　　ˊWhen did you °say he was °coming?

The 'house is to be °finished by ˏFebruary.　　ˊWhen is it °due to be °finished?

It's a ˇnuisance │ ˏhaving to ˏwait so ˏlong for ˏTom.　　ˊWhen was it he °wanted to °see you?

So we ˇshan't arˇrive before ˇseven.　　ˊHow long did you °say the °journey °took?

● 'Where are you ˏstaying?　　ˊWhere? ‖ (At the ˇGrand.)

'Who's °Archibald ˏSimpson?　　ˊWho, did you °say? ‖ (Or ˏhow?)

'When's he arˏriving?　　ˊWhen's he arˇriving? ‖ (Or ˏwhere?)

'Why's she °giving ˇup?　　ˊWhy's she °giving °up? ‖ (ˇBusiness ˏreasons.)

● ˏHow did he find ˇout?　　ˊHow did he find °out? ‖ (Through ˇMax, │ I iˏmagine.)

'Whose responsiˏbility ˏis it?　　ˊWhose re°sponsi°bility? ‖ (Why, ˇmine.)

Yes-No Questions

'Does it ˏmatter?　　ˊMatter? ‖ ('Not in the ˇslightest.)

ˉDo you ˏmean it?　　ˊMean it? ‖ (Most ˇcertainly I ˏdo.)

● 'Can you ˏmake me one?　　ˊMake you one? ‖ (With ˇpleasure.)

ˉIs that ˏyour little °boy?　　ˊMy little °boy? ‖ (ˇNot ˇlikely!)

Is he ˏangry °with me?　　ˊAngry °with you? ‖ (Of ˇcourse he's ˏnot.)

But 'dare we ˇrisk it?　　ˊDare we °risk it? ‖ (We've ˇgot to ˏrisk it.)

'Can we afˏford it?　　ˊCan we af°ford it? ‖ (We shall ˇhave to.)

ˏDid you °make the °fire up?　　ˊDid I °make the °fire up? ‖ (Of ˇcourse I ˏdid.)

ˏCould she °help °breaking it?　　ˊCould she °help °breaking it? ‖ (You ˇknow she ˏcould.)

Verbal context	*Drill*
ˏWill he a°gree to your °plan?	′Will he a°gree to my °plan? ‖ (No ˋdoubt aˏbout it.)
'Wasn't it ˏstupid!	′Was it so °stupid, I °wonder?
Well 'that's ˏthat.	′Finished?
So ˋthat's your ˏnew ˏhat.	′Like it? ′Suit me?
⁻D'you 'mind if I ˏsmoke?	′Must you?
I'll 'give you a ˋhand.	′Would you?
'Have aˏnother one.	′May I?
What 'lovely ˏcherries!	′Want °some?
It's 'going to °turn ˋcold.	′Think so?
ˋJohn'll ˏdrive you ˏhome.	′Can he °drive?
I've been 'thinking about ˋTom.	′Seen him °lately?
The 'cream was deˋlicious.	′Eaten it °all?
'Why not °ask the ˋconsul to ˏhelp you?	′Could we, d'you °think?
'Have a cigaˏrette.	′Are there °any?
I'm ˋglad they've enˏjoyed their ˏstay.	′Have they en°joyed it?
ˋDavid's ˏhome.	′Seen °anything °of him?
I thought 'Charles was ˋnever ˏgoing to ˏanswer.	′Did he °answer, °ever?
I ˋlike ˏBarbara.	′Do you?
The ˋprimroses are ˏout.	′Are they?
We must ˋgo ǀ ˏnow.	′Must we?
The ˋgovernment was to ˏblame.	′Was it?
The com'mittee °should have known ˏbetter.	′Should they?
'Won't you be ˏcold?	′Will I?
I'm a'fraid you °can't come ˏin.	′Can't I?
I 'daren't °promise ˏanything.	′Daren't you?
'Jack's not ˋfree.	′Isn't he?
Jane 'never °tells me ˋanything.	′Doesn't she?
You ˋneedn't °pay ˇnow.	′Needn't I?

Commands and Interjections

ˋDon't.	′Don't? ‖ (Why ˋnot?)
ˇCareful.	′Careful? ‖ (What ˋfor?)
ˋStop it.	′Stop it? ‖ (I'm ˏnot ˏdoing °anything.)
ˋWait a ˏbit.	′Wait a °bit? ‖ (But we've been ˏwaiting °ages alˋready.)

Verbal context	*Drill*
˅Telephone me, ₒthen.	ʹTelephone you? ‖ (How ˅can I?)
˅Think aₒbout it.	ʹThink a°bout it? ‖ (ʻWhy?)
ˋGive them ₒto her.	ʹGive them °to her? ‖ (ʻNo ˅fear!)
ˋKeep them ₒfor me.	ʹKeep them °for you? ‖ (I'd be ˋglad to.)
ˋHold it ₒfor me.	ʹHold it °for you? ‖ (A ˋpleasure.)
● ˋBuy me a ₒcouple.	ʹBuy you a °couple? ‖ (ˋCertainly.)
ʹShow me those ˎpapers.	ʹShow them °to you? ‖ (But I ˏhaven't °got them ˋhere.)
ˋRot!	ʹRot? ‖ (ˏWhat d'you ˋmean?)
ˋRubbish!	ʹRubbish? ‖ (But I ˏtell you I ˋhave ₒseen it.)
ˋPity!	ʹPity? ‖ (It ˏserves him ˋright.)
ˋMarvellous!	ʹMarvellous? ‖ (ˏHow d'you make ˋthat out?)
ˋExcellent!	ʹExcellent? ‖ (ˏWhat's so ˋexcellent aₒbout it?)
ˋWonderful ₒnews!	ʹWonderful °news? ‖ (ʹNothing of the ˎkind.)

Tune ⎯⎯ ╱   **Low Pre-Head+High Rise (+Tail)**

or

╱

Statements

He's ʹgoing on ˅holiday.	Aʹlone?
Not a ˅word from ˅Esther.	Surʹprised?
I've ʹgiven ˅up ₒsmoking.	For ʹgood?
ʹWhat d'you °think of the ˋcar?	Your ʹown?
I've ʹjust °met her ˋhusband.	You ʹlike him?
I'll ask ˋJoan to ₒlend us a ₒcorkscrew.	She's ʹgot one?
Have you ʹseen my ˏpen °anywhere?	You've ʹlost it?
Ask ˋBill to ₒplay the piₒano.	He's ʹcoming?

Verbal context	*Drill*
It's 'turning ˋcolder.	You ˊthink so?
I'll 'make you a ˋpresent of it.	You ˊmean °that?
I'm 'glad to say °Betty's ˋsafe.	You've ˊheard from her?
ˋTell me about this ₒnew ₒproject.	You're ˊinterested?
Mike's 'late aˋgain.	He's ˊoften °late?
We shall 'have to reˋturn it.	Imˊmediately?
● 'Pass me the ˏpaper.	The ˊTimes, d'you °mean?
'How about a °game of ˏbridge?	At ˊthis °time of °night?
'Agnes °looks quite ˋill.	She's ˊworrying about °something?
'What d'you °think of my ˋcoat?	It's a ˊnew one?
'Shall we go ˏswimming?	In Ocˊtober?
She's 'just off to the °Smiths' ˏparty.	She's been inˊvited?
● ˉHas ˏMichael ar°rived yet?	You were exˊpecting him?
John'll 'have to °give me that ˏmoney ₒback.	And if he reˊfuses?
He must 'make up his °mind at ˋonce.	At ˊonce?
He 'can't make °head or ˋtail of it.	He ˊcan't?
He'll be 'home for ˏChristmas.	For ˊChristmas?
It ˋmust be ₒright.	It ˊmust be?
It's an outˋrageous sug ₒgestion.	Outˊrageous?
'Let me °have it by ˏFriday.	By ˊFriday?
'Shall we °go to ˏgether?	To ˊgether?
It's 'painted on °both ˏsides.	On ˊboth °sides?
He 'really inˋsulted me.	Inˊsulted you?
They 'don't ˏlike it.	They ˊdon't °like it?
I'm a'fraid my ˋwatch had ₒstopped.	Your ˊwatch had °stopped?
I 'stopped °smoking a ˋlong time a ₒgo.	A ˊlong time a°go?
You ˋmust have ₒknown him.	I ˊmust have °known him?
● I shall 'send it off to°morrow after ˏnoon.	To ˊmorrow after°noon?
I ˋoffered it ₒto him.	You ˊoffered it °to him?
My ˋmother's ₒvery ₒill, I'm a ₒfraid.	Your ˊbrother's °ill, did you °say?
The po'tatoes are °too ˋsalt.	The poˊtatoes? ‖ (Or the ˋpeas, d'you ₒmean?)

WH-Questions

He 'sat on the ˋfloor.	On ˊwhat?
ˏGive it to °Anthony's ˋbrother.	To ˊwho?
I'm ˋflabbergasted.	You're ˊwhat?

Verbal context	*Drill*
He must be 'made to o͜o͜bey.	He must be 'what?
They'll be 'back by ˋFriday.	By 'when?
He'll 'meet us at °three fif͜teen.	At 'what °time?
● It's 'four °hundred feet ͜tall.	It's 'how °tall?
My ˋknife's ͜broken.	Your 'what's °broken?
That's ˋMarjorie's ͜grand pi͜ano.	That's 'whose °grand pi°ano?
● I 'told him about your sucˋcess.	About my 'what?

Yes-No Questions

● 'Would you ͜like one?	Would 'I °like one? ‖ (I'd ˋlove one.)
Is ͜that your °brother?	Is 'that my °brother? ‖ ('No, it's ˋnot.)
Did 'Bob °talk to ͜you?	Did 'Bob °talk to me? ‖ ('Yes, he ˋdid.)
'Won't °Liz be sur͜prised!	Won't 'Liz be sur°prised? ‖ (ˋNot ˇhalf!)
'Can I °ask you a ͜question?	Can 'you °ask me a °question? ‖ (ˋCertainly!)
'Could they ͜help it, d'you °think?	Could they 'help it? ‖ (Of ˋcourse they ͜could.)
‾Do you ͜want to °go?	Do I 'want to °go? ‖ ('Raˇther!)
'Didn't °Peter play ͜Hamlet °once?	Didn't 'who play °Hamlet?
'Don't you have a ͜light in your °garage?	Don't we have a 'what in our °garage?
'Can you °see my ͜glove °anywhere?	Is 'this the one?
We had a ˋmeeting | ͜last ͜night.	Should 'I have °been there?
I 'don't know ˋwhat I shall ͜do.	Can 'I °help at °all?
If 'only I °had enough ˋcapital!	Won't 'anyone °lend you the °money?
It's going to ˋfreeze | to͜night.	D'you 'think °so?
I 'liked it °very ͜much.	Were the 'others °pleased?
It's en'tirely up to ˋyou, ͜Bob.	Would you 'mind if I re°fused?
'Where can we °get a ͜gramophone?	Could we 'hire one, d'you °think?
'My °knife's ˋhopeless.	Well would 'mine °cut any °better?
I ˋwish you °wouldn't keep ˇjostling me.	Is it 'my °fault if you're °clumsy?
That's 'very ͜funny.	May we 'all know °what's a°musing you?
I've in'vited ˋeveryone.	Oughtn't 'I to have °been con°sulted?
● 'How d'you °like my ͜song?	D'you 'always °sing as °flat as °that?
I 'don't know ˋwhat up͜oset her.	Was it the ex'citement, d'you sup°pose?

Commands and Interjections

| Well re'mind me, ͜then. | Re'mind you? ‖ (What aˋbout?) |

Verbal context	*Drill*
Be ˎnice to them.	Be ˊnice to them? ‖ (Why ˎshould I?)
Re'member your ˎmanners.	Re'member them? ‖ (I've ˏnever forˎgotten them.)
Ex ˋplain it ₒto him.	Ex'plain it °to him? ‖ (What ˎfor?)
● 'Take them aˎway.	Take 'both of them a°way?
⁻The ˎbrute!	The 'brute? ‖ ('How ˎso?)
● Fan ˋtastic!	Fan'tastic? ‖ (What's fan'tastic aₒbout it?)
Co ˋlossal!	Co'lossal? ‖ ('Not ˇreally.)
'How ˎcharming!	How 'charming? ‖ ('Surely ₒnot.)
⁻Con ˎfound it!	Con'found it, did you °say?

Note: All the drills given above with the tune
LOW PRE-HEAD+HIGH RISE (+TAIL)
can be said with emphasis if the low pre-head is replaced by the high pre-head (see Chapter I, p. 36). With this feature marked the last drill in this section would read
⁻Con'found it, did you °say?

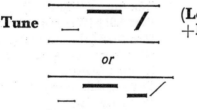

Tune   **(Low Pre-Head+) High Head +High Rise (+Tail)**

Statements

I've 'just had a °new ˎsuit ₒmade.	'Good ˊfit?
'Alan's not ˎhere, I'm aₒfraid.	He's 'gone ˊhome?
Oh 'take it aˎway.	You're 'not ˊinterested?
We're 'going ˎshopping.	'Right aˊway?
('When are you °coming to ˎstay with us?)	'Sometime ˊsoon?
('What does it ˎcost?)	'Seven ˊpounds °still?
'Where's my ˎnewspaper?	You 'want it ˊback?
'What's this I °hear about ˎGeorge?	He 'hasn't ˊtold you?
I 'bought that °house ˎafter ₒall.	You 'don't reˊgret it?

Verbal context	*Drill*
They'll 'have to sell ⟍up.	You 'really ⟋think so?
We'd 'better °send him a⟍nother ₒbill.	He 'hasn't ⟋paid for it °yet?
'Mine's a ⟍whisky.	You'd 'like some ⟋soda °with it?
'That won't °work at ⟍all ₒwell.	You've 'got a ⟋better sug°gestion?
'Come on ⟍Friday.	'Not before ⟋then?
We can ⟍count on ⟎Phillip.	He's 'definitely ⟋going?
'Let's °go to the ⟍pictures.	You've 'got enough ⟋money?
No, ⟍you ₒtake the ₒcar.	It 'won't incon⟋venience you?
I 'had to re⟍turn that ₒsquash ₒracquet.	You can 'borrow a⟋nother one?
'No more ⟍cake, °thank you.	A'nother °cup of ⟋tea?
'Take the °scissors by ⟍all ₒmeans.	Your 'wife °won't be ⟋needing them?
⟍Why have you °brought ⟍that ₒfile?	It's 'not the °one you ⟋want?
● 'Why not °ask ⟍Jennie?	You 'think she °might a⟋gree?
He swears he'll 'never °speak to her a⟍gain.	You 'think he °really ⟋means it °this time?
⟍No good °asking ⟎Kenneth.	He 'won't be °able to ⟋help?
I'm a'fraid he's al°ready ⟍gone.	My message 'didn't °reach him in ⟋time?
● It 'isn't ⟍fair.	'Not ⟋fair? ‖ ('Why ⟍not?)
I ⟍don't sup°pose it's ⟎true.	'Not ⟋true? ‖ ('How ⟍so?)
And 'that's not ⟍all he ₒsaid.	'Not ⟋all? ‖ (Well what ⟍else did he ₒsay?)
It's 'much °too ⟍big.	'Too ⟋big? ‖ (In 'what re⟍spect?)
● I'd like 'two ⟍dozen.	'Two ⟋dozen, sir? ‖ (⟍Certainly.)
I ⟍can't get the °car to ⟍start.	It 'won't ⟋start?
I've got the com'plete ⟍set.	You've got the com'plete ⟋set?
He's ⟍not much ⟎use.	'Not much ⟋use?
I 'felt °something ⟍move.	'Something ⟋move? ‖ (⟍When?)
'I should ⟍fry them.	'You would ⟋fry them? ‖ (⟍Why?)
⟍That was ⟍your lookₒout.	'That was ⟋my look°out?
They 'live near ⟍Eastbourne.	They 'live near ⟋Eastbourne?
We 'start to⟍morrow.	You 'start to⟋morrow?
He's 'very ⟍busy ₒthese ₒdays.	He's 'very ⟋busy, did you °say?
It's ⟍up to ⟍Peter to deₒcide.	It's 'up to ⟋Peter, did you °say?
⟍Mother's ₒlooking ₒfor you.	'Looking for ⟋me?
Take it 'three °times a ⟍day.	'Three °times a ⟋day?
They're 'not to be ⟍trusted.	'Not to be ⟋trusted?
They 'took what they ⟍wanted.	They 'took what they ⟋wanted?
You 'won't °know the ⟍difference.	I 'won't °know the ⟋difference?

Verbal context	*Drill*
I 'put them °back in the ˋairing ‚cupboard.	You 'put them °back in the ´airing °cupboard?
I ˅don't see what °good it'll °do to ˅Max.	You 'don't see what °good it'll °do to ´Max?

WH-Questions

'What ˅is it?	'What ´is it? ‖ (Why, a ˅pomegranate.)
● 'How °many ˏchildren has he ‚got?	'How ´many? ‖ (ˋSix, │ I be‚lieve.)
What ˅reason did he ‚give for his be‚haviour?	'What ´reason? ‖ (ˋNone, │ of ‚course.)
And why ˅shouldn't he ‚go if he ‚wants to?	'Why ´shouldn't he? ‖ (Because I 'need him ˋhere.)
'How ˅old is she?	'How ´old, did you °say? ‖ (She's ˅ten.)
'What's that ˋbowl ‚for?	'What's it ´for? ‖ (For the ˅flowers.)
● 'What would °you recom˅mend?	'What would ´I recom°mend? ‖ (The ˋsteak, │ I ‚think.)
'When did you ‚see him?	'When did I ´see him? ‖ (On ˅Sunday.)
'What's the °crowd ‚looking °at?	'What's the °crowd ´looking °at? ‖ (The ˅Cup ‚Final │ on ˅television.)
˅Now ‚what have you been ‚up to?	'What have I been ´up to? ‖ (ˋNothing.)
'How °much did you ˋgive for it?	'How °much did I ´give for it? ‖ (A ˅pound.)
‚Why don't you °write to the ˋsecretary?	'Why don't I °write to the ´secretary? ‖ (But I ˅have.)
I 'can't °come before ˅Tuesday.	Be'fore ´when?
He 'speaks °Hindu˅stani.	He 'speaks ´what °language?
I've walked 'ten ˅miles │ to‚day.	You've 'walked ´how far to°day?
They 'got it for a °mere ‚song.	For a 'mere ´what?
I 'told him to ˅scram.	You 'told him ´what?
We 'met him °last ˅summer.	You 'met him ´when?
It's 'warmer in the ˋkitchen.	It's 'warmer ´where?
He 'borrowed °five ‚pounds.	He 'borrowed ´how much?
It's 'number e˅leven.	It's 'number ´how many?
I'm to 'stay there °six ‚weeks.	You're to 'stay there ´how many °weeks?
'That °parcel's from ˅Jennifer.	'That one's from ´who?
● I waited there 'two °solid ‚hours.	You 'waited there ´how long?
We 'used to ˅braise them.	You 'used to do ´what to them?
He 'works in his ˃den │ 'all ‚day.	He 'works in his ´what all °day?
I'm a'fraid you'll be ˅angry.	You're a'fraid I'll be ´what?

Verbal context	*Drill*
I dis'covered them up`stairs.	You dis'covered them ′where?
I've ˇeaten °more than ˇTubby.	You've 'eaten °more than ′who?
The ˇblue one's °larger than the ˇblack.	The 'blue one's °larger than ′which one?
They be'haved like a °couple of °stuffed `dummies.	They be'haved like a °couple of ′what?

Yes-No Questions

'Is it ˌraining?	'Is it ′raining? ‖ (I'm 'not `sure.)
'Have you °answered his ˌletter?	'Have I ′answered it? ‖ (No, 'not ˌyet.)
'Have you ˌfinished it?	'Have I ′finished it, did you °say? ‖ (ˇNearly.)
'Will he °turn ˌup, d'you °think?	'Will he turn ′up? ‖ (ˌOh I should ˌthink so.)
'Did you enˌjoy the °concert?	'Did I en′joy it? ‖ (It was su`perb.)
'May I °shut the ˌwindow?	'May you °shut the ′window? ‖ (By `all ˌmeans.)
'Would you °like to ˌtry?	'Would I °like to ′try? ‖ (I'd `love to.)
'Will you be a°way ˌlong?	'Will I be a°way ′long? ‖ (About a `week.)
'Can't you be ˌsensible?	'Can't ′I be °sensible? ‖ (What have `I done ˌwrong?)
'Do the °others ˌlike it?	'Do the ′others °like it? ‖ (ˇSome of them.)
‾Wasn't 'Toynbee's °lecture `terrible!	'Wasn't ′whose °lecture °terrible?
`Isn't he eˌgregious!	'Isn't he ′what?
● Won't your 'wife be °rather ˌcross?	'Won't she be °cross with ′me, d'you °mean?
'Shouldn't the °doors be °double ˌlocked?	'Shouldn't the °doors be ′double °locked?
('What's it °like out`side?)	'Still ′snowing?
I 'can't find the °right sized `screw.	'Won't ′this one °do?
At 'last you've ar`rived.	'Been here ′long?
What de'licious ˌstrawberries!	'Want some ′more?
'Julia was in the `tennis ˌfinal.	'Did she ′win?
Do the 'eggs or the ˌflour ˌgo in ˌfirst?	'Does it ′matter?
`Now ˌwhat have you ˌlost?	'Seen my ′hat °anywhere?
‾Hulˌlo, Mrs. °Stevenson.	'Back al′ready, Mr. °Tompkins?
Oh 'dear oh ˌdear!	'Something the ′matter, °Joan?
('Welcome `back, ˌTom!)	'Had a °good ′holiday?
'What d'you °think of these `photos?	'Take them your′self?
What a 'charming ˌspot this ˌis!	Have you 'been here be′fore?

Verbal context	*Drill*

What a de'lightful ˎmeal! — Will you 'have some more ˊcoffee?

(We're 'going to °play ˋbridge.) — Would you 'care to °make a ˊfourth?

I've got Dr. ˋElliott ˳staying with me. — Is there 'any °chance of ˊmeeting him?

'Could I ˊtalk to you °sometime? — 'Are you °free ˊnow?

I've got a ˋdreadful ˳cold. — 'Doing °anything ˊfor it?

Would you 'like anything ˎwith your °bread and °butter? — Have you 'got any °strawberry ˊjam?

● 'Anybody °want a ˊlift? — Are you 'going near °Charing ˊCross, by °any °chance?

I ar'rived this ˋmorning. — Did 'someone °meet you at the ˊstation?

Have you 'finished e°xamining my ˎshoe? — 'May I have a °look at the ˊother one?

I 'seem to have ˋfar ˳too much ˳string. — 'Mightn't it be °better if you ˊcut it?

Commands and Interjections

ˏGet ˋrid of it. — 'Get ˊrid of it? ‖ (ˋWhy?)

'Please don't ˎworry. — 'Don't ˊworry, did you °say?

'Take it ˋhome. — 'Take it ˊhome? ‖ (Is 'that ˊwise?)

ˋHave a ˇheart. — 'Have a ˊheart? ‖ (Why ˋshould I?)

ˏTry aˋgain. — 'Try aˊgain? ‖ (ˋWhen?)

'Try the °second °phrase aˋgain. — 'Try the ˊsecond °phrase a°gain? ‖ ('Not the ˊthird?)

'Put it in ˎhere. — 'Put it in ˊthere? ‖ (Is ˊthat what you °said?)

● 'Tell me the ˎtime, ˳please. — 'Tell you the ˊtime? ‖ ('Ten past ˋsix.)

'Come over ˎhere a °minute. — 'Come over ˊthere a °minute? ‖ (What ˋfor?)

'Send it by °registered ˎpost. — 'Send it by ˊregistered °post? ‖ (⌐Is it ˊworth it?)

Con'sider the exˋpense. — Con'sider the exˊpense? ‖ (ˏHow d'you ˋmean?)

'Tell me °what it's ˎused ˳for. — 'Tell you °what it's ˊused °for? ‖ (ˋCertainly.)

● 'Leave the °key with Mrs. ˋAtkins. — 'Leave it with Mrs. ˊJoyce °Atkins?

'Mix it with °half a pound of ˎsugar. — 'Mix it with °half a pound of ˊsugar? ‖ (ˊCastor | or ˎgranulated?)

'Well ˋdone! — 'Well ˊdone? ‖ (It was ˋnothing, | ˏreally.)

'What a ˋshame! — 'What a ˊshame? ‖ (I'm 'not so ˋsure.)

'Stuff and ˎnonsense! — 'Stuff and ˊnonsense? ‖ (Oh I ˳don't ˎknow.)

Verbal context	Drill

● The 'silly young ˎfool!
The 'very iˎdea of such a ˳thing!

'Silly young ʹfool? ‖ (ʽWho? ‖ ʹJohn?)
The 'very iʹdea of such a °thing? ‖ (ʽWhy? ‖
What's ˎwrong?)

Note: All the relevant drills given above with the tune
    (LOW PRE-HEAD+) HIGH HEAD+HIGH RISE (+TAIL)
can be said with emphasis if one or both of the following features are used:
(*a*) the high pre-head instead of the low pre-head (see Chapter I, p. 36);
(*b*) the emphatic form of the high head (see Chapter I, p. 37).
The following drill is marked to show both these features:
    ⁻Is there 'any 'chance of ʹmeeting him?

8 *The Jackknife*

Attitude

In STATEMENTS: impressed, awed, complacent, self-satisfied, challenging, censorious, disclaiming responsibility.

In WH-QUESTIONS: challenging, antagonistic, disclaiming responsibility.

In YES-NO QUESTIONS: impressed, challenging, antagonistic.

In COMMANDS: disclaiming responsibility, sometimes hostile.

In INTERJECTIONS: impressed, sometimes a hint of accusation.

Tone marks used in JACKKNIFE drills

A Stressed, accented syllables (Nucleus, Head)
[^] (i) without Tail: medium rising to high, then falling to very low pitch.
  (ii) with Tail: *either* medium rising to high pitch *or* medium level pitch; the rise-fall is completed by the tail syllable(s).
['] Relatively high level pitch.
[°] Relatively high level pitch, the same pitch as the *preceding* ['].

B Stressed, unaccented syllables (Tail)
[˳] Very low level pitch, the same pitch as the end of the *preceding* [^] or the *preceding* [˳].

Tune ⟋ ⎯ *or* ⎯ ⟍ **Rise-Fall + Tail**

Verbal context	*Drill*

Statements

'How °many did she 'give you, ₒBobby? — ^Seven. ^Twenty. ^Thirty. ^Masses.

It's 'good, | 'isn't it? — ^Marvellous. ^Wonderful.

● ⎯Can you ‚see? — ^Perfectly. ^Easily.

'Wasn't it a ₒgood ₒlecture! — ^Very ₒgood. ^Excellent.

Have you 'ever been to ‚York? — ^Many ₒtimes. ^Often.

It was 'better the ˇsecond ₒtime, | ‚wasn't it? — ^Much ₒbetter. ^Very much ₒbetter.

Now re'member what I've 'said, ₒPeter. — ^Yes, ₒDaddy.

You 'won't °tell a 'soul, | 'will you, ₒJohn? — ^No, Mr. ₒHarris. ^No-one, ₒFrank.

It's 'rather 'difficult, | ‚isn't it? — ^Terribly ₒdifficult. ^Awfully ₒdifficult.

She was ‚wearing °purple 'stockings. — ^Purple! ‖ (Now ^there's a ₒthing!)

We're having 'strawberries for ₒtea. — ^Strawberries! ‖ ('Oh, ^good!)

I got 'ten 'pounds for it. — ^Ten ₒpounds! ‖ (You ^were ₒlucky!)

I've 'written 'all my ₒletters. — ^All of them! ‖ (You ^have been ₒquick!)

It's 'Peter's ₒturn, I ₒthink. — ^Peter's ₒturn! ‖ (Well I 'like ^that!)

He 'doesn't °show much ˇgratitude. — ^Gratitude! ‖ (Is ^that what you ex₀pect?)

And 'Jack °paid for the ice'cream. — ^Jack ₒpaid for it! ‖ (‚What's come 'over him?)

You'd 'better °say you're 'sorry. — ^I'd ₒbetter say I'm ₒsorry! ‖ ('What about ^Frank?)

It'll be 'abso°lutely di'sastrous. — ^Clearly. ‖ (But 'what can 'I ₒdo?)

'What was the 'maths paper ₒlike? — ^Simple. ^Easy. ^Horrible.

A ^lovely ₒcake! ‖ 'Who ‚made it? — ^I did. ^Janet ₒdid.

⎯Are you ‚sure? — ^Certain. ^Positive. ^Dead ₒsure.

You've 'won a'gain. — ^Naturally. ‖ (I'm ^good at ₒdarts.)

'Whose is the °new 'car? — ^Peter's. ^Michael's. ^Anthony's.

'Who's °got it 'wrong? — ^No-one. ^None of us. ^None of us ₒhas.

Did you 'catch your ‚train? — ^Comfortably. ‖ ^Loads of ₒtime to ₒspare.

'Anyone °still 'need this? — ^I do. ‖ (For ^one.)

You have 'sandwiches for °lunch? — ^Frequently. ‖ ('What's so °odd about ^that?)

Verbal context	*Drill*
I'm a'fraid I've ˋlost.	^Surely ₒnot.
You'll ˇmake a ˇmess of it.	^Probably. ‖ (But I'm ˇstill going to ˇtry.)
The ˇtrouble with ˇyou ₒis ǀ you're ˋlazy.	^You can ₒtalk. ^You're a ₒfine one to ₒtalk.
Must she 'type it °out aˏgain?	^Obviously she ₒmust. ‖ (It's ^full of misₒtakes.)
I ˋdo wish I could ˏwin.	^Everybody ₒdoes. ‖ (But it's ˇno good ˇwishing.)
You ˏcan't do ˏthat.	^Certainly I ₒcan.
(There's ˏno ˏhurry a°bout it.)	^Friday would be ₒtime enough.
The comˇmittee won't ₒhelp.	^We'll have to ₒdo it, ₒthen.
'How °early did you ˋget there? ‖ ˇTen?	^Earlier. ^Earlier, in ₒfact.
'Was it as °good as the ˏlast °concert?	^Better. ^Just as ₒgood.
● 'Is he as °tall as his ˏfather?	^Taller, ₒeven.
Did 'any of the ˏparents turn °up?	^Masses ₒof them. ^None of them. ^All of them ₒcame.
'How °soon d'you ˋwant them? ‖ By ˇTuesday?	^Sooner, I'm aₒfraid.
'May I °take this ˏchair?	^Certainly. ^Surely.
'Will you ˏhelp me?	^Willingly. ^Gladly.
'Who told the °boss I was ˏlate?	^Nobody.
'What are ˏyou ₒup to, ₒJohnnie?	^Nothing, ₒDaddy.
'Which would be the ˋbetter?	^Either would ₒdo.
● I was 'very ˋcross with him.	^Naturally. ‖ ^Anyone ₒwould be.

WH-Questions

I ˇcan't °see you toˇday.	^When, ₒthen?
I've 'left my ˋhat beₒhind.	^Where, ₒpray?
'Come over ˋhere a ₒminute, ₒFrank.	^Now ₒwhat? ^Now what's the ₒmatter?
'Would you mind °passing the ˏbook?	^What ₒbook? ^Which ₒbook?
D'you 'see that ˏman over °there?	^Which ₒman? ‖ (I can see 'ten at ^least.)
I shall want ˇmore than ˇthat.	^How much ₒmore?
I 'know it for a ˋfact.	^How d'you ₒknow?
'Someone's ^bound to ₒhave one.	^Who, may I ₒask?
You'll just ˏhave to ˋwait.	^Why, for ₒheaven's ₒsake?
(If you ˇtell ˇFrank, ǀ 'he'll tell ^Maud.)	^Then ₒwhat should we ₒdo?
Oh I ˋam ₒsorry.	^Now ₒwhat have you ₒdone ₒwrong?

Verbal context	*Drill*
I 'go there °quite ˅often.	^How ₒoften, if you ₒdon't mind my ₒasking?
There ˅must be ˅someone who'll ₒhelp.	^Who, ₒthough?
You ˅made a °mess of ˅that.	^How ₒdid I?
● ˅Surely ˅one of these ₒscrews will ₒfit.	^Which of them, ₒthough?

Yes-No Questions

● He 'shot an ˅elephant.	^Did he? ^Did he, ₒnow?
You ˏcan't go in ˏthere.	^Can't I? ‖ (We'll ^see about ₒthat.)
I'll 'punch your ˅head.	^Will you? ‖ (And 'who'll ^help you?)
They've 'nowhere to ˅live.	^Haven't they?
I 'wouldn't put ˅up with it.	^Wouldn't you?
I've ˅finished ₒpainting the ˏkitchen.	^Have you, ₒnow? ‖ (You ^have got a ₒmove on.)
You'd 'better °mind your ˅manners.	^Had I, inₒdeed!
He 'wants it by ˅Saturday.	^Does he, by ₒJove!
What a 'beautiful ˏday!	^Isn't it! ‖ ('Just like ^summer.)
'What d'you °think of my ˅roses?	^Aren't they deₒlightful!
'Jean's come ˅second in her eₒxams.	^Hasn't she ₒdone ₒwell!
It rained 'all ˅day.	^Wasn't that a ₒpity!
I ˅don't think °much of the ˅photos.	^Haven't they made a ₒmess of them!
I ˏthought she'd ˅never ₒcalm ₒdown.	^Didn't she get worked ₒup about it!
'John's ˅manager | ˏnow.	^Hasn't he got ₒon in the ₒlast few ₒyears!
She ˅says she can ₒplay.	^Can she, ₒthough?
'I think we should ˏrisk it.	^Dare we ₒrisk it?
He was in˅tending to ₒgo.	^Did he ₒgo, in ₒfact?
We could ˅always °give them °bread and ˅cheese.	^Have we ₒany, ₒthough?

Note: Examples of this tune used for question tags in sentences like

^Awful, \| ^wasn't it?

are given in Chapter V, Section 14.

Commands

D'you 'think they'd ˏhelp me?	^Ask them.
I'd 'like to °borrow your ˅shears, | if I ˏmay.	^Take them.

Verbal context	*Drill*
I ˏdon't ˋwant to ˳play.	^Don't, ˳then. ^Don't ˳play, then.
He ˏsays he °won't ˋpay.	^Make him ˳pay. ^Give it to him, ˳then.
She'd pre'fer to °go ˋcamping.	^Let her, ˳then.
'May I °take this ˏpaper?	^Do, my ˳dear.
'Would you ac°cept a ciˏgar?	^Offer me ˳one. ‖ ('Then you'll ^know.)
But ˏwho's going to ˋbreak it ˳to him?	^You ˳tell him. ‖ (ˏYou're his ˏcousin, °aren't you?)
The 'sponge looks deˋlicious.	^Try a ˳piece of it.
● I ˋhate it. ‖ But ˏwhat can I ˋdo?	^Tell them you ˳hate it.
Their 'phone is °out of ˋorder.	^Write to them, in ˳that case.
My ˋshoes are ˳too ˳tight.	^Loosen them a ˳bit, then.

Interjections

You can 'borrow my ˋJaguar.	^Thank you! ‖ ^Most ˳kind of you.
I've 'got a ˋknighthood.	^Splendid! ‖ (Con'gratu^lations!)
He's an 'M.ˋP. | ˏnow.	^Never! ‖ (You ^do surˏprise me!)
It's ˋafter eˇleven.	^Gracious! ‖ (‾Is that ˏreally the °time?)
He 'says it's ex'pensive.	^Nonsense! ‖ (It's 'very ^cheap.)
He's 'only °thirty ˋthree.	^Fancy! ‖ (I'd have 'said he was ^older.)
He's ˏspilt the °whole ˋbowlful.	^Goodness! ‖ ^What a ˳mess!
● ‾Did you ˏfinish that °job?	^Heavens, ˳yes! ‖ ^Ages a˳go!
Well why ˋcan't I ˳use my ˳fingers?	^Please, ˳Eric! ‖ ('Think of your ^manners.)
They've 'broken their en'gagement.	^There's a ˳fine ˳thing!
I ˋhaven't ˇbroken my ˳leg | 'after ˋall.	^That's a ˳good ˳job!

Tune ⋀ Rise-Fall only

Statements

Have you 'heard about ˏPat?	^Yes. ‖ ('Isn't it ^scandalous!)
'Have a ˏsandwich, ˳Mary.	^Ham! ‖ (I aˋdore ˏham.)
● Did you 'see any ˏlions?	^Lots. ^Scores.
'Who °painted ˏthis?	^Me. ‖ (^Aren't I ˳clever!)
'Who was °top of the ˏclass?	^Jane. ^Don. ^Hugh. ^Keith.

Verbal context	*Drill*
'What was the ˏfood ˳like?	^Grand. ^Fine. ^Great.
'What did you °have to `drink?	^Wine. ^Gin. ^Beer.
I took `ten | at the ˏninth °hole.	^Ten! || (A ^cricket ˳score!)
I've 'asked `Jill to ˳stand ˳in.	^Jill! || ('Why ^her?)
We've 'painted the °bathroom `red.	^Red! || (Why ^that ˳colour?)
'I thought he was a °bit `dull.	^Dull! || (He 'certainly ^was!)
'Isn't it a °bit ˏcold in °here?	^Cold! || (It's 'like an ^ice ˳box.)
I 'think `I'll have a ˳try.	^You! || (^That's a ˳new iˏdea.)
Did you 'have to °wait ˏlong?	^Weeks. ^Months. ^Years.
'Whose is the `new ˳bike?	^John's. ^Jack's. ^Tom's.
'Where are you °going for your ˏholidays?	^France. ^Spain. ^Greece.
'Was your °car ˏnew | or 'second ˏhand?	^New. || ('Brand ^new.)
● 'Have you any ˏdoubts a°bout it?	^None. || ('None whatso^ever.)
'What's it ˏmade of?	^Gold. || ('Eighteen ^carat.)
Well 'how `soon d'you ˳want it?	^Now. || (This 'very ^minute.)
You ˏdo know the °way, | `don't you?	^No. || (I ^don't.)
Well ˏwhere shall we `hold the ˳meeting?	^Here. || (ˏAny obˏjections?)
And 'whose is ^this, may I ˳ask?	^Mine. || (And ˏwhat's ˏwrong with it?)
'Which d'you pre`fer?	^These. || (^Obviously.)
'Where d'you think `you're ˳going?	^Home. ^Out.
‾D'you 'weigh as °much as °twelve ˏstone?	^More.
You'll need as 'little as °four ´yards?	^Less.
● ‾Is it ˏcheaper by °coach?	^Much.
'Can you get as °many as ˏeight in °there?	^Nine.
'Is it a ˏbig °house?	^Huge.
It'll be 'abso°lutely diˏsastrous.	^Quite. || (But 'what can ^I ˳do?)

WH-Questions

You could ˈsurely find the °money ˇsomewhere.	^Where?
You'll ˈhave to ac˳cept.	^Why?
● ^You ˳pay for it.	^How?
ˇSomeone'll ˳have to ˳go.	^Who?
Well ^borrow a ˏruler.	^Whose?
'Come and °see me a`gain.	^When?
Only ˇone of them is ˳yours.	^Which?

Verbal context	*Drill*

Commands

'May I °take this ‚newspaper? ^Do. ^Please.

⁻Could I ‚manage it, d'you °think? ^Try.

● 'What °ought I to `do? ^Wait. ^Stay. ^Fight. ^Come. ^Go.

'How d'you ad°vise me to `get there? ^Fly. ^Walk. ^Swim.

'Who are the `flowers ₒfrom? ^Guess.

(I can 'tie my °own ^tie, ₒDaddy.) ^Look. ^Watch.

'Shall we ‚dance? ^Let's. ‖ ('That's what we ˇcame ₒfor.)

Interjections

● `John's got it | ‚now. ^Oh! ‖ ('That's ^different.)

You can 'have it °back on `Sunday. ^Fine! ‖ (That's ^plenty ₒsoon enough.)

I've `finished. ^Good! ‖ (You were 'quicker than I ex-
^pected.)

I'll intro`duce you ₒto him. ^Thanks! ^Great!

Have you 'seen my °gold ‚watch? ^Gosh! ‖ ^Gold!

I've 'just got en°gaged to `Sheila. ^Well! ‖ (⁻You ^are a ₒdark ₒhorse.)

'You can `drive | if you ‚like. ^Right!

'Have a °glass of cham‚pagne. ^Grand! ^Cheers!

Tune ‾ ∧

or

‾ ／

Low Pre-Head+Rise-Fall (+Tail)

Statements

He's got 'two `wives. I ^know. I ^know he ₒhas.

⁻Did you ‚like it? E^normously. Im^mensely. Tre^mendously.

You can `keep it | if you ‚want to. You ^are ₒkind.

They can 'have a °week ‚off. They ^will be ₒpleased.

'What d'you °think of my °new `dress? It ^does look ₒnice. It's ^gorgeous.

'Was it °well ‚acted? Sur^prisingly ₒwell. A^mazingly ₒwell
ₒacted.

Verbal context	*Drill*
Did you 'have a °good ,time?	A ^marvellous ₒtime.
'Ever been to °Box 'Hill?	On ^several ocₒcasions. ‖ It's a ^charming ₒspot.
I 'find the re°port en'couraging.	Ex^tremely enₒcouraging.
'Only °three 'pounds I ₒpaid.	It's a ^bargain, ₒJack.
Will I 'do?	You look ^lovely, my ₒdear.
(I 'wonder he puts ^up with it.)	It's a^mazing how ₒpatient he ₒis.
I ex'pect you've 'heard about ₒBill.	Yes, I was ^very surₒprised. ‖ And ^pleasantly ₒso.
He won a 'gold 'medal.	A ^gold one!
I 'have to be °back by 'Sunday.	By ^Sunday! ‖ (^So ₒsoon!)
You can 'have it for 'nothing.	For ^nothing! ‖ (^How ₒkind!)
It was 'all °rather a'musing.	A^musing! ‖ (It was 'downright in^sulting.)
I 'met him in 'Oxford ₒStreet.	In ^Oxford ₒStreet! ‖ ('What was he °doing ^there?)
I 'made it with°out 'sugar.	With^out ₒsugar! ‖ ('How did you °manage ^that?)
I 'did it on my 'own.	On your ^own! ‖ ('Well ^done!)
I've 'no 'choice in the °matter?	Pre^cisely. ‖ ('No choice at ^all.)
You can have what'ever you ₗlike.	I ^know I ₒcan.
He 'wishes he could 'come, │ ₗnow.	Of ^course he ₒdoes. ‖ But he ^can't.
Will you 'win, d'you °think?	I'm ^bound ₒto. I'm ^bound to ₒwin.
‾Can you 'manage it aₗlone?	I'm ^sure I ₒcan.
(I 'knew he'd get ₗon.)	I've ^always ₒsaid so.
'Anyone °get it 'right?	We've ^all got it ₒright.
‾Is it too ₗlate to °give up °smoking?	It's ^never too ₒlate.
‾D'you ₗreally °know the °way?	I'm ^positive. I'm ^positive I ₒdo. I'm ^positive I ₒknow the ₒway.
‾D'you know 'Fred ₗHarris?	In^deed I ₒdo. ‖ He's my ^brother in ₒlaw.
'How did you ^manage it?	It was ^easy, my ₒdear ₒchap.
'Shall we °try the ₗcrossword?	I've already ^done it.
ₗWhy don't you 'like it?	I ^do. But I ^do ₒlike it.
Is it 'my °turn?	No, ^mine. No, it's ^Alison's.
'May I °have some more ₗtrifle?	There ^isn't any ₒmore. ‖ You've ^eaten it ₒall.

Verbal context	*Drill*

He's 'going to °get it ‸mended.
I should ^hope ₒso. ‖ (‚He ‚broke it.)

Have you 'got all you ‚want?
By ^no ₒmeans. ‖ I want ^lots ₒmore.

(What'ever were you ^thinking ₒof?)
I'm sur^prised at you.

● I 'thought you °didn't ‸like ₒspinach.
On the ^contrary. ‖ I ^love it.

Well they ˅said they'd ₒbring it.
But they ^haven't ₒbrought it.

He ‚doesn't speak ‚French, °does he?
Of ^course he ₒdoesn't. ‖ You should ^know ₒthat.

‚Why didn't you °bring the ‸screws?
I thought ^you'd ₒtaken them.

‚Why be so ‸rude to him?
I just ^felt like being ₒrude to him.

(I ˅shouldn't buy ˅that.)
It's so ex^pensive.

'Why didn't you ^tell me?
You didn't ^ask me.

You don't ˅have to ac₀cept.
No but I'd ^like to.

I 'don't ‸want to ₒplay, | ‸really I ₒdon't.
I ^know you ₒdon't. ‖ But you'll just ^have to.

(I've ‸not only ˅written my ₒletter.)
I've ^posted it.

It was so ^obvious, | ^wasn't it?
My ^brother ₒnoticed it. ‖ (And 'he's ^very unob₀servant.)

(To'morrow °morning's ^hopeless.)
To^night ₒwouldn't be ₒsoon enough.

(It's ‸useless | ‚writing him a ‚letter.)
A ^telegram wouldn't ₒreach him in ₒtime.

There'll be about ‸ten, I sup₀pose.
There'll be ^more.

I 'doubt whether there'll be ‸time.
There most ^certainly ₒwon't be ₒtime.

You should at ‸least have ˅drawn the ₒgame.
I should have ^won. ‖ By a ^street.

'Can I have ‚ten °bottles of °beer?
You can have ^fifty.

'Shall we be in ‚time?
We'll be a^head of ₒtime.

It was 'rather ‸odd, | ‸wasn't it?
It was in^credible.

'Can I have a ‚word with you?
By ^all ₒmeans.

'Why did you °pay in ‸cash?
They in^sisted ₒon it.

(˅I ₒcan't ad₀vise you.)
It's your ^own re₀sponsi₀bility.

'Shall I °go or ‚shan't I?
As you ^like. ‖ It's for ^you to de₀cide.

‚Where does he ‸get them ₒfrom?
I couldn't ^say. I don't ^know.

'What would ‸you do a₀bout his pro₀posal?
I should ig^nore it.

'Would you °mind ‚helping?
I should be ^glad to.

I 'hoped you'd be °here ‸earlier.
You should have ^told me.

(It's ‸not ˅my de₀cision.)
It's the com^mittee's.

(I'd ˅like to ₒhelp.)
But it's im^possible.

Verbal context	*Drill*

WH-Questions

^You must ₒask him.	Why ^me?
I'm 'sending ˋPeter | ˏthis °time.	Why ^Peter? || ('Why not ^Paul?)
ˇThat's not the ₒway to ₒdo it.	Well ^how, ₒthen?
You'll ˋhave to °give them ˇsome.	How ^much, ₒthough?
(I ˋtold him he was ₒbeing ˏfoolish.)	What ^more could I ₒdo?
I 'couldn't be °more ˏangry.	But ^why, for ₒheaven's ₒsake?
● 'Why should ˏyou do the ₒdonkey work?	Who ^else is there to ₒdo it?
I'll ˋsend it ₒto you.	Just ^when, if that ₒisn't a ₒrude ₒquestion?
● I'll ˋmake it ˇsoon, | I ˋpromise.	Yes but ^how ₒsoon?
You can have ˇone of them.	Yes but ^which, may I ₒask?

Yes-No Questions

You don't know 'what you're ˏtalking aₒbout.	Oh ^don't I?
'I should keep ˋquiet aₒbout it.	Oh ^would you?
He 'doesn't °want to ˋpart with it.	Oh ^doesn't he?
It was a ˋshame | he ˏhad to give ˏup.	Yes, ^wasn't it?
It would be ˋnice | to have a ˏcar.	Yes, ^wouldn't it?
● You 'ought to a^pologise.	Oh ^ought I, inₒdeed?
'Arthur had a ˋrise | toˏday.	Is ^that why he's so ₒcheerful?
They've 'given him a ˋtravel ₒscholarship.	Now ^isn't that ₒsplendid!
'Jean's going to °wear a biˋkini.	Won't ^that be a ₒfine ₒsight!
'What price °poor old ^Peter!	Oh ^doesn't he ₒlook ₒill!
I'm 'getting ˋold, I'm aₒfraid.	Aren't ^all of us ₒgetting ₒold!
● 'Everything's so ^dear.	Aren't po^tatoes a ₒprice!
'What an °odd ˋpair they ₒare!	Didn't ^Janet look a ₒfright!
ˋIf you were ˇlate | you should a'pologise.	But ^was I? But ^was I ₒlate?
ˏAll ˏright. || I'll ˋgive it to you.	D'you ^mean ₒthat? || Can I ^count on it?
I ˇcould ₒplay.	Well ^will you, ₒthen?
I simply 'don't underˏstand her.	Does ^anyone?
'All ˏright. || I'll ˋhave it.	D'you ^really ₒwant it?
He was 'cross because you ˋbeat him.	Is ^that ₒall it ₒwas?
I'm at my 'wits' ˏend.	Could ^I ₒhelp at ₒall?
He 'didn't °like their ˋattitude.	Would ^you have ₒliked it?
'That's ^silly. || 'Betty's ^hopeless.	Would ^Pamela be a ₒbetter ₒchoice, then?
She ˇought to be ₒable to ₒget it.	Yes but ^can she?

Verbal context	*Drill*
He ˇmay still ₒcome.	Is it ^likely, ₒthough?
He ˇsays he's ₒinterested.	Is he ^really ₒinterested?
(It's ˈall very °well to ˇcriticise.)	But could ^you do ₒany ₒbetter?
No ˇthat's not the ₒone I ₒwant.	Well then is ^this the ₒone you ₒhad in ₒmind?

Commands

ˈMay I °help my‚self?	Yes, ^do.
I don't ˇreally ₒwant to ₒgo.	Re^fuse, ₒthen.
ˈThis is °rather a ˋdreary ₒparty.	Let's ^go, ₒthen.
She ˋnever ₒanswers ₒletters.	Well ^phone her, ₒthen.
ˈMay I have a °few ‚grapes?	Take ^all of them.
He's ˈtaken my umˋbrella.	Go ^after him. ‖ And get it ^back.
ˈWouldn't you °like to ‚fetch it °for her?	No, ^you ₒfetch it.
ˈCan I °tell ‚Malcolm?	By ^all means ₒtell him.
‾Would ‚Harris sub°scribe, d'you sup°pose?	Sug^gest it ₒto him.
ˈDon't °talk with your ‚mouth ₒfull.	Don't ^you do it, ₒthen.
ˈDon't look so °disapˋproving.	Be^have yourself, ₒthen.
ˈDon't °treat me like a ‚baby.	Be ^sensible, ₒthen.
(ˈMost of these °sums are ^wrong.)	Take ^this one, for ₒinstance.
He's ˋvery °keen to ˇbuy.	Then ^sell it ₒto him, in ₒthat case.
ˈJackson's °worse than ^useless.	Dis^miss him, if he's ₒso unsatisₒfactory.
And the ˈletter from ˊStevens?	Just ig^nore it.
● ˈNobody °seems at ^all ₒkeen.	Well give ^up the iₒdea.
She ˇwon't do it without °being ˇprompted.	Then re^mind her aₒbout it.
I ˇought to inₒvite her.	Well then in^vite her.
But the ˋpurchase tax ₒmay come ₒdown.	In that case ^wait a bit beₒfore you ₒbuy.

Interjections

Did you ˈpass your e‚xam?	Of ^course! Of ^course I ₒdid!
ˈOver a °thousand ^pounds we've colₒlected.	Good ^gracious! ‖ A ^record!
He's ˈdue ˋhome │ to‚morrow.	How ^marvellous!
Will you ˈlend a ˊhand, °Tom?	With ^pleasure! Why, ^certainly!
ˋHullo, │ ‚Ted.	Good ^evening, ₒGeorge.
I've ˈleft it at ˋhome.	Well ^really, ₒFrank! ‖ You ^are a ₒnuisance!
ˈTerry knocked a po°liceman's ˋhat off.	The ^devil he ₒdid!

Verbal context	*Drill*

'Hullo, | ,Michael.

Oh ^there you ₀are, ₀Freddie. ‖ Good ^morning.

The 'front ˋwheel came ₀off.
● The ˋpetrol ₀tank was ₀empty.
I'm ˋso sorry I was ,rude.

Well ^what an ex₀traordinary ₀thing!
No ^wonder the ₀car wouldn't ₀start!
I should ^think so, in₀deed!

Note: All the drills given above with the tune

LOW PRE-HEAD+RISE–FALL (+TAIL)

can be said with emphasis if the low pre-head is replaced by the high pre-head (see Chapter I, p. 36). With this feature indicated the last drill in this section would read

⁻I should ^think so, in₀deed!

Tune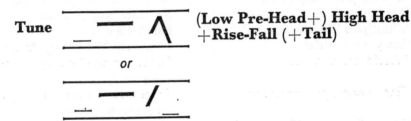

(Low Pre-Head+) High Head +Rise-Fall (+Tail)

or

Statements

'Have °some?
Did you 'like it?
Are you 'fond of him?

'Smoked ^salmon! ‖ ('What a ^treat!)
I 'simply ^hated it.
I 'just can't ^tell you ₀how much he ₀means to me.

'What was the ˋparty ₀like?

'First ^rate. ‖ I 'don't know ^when I've en-₀joyed myself so ₀much.

'How °much did you ˋget for it?

'Five °thousand ^pounds. ‖ (^Much more than I ex₀pected.)

I can ˋget you one, | if you ,like.
⁻Did you en,joy the °film?

'That would be ^wonderful.
'Very ^much. ‖ 'More than I ^thought I ₀would.

'Was he ,really so °bad?

'Abso°lutely ^terrible. ‖ I could 'hardly be^lieve it.

,What about his ˋcabbages?

I've 'never seen °anything ^like them. ‖ They're 'simply e^normous.

Verbal context	Drill
'Didn't you ˌfinish it?	No, it was 'more °difficult than I'd ^thought.
I got 'two °hundred ˋpounds for it.	'Two ^hundred! ‖ (As 'much as ^that!)
He weighs 'eighteen ˋstone.	'Eighteen ^stone!
He's 'emigrating to °Argen^tina.	'Argen^tina! ‖ ('Why ^there?)
● 'Is he getting ˌfatter?	'Getting ^fatter! ‖ (He's ^huge!)
I 'made this °cake myˋself.	'Made it your^self! ‖ ('Good for ^you!)
We'll have 'coffee in the ˌsummer ₒhouse.	'Coffee in the ^summer ₒhouse! ‖ (^How ₒnice!)
Catch the 'three o°clock from ˋEuston.	The 'three o°clock from ^Euston! ‖ (But it's ˌnearly °that alˋready.)
'Would you mind °cleaning the ˌwindows?	'That's ^soon ₒdone.
'How did your °party go ˋoff?	'Very ^well, I'm ₒglad to ₒsay.
'After ˋyou, ₒCecil.	No, 'after ^you, ₒClaude.
Is 'that your °last ˌword?	I'm aˈfraid it ^is.
'Did you comˌplain?	I 'certainly ^did. ‖ 'Very ^much so.
I should 'ask for a ˋrise.	I most 'certainly ^shall. ‖ Beˈfore the ^day's out.
⌐But ˌhow did you ˋmanage it?	There was 'nothing ^to it. ‖ It 'couldn't have been ^simpler.
(I had a 'letter from ˋFrank │ toˌday.)	He's 'asked me to go ^out with him.
It's 'abso°lutely riˌdiculous.	I 'quite a^gree with you. ‖ I 'couldn't a°gree ^more.
John ˋfailed his ₒdriving test.	I'm 'not sur^prised. ‖ He's 'no °road sense at ^all.
● 'Did you °save ˌtime?	I was 'able to °do it in ^half the ₒtime.
⌐D'you ˌreally °need it?	'Yes, I ^do. Inˈdeed I ^do.
Of ^course he'll aₒgree.	'That's what ^you ₒthink.
He said 'only ^he could ₒuse it.	'That's all ^he ₒknows.
'Would you mind °lending me a ˌhand?	'You're a ^nuisance. ‖ ('Can't you °see I'm ˌbusy?)
'Why didn't you ^tell me?	I 'thought you ^knew.
I'm exˋtremely ˌsorry.	I should 'think you ^are.
Jane was ˋterribly upˌset.	You can 'hardly ^blame her.
'Why not this ˋmorning?	Because there 'isn't ^time. ‖ We're 'late as it ^is.
(It's ˈmuch too late ˇnow.)	You should have 'told me be^forehand.

Verbal context	Drill
I'm 'having my `house ₒpainted.	And 'not before ^time. ‖ It's an 'absolute dis^grace.
So you 'think I'm dis^honest.	'Not at ^all. ‖ The ac'counts °just don't ^balance.
They're 'sending you to `India.	I 'don't be^lieve you. ‖ I'm 'due for °three months' ^leave.
I 'don't `like the ₒman.	You've 'never °even ^spoken ₒto him.
So you 'had to give ^up.	It was 'not like °that at ^all.
● 'Why didn't you ^call for me?	We 'thought you'd al°ready ^gone.
(I'm `not staying ˅there aₒgain.)	You 'can't even °have a ^bath when you ₒwant one.
He 'thinks you're a`fraid.	He can 'think what he °jolly well ^likes.
Well 'sometime `next week, ₒthen.	I 'don't think you °quite under^stand. ‖ I 'never want to °see you a^gain.
(What'ever made you ^take such a ₒrisk?)	It 'wasn't as if you °hadn't been ^warned.
I ˏcan't `do it.	You 'aren't ^trying.
(It's ˏnot a very ˏdifficult °game.)	My 'small ^son can ₒplay it.
'Hasn't °Tim ^grown!	He 'has in^deed.
'Can I have a °box of ˏmatches?	You can 'have a ^hundred.
I `hope we're °not ˅late.	We'll be 'far too ^early.
‾Have you ˏfinished it?	I 'haven't be^gun it.
D'you 'think there'll be ˏtime?	There'll 'jolly well ^have to be.
'One °lump ‖ or ˏtwo?	I 'usually °take ^three.
'Read any of 'Hacket's °books?	I've 'never °even ^heard of him.
'Was it a ˏgood °show?	It was the 'best they've °ever ^done.
Are you as 'heavy as °twelve ˏstone?	'Very °nearly thir^teen.
(`Sorry I can't ₒhelp you with ˏyours.)	I 'haven't °finished my ^own.
He has a 'good `opinion of himₒself.	And he 'doesn't °hesitate to ^show it.
`Strange, ‖ `wasn't it?	It was 'absolutely °unbe^lievable.
● I was 'absolutely ˏlivid.	I 'don't ^blame you. ‖ It's e'nough to °make a ^saint ₒangry.
'Which ˏracquet shall I ₒtake?	You can 'take ^either. I 'don't ^mind.
Would you 'keep it or ˏsell it?	'I should ^sell it.
The 'whole thing's ˏstupid.	'That's what ^I ₒthink.
I a'fraid °Tess will be up`set.	'Very ^likely. ‖ She 'often ^is.
‾D'you 'mind if I ˏjoin you?	'Not at ^all. 'Not in the ^least.

Verbal context	*Drill*
He's 'threatened to re'sign.	I 'couldn't °care ^less. ‖ He can 'do what he ^likes.
'How °much should I 'take?	As 'much as you ^need.
'Which one shall I 'choose?	It's 'up to ^you. ‖ You must 'make up your ^own ₒmind.
'When can I ‚borrow it?	'Any °time you ^like.
You 'won't 'tell anyone, │ 'will you?	'Nobody at ^all. ‖ I 'wouldn't ^dream of it.
'Can you °lend us some ‚money?	I 'wish I ^could. ‖ 'Nothing would °give me °greater ^pleasure.

WH-Questions

'Don't for°get to °bring your 'camera.	'Which ^one?
You'll 'have to ^pay for it.	'What ^with?
('I'm not ₒlending him the ₒmoney.)	'Why ^should I?
I 'won't 'hear of your ₒbuying one.	'Why ^not, for ₒheaven's ₒsake?
You were 'quite put 'out about it, ₒthen.	Well 'who ^wouldn't have ₒbeen?
‾Would ‚Max have a °game?	'Why not ^ask him?
He's 'rather a 'nuisance.	'Why not ^tell him ₒso?
(I've 'said I'm ‚sorry.)	'What else ^can I ₒsay?
‾Would you 'mind washing ‚up?	'Why can't ^you ₒdo it? ‖ 'Why should ^I do ₒall the ₒdirty ₒjobs?
If you 'ask 'me │ it's 'worse than ^useless.	'Who asked for ^your ad₀vice? 'Who asked ^you to ₒstick your ₒnose in?
It's 'half an °inch too ^big.	'What °difference does ^that ₒmake?
So you're 'going to re'sign.	'Where did you °get ^that i₀dea from?
I'm 'terribly ₒworried a₀bout it.	'Why should it °worry ^you?
But we ‚may not 'win │ ‚that way.	'What does it °matter if we ^don't? ‖ (It's ‚only a ‚game.)
‚How about 'phoning them?	'What's the °good of doing ^that?
'How °many d'you ^want?	'How many can you °let me ^have?
I 'can't under'stand her.	'Who ^can?
I 'don't be°lieve a ‚word of it.	'Who ^does?
I've 'never 'seen you so ₒangry.	'How would ^you have ₒliked it?
You 'certainly en'joy your₀self.	Why 'ever ^shouldn't I?
'Where's ‚Jane?	How on 'earth should ^I ₒknow?
I could 'do with 'twice my ₒpresent ₒsalary.	'Which of us ^couldn't?

Verbal context	*Drill*
● I've ˈhad this °pain for ˋdays.	ˈWhy don't you ^do something a˳bout it?
● I ˈdon't think °Bill ˋknows.	ˈWhy not °write and ^warn him, ˳then?
ˈHelp me °put it ˏright, °will you?	Why should ˈI °suffer for ^your mis˳takes?
You ˋought to do ˇsomething a˳bout it.	ˈWhat can ^I ˳do? ‖ ˈWhat can °one man °do on his ^own?
Yes-No Questions	
I'm ˋterribly ˳lazy | ˏthese days.	ˈAren't we ^all!
ˌYou seem ˳very ˏbusy, °Alan.	ˈDon't I ^know it! ‖ (ˈUp to my ^eyes!)
ˈThis is my °new ˋwatch.	ˈIs it ^really?
● You seem ˌvery ˏhappy about °something, °John.	ˈWouldn't ^you be ˳happy? ‖ (I've ˈjust won a °hundred ^pounds.)
ˈWasn't °Charles a ˋbore to˳night!	ˈIsn't he ^always?
ˈLarry will be ˋterrible | as ˇHamlet.	ˈCan you i^magine him! ‖ ˈIsn't it ri^diculous!
And ˈthis is ˋCharles, | the ˋeldest.	ˈHasn't he ^grown! ‖ And ˈisn't he °like his ^father!
He ˋchanged his ˇmind | at the ˈlast ^minute.	Isn't that ˈjust what you'd ex^pect him to ˳do?
He walked ˈright across the ^flower ˳bed.	ˈWouldn't you °think he'd know ^better?
Shall I ˈmention it to ˏFreda?	Is it ˈworth ^while, d'you ˳think?
They're ˋnot much °good ˇnow.	ˈWere they ^ever much ˳good?
You're ˋnot ˇreally ˳leaving, | ˏare you?	Now ˈis it ^likely?
ˈWhat do ˋyou think, ˳Terry?	ˈDoes it °matter ^what I ˳think?
She's ˈgoing to °have a ˋshot at it.	ˈWill she suc^ceed, ˳though?
ˈCan we afˋford to ˳buy it?	ˈCan we af°ford ^not to?
We could ˋtry aˇpologising.	ˈWould they be con^tent with ˳that?
It's a ˇfaster ˳car.	But ˈis it °any ^safer?
We ˋcan't de°cide this ˇnow.	ˈOught we to be dis^cussing it, ˳even?
It's a ˈvery in°genious ˎplan.	ˈIs it °really ^practicable, ˳though?
Perˈhaps someone'll ˋgive us the ˳money.	ˈDare we °even ^hope for ˳such a ˳thing?
You ˋcertainly ought to ˇsit for the e˳xam.	But have I ˈany °chance of ^passing?
I ˈdon't know ˋhow to ˳tackle him.	ˈCould we ap°proach his ^wife, per˳haps?
ˈCouldn't we ^borrow a ˳copy?	D'you ˈknow °anyone who's ^got one?
● ˈShould we go ˏon?	ˈIs there °really much ^point in it?
(ˇI'm not ˳going to ˳help him.)	Is there ˈany °reason °why I ^should?

Verbal context	*Drill*

ˋEveryone apˇproves of the iˌdea. | But 'will they °all ^help? ‖ And 'are they °likely to pro°vide the ^money?

Commands

'May I take this °last ˌcake? | 'Please ^do.
'So far I °haven't had ˋtime. | 'Start ^now, ˌthen.
'Thank you °very ^much. | 'Don't ^mention it.
'Which one shall I ˌbuy? | 'Please your^self.
'This °pen's ˋuseless. | Well 'try a ^different one.
(ˋDon't thank ˇme.) | 'Thank my ^secretary.
But I've alˌready ˋseen that ˌfilm. | Pre'tend you ^haven't, in ˌthat case.
‾Would I ʹlike it, d'you °think? | 'Try it and ^see.
‾Could you ˌhelp? | 'You fight your ^own ˌbattles.
'Shall we in°vite ˌPat ǀ or ˌIan? | 'Let's in°vite ^both of them.
I ˇasked him ǀ but he 'didn't reˋply. | Well 'ask him a^gain, ˌthen.
May I 'have some more ˌpie? | 'Help your^self. ‖ Take as 'much as you ^like.

'May I °turn the ˌradio °on? | 'Make yourself at ^home.
I ˋcan't go ǀ ˌyet. ‖ It's ˋraining. | 'Wait until it ^stops, ˌthen.
'That's a ^silly ˌplan. | 'You sug°gest a ^better one.
Oh he's ˌnot such a ˌbad °chap. | Well 'you °mark my ^words. ‖ (He'll 'come to °no ^good.)
Praps ˋyou'd ˌbreak it to him. | 'You °do your ^own ˌdirty ˌwork.
I'm 'quite enˋjoying ˌthis. | Then for 'heaven's °sake ^look as ˌthough you ˌwere.
We 'ought to stay ^in toˌnight. | 'You stay °in by ^all ˌmeans. ‖ ('I'm going ^out.)
'My head's ˋterrible ǀ this ˌmorning. | 'Try taking °more ^water ˌwith it.
We ˋought to °ask ˇJohn. | Well 'go a°head and ^ask him.
It's ˋnot ˇmuch of a ˌcut. | Then 'don't make °so much ^fuss aˌbout it.

'May I °borrow this ˌbook for a °while? | 'Keep it as °long as you ^like.
I'm 'going to ^risk it, ǀ in ^spite of what you ˌsay. | 'Don't °say I °didn't ^warn you, ˌthen.
I'm ˋterribly ˌsorry. | 'Don't °give it a°nother ^thought.

Verbal context	*Drill*

Interjections

I'm ˋawfully ˏsorry.	'No ˆdoubt! ‖ (But it's 'too ˆlate for aₒpologies.)
'John may ˋtreat us.	'Not ˆhim! ‖ (He's ˆfar too ₒmean.)
'Sally's °just had ˋtriplets.	'My ˆgoodness! 'Good ˆheavens!
Your 'father looks ˋvery ₒwell.	'By ˆJove he ₒdoes!
I've ˏmissed my ˋturn.	'Serves you ˆright! ‖ (You should 'pay more atˆtention.)
I got 'really ˏcross with them.	'Well ˆdone! 'Good for ˆyou!
● 'Thank you °very ˋmuch.	'Not at ˆall. ‖ 'Thank ˆyou.
'Will you °say you're ˏsorry?	'Not ˆI! ‖ 'On the ˆcontrary.
ˋHullo, │ ˏDavid.	Good 'afterˆnoon, ₒFrank. ‖ (ˏBit ˏlate, °aren't you?)
May 'I come ˏtoo?	The 'more the ˆmerrier.
At ˋleast he aˇpologised.	'So I should ˆthink. 'So I should ˆhope.
'Nikki's °not ˋcoming.	'So much the ˆbetter.
'Can't you °get a ˏflat?	If 'only we ˆcould!
He said 'nothing °more aˋbout it.	How 'very peˆculiar! ‖ ('He was °so ˆkeen on it.)
We 'ought to be °going ˋhome.	The 'sooner the ˆbetter.
You ˇwill ₒcome, │ ˋwon't you?	With the 'greatest of ˆpleasure!
⁻Let ˏme ₒcarry it ₒfor you.	'Thank you °very ˆmuch. ‖ ('That ˆis ₒkind of you.)
I 'won't have °anything to ˏdo with it.	'More °fool ˆyou!
He won 'ten °thousand ˋpounds.	What an ex'traordinary °piece of ˆluck!
'Many °happy re°turns of the ˋday!	How 'very °nice of you to reˆmember!
He 'took me °in ˆproperly.	If 'only you'd °taken some °expert adˆvice!

Note: All the relevant drills given above with the tune

(LOW PRE-HEAD+) HIGH HEAD+RISE–FALL (+TAIL)

can be said with emphasis if one or both of the following features are used:
(*a*) the high pre-head instead of the low pre-head (see Chapter I, p. 36);
(*b*) the emphatic form of the high head (see Chapter I, p. 37).
With both of these features indicated the last drill in this section would read

⁻If 'only you'd 'taken some 'expert adˆvice!

9 *The High Dive*

Attitude

In STATEMENTS: appealing to the listener to continue with the topic of conversation; expressing gladness, regret, surprise.

In QUESTIONS: very emotive, expressing plaintiveness, despair, gushing warmth.

In COMMANDS: pleading, persuading.

In INTERJECTIONS: intensely encouraging, protesting.

Tone marks used in HIGH DIVE drills

A Stressed, accented syllables (Nucleus, Head)
['] High falling to very low pitch.
[͵] (i) without Tail: low rising to medium pitch.
    (ii) with Tail: low level pitch; the rise is completed by the tail syllable(s).
['] Relatively high level pitch.
[°] Relatively high level pitch, the same pitch as the *preceding* ['].
[₀] Low level pitch, the same pitch as the end of the *preceding* ['] and the beginning of the *following* [͵].

B Stressed, unaccented syllables (Tail)
[°] Level pitch, never above medium, higher than the lowest possible, and higher than the *preceding* [͵] or an *immediately preceding* [°].

Verbal context	*Drill*
Statements	
● 'Which are `our ₀places?	`There's ͵yours. ‖ ('Next to `Peter.)
'Who'd `help?	`Julian's the most ͵likely one.
'Who can we `ask?	`Jackson's your ͵man.
'How do we `get there?	`Frank's got a ͵car. ‖ (Perhaps 'he'll °give us a `lift.)
'Where could I `get a ₀copy?	`Smith's is the ͵best °bet.
'What was she `like at ₀school?	`French was her ͵best °subject.
● 'How can we `get to his ₀house?	`Walking's the ͵easiest °way.
'What d'you °do in your °spare `time?	`Fishing's my ͵favourite relax°ation.
'How was the `game?	`Andrew was the ͵winner.
'Any i°deas for the ⸍holiday?	`Scotland would be ͵pleasant.

Verbal context	Drill
'How about °asking `Jack?	`That's what I'll ,do. ‖ ('Good i`dea!)
'Which d'you recom`mend?	`This one's the ₒmost ,useful.
He 'only °charged a `pound.	`That was ₒvery ,reasonable.
'Isn't he °like his ^father!	`Most people ₒtell me ,that.
'Where can we °buy e`nough of them?	`Selfridge's have got a ₒgood ,stock. ‖ ('Try `there.)
And 'what about `vegetables?	`Celery would be ₒrather ,nice.
'When can you `come?	`Saturday would be the ₒmost con,venient °day.
● 'Where could we `sleep?	`Frances has got a ₒcouple of ₒspare ,beds.
‚Where have they `got to?	Oh `there's ,Tom. ‖ ('Talking to `Jane.)
⎺Is ,that °Bill?	Yes `that's ,him.
'Which is `which?	The `blue one's ,yours.
(You 'asked when to `plant them.)	Well `now's the ,time.
I 'haven't °got a `knife.	Oh `here you ,are. ‖ ('Catch hold of `this one.)
'Which `fuel would you ad₀vise?	Well `oil's the ,cheapest.
'Why are they so `cross with me?	Being `rude won't have ,helped °matters.
● 'I'm from `Sheffield.	(‚Really?) ‖ My `mother came from ,there.
I'm a `bank ₒmanager.	(‚Really?) ‖ My `brother works for ,Barclays.
'Where should I `stay?	Well the `Grand's a very ,comfortable ho°tel.
D'you 'like my °new ,raincoat?	Yes `I've got ₒone like ,that.
And now 'what about `fruit?	Well `pears are ₒpretty ,plentiful at the °moment.
I 'need a `hobby.	You know `painting's ₒvery re,laxing. ‖ ('Try `that.)
'Who'd `know about such ₒthings?	Well `Allen's the man we ,usually °ask.
● But your 'sister said `no.	Oh `no-one ₒlistens to ,her.
Have you 'ever seen a ,warming °pan?	Yes my `grandma's got ₒone of ,those.
'Where shall we `meet?	Well `my house is the ₒmost ,central. ‖ ('How about `there?)
We're 'one `short │ for ,doubles.	My `cousin likes ₒplaying ,tennis. ‖ (Shall I 'ask `him?)
● 'Where can I `get Bra₀zilian ₒcoffee?	Well the `supermarket's got a ₒfresh sup,ply.
● She's a `pleasant ₒgirl, │ `isn't she?	Yes I `like ,Barbara.

Verbal context	*Drill*
ˋTake a ˳handful.	(ˋThank you.) ‖ I'm ˋfond of ˏpeanuts.
● 'How's ˋFreda ˳getting ˳on?	She's ˋdreading her ˏdriving °test.
● ˏWhy not °ask ˋJanet?	No I'd ˋhate to ask ˏher a °favour.
'Piece ʹmore, °Alice?	(ˋYes, │ ˏplease.) ‖ I aˋdore your ˳fruit ˏflans.
(ˋThanks │ for the ˏcopy of his ˳new ˏnovel.)	I shall enˋjoy ˳reading ˏthat.
'How about a ˋrubber, ˳Tony?	I'd ˋlove ˏthat. ‖ I'm ˋvery keen on ˏbridge.
'How about the °Moonlight Soˋnata?	(ˋLovely!) ‖ I'm ˋawfully fond of ˏBeethoven.
● He had at ʹleast ˇtwo ˳helpings.	(I'm 'not surˋprised.) ‖ He's ˋmad on ˳apple ˏpie.
● Are you 'going by ˏcar?	No I ˋloathe ˳driving at ˏnight.
You 'don't °mind not ʹcoming?	(ˈNot at ˋall.) ‖ I'd preˋfer to ˳stay at ˏhome.
ˏWhy are you so ˋmiserable?	Oh I ˋhate ˳getting up ˏearly.
I've alˈready ˋtelephoned your ˏmother.	('Thanks very ˋmuch.) ‖ I apˋpreciate your conˏcern.
'Going out in ʹthis °weather?	Yes I ˋlike ˳walking in the ˏrain.
I had 'five ˋyears with ˳Nelson.	(ˏReally?) ‖ I should have ˋhated ˳working with ˏhim.
● 'Have some ˋmore.	(ˋThanks.) ‖ I'm ˋpartial to ˳Indian ˏcurry.
Does 'Mary ˏknow yet?	No and I'm ˋdreading ˳having to ˏtell her.
It was ˋFreddie's ˳fault.	I ˋthought ˏso.
● It's a ˋlovely ˳present, ˳Dick.	I ˋhoped you'd ˏlike it.
(What ˋmore can I ˳do?)	I've ˋsaid I'm ˏsorry.
● 'Look at the ˋweather.	(ˈAh ˏwell!) ‖ I ˋthought it would ˏrain.
'Bill's been proˋmoted.	(Oh ˋgood!) ‖ I ˋknew he'd get ˏon.
It's an ˋexcellent ˳photo.	(ˋFine!) ‖ I was ˋsure you'd apˏprove.
Good ˋmorning, ˳George.	(Oh ˋhullo, │ ˏDick.) ‖ I was ˋhoping to ˏsee you.
ˋJohn was the ˏwinner.	Yes I ˋheard he'd ˳pulled it ˏoff.
It was ʹquite an ˇaccident.	But I ˋtold you ˳not to ˏtouch it.
'Did you ˏsee °Arthur?	Yes and I ˋtold him about the ˏmeeting.
Yes ˋthat's ˳Ben ˏSmith.	(ˋWell, now!) ‖ I ˋthought his ˳face was faˏmiliar.
ˉDid you 'call at the ˏbank?	(ˉOh ˏdash it!) ‖ I ˋknew there was ˳something ˏelse I had to °do.
She was 'quite exˋhausted by the ˳trip.	Well I ˋbegged her ˳not to underˏtake it.

Verbal context	*Drill*
ˋNo news from ˅Peter, I'm a₀fraid.	And he ˋpromised he'd ₀write at the week-ˎend.
● So you've ˋheard from ₀Archie.	Yes and he ˋtold me you'd be ₀dropping ₀in to ˎsee me.
● 'Don't inter ˋrupt, ₀Jake.	I ˋbeg your ˎpardon. ‖ (I 'thought you'd ˋfinished.)
('Won't you °come for a ˎwalk?)	I ˋknow you'd en ˎjoy it.
● Oh ˋthere you are, ₀Tony.	('Hullo, │ ˎAlf.) ‖ I ˋhope I'm ₀not ˎlate.
'Was it ex ˋpensive?	I for ˋget how ₀much he ˎpaid for it.
So ˋyou ₀borrowed ₀my ₀copy.	I ˋdo hope you ₀didn't ˎmind.
'Did you ˎsee °David?	Yes he ˋknows you'll ₀be a bit ˎlate.
Not a ˋword from ˅Alf ₀yet.	Oh I ˋwish he'd ₀make up his ˎmind.
('Do let me ₀into the ˎsecret.)	I ˋpromise not to ₀tell anyone ˎelse.
● I really ˋmust go │ ˎnow.	(˅Good ˎbye, then.) ‖ I ˋdo hope you have a ₀comfortable ˎjourney.
It's a mag ˋnificent ₀present.	I'm ˋglad you ˎlike it.
So you en ˋjoyed the ₀concert.	Yes I was a ˋmazed how ˎgood it °was.
Per'haps you °misunder ˋstood him.	No I'm ˋsure he said ˎTuesday.
(I 'don't want to °hear any ˎmore.)	I'm ˋtired of ex ˎcuses.
He 'played the so°nata rather ˋwell.	And I felt ˋsure he'd make a ˎmess of it.
● 'Fred's °answer was ˋwrong.	(ˎFunny!) ‖ He was ˋsure he'd ₀got it ˎright.
He 'couldn't have been °more ˋangry.	I'm sur ˋprised he ₀felt like ˎthat.
ˎHelp? ‖ ˋCertainly.	('Thanks.) ‖ I was ˋsure I could ₀count on ˎyou.
('Don't °try to dis ˅suade me.)	I'm de ˋtermined to ₀carry ˎon.
'Max °came after ˋall, then.	Yes we were ˋthankful he ₀changed his ˎmind.
'Wasn't it ˎtragic about ₀Jim ₀Smith!	Yes I was ˋshocked to ₀hear that he'd ˎdied.
Jack 'lost his ˋtemper.	('Oh ˎdear!) ‖ I was a ˋfraid he'd ₀do something ˎsilly.
And 'what was ˋTom's re₀action?	He was an ˋnoyed at being ₀kept ˎwaiting.
● It's 'sheer °highway ˋrobbery.	I'm ˋsorry you ₀feel it's ₀too ex ˎpensive.
'What an ˋappetite he's ₀got!	I'd be a ˋshamed to eat as ₀much as ˎthat.
I've ac ˋcepted your ₀parents' invi ˎtation.	They were de ˋlighted you'd be ₀able to ˎmanage it.

Verbal context	*Drill*
Your 'cooking's quite `good, | ‚really.	Well I'm `grateful for those ₒfew ₒkind ‚words.
Oh `there you are, ₒPeter!	I'm `sorry I couldn't ₒget here any ‚earlier, °John.
(Yes he 'told me at the `meeting.)	I'm sur`prised he ₒdidn't ₒmention it to ₒyou at the ₒsame ‚time.
'Any re°ply from ʹBrown?	Yes he's ac`cepted your ‚offer.
('Shall I °change your ‚library books °for you?)	I've `got to change my ‚own. || (They're 'over`due.)
Did they 'have any ‚luck?	Yes they've `found that ₒbottle of ‚acid.
'How're you °getting `on?	I've `finished ₒpainting the ‚kitchen.
(`Don't ₒoffer to ‚help him.)	He in`sists on ₒdoing it by him‚self.
‚Where are you `off to?	(To see `Frank.) || I `shan't be ‚long.
We 'can't °leave till `Tuesday.	Well it `can't be ‚helped.
'Trust `you to do ₒsomething ₒsilly.	But I `couldn't ‚help it.
● I'm `so ‚sorry.	It `doesn't ‚matter. || There's `no real ‚harm done.
'Shall I go °back for it ‚now?	No I `shouldn't ‚bother.
I feel `very ₒbad about it.	But it `wasn't ‚your fault.
(Let `me have a ₒshot at it.)	It `shouldn't take ‚long.
('Go ahead and `ask him.)	I `don't think he'll ‚mind.
But he ‚says he'll re`sign.	Oh I `shouldn't take him ‚seriously.
(Good `morning. || `Do sit ‚down.)	I `won't ₒkeep you a ‚second.
John 'sounded so `cross.	(`Don't ‚worry.) || He `doesn't ₒreally ‚mean it.
I feel `terrible aₒbout it.	But you `mustn't ₒlet it up‚set you.
What'ever ‚next, I'd ₒlike to ₒknow!	You `needn't preₒtend to be ₒso sur‚prised. || (You've ‚known all a`long.)
A 'right mess `you've made of ₒthings!	I `do a‚pologise.
('Please say ‚yes.)	I `do so ₒwant to ‚go.
`I ₒbroke it, I'm aₒfraid.	(‚Really, ₒJohn!) || You `must ₒtry to be ₒmore ‚careful.
I'll 'do it °right a`way.	Thank you `so ‚much.
● ⁻But ‚why didn't you `tell me?	I'm `so ‚sorry. || (⁻I ‚thought I `had.)
'What's the `matter, ₒMay?	Oh I'm `so ‚tired.
⁻Hul`lo? || ⁻Who's `there?	It's `only ‚me. || (`Jonathan.)
(I'll `have to ₒgo, | I sup‚pose.)	But it's `such a ‚bore.

Verbal context	*Drill*
He's ˇfailed, │ I'm aˏfraid.	I'm not a ˇbit surˏprised. ‖ (He ˏdidn't work ˇhard e∘nough.)
So he 'had to ˇwait a few ∘minutes.	Yes and he was ˇso anˏnoyed.
How ˇare you, ∘Bill?	('Rather ˇpoorly.) ‖ I've got a ˇshocking ˏcold.
He's 'getting ˇbetter.	I'm ˇso reˏlieved. ‖ I've been ˇterribly ˏworried.
You can 'borrow it ˇany ∘time.	That's exˇtremely ˏkind of you.
'How did he °come to ˇbreak it?	It was ˇquite an ˏaccident.
He's ˇvery disap∘pointed.	Oh he'll ˇsoon get ˏover it.
('Don't stop ˇnow.)	We ˇstill need some ˏmore.
ˏWhat's °happened to ˇJill?	It's ˇalways the ˏsame. ‖ She's ˇnever on ˏtime.
● You ˏdon't ˏmind, °do you?	No I ˇquite underˏstand.
ˏWhat was that ˇnoise?	('Don't ˏworry.) ‖ It was ˇonly a ˏfirework.
'Isn't °Frank ˇtiresome!	Yes I thought he'd ˇnever stop ˏgrumbling.
(ˇWhy ˏdon't you ∘go?)	I'd ˇgladly sit ˏin for you.
It was a ˇterrifying ex∘perience.	I ˇdo feel ˏsorry for you. ‖ I know ˇjust what it's ˏlike.
'Will he be all ˏright?	Yes there's ˇnothing to ˏworry about.
('Please write it ˏdown for me.)	I've got ˇsuch a ∘shocking ˏmemory.
D'you 'need it at ˏonce?	No ˇany time'll ˏdo.
ˏHow did ˇthis get ∘broken?	I'm ˇterribly ˏsorry about it. ‖ (I ˇdropped it.)
It's 'all so disˇcouraging.	I know eˇxactly how you ˏfeel.
● 'Thanks for inˇviting me.	We were ˇso glad you could ˏmake it.
(Are you ˊsure there'll be e°nough?)	I'd ˇwillingly ∘fetch some ˏmore.
(He's a ˇwonderful old ∘chap.)	He ˇstill does a ∘full day's ˏwork.
('Keep ˏtrying.)	It's ˇjust a ∘matter of ˏpractice.
So you ˇcalled on ∘June.	Yes and she was ˇvery ∘pleased with the ˏpresent I °brought her.
● ˇSorry I ∘haven't reˏturned it.	That's ˇquite all ˏright. ‖ I'm in ˇno par∘ticular ˏhurry °for it.
You'll 'have to °wait a bit ˇlonger.	But I've alˇready been ∘waiting a ˏyear.
It was a 'real ˇmystery.	Yes I've ˇoften ∘wondered how he ˏdid it.

Verbal context	*Drill*
I ˋwish he'd ₒmind his own ˏbusiness.	But he was ˋonly ₒtrying to ₒbe a bit ˏhelpful.
'What °made him so ˋangry?	I ˋonly asked ₒhow much he ˏpaid for the °house.
● It's an 'abso°lute ˋscandal.	There's ˋno need to ₒget so worked ˏup about it.
ˋYou ₒtell her.	No I'd ˋmuch rather you ₒdid it your ˏself.
(Why ˋshouldn't he ₒgo to the ₒmatch?)	He ˋneeds a ₒbit of ₒrelax ˏation.
'Any sug ˊgestions?	The 'roast ˋlamb's very ˏnice, sir.
I can see ˋtwo men at the ₒbar.	Well the 'tall ˋdark man is ₒTom's ˏbrother.
'Who can we °get to stand ˋin?	Well 'Joan ˋBennett plays a ₒreasonably ₒgood ˏgame.
'Who are ˋyou?	'Barry ˋJones is my ˏname.
'Which would ˋyou ₒbuy?	Well I think 'Andrew ˋHarrod's are the ₒbest ₒvalue for ˏmoney.
● 'How do we ˋget there?	'Going by ˋunderground would be the ˏquickest.
● 'Where shall we go ˋthis year?	'Somewhere in ˋDevon would make a ₒpleasant ˏchange.
(Why 'do we in ˋvite the ₒGreens?)	I 'can't ˋbear ˏAlice.
Well 'how about ˋJulia?	No I 'don't ˋfancy asking ˏher a °favour.
'Don't you °get a bit ˏlonely?	No I 'quite ˋlike ₒbeing on my ˏown.
(ˋDon't invite ˇRobinson a ₒgain.)	I 'can't ˋstand people who ₒsmoke during ˏmeals.
● 'How did your ˋholiday ₒgo?	You know, I 'quite en ˋjoyed ˏcamping.
'How can you ˋeat such ₒstuff?	Well I'm 'rather ˋfond of ₒjellied ˏeels.
ˋDavid'll be ₒhere │ to ˏmorrow.	(ˋGood!) ‖ I've been 'looking ˋforward to ₒmeeting ˏhim.
Was the 'meal any ˏgood?	Yes I 'rather ˋliked Joan's ₒcontinental ˏcooking.
'What upset the ˋSmiths?	Well they 'didn't ˋlike having to ₒwait such a ₒlong ˏtime.
('Lend me your ˏscissors, °will you?)	I just 'can't ˋthink what I've ₒdone with ˏmine.
He's 'over ˋninety, │ I ˏgather.	(ˋNever!) ‖ I'd ˋno iˋdea he was ˏthat old.
(We 'need a ˋskeleton.)	But I've 'no iˋdea where to ˏget one.

Verbal context	Drill
'How about °asking `Tim?	(‚Good i`dea!) ‖ I 'hadn't `thought of ₒasking ‚him.
My 'tulips got °first `prize.	('Well `done!) ‖ I 'didn't `know you were so ‚good at °gardening, °Jim.
● He's ac`cepted your ‚offer.	(‚Really?) ‖ I 'didn't `dream he'd ₒtake me ‚seriously.
He just 'cut me `dead.	(‚Really?) ‖ I 'can't under`stand his be-ₒhaving like ‚that.
¯Do they ‚know about it °yet?	Yes I've 'just `told ‚Peter. ‖ (And 'he's °going to tell `Frank.)
'Will you make a ‚fourth?	I 'don't `play ‚bridge.
'Will you ‚lend me a °couple?	(˅Sorry.) ‖ I've 'only `got ‚two.
'Have a ciga`rette, °Max?	('No, ‖ ‚thanks.) ‖ I've 'given `up ‚smoking.
(I've 'scrubbed and ‚scrubbed.)	But I 'just can't `shift this ‚stain.
● Can you 'let me have °six of the ‚large °glasses?	(˅Sorry.) ‖ I 'haven't `got ₒmany of ‚them.
● ¯Haven't you ‚read that °article?	No I 'don't °often `see the ‚Times.
('Can I °borrow your ‚rubber?)	I 'seem to have mis`laid ‚mine.

WH-Questions

'Can't you work it °out for your‚self?	(Oh `come ‚on.) ‖ `What's the ‚answer?
It was `my ₒtreat.	(No `really.) ‖ `How much ‚was it?
Did you ⸝call, `Frank?	Yes `what's the ‚time, °please?
(`So sorry to ₒhear you were un‚well.)	`How d'you ‚feel, °Martha?
I'm `so up‚set, °Daddy.	`What's the ‚matter, °darling?
[Pouring a guest a cup of coffee]	`How d'you ‚like your °coffee? ‖ ('Black or ‚white?)
You owe me 'ten ‚pounds.	Just `how d'you make ‚that out?
Your ⸝cap? ‖ It's `here ˅somewhere.	('Don't play the ‚fool.) ‖ `What have you ‚done with it?
‚How °big did you °say it was?	Oh `why don't you ‚listen, °Charles?
● I 'have to go `out ‖ ‚now.	`When will you be ‚back, d'you °think?
(I'm `so glad you could ‚come.)	`What'll you have to ‚drink, my °dear?
(You ‚said you `would go, ‖ ‚yesterday.)	`What's made you ₒchange your ‚mind?
He `knows, ‖ ap‚parently.	Now `who on ₒearth could have ‚told him?
`Sorry I'm ‚late.	Oh `why can't you ₒcome on ‚time for °once?

Verbal context	*Drill*

He's 'broken his ˋright leg | ˌthis time. — ˋWhy is he ₒalways so unˌfortunate?

(ˌFirst he says ˌone thing, | ˌthen aˋnother.) — ˋHow am I to ₒknow what he ˌreally °thinks?

(I've ˌlost Bill's ˋwatch.) — What ˋshall I ˌdo, °James?

● ˌThree ˋthousand he ₒpaid for it. — When ˋwill the ₒpoor ₒfool learn ˌwit?

Not a 'single ˎpenny will I ₒgive. — How ˋcan you be ₒso hardˏhearted, °Father?

(ˋLook at the ₒmess you've ₒmade.) — When ˋare you going to ₒlearn to ₒwipe your ˌshoes?

Yes-No Questions

Perhaps ˋI could ₒhelp. — ˋDo you ₒthink you ˌcould?

(You can ˋstill make it in ˌtime.) — ˋWon't you ₒchange your ˌmind?

● ˋCome and have a ˌgame, °Phil. — ˋWill you stop ˏbothering me? ‖ ˋCan't you see I'm ˏbusy?

I tell you I 'won't ˎlisten. — ˋMust you ₒbe so ₒobstinate?

ˊLost °something, °Ron? — Yes ˋhave you ₒseen my ˌcheque book °anywhere?

You ˋwill come ˏwith me, | ˋwon't you? — ˋCan't you ₒgo by yourˏself for °once?

You 'owe me a ˋpound. — ˋWould you mind ₒwaiting till ˌFriday?

You look ˋworried, ₒPeggy. — ˋWould you mind ₒtelling me the ˌtime? ‖ (I've an ˏawful °feeling I'm ˋlate.)

'May I °have another ˌbun? — ˋDo you really ₒthink you can ˌeat it?

ˏWhat d'you want ˋnow, ₒJean? — ˋCan I have aₒnother piece of ˌtoffee?

Commands

It's 'all so deˋpressing. — ˋCheer ˌup. ‖ (It ˇcan't last for ˇever.)

ˏWhat's the ˋmatter? — ˋBe ˌcareful. ‖ (You ˏnearly ˋhit me | with ˌthat.)

I've got a ˋvery sweet ₒtooth. — ˋGo ˌeasy with the °sugar. ‖ (That's ˏall we've ˋgot.)

(But it's a ˋnice ₒpudding.) — ˋEat it ˌup. ‖ (There's ₒa good ˌboy.)

● I'm aˋfraid I've ˋlost it. — ˋNever ˌmind. ‖ (I've ˋgot aₒnother one.)

Why ˋshould I aₒpologise? — ˋHave some ˌsense. ‖ (It's the ₒonly thing you ˋcan do.)

(ˋSorry I forₒgot your ˌbirthday.) — ˋDo forˏgive me.

ˇQuickly. — ˋWait a ˌminute. ‖ (There's ˋno ˌhurry.)

Verbal context	*Drill*
We can have ‚one more °game, | ‛surely.	‛Have a ‚heart, man. || (I'm ‚dead ‛tired.)
‛Lend me a ‚pound, °Max.	‛Don't be ‚silly. || (‛I'm broke, | ‛too.)
‚What's all the ‛knocking a₀bout?	Oh ‛don't just ‚sit there. || ‛Open the ‚door.
I'll have 'nothing to ˎdo with it.	Now ‛do be ‚reasonable, °Charles.
I'm ˅almost ₀ready.	‛Please hurry ‚up. || (We're al'ready ˅ten minutes ₀late.)
● ‚What's up°setting ‛you?	‛Do shut the ‚door. || (There's ‛such a ‚draught.)
He ‚said he'd ‛sue me.	‛Don't take ₀any ‚notice °of him. || (He ‛always ₀talks like ‚that.)
I'm ‛dreadfully disap‚pointed.	‛Don't let it ₀get you ‚down.
● I really ‛must go | ‚now.	Oh ‛please ₀stay a little ‚longer.
'Shall I °get you some ‚more?	No ‛please don't ₀bother on ‚my ac°count.
It's my e‛xam | to‚morrow.	‛Let me know ₀how you get ‚on. || (I'll 'keep my ‛fingers ₀crossed ₀for you.)
Oh it's ‛awful. || I can't ‛bear it.	Now ‛don't take it ₀too much to ‚heart.

Interjections

Will you 'call at the ‚chemist's °for me?	‛All ‚right. || ('On my way ⁄home °do?)
I ‚thought I °asked you to °make up the ‛fire.	‛All ‚right. || (‛Don't go ‚on a°bout it. || I was ‛just ‚going.)
[Coming across something totally unexpected]	‛Hul‚lo. || (‚What's ‛this?)
I've in'vited him for ‛tea.	‛Jolly ‚good! ‛Good ‚show!
● 'See you on ‚Friday.	‛Right you ‚are. ‛Righ‚to.
You can 'stay if the ˎothers ₀do.	‛Fair e‚nough.
I'm de‛termined to ₀carry ₀on.	‛That's the ‚stuff! ‛That's the ‚spirit!
‚That's the ‛second time he's ₀failed.	‛Poor old ‚Peter! || (He'll ‛never ‚make it.)
● We go ‛that way.	‛Half a ‚minute. || (‚How d'you ‛know?)
And we'll have a 'new ‚carpet.	‛Just a ‚second. || (‚Where do we °get the ‛money?)
I ‛lost, | I'm a‚fraid.	‛Jolly hard ‚lines! ‛Better luck ‚next time!

10 *The Terrace*

Attitude

In ALL sentence types: (in non-final word groups) marking non-finality without conveying any impression of expectancy.

In STATEMENTS AND INTERJECTIONS: (in final word groups) calling out to someone as from a distance.

Tone marks used in TERRACE drills

A Stressed, accented syllables (Nucleus, Head)
[ꞌ] Mid level pitch.
[ꞌ] Relatively high level pitch.
[°] Relatively high level pitch, the same pitch as the *preceding* [ꞌ].

B Stressed, unaccented syllables (Tail)
[°] Mid level pitch, the same pitch as the *preceding* [ꞌ].

Tune — — Mid-Level (+Tail)

Verbal context	*Drill*

Statements

Verbal context	Drill
(ꞌFirst | I 'cleaned my ꞌshoes.)	ꞌThen | I went 'out for a ꞌwalk.
(⌐Are you ˏstill °eating that °chocolate?)	ꞌSoon | you 'won't have °any ꞌleft.
(It's ꞌno use °ringing ˅John.)	ꞌJohn | is aꞌway on ꞌholiday.
(⌐Why ˏever °give him ꞌsix?)	ꞌSix | is ꞌfar too ₒmany.
'What are the ꞌphotos ₒlike?	ꞌSome | are 'very °good inꞌdeed.
Well 'what about ꞌSmiths?	ꞌTheirs | are 'far too exꞌpensive.
'Alan says ꞌyou ₒbroke it.	ꞌThat | is a 'downright ˏlie.
But I ˏonly ₒdid it ˏonce.	ꞌOnce | is 'once too ꞌoften.
(What's ꞌyour ₒcoffee ₒlike?)	ꞌMine | tastes 'much too ꞌsweet.
● Let's ˅hope ₒso.	ꞌHope, | that's 'all you ꞌcan do.
(Ask ꞌChris to transₒlate it.)	ꞌFrench, | he's 'very ꞌgood at.
If 'only he'd °stop ꞌtalking | and ꞌdo ₒsomething!	ꞌTalk, | that's 'all he ꞌever ₒdoes.
(ꞌDon't let's °stop for ˅tea.)	ꞌTea | we can 'have when we get ꞌhome.
(ꞌDon't °bother with those °papers ˅now.)	ꞌThose | you can 'take ꞌany time.

Verbal context	*Drill*

'Will you °have a ′beer, °Peter?

(‵Yes, | ‚please.) ‖ >Beer | I can 'drink at ‵any ₒhour of the ₒday.

‾D'you ‚like your °job?
'What d'you °do on ‵Saturdays?
'Why not ‵buy a ₒhouse?
('What's the ‵matter, ₒAndrew?)
(I 'borrowed ‵Jim's | to be‚gin with.)
'How °often d'you ‵play?
How on ‚earth did you ‵manage?

>Sometimes | I ‵hate it.
>Often | I 'go to a ‵football ₒmatch.
>Frankly | I 'can't af‵ford to.
>Lately | you've 'hardly °played at ‵all.
>Finally | I ‵bought a ₒpair.
>Generally, | at least 'twice a ‚week.
>Fortunately | I'd got a 'couple of ‵spare ones.

(No, it ‵can't have been ‵yesterday.)
And 'what did ‵Len ₒsay?
● How's ‵Tim be₀having?
(At >first | I a'greed to ‚help.)
‵Here you ‚are. ‖ ‵Twenty.
('Let's ask ‵Alec to ₒplay.)
What's your ‵brother's o₀pinion?
I thought ‵everyone had been ₒtold.
'Why do ‵you play ₒsquash?
But you're so ‚very ‵clever.
● But he ‚only ₒgave me ₒten ‚pounds.

>Yesterday | I stayed ‵in all ₒday.
>Naturally | he was 'quite ‵pleased.
>Recently | he's been 'very con‵siderate.
>Afterwards | I 'thought ‵better ₒof it.
>Twenty | is ‵far too ₒmany.
>Alec | is 'rather ‵good at the ₒgame.
>He thinks | we 'ought to go a‵head.
>John says | he knew 'nothing a₂bout it.
>I play | to 'try to °keep ‵fit.
>Flattery | will 'get you ‚nowhere.
>Some °people | 'don't know °when they're well ‵off.

('Jane's re°turning to‵day.)
‚Why not °go by ‵air?
'How did you get ‵on with the ₒMartins?

>Antony | will be 'back on ‵Tuesday.
>Air °travel | I find 'so ‵frightening.
('Very ‵well.) ‖ >Henry °Martin | I've 'met °somewhere be‵fore.

Tune	▁ ▬ ▁	**Low Pre-Head+Mid-Level (+Tail)**

Statements

Will it ′help, d'you °think?
'See anything of ‚Tom °nowadays?

Indi>rectly | it 'certainly ‵will.
Oc>casionally | I run 'into him on the ‵train.

Verbal context	*Drill*
ˇDon't tell ˇGreta.	Un>fortunately | she al'ready `knows.
'Didn't he °come from ,Somerset?	O>riginally | I be'lieve he `did.
'Where's `Arthur?	By >now | he should be 'on his °way to `Leeds.
'Couldn't you ,help a °bit?	At >present | I'm 'far too `busy.
So he's 'giving `up ₒsmoking.	Since >Easter | he 'hasn't °smoked at `all.
('Hard `luck, ₒJohn.)	For a >moment | I 'thought you'd suc-`ceeded.
'What did you `think of it?	For the >most part | it was 'very `good.
But you ,said he was `married.	For a >long time | I 'thought he `was.
Oh ,don't ,worry him a°bout it.	If >you can °do it | 'so can ,he.
Yes, we've been 'playing `bingo.	What you >see in the °game | I just 'can't ,think.
● I'll >give him | a 'piece of my `mind.	I >hope | you'll do 'no such ,thing.
● Jane's for'gotten her um`brella.	Yes, she >left | in 'such a `hurry.
● 'Fancy °Max a`pologising!	He a>pologised | because he 'jolly well `had to.
'How about to`morrow?	To>morrow | will be 'too `late.
'How about °asking the `Jacksons?	The >Jacksons | are the 'very ,last people to ₒask.
(No, 'no po,tatoes, °thank you.)	Po>tatoes | make me 'put on `weight.
(Mr. >Jones | I 'don't get ,on with.)	But his >sister | I 'like e`normously.
So he's 'reading ge`ography.	Yes, ge>ography | he's 'pretty `good at.

WH-Questions

It's >only a ˇtemporary ₒjob.	E>ventually | 'what sort of °job would you `like?
(Your >references | are 'really `excellent.)	And now >finally | 'when can you ,start?
He's 'living in `Sunderland.	O>riginally | 'where did he `hail from?
What a 'difficult situ`ation!	As a >friend | 'what would you ad°vise me to `do?
● But I 'get so `airsick.	In >that case | 'why not °go by `train?
Anything ᐟelse you °want to `know?	For the >record | 'what's your ,home ad-ₒdress?
'Any sug'gestions?	On >Saturday | 'how about °going to the `theatre?

Verbal context	*Drill*
(He 'may not ˇwant to ₒplay.)	And in ›any °case | 'how d'you °know he'll turn ˇup?
'Jack can't ˇmake it, I'm aₒfraid.	With ›Jack a°way | 'how shall we ˇmanage?
'Why not hang °on till ˇChristmas?	By ›Christmastime | 'how °much of it will be ˇleft, d'you ₒthink?
● In'vite him a°gain in ˇJanuary.	But in ›January | ˌwhere will he ˇbe?
So you reˇfused his ₒoffer.	In ›my po°sition | 'what would ˇyou have ₒdone?
I 'really ˇneed it | ˌnow.	Since you ›need it | 'why not °ask him to reˇturn it?
'Take it °back to ˇHarringtons.	And when I ›get there | 'who shall I ˌask for?
But a ˌletter °takes so ˇlong.	Well if it's ›urgent | 'why don't you ˇwire him?
● I'm not ˌvery °interested.	If ›that's how you °feel | 'why °bother about it at ˇall?

Yes-No Questions

● Well, ˇwhat time, ₒthen?	Shall we say ›ten | or 'ten ˌthirty?
'Have a cigaˌrette.	Is that your ›last | or have you 'got a°nother ˌpacket?
ˇAll ˌright. || I'll ˇcome.	Can you come to›day | or 'must it be °next ˌweek?
It 'doesn't °matter a ˇbit.	D'you ›mean that | or are you 'just being ˌnice aₒbout it?
It 'costs about °twenty ˇpounds.	Is that ›reasonable | or d'you 'think it °too ˌdear?
ˇI can't ₒdo it.	In ›that case | shall ˇI have a ₒtry?
'When would you °like me to ˇstart?	If it's con›venient | 'can you start °early on ˌWednesday?
(Lunch 'won't be °ready till ˇone, I'm aₒfraid.)	In the ›meantime | 'would you °care for a ˌdrink?
Yes, I'm ˇquite ₒwilling to be ₒon the comₒmittee.	And when ›necessary | 'would you °act as ˌsecretary?
I shall ˇlike ₒusing the ₒnew ˌmower.	If you're ›so keen | would you 'like to cut ˇmy grass | ˇtoo?

Verbal context	*Drill*
I ˘don't know about ˇTuesday.	Well if ˃that's no °good | 'can you °manage ˋWednesday?
● He's 'promised it for Juˋly.	Juˀly, | will 'that be ˋsoon enough, d'you ₒthink?
I'm to call 'back at ˌlunchtime.	By ˀlunchtime, | 'will it be ˋready, d'you supₒpose?
'Why not °try ˋBennetts?	But ˀBennetts, | 'are they an efˋficient ₒfirm?
● It'll be ˇdifficult, you ₒknow.	But do ˀyou | con'sider it °worth ˋtrying?
Commands	
(She'll ˘tell you ˇsoon, | I'm ˋsure.)	Till ˀthen, | pre'tend you know °nothing aₒbout it.
● 'When d'you ˌwant me?	If you ˀcan, | come 'right aˋway.
I shall be ˘going there ˇsometime.	Well when you ˀdo, | 'go by ˋtrain.
So you're ex'pecting ˋThomson.	Yes and when he arˀrives, | 'show him °in imˌmediately.
'Can I °stay a bit ˌlonger?	By ˀall means, | 'stay as °long as you ˋwish.
'Any sug'gestions, °George?	At ˀWhitsun, | 'let's have a °week in ˋParis.
And 'what about ˋThursday?	On ˀThursday, | 'let's stay at ˀhome | and 'watch ˋtelevision.
And 'how's the ˋskirt?	For ˀmy taste, | 'cut it a °bit ˋshorter.
(Oh there's ˌno real ˌharm done.)	But in ˀfuture, | 'mind your own ˌbusiness.
(I'll 'send you a °better one ˋlater.)	In the ˀmeantime, | 'make the °best of ˋthis one.
● 'Which °car shall I ˋuse?	If you've a ˀchoice, | 'use the °old ˋmini.
'What would ˌyou adₒvise, ₒAllan?	Since you ˀask me, | don't have 'anything to ˋdo with it.
It ˘isn't very atˇtractive, | ˋis it?	If you disˀlike it, | 'don't ˋhave it.
● Won't 'forty be eˌnough?	To be on the ˀsafe °side, | 'take °one or two ˋmore.
(I'll ˘get a °new one ˇsoon.)	But for the time ˀbeing, | 'make °do with that ˋold thing.
(ˋDon't stand °any of ˇhis ₒnonsense.)	If ˀnecessary, | 'write to his ˋboss aₒbout him.
'How °many shall I ˋgive him?	If ˀpossible, | 'give him a °couple of ˋdozen.

Verbal context	*Drill*
But he was ex˖tremely of˅fensive.	In the ˀcircumstances, | ˈdon't take °too much ˅notice.
ˈCan I bring ˏtwo °guests?	As far as ˀI'm con°cerned, | bring as ˈmany as you ˅like.
You must ˈdo it ˅my way.	If ˀthat's how you °want it, | ˈdon't ask ˏme to ˳help a˳gain.

Note: All the drills given above with the tune
LOW PRE-HEAD+MID-LEVEL (+TAIL)
can be said with emphasis if the low pre-head is replaced by the high pre-head (see Chapter I, p. 36). With this feature marked the last drill in this section would read
‾If ˀthat's how you °want it, \| ˈdon't ask ˏme to ˳help a˳gain.

Tune ▬▬ ▬ ‒ **(Low Pre-Head+) High Head +Mid-Level (+Tail)**

Statements

What re˅action did you ˳get?	ˈJohn and ˀGeorge | seemed ˈrather ˅keen.
ˈWhere shall we ˅eat?	The ˈFox and ˀHounds | does a ˅splendid ˳lunch.
But ˈisn't it ex˖pensive?	No, the ˈcheapest ˀseat | costs ˈless than a ˅pound.
ˈHow did you get ˅on?	ˈPlaying °chess with ˀJohn | is ˈquite an ex˅perience.
But ˖where does he °get the ˅money?	ˈWhere he °gets the ˀmoney from | is ˈno con°cern of ˏours.
● ˏWon't you °have some °coffee?	(ˀNo, | ˏthanks.) || ˈDrinking °coffee at ˀlunchtime | ˈmakes me so ˅sleepy.
ˈWhich °month would you pre˅fer?	ˈJune or Juˀly, | it's ˈall the ˅same | to ˏme.
ˈWhy not °travel over˅night?	ˈSleeping on a ˀtrain | I ˈfind im˅possible.
˅Now ˳what have you been ˳up to?	I sup ˈpose I ought ˀreally | to make a ˈclean ˏbreast of it.
● ˈShall we go to˒day?	No, it would ˈprobably be ˀwiser | to ˈwait till ˅Saturday.
‾Didn't you ˏsee °John?	No, by the ˈtime I ˀgot there | he'd ˅gone.

Verbal context	_Drill_
'Won't you ,really °have one?	Well 'since you in›sist, | ⁻I ˏthink I ˋwill.
'Didn't Fred exˏplain it °to you?	Yes but 'what he was ›getting at | I simply 'couldn't make ˏout.
'What d'you °think of my ˋpainting?	If you 'don't mind my ›saying so, | it's a 'terrible ˋmess.
You ˏwill °come, | ˏwon't you?	As 'far as I can ›see, | I 'shan't be ˋfree.
But he alˏready ˋknows.	'All the ›same, | you'd 'better conˏfirm it ˏwith him.
(I don't ˇwant to ˏask her.)	But 'sometime ›soon, | I shall ˋhave to.
I 'thought you °didn't ˋdrink ˏcoffee.	As a 'general ›rule, | I ˋdon't.
'What was ˋFrank's reˏaction?	'Not un›naturally, | he 'didn't °like it a ˋbit.
● But I ˏthought you'd ˋlike one.	As a 'matter of ›fact, | I've al'ready got ˋtwo.

WH-Questions

He 'missed the ˋtrain.	For 'heaven's ›sake, | 'what's he °going to ˋdo?
You 'owe me °ten ˋpounds for it.	With 'all °due res›pect, | 'how d'you make ˋthat out?
'When °ought we to ˋleave?	So as to 'get there ›early, | 'how about °travelling over'night?
'What would ˋyou do, ˏGerry?	In 'view of °all the ›circumstances, | 'why don't you °start aˋgain?
He ˋdid ˏknow. || I 'told him my'self.	'If that's ›so, | 'why did he com°plain that he ˋdidn't?
But he ˏmay reˋfuse.	Sup'posing he ›does, | 'what ˋdifference will it ˏmake?
Oh ˏhe'll °contact ˋyou.	Yes but in 'case he for›gets, | 'what's his ˏphone ˏnumber?
● It's ˏso exˋpensive.	Pro'vided you can af›ford it, | 'what does it ˋmatter ˏhow much it ˏcosts?
To be ˇfrank, | I'm 'not very ˋkeen on ˏporridge.	If you 'didn't ›want it, | 'why didn't you ˋsay so?
'Let's get a °new ˋcar.	If you 'don't mind my ›asking, | ˏwhere's the ˋmoney ˏcoming from?
D'you 'think we'll °pull it ˏoff?	Since 'Fred and ›Tom are °willing, | 'what's to ˋstop us?

Verbal context	*Drill*
I 'like them `both.	But 'if you °had to ⟩choose, | 'which would you pre`fer?
('Let's carry `on.)	When 'all is °said and ⟩done, | 'what have we °got to `lose?
D'you 'like my ˏsuit?	If it's 'not a °rude ⟩question, | 'how much did you `pay for it?
We shall 'have to a`bandon ˏthat i°dea.	But 'why was ⟩Charles | so 'violently op-`posed to it?
● He 'fooled ⟩me | com`pletely.	'How could ⟩you | with 'all your ex⟩peri-ence | be 'so °taken ˏin?
'Isn't that °man a ˏfool!	'How in the ⟩world | did we 'never °realise it beˏfore?
He gave us a ⟩week | from the 'date of his `letter.	'When was the ⟩letter | 'actually `dated?
I was 'foolish to `try.	'Why did you ⟩do it | if it 'wasn't `necessary?
What an ex'traordinary ˏparty!	Who'ever was that ⟩girl | with the 'purple ˏhair?
● 'How shall we `feed them?	'Why don't you en⟩courage them °all | to 'bring `sandwiches?
He was `cross aˌbout the ˏbill.	Well 'who can ⟩blame the °man | for 'wanting his `money?
(It's a'bout the `play we're ˌdoing.)	'Where's the °best ⟩place | to 'hire ˏcos-tumes ˌfrom?
I 'must get °rid of this °colour `television.	What'ever °made you ⟩think | you could 'possibly afˏford it?
I feel `so ˏsorry for him.	'When did you °first ⟩know | that his ⟩wife | was so 'terribly ˏill?
(I'm 'clearing this ˏcupboard.)	Now 'which of these °various ⟩bottles | d'you 'really °want to ˏkeep?

Yes-No Questions

'Shall we ˏgo now?	Well 'are you ⟩sure | you 'know the ˏway?
'Frank's got a °new `car.	'Did he ⟩say | 'how much he ˏgave for it?
Shall we ⟩go?	'Don't you ⟩think | it would be 'wiser to `wait a ˌwhile?
`John's ˌtaking them | in his `car.	D'you 'think he ⟩knows | 'how to ˏget there?

Verbal context	*Drill*
What's the ˋmatter, ₒPeter?	Did I 'hear you ˎsay │ you'd 'lost the ˏkeys?
I 'shan't be ˋfree, I'm aₒfraid.	But 'didn't you ˎsay │ you could 'come on ˏSaturday?
Yes, they've ˋbought that ₒhouse.	D'you 'happen to ˎknow │ 'how much it ˏcost them?
ˇSorry. ‖ 'Mine's ˋbroken.	Have you 'any iˎdea │ 'where I can °find aˏnother one?
D'you 'like these °new ˏcurtains?	'Would you mind ˎtelling me │ 'where you ˏgot them °from?
'Seen my ˊsaw °anywhere?	'Can't you reˎmember │ 'where you °had it ˏlast?
● What's ˋwrong, ₒJim?	'Would it be ˎpossible │ to 'have the ˏwindow °shut?
I ˇmay have a ₒcopy │ ˏsomewhere.	'If you ˎhave, │ 'could I ˏborrow it °sometime?
I shall be ˋseeing ₒFrank │ ˌlater ˏon.	'When you ˎdo, │ 'will you °tell him I ˏphoned?
● 'Shall we ˏwalk there?	In 'case it ˎrains, │ 'hadn't we °better take the ˏcar?
'Why d'you ˋask about that ₒbook?	'If you've °still ˎgot it, │ 'would you pass it °on to the ˋBrowns?
'Have a ˋwhisky, ₒAlan.	If it's 'all the °same to ˎyou, │ 'can I °have another ˏbeer, °George?
‾Any ˊother sug°gestions?	'Sometime ˎsoon │ 'could we °go to the ˏtheatre a°gain?
Well, ˋwhen, ₒthen?	'All things conˎsidered, │ 'can we make a °start on ˋFriday?
It's ˋnot very ˇgood.	But in 'all your exˎperience, │ have you 'ever seen a ˏbetter one?
'What d'you ˋwant, ₒAgnes?	'Sorry to ˎbother you │ but 'could you °tell me the ˏtime?
Have you 'got any °offwhite ˏpaint?	'Must it be ˎoffwhite │ or will ˋordinary ₒwhite ₒdo?
I could 'lend you ˋmy ₒracquet.	Have you 'got it ˎwith you │ or will you 'have to go ˋhome ₒfor it?

Verbal context	*Drill*
● 'Anything 'else I can °do for you?	'Can you °call at the >Post °Office | or is 'that a bit °out of your `way?

Commands

'What about `Andrew?	'Ring him >up | and 'tell him we °shan't be `needing him.
● I `don't feel like °going ˇout.	Well then 'let's stay at >home | and 'look at `television.
But I ˏcan't leave ˳Tommy ˏhere all the °morning.	Well 'give him a >pound | and 'pack him °off to the `swimming ˳pool.
'Anything 'else to be °done?	Yes 'call at the >butcher's | and 'buy me a °couple of ˏchops.
D'you 'want it 'back?	No 'keep it for your>self | or 'pass it °on to `Adrian.
'What are the al`ternatives?	'Go by the °morning >train | or 'catch the °afternoon ˏcoach.
'How shall we `go?	'If there's >time, | 'let's `walk.
I ˇmight ˳see her.	'If you >do, | please 'tell her I `phoned.
But ˏTed's °very much a`gainst it.	No matter 'what he >says, | 'just you carry `on with it.
I'm 'calling on °Peter to`night.	'When you >see him, | 'say I'll be °back on `Sunday.
'Can I tell ˏAnn?	Yes but what'ever you >do, | 'don't let °on to `Alice.
● But ˏJoan's ex`pecting us.	'Even if she >is, | 'let her ˏwait a ˳bit.
'What d'you ad`vise, ˳doctor?	For the 'time >being, | 'stay in`doors.
'What's to be `done?	'Sometime >soon, | 'write to him and ex-`plain.
'What have I °done `now?	For 'goodness >sake, | 'keep `quiet a ˳minute.
But she's so ˏvery `rude.	For the 'sake of °peace and >quiet, | ig`nore her ˳shocking be˳haviour.
● 'Which is the °quickest `way?	Take the 'first on the >left, | 'just past the `station.
And the 'pills?	Take them 'three times a >day, | 'after ˏmeals.

Verbal context	*Drill*
'What about this °waste `paper ₒbasket?	Leave it 'just where you ⁾found it, | by the 'side of the `bookcase.
'Where shall we `keep it?	'Put it in that ⁾cupboard | in 'Alfred °Johnson's `office.

Interjections

● They've 'gone on a `cruise.	'How ⁾wonderful | to be 'able to af`ford such a ₒholiday!
'Thank °heavens they've `gone.	Yes 'good⁾bye | and 'good ˎriddance!
(`Too late ˇnow, I'm aₒfraid.)	'What a ⁾pity | you 'didn't °mention it be`fore!
We 'all hate the `sight of him.	'How ex⁾traordinary | he 'keeps on `coming!
We must be `off | ˎnow.	Well the 'best of ⁾luck | to `all of you!
'Jack's °changed his `mind.	How 'terribly an⁾noying | for `everyone!
● 'Isn't the °weather `gorgeous!	And what a 'perfect ex⁾cuse | for doing 'abso°lutely ˎnothing!
And I 'had to °do it a`gain.	'What a gi°gantic ⁾fuss | about 'nothing at ˎall!

Note: All the relevant drills given above with the tune

(LOW PRE-HEAD+) HIGH HEAD+MID-LEVEL (+TAIL)

can be said with emphasis if one or both of the following features are used:

(*a*) the high pre-head instead of the low pre-head (see Chapter I, p. 36);

(*b*) the emphatic form of the high head (see Chapter I, p. 37).

The following examples are marked for these features:

⁻Well the 'best of ⁾luck \| to `all of you.

'Playing 'chess with ⁾John \| is 'quite an ex`perience.

V Intonation Drills
TONE GROUP SEQUENCES

1 Low Bounce | High Drop

ALTERNATIVE QUESTIONS

Verbal context — *Drill*

● 'This box ˎis ˳heavy.

D'you 'want a ˏhand │ or can you ˋmanage?

Well ˋanyway, │ ˇFrancis has got eˏnough ˳copies.

Wasn't 'he °short ˏtoo │ or have you 'given him some °spare ones ˋsince?

It's an ˋexcellent bit of ˳work.

D'you 'really ˏmean that │ or are you 'just being ˋnice aˏbout it?

ˏYes, Jones? ‖ What ˋis it?

Can you 'see °Smith ˏnow, sir, │ or d'you 'want him to °come back ˋlater?

● Well ˇBob's ˳car's aˏvailable.

Will there be 'room for ˏall of us °in it │ or d'you 'think I should bring °mine as ˋwell?

Would you 'like a ˏchocolate?

Is 'that the °last ˏone │ or are there some 'more underˋneath?

'Well ˋdone, ˳Jim! ‖ You've ˋbeaten me.

Would you 'care for aˏnother °game │ or have you had eˋnough for toˏnight?

'Wasn't °Mark's a fanˆtastic ˳story!

Was he 'telling the ˏtruth, d'you °think, │ or was it 'just his imagiˋnation at ˳work aˏgain?

Yes I ˋpaid the ˳bill. ‖ 'Six ˋpounds it ˳was.

Have you got 'change for °two ˏfivers │ or shall I ˋowe it to you for the ˳moment?

'What shall we °do this ˋevening, ˏDick?

Would you 'care for a °game of ˏchess │ or shall we 'just °sit and ˋgossip?

D'you 'mind if I ˏsmoke?

('Not at ˋall.) ‖ Can I 'offer you a cigaˏrette │ or d'you preˋfer your ˋpipe?

'Hadn't we °better ring him ˏnow?

'Can't that °wait till °after ˏtea │ or d'you supˈpose he'll have ˋleft by ˳then?

'Something the ˊmatter?

'Wasn't that a °knock at the ˏdoor │ or 'am I iˋmagining ˳things?

'Wasn't °Dan ˋtouchy!

⁻Does he ˏusually be°have like °that │ or has 'something upˋset him?

Verbal context	*Drill*
'What °time shall we ˎmeet?	⁻Shall we say 'five oˎclock | or is 'that too ˋearly ₀for you?

2 Low Bounce | High Drop

NON-FINAL WORD GROUPS

I'm most ˋgrateful for your ₀help.	Well if 'that's ˎall, | then I 'think I'll be ˋgoing.
'Fancy going °out in ˋthis ₀weather!	'Rain or ˎshine, | they ˋalways go ₀out on ₀Sunday after₀noons.
So you ˋdid go to their ₀house.	Yes and 'when I ˎgot there, | there was 'no-one ˋin.
'Don't de°cide ˎnow. ‖ 'Think a°bout it aˋgain.	'Since you inˎsist, | I'll ˋsleep ₀on it.
You ˋlike ˎPeter, | ˋdon't you?	Yes after 'only a ˎweek, | we've become the ˋbest of ₀friends.
⁻Wasn't ˎJohn any °help?	No 'first he said ˎone thing | and 'then aˋnother.
● ⁻Would you ˎlike one?	As a 'matter of ˎfact, | I've al'ready ˋgot one.
How ˋwas your ₀uncle?	As 'soon as I ˎsaw him, | I 'knew his °illness was ˋserious.
But ˎnine o₀clock will be ˎsoon enough, | ˎwon't it?	So as to be in 'plenty of ˎtime, | you'd 'better °leave beˋfore that.
'Have you seen ˎPeter °lately?	'When I was in ˎLondon, | I had ˋlunch with him a ₀couple of ₀times.
I've de'cided to ˎsack him.	'After you've °heard what ˎhappened, | you'll 'change your ˋmind, I ₀think.
But I ˎthought you were on your °way to ˋLondon.	No by the 'time I °got to the ˎstation, | the 'train had al°ready ˋgone.
Well I'm 'not ˋsure. ‖ I 'don't °trust him a ˋbit.	'Whether we °trust him or ˎnot, | we've just ˋgot to be₀lieve him.
D'you 'mind °waiting a bit ˎlonger? ‖ He's ˋbound to be °back ˇsoon.	If he's 'not here in a °quarter of an ˎhour, | I shall 'have to °leave withˋout ₀seeing him, I'm a₀fraid.

Verbal context	*Drill*
ˏWhy were you so ˋcross with ₒAlec?	No 'sooner had we got °everything fixed ˏup | than he 'wanted to °cry ˋoff.
I ˋlove ₒsalted ˏalmonds.	'As you're so ˏfond of them, | 'why not ˋbuy some?
We really ˟must tell him ˇsoon.	'If it's so ˏurgent, | 'what about °ringing him °up ˋnow?
No I've got ˋnothing on | ˏlater.	Well 'after the ˏclass, | 'why don't we °drop in at the °George for a ˋdrink?
And 'what about ˋTim?	'When you ˏcan, | 'write to him aˋgain.
The 'train doesn't °leave until ˋfive.	Well 'while we're ˏwaiting, | 'let's go and °have a cup of ˋtea.
● 'Which day's ˋbest, d'you ₒthink?	'If you can ˏmanage it, | 'go on a ˋSunday.
I 'told him ˋpersonally about the ₒmeeting.	So that he 'doesn't forˏget, | 'drop him a °line to conˋfirm the ₒdate.
'What about this °old ˋdeed? || 'Shall I get ˏrid of it?	Beˈfore you desˏtroy it, | 'show it to your soˋlicitor.
'Peter °doesn't ˋknow | ˏyet.	Well 'when he °comes ˏback, | ˋtell him aₒbout it.
'What shall I ˋdo about his ₒoffer?	'As it's so °very ˏreasonable, | 'go a°head and acˋcept it.
I 'shan't keep you °much ˏlonger.	Since you're 'obviously °very ˏbusy just °now, | 'shall I come °back toˋmorrow?
D'you 'really ˏlike her?	⁻In ˏsome °ways, | I ˋdo.
'Any time to °spare on ˋSunday?	⁻For ˏonce in a °while, | I ˋhave.
'What was the °meal ˋlike?	⁻On the ˏwhole, | it was ˋexcellent.
Have you 'got any °tinned ˏpeas?	⁻At the ˏmoment, | we're 'right ˋout of them, ₒmadam.
ˇI ₒthink | ˋJames ₒbroke it.	⁻If that's ˏso, | 'what's to be ˋdone aₒbout it?
He's got ˇvery °good seˇcurity.	⁻In ˏthat case, | ˋlend him the ₒmoney.
'Can I °borrow the ˏcar? || ˇMark's quite aₒgreeable.	⁻If ˏMark doesn't °mind, | 'carry ˋon.
I 'may °go to the ˋclub.	⁻If you ˏdo, | keep an 'eye out for ˋAdrian.

3 Low Bounce | Low Bounce

	NON-FINAL WORD GROUPS
Verbal context	*Drill*

● ˇSorry. ‖ He's ˋout.

'When he comes ˏback, | 'would you °tell him I ˏphoned?

Yes I ˋam ₀going to the ₀meeting.

'If you see ˏChristine °there, | 'could you °give her this ˏletter?

'Anything you °want in ʹtown?

If you're 'passing the ˏbutcher's, | would you 'buy a °pound of ˏsausages?

'How about ʹme going to ₀fetch them?

If you're 'sure you °don't ˏmind, | 'do you °think you ˏcould?

'Come ˏon. ‖ 'Let's ˋgo.

If the 'Smiths are °going as ˏwell, | 'oughtn't we to ˏwait °for them?

Yes I'll ˋcertainly ₀call at the ₀grocer's.

'After ˏthat, | 'would you mind col°lecting my °suit from the ˏcleaner's?

I 'don't °think I can ˋdo it.
Well I'm a 'bit °short of ˋmoney.

⁻In ˏthat case, | ⁻shall ˏI have a °try?
⁻If ˏthat's °all that's °worrying you, | ⁻can I ˏlend you °some?

4 Switchback | High Drop

	NON-FINAL WORD GROUPS

I've 'broken a°nother ˋcup.
(ˇOnce | he em'ployed ˋsix men.)
(In the ˇmorning, | he 'seemed ˋbetter.)
(No it ʹwasn't ˇMonday I ₀saw him.)
'How d'you ʹgo to the ₀office?
⁻D'you ˏlike your °job?
I 'won't put ˋup with it.
(We're 'going to ʹItaly, | ˏthis year.)
'Got a °full ʹteam °yet?
(For a ˇlong ₀time | I 'tried to ˋborrow a ₀cloak.)
(ˋSorry I was ˏout when you °called.)

ˇSoon, | you 'won't have ˋany ₀left.
ˇNow, | he 'works on his ˋown.
ˇLater, | I 'heard he'd °had a reˋlapse.
ˇMonday, | I stayed ʹin all ₀day.
ˇOften, | I ˋwalk.
ˇSometimes, | I ˋloathe it.
ˇFrankly, | I 'don't ˋblame you.
ˇLast ₀year, | we 'went to ˋAustria.
ˇSo ₀far, | we're 'two men ˋshort.

ˇFinally, | I was 'forced to ˋbuy one.
ˇUsually, | I'm at ˋhome on ₀Mondays.

Verbal context	*Drill*
('Help your°self to the ˏwhisky.)	˅Personally, | I 'never ˋtouch the ₒstuff.
Does 'Arthur °really ˏneed it?	Apˇparently, | he ˋdoes.
● It's 'too ˋdear, | ˏJohn says.	In ˇmy oₒpinion, | he's 'abso°lutely ˋright.
D'you 'like my ˏtie?	Since you ˇask me, | ˋno.
‾Shall I ˏgo to the °meeting?	If you ˇcan ₒgo, | you 'ought.
'What's the °Lake District ˋlike?	When the ˇweather's ₒgood, | it's deˋlightful.
(He 'told me to °mind my own ˋbusiness!)	Well after ˇthat, | I 'let him get °on with it aˋlone.
So the 'soup was ˋterrible.	Yes but in ˇother resₒpects, | it was an ˋexcellent ₒmeal.
So you 'rang him at ˋonce.	Yes and when I ˇsaw him, | I reˋpeated my reₒquest.
'What should I ˋdo, ₒGeorge?	If ˋI were ˇyou, | I'd 'wait and °see what ˋhappens.
I ˋlove ˏgardening.	ˋIf you're so ˇkeen on it, | 'why °live in a ˋflat?
ˏWhat's °happened to ˋyour ₒcar?	With the ˇcost of °living what it ˇis, | I 'can't af°ford to ˋrun it.
And 'how was ˋyour ₒChristmas?	What with ˇone thing and aˇnother, | 'rather disapˋpointing.
D'you 'like my °new ˏsuit?	If you ˇdon't mind my ˇsaying ₒso, | it's ˋterrible.
'My °watch is ˋterrible.	˅Mine's | ˋfine.
('Don't give me ˏtoo °many.)	˅Six | is ˋample.
'Aren't °vegetables ˋdear!	˅Beans | are a terˋrific ₒprice.
‾What a 'wretched ˋsummer!	˅August | was a ˋterrible ₒmonth.
('Why won't they °make up their ˋminds?)	˅Peter's | the ˋobvious ₒchoice.
I shall 'never °speak to him aˏgain.	˅Never | is a ˋvery ₒdangerous ₒword to ₒuse.
'Why do °people play ˏgames?	˅I ₒplay | for ˋexercise.
Well 'whose °fault ˋwas it, ₒthen?	˅Dad ₒsays | it was ˋyours.
('Don't use ˇthat ₒknife.)	˅That ₒknife | 'won't cut at ˋall.
'Fred's made a°nother comˋplaint.	˅Some ₒpeople | are ˋalways comₒplaining.
The 'party was ˋfun, | ˋwasn't it?	˅Margaret's ₒparties | 'usually ˋare.
'What d'you °think of ˋCubism?	˅That sort of ₒart | is 'quite beˋyond me.

Verbal context	*Drill*
'Max is `always ₀late.	ˇYou on the ₀other hand | are 'always `early.
'Did you °like the ,people in °France?	ˇMost of the ₀ones I ₀met | were `charming.
'What was the °meal `like?	The ˇsoup | was `terrible.
'What did your `parents ₀think?	My ˇfather | was de`lighted by the ₀news.
'Why not °ask the `Browns?	So ˇyou ₀think | they'd be sympa`thetic.
I've 'got to work `late, I'm a₀fraid.	So ˇthat ₀means | 'I can't °go to the `party.
'How °much to go `in?	The ˇcheapest ₀seat | costs a `pound.
'When will she be `out of ₀hospital?	The ˇdoctor ₀thinks | in 'ten days' `time.
'How °much do we `need?	Well ˇmy ₀estimate | is about 'half a `ton.
(ˇI ₀think | it'll `do.)	But my ˇfather's con₀vinced | it's 'too `big.
'Didn't Frank a,gree to the °plan?	Yes but ˇPeter | was 'very °much a`gainst it.
● ‾Did you ,eat °well?	The ˇfood in ˇParis | was su`perb.
'Who's `next?	Well ˇFred and ˇI ₀think | it's `our ₀turn.
‾What did `you people ₀think of those ₀plans?	Well in ˇTom's o°pinion and ˇmine | they're 'worse than `useless.

5   Switchback \| Switchback

● They `all ₀got it ₀wrong.	Well ˇJames | came ˇclose.
I'm ˇnot going to a ˇpologise.	Well ˇsomehow | you've ˇgot to °calm him ˇdown.
(Yes he ˇpassed all ₀right.)	But ˇmind ˇyou, | he could have ˇdone even ˇbetter.
I ,don't think I'll ₀go to,day.	ˇSometime ˇsoon | you'll ˇhave to ₀go, you know.
And ,that's not `all. || It's ,horribly ex-`pensive.	No matter ˇwhat you ˇsay, | I'm ˇquite de-°termined to go ˇon with it.
I ,just can't af`ford a ₀car.	If you ˇwanted one ˇbadly e₀nough, | you'd ˇfind the °money ˇsomehow.
I `shan't buy the ₀shirt | ,this month.	ˇLeave it till ˇnext ₀month | and you'll ˇhave to pay ˇmore.

Verbal context	*Drill*
Your ˅conduct | was 'inex˅cusable.	Be˅fore you °jump to con˅clusions, | for ˅goodness sake °hear me ˅out.
He's ˏsuch a ˅fool. ‖ I can ˏhardly be ˅civil ˳to him.	How˅ever much he °gets on your ˅nerves, | ˅try and be po˅lite to him.

6 Take-Off \| High Drop

NON-FINAL WORD GROUPS

Count from 'thirteen to ˎtwenty.	ˏThirteen, | ˏfourteen, | ˏfifteen, | ˏsixteen | ˏseventeen, | ˏeighteen, | ˏnineteen, | ˅twenty.
But the as'sistant was so ˅rude.	In ˏthat case, | 'why didn't you °ask to see the ˅manager?
● He 'thinks it's ˎyour ˳fault.	If ˏthat's what he °thinks, | he can 'think a˅gain.
'Poor °old ˅Tom! ‖ He's got a ˅terrible ˳black ˳eye.	In ˏmy o°pinion, | he deserved 'all he ˅got.
(For a ˏlong °time | it looked ˅hopeless.)	But when ˏPhillip took a °hand, | the 'difficulties were ˅soon over˳come.
˳That's my 'final ˎoffer.	If ˏthat's the °way you °want it, | there's 'nothing °more to ˅say.
Count from 'seventy °one to °seventy ˎsix.	ˏSeventy ˏone, | ˏseventy ˏtwo, | ˏseventy ˏthree, | ˏseventy ˏfour, | ˏseventy ˏfive, | 'seventy ˅six.
(At 'first he was ˅very luke˳warm.)	But ˏafter I'd ex˳plained the °matter °to him, | he was 'quite ˅keen.
Are you 'willing to be ˏchairman a°gain?	Unless ˏanyone obˏjects, | I'm ˅very ˳willing.
D'you 'want to know °right aˏway?	No be˳fore you de˳cide, | ˅sleep on ˳what I've sug˳gested.
(He was 'quite ready to ˅bluff it ˳out.)	But as ˏsoon as I ˏtackled him a°bout it, | he ad˅mitted he was ˳wrong.

7 Take-Off | Long Jump

Verbal context	*Drill*

He com͵pletely igˋnored your reₒquest.

For ͵two ͵pins, | I'll ͵tell him what I ˋthink of him.

ˇJack ₒsays | ˋfares are ₒgoing ₒup aₒgain.
'Didn't you a͵pologise °to him?

If ͵that's ͵so, | it's a ͵downright ˋscandal.

I ͵went ͵up to him | and he ͵just ˋsnubbed me. ‖ (So I ˋdidn't.)

● She ͵knew about the °dangers, | ˋsurely.

͵Bill ͵warned her a°bout them | but she ͵just took °no ˋnotice.

I'm ˋvery disₒsatisfied ₒwith it.

If ͵I were ͵you, | I'd ͵send it ˋback.

Well 'what did ˋyou ₒthink of the ₒplay?

͵Since you ͵ask me, | I must confess I ͵rather ˋliked it.

But ͵surely your ͵husband was °there to look °after you.

For ͵all that ͵Simon °cares, | I ͵might have been °squashed ˋflat.

(So I ͵rang him ͵up | and ͵told him I was ˋcalling ₒfor it.)

And ͵when I ͵got there, | he ͵gave it me without °any ˋargument.

'Let's go and ˋmeet her. ‖ She's 'due at the °station at ˋten.

By the ͵time we ͵get there, | it'll be ͵much too ˋlate.

Oh he ˋnever ₒanswers my ₒletters.

In͵stead of ͵writing °to him, | ͵why not drop °in at his ˋoffice?

Well ˋask him aₒbout it.

But ͵if he re͵fuses, | ͵what's to be ˋdone?

ˉWhat͵ever ˋnext! ‖ ˉHe ͵wants to °buy a ˋcar.

If he's ͵got the ͵money, | ͵why not ˋlet him?

I sup'pose I shall ˋhave to ₒgo. ‖ ˋWhat a ₒbore!

If you ͵feel like ͵that a°bout it, | ͵why ˋbother?

8 High Bounce | Low Drop

(I can 'usually ˋdo ₒcrosswords.)
(In 'winter I °play ͵squash.)
(The 'snow °stopped about ͵midnight.)

But with 'this one | I'm 'all at ͵sea.
And in 'summer | I ͵swim a ₒlot.
And in the 'morning | it had 'all ͵gone.

Verbal context	*Drill*
(I worked 'all ˎday on the ˳car.)	And when I'd 'finished, │ it ˏstill ˳sounded no ˳better.
I 'need your ˋhelp.	If you're in 'trouble, │ I'll ˏcertainly ˳help.
I reˋfuse to aˎˎpologise.	In 'that case, │ I've got 'nothing °more to ˏsay to you.
I aˋdore ˳rice ˏpudding.	What you 'see in it, │ I just 'can't ˏthink.
('Una said ˋshe'd sit ˳in for us.)	But whether she 'meant it, │ I ˳haven't the 'faintest iˏdea.
Well that's ˇmy oˎˎpinion.	If 'you °think so, │ that's 'all that ˏmatters.
(Yes I ocˇcasionally ˳watch ˳television.)	But 'usually, │ I'm ˏfar too ˳busy.
● But ˎcan we afˋford it?	If it's the 'money that's °bothering you, │ ‾that's ˏeasily ˳settled.
('What'll you °have to ˏdrink?)	You can have 'tea, │ or 'coffee │ or ˏcocoa.
'When can you ˏstart?	On 'Tuesday, │ or 'Wednesday │ ‾or ˏFriday.
'Which °way will you ˋgo?	Through 'Belgium, │ 'Holland │ ‾and ˏGermany.
'What can she ˏdo?	She can do 'shorthand, │ and 'typing, │ both in 'English and ˏFrench.
(Well 'what would you °like to ˏhear?)	I've got some 'Bach, │ or De'bussy, │ or if you pre'fer it, │ I've got a 'new ˏjazz ˳record.
'What shall I ˏtake?	You'll need py'jamas, │ your 'shaving °kit │ and a ˏtoothbrush.

9 High Drop │ High Drop

	QUESTION TAGS
They ˇcan't ˳go │ ˋafter ˳all.	'Pity, │ ˋisn't it?
What a 'terrible ˋaccident!	'Shocking, │ ˋwasn't it?
‾I ˏdid enˎjoy the ˳match.	'Very good ˳game, │ ˋwasn't it?
It 'looks like ˋrain.	It 'does, │ ˋdoesn't it?
'Was I °glad to get ˋhome!	You 'were ˳tired, │ ˋweren't you?
‾She's ˏvery good ˳looking.	Yes she 'is, │ ˋisn't she?
It 'served him ˋright.	Yes it 'did, │ ˋdidn't it?

Verbal context	Drill
They 'don't 'need ˎboth of them.	No they ˋdon't, | ˋdo they?
You're 'not very ˋgood at it, | ˋare you?	No I'm ˋnot, | ˋam I?
ˏWhere did you ˋsee him, ˎthen?	In the ˋHigh Street, | ˋdidn't we, ˎGeorge?
At 'last °Max has ˋfinished.	'Now it's ˋyour turn, | ˋisn't it?
● It 'doesn't °help at ˋall.	'Not in the ˋslightest, | ˋdoes it?
ˋNone of us ˎwants to ˎgo.	'Someone'll ˋhave to ˎgo, | ˋwon't they?
But we 'still need ˇPaul's ˎhelp.	'More than °ever be'fore, | ˋdon't we?
ˇThese ˎdays | he ˋrarely ˎgoes there.	And he 'used to en'joy the ˎtrip, | ˋdidn't he?
ˇI can't ˎlend you one.	Then I must 'ask °someone ˋelse, | ˋmustn't I?
Oh the ˋsun's gone ˎin.	And it 'looks a °bit like ˋrain, | ˋdoesn't it?
The ˏparcel °hasn't ˋcome.	Well you'd 'better en°quire at the ˋstation, | ˋhadn't you?

10   Take-Off | High Drop

QUESTION TAGS

He 'says I'm ˇjealous.	You're ˏnot, | ˋare you?
ˋTry it ˎthat way.	It ˏmay come °off, | ˋmayn't it?
Don't take 'any ˏnotice ˎof them.	They can't ˏalways be °right, | ˋcan they?
But ˏwhy was he so ˋrude to you?	It wasn't ˏmy °fault, | now ˋwas it?
I'm sur'prised at ˏPeter.	He ˏoughtn't to have made ˏthat mis°take, | ˋought he?
He 'says he's °got an ap'pointment. ‖ At ˋfive.	But he could ˏcome on ˏafterwards, | ˋcouldn't he?
We'll ex'cuse them, | ˏthis time.	They ˏdon't let us ˎdown ˏoften, | ˋdo they?
● He's no ˏreason to be °cross with you.	I'm ˏdoing the ˎbest I ˏcan, | ˋaren't I?

11   Low Bounce | High Drop

QUESTION TAGS

It 'doesn't °matter a ˏscrap.	'Not ˏreally, | ˋdoes it?
ˋThank you | for ˏlending me your ˏcamera.	'Take good ˏcare of it, | ˋwon't you?

Verbal context	Drill
ˋHang the exˏpense. ‖ 'Let's take a ˋtaxi ˏhome.	We 'don't have a °night out ˏoften, │ ˋdo we?
'Off al'ready?	It's 'time we were °getting aˏlong, │ ˋisn't it, ˏHenry?
He's a ˋmarvellous old ˏchap.	You 'wouldn't ˋthink he was ˏseventy, │ ˋwould you?
● ˋThanks │ for ˏhaving me.	⁻Come again ˏsoon, │ ˋwon't you?
He's 'on the ˋshort list.	⁻That's ˏvery en°couraging, │ ˋisn't it?
They ac'cused me of °telling ˋlies.	⁻You ˏdidn't tell °lies, │ ˋdid you?
ˇOlive ˏsays │ it's ˋvital to the ˏplan.	⁻But it's ˏnot im°portant, │ ˋis it?

12   Switchback │ High Drop

QUESTION TAGS

ˇThey ˏsay │ they 'gave us ˋeight ˏpounds.	ˇSeven, │ ˋwasn't it?
I ˏthink you've ˋdone it.	ˇAlmost, │ ˋhaven't I?
ˇPeter ˏsays │ ˋall fruit's ˏplentiful.	ˇPlums ˏaren't, │ ˋare they?
He ˋalways ˏgets it ˏwrong.	ˇMost ˏtimes, │ ˋdoesn't he?
I'll 'give her a °good ˋtalking to.	ˇThat won't imˏprove things, │ now ˋwill it?
In ˇhis oˏpinion, │ ˏvegetables are °very ˋreasonable.	ˇCabbages aren't ˏall that ˏcheap, │ ˋare they?
It's ˋnone of ˇmy ˏbusiness.	ˇYou're not ˏbeing very ˏhelpful, │ ˋare you?
⁻But ˏwhy °pick on ˋme?	ˇSomebody's ˏgot to ˏstay beˏhind and ˏhelp, │ ˋhaven't they?
ˇDaddy ˏsays │ it's ˏtoo ˋbig.	It's ˇnot too ˏbig, │ ˋis it?
So you 'think they'll ˋhelp us.	Well they ˇmight, │ ˋmightn't they?
I ˇthink I could ˏeat aˏnother one.	You don't ˇreally ˏwant it, │ ˋdo you?
He's ex'pecting it this °afterˏnoon.	But he ˇcan't ˏhave it by ˏthen, │ ˋcan he?
It's ˋvery ˇdifficult, you ˏknow.	But ˋnot imˇpossible, │ ˋis it?
ˋGoodness! ‖ It's ˏnearly °six o'clock.	You'd ˋbetter °hurry ˇup, │ ˋhadn't you?
Come at 'two or °two ˏthirty.	You ˋdon't give me °much ˇchoice, │ ˋdo you?
● 'What did you °think of the ˋlecture?	It ˋwasn't e°xactly senˇsational, │ ˋwas it?

13 Low Drop | Low Drop

Verbal context

Drill

What a 'very °nice ˎhouse!	ˎYes, | ˎisn't it?
It'll 'never be °ready in ˎtime.	ˎNever, | ˎwill it?
What 'hideous ˎcurtains!	ˎTerrible, | ˎaren't they?
'Jane thought I ˎmeant it.	But you ˎdidn't, | ˎdid you?
He paid 'ten ˎpounds ₒfor it.	It was a riˎdiculous ₒprice, | ˎwasn't it?
They 'offered it to ˎPeter.	'Peter had ˎgot one, | ˎhadn't he?
She's 'left us ˎsix.	'Six isn't sufˎficient, | ˎis it?
She's 'now °sent it ˎoff.	But 'not ˎsoon enough, | ˎhas she?
● 'Where's the ˎmoney ₒcoming from?	It's 'very ˎdifficult, | ˎisn't it?
ˏWhy didn't he °ask ˋme?	You'd have 'gone at ˎonce, | ˎwouldn't you?

14 Jackknife | Jackknife

'What a ^film!	^Awful, | ^wasn't it?
'Which of you °broke my ˎpipe?	^None of us, | ^did we?
ˇI ₒthink | it would be ˇfoolish.	^Terribly ₒfoolish, | ^wouldn't it?
‾What ^weather we're ₒhaving!	It's ^horrible, | ^isn't it?
I was deˇlighted to ₒhear about ₒBert.	He ^did do ₒwell, | ^didn't he?
We 'go through ˇStoke, | ˏdon't we?	Of ^course we ₒdon't, | now ^do we?
I 'had to stay ˇin | toˏday.	You're ^always ₒgetting into ₒtrouble, | ^aren't you?
Jane's ˇterribly upₒset.	That's 'quite under^standable, | ^isn't it?
● It's ˏnot all ˏthat °serious.	You 'don't °really ^care, | ^do you?
I'm aˈfraid you've ˇfailed.	I shall 'have to °try a^gain ₒthen, | ^shan't I?

15 Low Drop | Take-Off

'Whose ˎbook is ₒthat?	ˎJohn's, | ˏisn't it?

Verbal context	Drill
If 'only the ˎweather had been ˳better!	ˎVery ˳wet, | ˏwasn't it?
'Max says it's ˋyour ˳turn.	It ˎisn't, | ˏis it?
'Who'll ˎhelp, d'you ˳think?	Mr. ˎRobinson ˳will, | ˏwon't he?
ˇFrank can ˳play.	But 'Arthur ˎcan't, | ˏcan he?
I've 'just °heard from ˎAnn.	She's 'gone to ˎGermany, | ˏhasn't she?
'Shall we °give him a ˋcouple?	He 'wouldn't be ˎsatisfied with ˳that, | ˏwould he?
I 'rang the °bell ˋseveral ˳times.	But there 'wasn't °any ˎanswer, | ˏwas there?
● Yes I ˋhave ˳finished my ˳course.	You 'took the e°xam in ˎJune, | ˏdidn't you?
They 'left °Greece last ˋFriday.	So they 'won't be °here until toˎmorrow, | ˏwill they?

16 High Drop | Take-Off

QUESTION TAGS

'Whose is ˋthis ˳painting?	ˋTom's, | ˏisn't it?
ˋDon't rely on ˇthat ˳clock.	It ˋgains, | ˏdoesn't it?
ˋFunny ˳business, | about ˏJill.	She reˋsigned, | ˏdidn't she?
Yes I 'called on him ˋpersonally.	He was surˋprised, | ˏwasn't he?
'How many did he ˋwant?	ˋSeven, | ˏdidn't he?
Have you 'heard about ˏFrances?	She's 'quite ˋill, | ˏisn't she?
They 'came about °one o'clock.	They 'weren't in ˋtime, | ˏwere they?
'What °time'll you get ˋback?	At about 'ten o'clock, | ˏwon't we, °Frank?
The 'meeting's in the °Small ˋHall.	That 'won't be ˋbig enough, | ˏwill it?
'Why didn't Len °mention it to ˋJean?	He 'told her °last ˋweek, | ˏdidn't he?
'Arthur's coming °home toˋday.	Yes he's 'due here at e°leven, | ˏisn't he?
● ˉWhen ˎdid we ˳last ˳meet?	'Sometime in ˋApril, | ˏwasn't it?
'What's °happened to the ˋSmiths?	They 'weren't inˋvited, | ˏwere they?
ˉD'you know ˏGeorge °Dixon?	'He's the °tall ˋdark ˳twin, | ˏisn't he?
ˋI'm a ˋLondoner.	You 'live in °Camden ˋTown, | ˏdon't you?
He's at the 'local compreˋhensive ˳school.	He 'teaches °French and ˋGerman, | ˏdoesn't he?
No ˇI didn't ˳go to the ˳cinema.	You'd 'seen the °film alˋready, | ˏhadn't you?
And I 'also °mentioned it to ˋBob.	'He °wasn't °very ˋkeen, | ˏwas he?

Verbal context	*Drill*
They 'want a ˎrise.	They ˋdo, | ˏdo they?
She's al'ready ˋgot one.	Oh she ˋhas, | ˏhas she?
What a 'lovely ˎdress!	You ˋlike it, | ˏdo you?
'I don't ˋneed a ₒcopy.	You've ˋgot one, | ˏhave you?
Yes I've ˋtold ˏMary.	Oh you've ˋseen her, | ˏhave you?
ˉDon't ˏwait for me.	You'll 'come on ˋlater, | ˏwill you?
They 'wouldn't °do at ˋall.	They were 'quite imˋpossible, | ˏwere they?
'How about °asking ˋDick?	You 'think he °might aˋgree, | ˏdo you?
The ˇmilk's ₒnearly ₒboiling.	'Keep an ˋeye on it, | ˏwill you?
'What'll you °have to ˋdrink?	'Make mine a ˋgin, | ˏwould you?
'Don't you ˏlike the °radio?	'Turn the ˋvolume ₒdown a ₒbit, | ˏwould you?
ˉDid you ˊcall, °Joan?	Yes 'come over ˋhere a ₒminute, | ˏwill you?

17 Take-Off | Take-Off

QUESTION TAGS

'Whose ˎturn is it?	ˏMine, | ˏisn't it?
Peggy ˏwants to °stay at ˋhome.	ˏThat doesn't °matter, | ˏdoes it?
I ˋcan't ₒplay. ‖ My ˋracquet's ₒbroken.	You could ˏborrow one, | ˏcouldn't you?
There's ˋno point in °asking ˇAudrey.	But she ˏmight ac°cept, | ˏmightn't she?
● Oh ˏall ˏright. ‖ ˋI'll ₒget it.	You ˏdon't ˏmind, | ˏdo you?
Oh 'let's get ˋout of ₒhere.	You're ˏnot ˏfrightened, | ˏare you?
'Why °bring me ˋthat ₒbook?	It's the ˏone you ˏasked for, | ˏisn't it?
He ₒsays he'll 'never °speak to me aˎgain.	He ˏdoesn't ₒreally ˏmean it, | ˏdoes he?

18 Low Bounce | Take-Off

QUESTION TAGS

They've ˎsent us ˋfour.	We 'don't need ˏso many, | ˏdo we?
● 'Write to him at ˋWarwick ₒStreet.	That's 'not his ˏhome ad°dress, | ˏis it?
I 'may be a °bit ˋlate toₒnight.	But you'll be 'home in °time for ˏdinner, | ˏwon't you?

Verbal context	*Drill*
'Now I really ˋmust go.	But you'll 'come aˋgain to‚morrow, │ ‚won't you?
‚Why've you ˚taken ˋthat one?	‾This ‚is ˚mine, │ ‚isn't it?
'Jack thinks ˋChristine ˳wants it.	‾She ‚doesn't ˚want it, │ ‚does she?
‾Hul‚lo, ˚Jean. ‖ You're ˋearly.	‾But not ‚too ˚early, │ ‚am I?
There ˋmay be ˇmoney ˳snags.	‾They'll not ‚bother us ˚much, │ ‚will they?

19 Switchback │ Take-Off

QUESTION TAGS

The 'course ˚finished on ˋTuesday.	ˇWednesday, │ ‚wasn't it?
The train ˋstops there ˇsometimes.	ˇRarely, │ ‚does it?
‾Does he ‚ever lend a ˚hand?	ˇSome ˳days, │ ‚doesn't he?
'They won't beˋlieve you.	ˇYou ˳do, │ ‚don't you?
It be˳gins at 'two o‚clock.	ˇHalf past ˳two, │ ‚doesn't it?
I 'didn't know ˋanyone at the ˳party.	ˇMarjorie was ˳there, │ ‚wasn't she?
‚Why not ˚ask ˋGeorge?	ˇHe ˳won't ˳know, │ ‚will he?
He speaks 'French and I˚talian ˋfluently.	ˇGerman and I˳talian, you mean, │ ‚don't you?
He 'came ˚home last ˋFebruary.	You mean last ˇMarch, │ ‚don't you?
(‚Why didn't ˋAdrian ˳come?)	You ˇdid in˳vite him, │ ‚didn't you?
I ‚think they're ˋall ˳mine.	The ˇgreen one ˳isn't ˳yours, │ ‚is it?
● I ‚tell you I ˋneed it.	But ˋnot ˇurgently, │ ‚do you?
'What's so ˚special about toˋday?	You ˋhaven't forˇgotten, │ ‚have you? ‖ (It's your ‚mother's ˋbirthday.)
She 'speaks ˚French ˋfluently.	But with a ˋshocking ˚English ˇaccent, │ ‚doesn't she?
Well ‚what d'you ˋsay to my ˳offer?	I ˋneedn't ˚make up my ˚mind imˇmediately, │ ‚need I?
Have you 'heard about ˆFrank?	He ˋhasn't ˚failed his e˚xam aˇgain, │ ‚has he?

20 High Drop | Take-Off

Verbal context

Drill

● 'Would you °like to ,come?
Ciga'rette, °Julian?
'What can I °do for `you, sir?
Would you 'care for some °more ,tea?
'Can I °lend you a ,hand?

`Yes, | ,please.
`No, | ,thanks. ‖ (I've 'just °put one `out.)
I'd 'like a °box of `chocolates, | ,please.
I've 'still `got some, | ,thank you.
I've 'just this °minute `finished, | ,thank you
   ₒvery ,much.

● He 'made me feel °so at `ease.
'Jenny `gave it ₒto me.
⌐I don't know ,when I've ₒlaughed so
   ₒmuch.
(I 'can't think °where they've `got to.)

Yes he's a `nice chap, | ,John.
She's a 'very `kind ₒperson, | ,Jenny °is.

He tells a `very good ₒstory, | does ,Alfred.
They're 'usually °so re`liable, | the ,Smith
   °twins.

'Don't you ⌐like it?
'What's her `cooking ₒlike?
'Whose turn `is it, ₒthen?
'What's in the `bottle?
You'll be °going there `soon, | ,won't you?
⌐D'you ,have to °be there?
It 'looks like `rain, | I'm a,fraid.

I `don't, | ,frankly.
It's 'quite `good, | ,really.
`Mine, | ,actually.
`Whisky, | of ,course.
Yes on `Tuesday, | in ,fact.
`Yes, | con,found it.
Then 'let's stay at `home, | in ,that case.

● 'Shall we tell ,Ann?
'Any °news of ,Gerry?
'Whose fault `was it, ₒthen?
'Can I °sell you a ,ticket?
⌐Is it ,much °further?
'How many °times did he `do it?
'What's °happened to `Muriel?
'Why did he re`fuse?
You've got ,more than ,three, | ,haven't
   you?
'How much ma`terial does it ₒtake?

She al'ready `knows, | ap,parently.
He's 'not °seriously `hurt, | the ,doctor °says.
`Betty's, | in ,my o°pinion.
I've al'ready `got one, | as it ,happens.
A 'couple of `miles, | at a ,rough ,guess.
`Three ₒtimes, | ,more fool ,him.
She's re`signed, | ,so it ,seems.
He 'hadn't got `time, | ,so he ,said.

Yes `seven, | in ,point of ,fact.
'Three and a °half `yards, | as ,near as
   ,matters.

Verbal context	*Drill*
● 'Which one can I ˋtake?	You can take ˋboth, | as ˏfar as ˏI'm con-°cerned.
'What are you °doing this ˋevening?	We're 'not doing ˋanything, | as ˏfar as I ˏknow.
'What's the ˋweather ₒgoing to ₒdo?	It's 'going to ˋrain, | acˏcording to the ˏforecast.
● 'When will they get ˋback?	Toˋmorrow, | I ˏthink.
'How much ˋholiday will you ₒget?	'Three ˋweeks, | I ˏhope.
‾You ˏwill °meet them, | ˋwon't you?	I shall ˋhave to, | I supˏpose.
‾Well ˏwhere did you °have it ˋlast?	I don't reˋmember, | I'm aˏfraid.
'Who got the ˋgoal?	The 'left ˋwinger, | I beˏlieve.
'Who's the °best person to ˋask?	'Andy McˋMillan, | I should ˏsay.
‾Which ˏtrain's she °coming on?	The 'ten ˋthirty, | I iˏmagine.
● 'Any °news of ˊTim?	He's 'coming ˋhome | ˏsoon.
You 'said you °wouldn't ˋplay.	Well I ˋwant to, | ˏnow.
He ˋwasn't very °good ˇyesterday.	And he was 'even ˋworse | toˏday.
'How're you °getting ˋon, ₒJim?	It's my 'final eˋxam | toˏmorrow.
I ˏdidn't ₒknow you ˏsmoked.	Yes I ˋdo, | ˏsometimes.
So you enˋjoyed ₒgoing to the ₒclub.	Yes and I'd 'like to go aˋgain | ˏsometime.
I saw ˋAlfred | ˏyesterday.	(How ˋnice!) || I 'don't sup°pose you ˋmeet very ₒoften | ˏnowadays.
'Why so ˋserious, ₒStephen?	I've got a ˋbone to ₒpick | with ˏyou.
'What's the ˋmatter?	It's a 'bit ˋchilly | in ˏhere.
● I ˏdon't think I'll ˏgo.	You 'said you ˋwould go, | ˏyesterday.
'When shall I ˋmeet you? || ˊFive?	Yes the 'meeting should be ˋover | by ˏthen.
'Why didn't you °buy one in ˋthis ₒcountry?	They're 'so much ˋcheaper, | in ˏFrance.
'How did ˋPeter reₒact?	He was 'frightfully ₒrude | to the ˏporter.
● 'Go by ˋbus.	It 'doesn't ˋrun | on ˏSundays.
‾D'you see ˏPaul these °days?	Yes I have ˋlunch with him | ocˏcasionally.
And 'what price ˋArthur?	We were 'all aˋstonished | by ˏhis per-°formance.
'Who'll °give me a ˋlift?	ˋI will, | if you ˏlike.
Shall I 'lend him ˏmine?	I'd be ˋawfully ₒgrateful, | if you ˏwould.
I 'thought of °going for a ˋwalk.	'I'll come ˋtoo, | if I ˏmay.
We had a ˋvery wet ₒfortnight.	(ˏHow ˋodd!) || 'Swiss weather's °pretty reˋliable, | in Juˏly.

Verbal context	*Drill*
Does the 'journey take ,that °long?	Yes it's a 'long `way, | to ,Wales.
Yes `that was ₀Andrew ,Brown.	(,Really?) ‖ I 'hardly `recognised him, | with his ,beard.
He's 'just become °managing di`rector.	Then I must con`gratulate him, | when I ,see him.
● ,Why bring a `mac?	It was `raining, | when I ,left this °morning.
‾Was he ,very °late?	Yes it was 'past `midnight, | ,when he came ,home.
I 'don't feel °very `well.	I should go `home then, | if I were ,you.
We `must suc₀ceed.	Yes it would be `awful, | if we ,failed.
(‿Sorry. ‖ I must `dash.)	I'm 'meeting my °wife at Vic`toria | in ,ten ,minutes.
How's `Rachel getting ₀on?	She's 'off to °South A`merica | in a ,month's ,time.
('Get on to `Jackson.)	You `can't go ₀wrong, | if you con,vince ,him.
You're a 'bit disap`pointed ₀then.	Yes I'd 'hoped to have `done the ₀job | by this ,after,noon.
● Well when `did he re₀tire?	'Sometime °last `Spring, | if I re,member ,rightly.
Is 'this the °biggest you've ,got?	No there's a `bigger one | on the ,kitchen ,table.
It 'must have been a `great ₀shock, | ,Peter's ,death.	Yes I was 'talking to him on the `phone, | ,yesterday ,morning.
‾But ,how can you af`ford to ₀stay at the ₀Grand?	Well it's 'not so °terribly ex`pensive, | ,out of the ,season.
'How're they `going?	They 'think they might `fly, | as ,far as New ,York.
● 'Who's `that?	'Andrew `Black, | I ,think his ,name is.
I'll 'bring it °round my`self.	('Thank you.) ‖ It's `good of you | to ,take so much ,trouble °over it.
He was com'plaining to the `manager.	It's `silly, | to ,make such a ,fuss.
I felt `very ₀sorry for ₀Tom.	Yes it was a `shame | he ,had to give ,up.
'Don't be °so im`patient.	But it's a `nuisance, | ,having to ₀wait so ₀long for ,Gerry.

Verbal context	*Drill*
⁻Did you ˎsay °anything to °Jim?	No I 'thought it °wouldn't be `kind │ to reˎmind him aₒgain so ˎsoon.
('How about °going in the `spring?)	It would be 'quite a `change │ to have an ˌearly ˌholiday.
⁻Whyˎever °go by `boat? ‖ It's so `slow.	Well it 'rather up`sets me, │ ˌtravelling by ˌair.
You `like ₒstaying with your ˎcousins, │ ˎdon't you?	Yes it's 'such `fun, │ ˌhelping them in their ˎshop.
● 'Why've you `moved?	It was so 'dreadfully ex`pensive, │ ˌliving in ₒcentral ˎLondon.
● I 'had to °cope a`lone.	It's a `pity │ you ˎdidn't ₒmention it ˎearlier. ‖ ('I could have `helped.)
He 'had to °leave at `seven.	It was a `shame │ he ˎcouldn't have ₒwaited aₒnother five ˎminutes.
'Why are you °looking so `miserable?	It's so `boring, │ ˌbeing at ₒhome aˎlone all °day.
⁻Oh I ˎam ₒsleepy!	(And no ^wonder!) ‖ It must have been `terribly faₒtiguing, │ ˌsitting in that ˎdeckchair °all °day.
● 'What shall I `do about those ₒshares? A 'letter °wouldn't be `quick enough.	`Sell them, │ of ˎcourse. 'Try getting him °on the `phone, │ in ˎthat case.
'What about the `pills? (The 'story's °still confi`dential.)	Take them 'six times a `day, │ to beˎgin with. So 'keep it °under your `hat, │ for the ˎmoment.
He in`sists on ₒdoing it aₒlone.	Well 'let him get `on with it, │ for the ˌtime ˎbeing.
'What shall I `do with it?	'Hang °on to it till `Monday, │ if ˎthat's ˎpossible.
● ⁻Whatˎever shall I `do? I `don't like °leaving the ˇJanes ₒout.	'Carry °on as `usual, │ if you ˎpossibly ˎcan. Well 'go a°head and in`vite them, │ if you ˌfeel you ˎmust.
'What shall I `say to them?	Don't say 'anything at `all, │ unless you ˌreally ˎhave to.
'When d'you °want me to `start?	Start 'right a`way, │ if ˎthat's conˎvenient °for you.

Verbal context	Drill
'Here I °am at ˌlast.	‛Hullo, | ˌStephen. ‖ ('Nice to ‛see you.)
'Now I °really ‛must ˳fly.	Well ‛goodbye, | ˌMabel. ‖ ('Have a good ˌtime.)

21   Long Jump | Take-Off

ADDED COMMENTS, RESTRICTIONS, CLARIFICATIONS

I ˌthought you °went by ‛car.	ˌSo I ‛do, | ˌnormally.
'What's to be ‛done?	You ˌought to °stay at ‛home, | of ˌcourse.
D'you 'like my °new ˌshirt, °Ann?	I ˌcan't say I ‛do, | parˌticularly.
And 'this is ‛Tommy's ˳drawing.	You know it's ˌrather ‛good, | for a ˌsix year °old.
'How many can I ‛have?	You can have as ˌmany as you ‛like, | so ˌfar as ˌwe're con°cerned.
⁻But you ˌsaid he was in ‛Canada.	ˌSo he ‛was, | the ˌlast time I ˌheard from him.
'Haven't you °nearly ˌfinished it?	I've ˌonly °just be‛gun it, | as a ˌmatter of ˌfact.
● But what ‛difference does it ˳make?	ˌAll the °difference in the ‛world, | if you ˌdon't ˳mind my ˌsaying °so.
'How did you get ‛on with him?	ˌRather ‛well, | ˌstrange as it ˳may ˳seem ˌnow.
You really ‛shouldn't have been so ˳cross with him.	But it was so ˌterribly ‛childish, | making ˌall that ˳fuss about a ˳broken ˌwindow.

22   High Drop | Switchback

ADDED COMMENTS, RESTRICTIONS, CLARIFICATIONS

'How much did ‛George ˳know?	‛Nothing, | his ˇbrother ˳says.
Well who ‛was to ˳blame?	‛Johnson, | in ˇmy oˌpinion.
'What was °Joan's re‛action?	She'd 'never ‛seen it beˌfore, | ˟so she ˇsaid.
● Does he 'still °work at ˌAshby's?	'Yes he ‛does, | as ˟far as I ˇknow.

Verbal context	*Drill*
It's 'raining °harder than ‘ever.	And by 'now it °should have cleared ‘up, | ac‘cording to the ˇweather ₒmen.
'How °many have you ‘got?	A 'couple of ‘dozen, | I ˇthink.
'Any °news of ′Anthony?	He'll be 'home to‘morrow, | I ˇhope.
'Can you ,manage it?	I ‘must ₒmanage it, | ˇsomehow.
'Don't you °go by ,underground?	I ‘do, | ˇusually.
'Didn't you °say you °couldn't ,play?	I ‘couldn't, | ˇyesterday.
I ,thought you °didn't ‘take ₒsugar.	I ‘don't ₒtake it, | in ˇtea.
'Larry's playing °Hamlet and ‘Bottom.	He'll be ‘terrible, | as ˇHamlet.
I 'thought you °said he was ‘ill.	'So he ‘was, | two ˇdays aₒgo.
You 'asked °Fred to ′give you the °money?	Yes he 'wouldn't a‘gree, | to ˇthat at ₒany rate.
,Come ,on. || ,Who'll volun‘teer?	‘I will, | if you inˇsist.
'Didn't you °have your °usual ,swim?	'No I ‘didn't, | not this ˇmorning.
He 'couldn't have been ‘pleasanter.	ₒGeorge can be 'absolutely ‘charming, | when he ˇchooses to ₒbe.
⁻But I ,thought you °didn't ‘eat ₒbreakfast.	I ‘don't, | during the ˇweek.
Well 'how often ‘do you ₒvisit her?	'Every ‘week, | as a ‘general ˇrule.
● 'Let's go and °see Pyg‘malion.	'Not a ‘hope, | un‘less you've al°ready ˇbooked.
'What are you ‘doing toₒmorrow ₒevening?	We're 'going to the ‘theatre, | if Don ‘doesn't have to °work ˇlate.
'Why don't you °go to ‘bed?	I ‘will, | if you ‘don't mind °doing the °washing ˇup.

23 High Drop | High Drop

⁻May I ,borrow this a °moment?	‘Yes, | ‘do.
'Shall we have a °game of ,tennis?	‘Yes, | ‘let's.
ₒMax was 'very ‘obstinate.	Then ‘you be ₒobstinate, | ‘too.
I 'don't see °any ‘point in it.	‘I don't, | ‘either.
'What did he ‘say aₒbout it?	He was ‘sorry, | ‘very.
And 'how about ‘Gerry?	He ‘didn't ₒcome, | ‘after ₒall.

Verbal context	*Drill*
'What about `Alice?	'She'll get a `free ₒcopy, | `naturally.
So you 'weren't °able to `go to the ₒcinema.	No but I'd `seen the ₒfilm, | `anyway.
'Why are you so `late?	I 'had to `work ₒlate, | `honestly.
'How did °Andrew re`act?	He was 'very up`set, | `obviously.
You ˏdon't `care for it ₒmuch, | `do you?	I 'like it a `lot, | `really I ₒdo.
When `will you ₒask him, ₒthen?	I'll in`vite him on `Sunday, | `honest I ₒwill.
● ¯Don't you ˏlike it?	`No, | I `don't.
'Does he write ˏoften?	`Yes, | he `does.
I 'wonder why `Jill didn't ₒcome.	You in`vited her, | of `course.
'Where's `Peter?	He's 'gone to `Manchester, | on `business.
Well when `can I ₒhave it?	I'll 'bring it to`morrow, | I `promise.
● You 'say you °gave it ˏback to him?	It's the 'absolute `truth, | I `swear it.
('That's ˏAlan.)	And 'this is `Charles, | my `elder ₒboy.
'Where does he `live?	In `Essex, | near `Chelmsford, I ₒthink.
'How's `Freda ₒgetting ₒon?	Her 'arm `isn't ₒbroken, | after `all.
You 'really °can't ˏlend me a °copy?	No this is the 'only °one I've `got, | I as`sure you.
¯Does he ˏknow?	`Surely, | he `must ₒknow.
I 'don't think I'll ˏanswer her ₒletter.	`Really, | you `must ₒanswer it.
'Thursday's im`possible.	`Well, then, | 'how about the `next day?
● ₒMabel was `very an`noyed.	`Naturally, | she `would be.
'How °many shall we `take?	`Obviously, | we shall need 'all we pos`sess.
I `can't be °there by `ten.	Well `anyway, | 'come as °soon as you `can.
(You `must ₒcome. || You'll `love the ₒpeople ₒthere.)	And be`sides, | I 'don't want to °go on my `own.
So you didn't `like the ₒpudding.	On the `contrary, | I `loved it.
('Thank you. || I'd `love to ₒcome and ₒmeet the ₒfamily.)	
(I was sur'prised he `asked me ₒfor it.)	'By the `way, | 'where d'you `live?
	'After `all, | it 'wasn't as °if he `needed it.

VI Dialogues for Intonation Practice

1 'Did you see O,thello on °television °last °night? ‖ — The
'opera, you ₒmean. ‖ 'No, | I 'didn't. ‖ I was 'out. ‖ — ˇI ₒsaw
it, | and 'quite en'joyed it. ‖ — ,Did you? ‖ I ,thought you
°didn't ap'prove of ₒtelevision. ‖ — I 'don't, | as a ,regular
,thing. ‖ But I 'happened to be °round at my ˇsister's, | and
ˇshe ₒwanted to ₒsee it. ‖ So 'I watched it 'too. ‖ — Have you
'thought any °more about ,getting a °set? ‖ — ,No, | I ,don't
think I ,shall. ‖ Though there's a 'good deal of ˇpressure, of
ₒcourse. ‖ — From your 'family? ‖ — From my 'daughter, |
in par'ticular. ‖ 'All her 'school friends ₒtalk about it so
ₒmuch. ‖ — 'I ,know. ‖ You'd ₒthink they 'never did °any-
thing ,else | but sit 'glued to the 'television ₒscreen. ‖ —That's
'mostly what I ob'ject to, | the 'time it ₒwastes. ‖ — It 'isn't
the ˇtelevision that ₒwastes the ₒtime. ‖ It's 'you. ‖ — I 'know
ˇthat. ‖ But I have a 'deep dis,trust of my₀self. ‖ So it's
'probably ›better | to a'void the oc'casion of ₒsin. ‖ 'Don't
you 'think? ‖

2 I 'say, | ,Arthur. ‖ 'Seen anything of °Jack ,Taylor °recently? ‖
— 'Naylor, did you °say? ‖ — No, 'Taylor. ‖ With a 'T. ‖
— 'Who's 'that? ‖ — Oh, ,you re₀member ,him. ‖ The 'man
who °gave you those 'driving ₒlessons, | 'just be°fore your
'test. ‖ — Oh, 'him! ‖ 'No, | I 'haven't, I'm a₀fraid. ‖ ,Why
d'you 'ask? ‖ — Well I was ˇwondering | if he'd got 'any °free
'time during the ₒnext few ₒweeks. ‖ — But you ,don't need
ₒmore ,lessons, °do you? ‖ I ,thought you 'passed your ₒtest. ‖
— 'So I 'did, | 'just after 'Christmas. ‖ No, ˇI don't ₒneed
,lessons. ‖ My 'sister 'Janet ₒdoes. ‖ — ,Oh? ‖ But 'didn't you
°say your ,father was °teaching her? ‖ — He ˇwas. ‖ But he
'couldn't °stand the 'pace. ‖ — 'Couldn't °stand the 'pace? ‖
'How's 'that? ‖ Janet ,mustn't go ₒfaster than ,thirty, |
'surely. ‖ She's a 'learner. ‖ — Oh, but 'you don't know
'Janet! ‖ At least 'not as a ˇdriver. ‖ ⁻She's got ,no i°dea of
275

°speed at ˋall. ‖ — You ₒmean she ʹreally ˏdoes °drive too
°fast? ‖ — ˇI'll say she ₒdoes! ‖ ʹEvery bit of ˇpractice, ‖
‾well it's ˏmore like an °inter°national ˋcar race. ‖ It just
ʹdoesn't ocˋcur to her │ that ʹgoing ˎfast │ can be ˋdangerous. ‖
— Well, ˋanyway, │ she sounds ˇconfident. ‖ — ˇConfident! ‖
ʹThat's °putting it ˋmildly. ‖ — And ˎconfidence │ ʹnot
°shared by ˋfather, I ₒgather. ‖ — ʹNot °one ˋbit! ‖ ˇSometimes, │ after an ˋhour's ˇdriving ₒwith her, │ he's ˏcome home
ˋpetrified! ‖ — And ʹnow he's re°fused to go ˋout with her
aₒgain? ‖ — Yes, but ˋnot be°cause of her ˇspeeding. ‖ —
Well, then, ˏwhy ˋdid he cry ₒoff? ‖ — Because when he ˋgot
back from ˇwork ₒyesterday │ the ʹengine was in ˋbits. ‖ —
Had ˏJanet had an ˏaccident? ‖ — ˏNo. ‖ She'd ʹmerely
deˋcided │ to ʹsee how things ˎwork │ ʹunder the ˎbonnet. ‖ —
Does she ˎknow °anything about °car °engines? ‖ — ˏNot a
ˋthing! ‖ ʹDad was ˎvery upₒset, │ as you can iˎmagine. ‖ —
ˋYes, │ he ˋwould be. ‖ It's his ʹone °real ˋjoy in ₒlife, │ that
ˏcar of his, │ ˋisn't it? ‖ — Well, ˋanyway, │ ʹthat was the °last
ˎstraw. ‖ ʹNo more °use of the ˎcar ₒfor her │ till she'd ʹpassed
her ˎtest. ‖ 'And you'd ʹbetter start ˎlooking │ for aʹnother
inˎstructor,' he ₒsaid. ‖ — And you ʹthought of °poor old
ˇTaylor. ‖ ʹLet's hope his ˇnerves'll ₒstand it. ‖ ˋAnd his
inˏsurance! ‖

3   ʹWhat ˎis there about ₒCopenₒhagen │ that ʹmakes you keep
°going ˎback there? ‖ — Well, it's ʹrather °difficult to ˋanalyse. ‖
ˇPartly the ₒplace itₒself. ‖ But ˇmostly, I supₒpose, │ the
ˋpeople. ‖ — You ˎlike the °Danes? ‖ — Oh, ˎvery ₒmuch. ‖ —
ˋWhy? ‖ ʹWhat is it that ˎmakes you ₒlike them? ‖ — I've
ˋoften ₒwondered ˏthat │ myˋself. ‖ They ʹseem to have a
°freshness of ˎmind, ‖ and a ˋgaiety, ‖ that's ʹmost atˎtractive. ‖
— Is ʹCopenhagen a °gay ˏcity, would you °say? ‖ — ˋYes, │ it
ˋis. ‖ But ˋdon't misunderˇstand me. ‖ It's ˋnot all cham°pagne
and ˇoysters. ‖ Or ʹeven °beer and ˋbonhomie! ‖ But ʹI've
always ˎfound it │ a ʹvery ˎhappy ₒplace. ‖ — ʹIsn't that a
°bit like ˏbeauty, °though, │ in the ʹeye of the beˎholder? ‖ I
mean, ʹmayn't you be pro°jecting your ˏown °pleasure │ on to

the 'city it‚self? ‖ — Oh, I'm ^sure. ‖ But ‚surely °that's what we `mean by a ₒhappy ₒplace. ‖ A place where we ʹhave been | and ʹcan be | `happy. ‖ — I'm 'not so `sure about ‚that. ‖ I ˇthink I can iₒmagine ₒsomewhere ‖ where ˟everything out-ˇside is ₒhappy, | but the ob'server's `miserable. ‖ — But then `surely, | ‚that's a °miserable `place. ‖ — De'pends how you de°fine your `terms. ‖ — Like 'everything `else, | `yes, | of `course. ‖ But ˟that's how ˇI would deₒfine it. ‖ And ˇTivoli | 'seems to ‚me | to be a 'very °good ‚symbol of ₒCopenₒhagen. ‖ — ʹTivoli? ‖ — `Yes. ‖ It's a 'sort of `pleasure ₒgarden, | 'right in the °very ‚centre of the ₒcity. ‖ — ʹRoundabouts and °things? ‖ — Well, ˇyes, | but 'much `more. ‖ `Restaurants, | and `gardens, | and ʹfountains, | and `lights, | and `theatres, | and `pantomime, | and `ballet, | and `music ₒhall. ‖ ˉIt's deₗlightful! ‖ 'Difficult to de°scribe `how deₒlightful. ‖ You must `go there | and 'see it for your`self. ‖ — I 'hope I shall be `able to, | ‚some °day. ‖ But ˟not ˇthis ₒyear. ‖ I've 'got to have a °wretched `chimney ₒknocked ₒdown | and 're`built. ‖ 'That'll °cost a `fortune. ‖ — ˉI can i^magine! ‖ ‚Still, | per'haps ‚next ₒyear. ‖

4 ˉD'you 'seriously ‚think | 'English'll be a °world ‚language °one °day? ‖ — I ‚think so, | `yes. ‖ Of ₒcourse, one ˟can't say ˇcertainly. ‖ There are 'too many `factors inₒvolved. ‖ But at ˟least it seems ˇlikely. ‖ — But ‚what about the `spelling? ‖ It's ‚so ap`palling. ‖ ‚No-one in their `senses, | `surely, | would ‚want to learn ₒEnglish ‚spelling, | ‚if they could a‚void it. ‖ — It's ‚not very ‚good, | `certainly. ‖ But in ˇtime, | it'll be `altered. ‖ — 'Who ‚by, I should ₒlike to ₒknow? ‖ — By `circumstances, | in ‚my o°pinion. ‖ I 'think it'll become `obvious, | 'even to `English ₒpeople, | that the 'spelling °simply `must be imₒproved. ‖ — I should have ˟thought if that were ˇgoing to ₒhappen | it would have 'happened al`ready. ‖ — ‚No. ‖ There are 'certain things °coming aˇlong | that'll make 'simplified ʹspelling | 'even `more deₒsirable. ‖ — 'Such ‚as? ‖ — Such as a `speech ₒrecogniser, for ₒinstance. ‖ — ˉA ‚what? ‖ — A `speech ₒrecogniser. ‖ A ma'chine that'll

°take dic,tation, as it °were | and im'mediately pro°duce a `typescript. ‖ — 'Is that ,feasible? ‖ — `Oh, | I ,think so. ‖ It's °certainly being ˅worked ₒon. ‖ And e˅ventually, | it'll be a `fact. ‖ — Yes, but 'where does °simplified `spelling come ₒin? ‖ — Well, if you °want the ma°chine to produce ˅ordinary ₒspelling, | it'll be a 'much more °complicated de`sign ₒjob. ‖ — So you °think it'll be to °everyone's ad˅vantage | to a'dopt the `simplified ₒstuff. ‖ — `Yes. ‖ — 'I think you're °opti-`mistic. ‖ — Well, 'come back in °twenty years' ,time, | and we'll `see. ‖

5   'Played any ´bridge °recently? ‖ — `No. ‖ 'Not for `ages. ‖ You see, it's 'difficult to get a `four, | ,nowadays. ‖ — 'How's `that? ‖ — Oh, 'didn't you ,know? ‖ 'Peter's `left us. ‖ — ,Left you? ‖ 'What's °happened to `him? ‖ — He's got a 'new ap°pointment in `Edinburgh. ‖ Be'ginning °last Oc`tober. ‖ — ,Really? ‖ `Oh, | of `course, | `yes. ‖ ˅I re₀member. ‖ Well, 'what about the `other ₒpeople ₒin the de₀partment? ‖ ¯Don't ,they °play? ‖ — 'None of them °seem at `all ₒkeen. ‖ — 'How disapˎpointing ₒfor you! ‖ You 'used to en`joy your ₒlunch-time ,games, | ,didn't you? ‖ — `Yes, | im`mensely. ‖ It was `great ₒfun. ‖ We in`variably ₒplayed the ₒsame ,four. ‖ And the 'same `partners, | ,usually. ‖ — So you °must have got to °know each other's ˅bidding | ex`tremely ₒwell. ‖ — Yes, our op˅ponents' | as `well as our ₒpartner's. ‖ — But 'didn't that °take some of the ,fun out of it? ‖ I mean, ^surely, ‖ if °everybody knew °who'd got ˅what, | there was 'no point in °playing the °cards at ^all! ‖ Or °not ˅much! ‖ — 'Don't you be^lieve it! ‖ For `one thing, | you could °never be °certain that °one of the ˅others, ‖ or 'all `three, | for ,that °matter, ‖ 'wasn't `bluffing. ‖ Or 'going `psychic. ‖ — 'Going ,psychic? ‖ What on ,earth does `that ₒmean? ‖ — Oh, ,you °know. ‖ 'Bidding the °cards you °hope your `partner's ₒgot. ‖ — You 'mean that °really ,happens? ‖ No `wonder I ₒnever ₒwon at ₒbridge! ‖ — So you see, we could °never be ˅quite sure of the ₒlie of the ₒcards, | in `spite of ₒall the con₀ventions we ₒliked to ₒthink we ₒplayed. ‖ — That's a`nother thing I could

₀never under₀stand. ‖ 'All those °wretched con'ventions! ‖ —
Oh, but they can be 'very 'helpful. ‖ — 'One or ˅two of
them, | per'haps. ‖ But ˅most con₀ventions, | ⁻well, they're
₀just a °lot of °mumbo 'jumbo. ‖ — ₐWhat d'you 'mean,
₀mumbo ₀jumbo? ‖ — Well, for ₀instance, calling 'two
˅hearts | when you've got 'only a °fair °hand in ˅diamonds |
seems 'plain 'crazy, | to ₐme. ‖ — Oh, 'come, ₀now. ‖ 'Don't
ex˅aggerate. ‖ 'Nobody plays a con₀vention like ₐthat. ‖ 'Not
even 'us. ‖ — Per'haps 'not. ‖ But 'why you don't ˅tell each
₀other | what ˅cards you've ₀got, | and have ˅done with it, |
I 'just don't 'know. ‖ — Because ₐthat would be 'cheating! ‖
Oh, you've been 'pulling my ˎleg. ‖ 'Still, | to ˅some ex₀tent, |
I aˆgree with you. ‖ — ⁻Aˎgree with me? ‖ ˎNever! ‖ — Yes,
'too many con'ventions by 'half. ‖ — And ˃some of them |
'pretty °senseless, 'too, | you 'must ad₀mit. ‖ — Well, ˅yes. ‖
And in 'any ₀case, | bridge is 'still a ₀game of ₐchance, | no
matter 'how ₀sensible its con₀ventions ₀may ₀be. ‖ Or 'sense-
'less, | for ₐthat °matter. ‖ 'After 'all, ‖ you can 'only °bid and
°play the °cards you're ˅dealt, | 'can't you? ‖ 'Care for a
ˊrubber? ‖

6   Oh, ˆthere you ₀are, ₀Peter! ‖ At ˆlast! ‖ — 'Sorry to be so
ₐlate, °Frank. ‖ I ex'pect you ˃thought | I was 'never ₀going to
turn ₀up. ‖ — Well, I'd be'gun to °have my ˅doubts, | I
'must ad₀mit. ‖ — Not 'half as °many as ˅me, | 'I'll be
₀bound! ‖ — And, you know, it's 'pretty 'chilly | ₌waiting
ₐhere. ‖ A˅nother °five ˅minutes | and I'd have 'needed
°treatment for ˆfrostbite! ‖ — Well, ₐwhy didn't you °wait in
the 'waiting₀room? ‖ You'd have been 'much warmer |
ₐthere. ‖ — 'No, I ˅wouldn't. ‖ The 'heating's ₀broken
₀down. ‖ 'Well, ₀now | ex'plain your₀self. ‖ 'What's been
°keeping you 'this ₀time? ‖ — Oh, it's 'been one of those
'days. ‖ 'Everything ₀seems to have gone ₀wrong. ‖ — ˆAll
your ₀days are ₀like that, | ˆsurely! ‖ — No, ˆhonestly! ‖
'Take this ˎmorning, for ₀instance. ‖ Aˎlarm clock ₀fails to go
₀off. ‖ 'Miss my ˎtrain. ‖ 'Late for the ₀office. ‖ 'Boss ˎearly for
₀once. ‖ 'Acid ˃comments | on per'sistent °unpunctuˎality. ‖

Un'pleasantness all ˏround. ‖ — Yes, but ˏthat was this ˋmorning. ‖ And in ˋany ˳case, | I ˏdon't sup˳pose you were an ˳hour late ˏthen, | ˏwere you? ‖ — Oh, ˋdon't rub it ˏin. ‖ And 'don't ex^aggerate, | ^either! ‖ —¯Ex ˏaggerate? ‖ 'Who's ex ˋaggerating? ‖ — ˋYou ˳are. ‖ It's ˇless than an ˳hour I'm late, | ˏactually. ‖ 'Fifty ˋminutes, | ap ˏproximately. ‖ —^Very ap˳proximately. ‖ ˇI ˳make it | fifty ^eight ˳minutes, | pre-^cisely! ‖ — Well, ˋmaybe it ˇwas a ˳bit more than ˳fifty. ‖ And in ˋany ˳case, | you're ˋperfectly ˇright. ‖ I ˋwasn't ˳that much ˳late this ˳morning. ‖ — ¯Well, ˏwhy so °late ˋnow, ˳then? ‖ — As I ˋsay, | it's been 'one of those ˋdays. ‖ A 'bad ˏstart | which 'nothing can re ˏtrieve. ‖ — But you 'battled on ˏvaliantly | against 'all the ˏodds. ‖ — ^Naturally! ‖ 'Hour after ˋhour, | 'working my °fingers to the ˏbone. ‖ A ˏmere half ˳hour for ˏtea, | and 'there I ˋwas, | 'work up to ˋdate | and 'ready to ˏleave. ‖ At 'five ˏsharp. ‖ ˋThen ˳what d'you sup˳pose ˳happened? ‖ — 'No i ˏdea! ‖ — I was ˋcollared. ‖ 'Well and °truly ˏcollared. ‖ — Who ˋby? ‖ — By the 'office °shaggy ˏdog. ‖ — ¯By ˏwho? ‖ — The 'office ... | — Oh, you mean, 'Bill ˋWhatsisname. ‖ ˋAnstruther, | ˏisn't it? ‖ — Yes, ˋthat's ˏhim. ‖ He's the o ˋriginal ˳shaggy ˳dog, | he ˋmust be. ‖ They go ˋon, | and ˋon, | and ˏon. ‖ His ˋstories, I ˳mean. ‖ — 'Which one ˋthis time? ‖ — The 'one about the ˋparrot | that 'plays the pi ˋano. ‖ — ˋNot very a ˇmusing, | ˋI ˳bet. ‖ — Oh, ˇquite a˳musing. ‖ That is, if you ˋhaven't °heard it be ˇfore. ‖ And 'I ˋhave, of ˳course. ‖ On ˋvarious oc˳casions. ‖ 'All °ten ˋminutes ˳of it! ‖ — So by the ˋtime he'd °dotted the °last ˇi | and ˋcrossed the °last ˇt, | ˋgoodness knows ˇhow many ˳times, | you'd ... | — Yes, you're 'abso-lutely ˏright! ‖ I'd 'missed my ˏtrain. ‖ For the ˋsecond ˳time to˳day. ‖ ˋVery frus˳trating! ‖ ¯Which re ˏminds me. ‖ 'Like to ˊhear about the pi°ano-playing °parrot? ‖

7   Have you 'ever done any ˋwork | with syn'thetic ˏspeech? ‖ — ˋYes, | a 'fair a ˋmount, | ˏactually. ‖ — ¯Does it 'really ˋmean | that ma'chines ˏtalk? ‖ — Well, it de'pends what you °mean by ˋtalk. ‖ ˋCertainly the ma°chines produce °sentences

elec˅tronically. ‖ — ^Do they, ₒnow? ‖ 'What does it ˋsound ₒlike? ‖ — Well, aˋgain, | it deˋpends. ‖ ˈIf you're °trying °really ˅hard | you can ˈget it °fairly ˋlifelike. ‖ — Well, ˈisn't °that what you ˌwant? ‖ — ˈNot ˋnecessarily. ‖ You see, we ˈuse them to °try and find ˋout about ₒspeech. ‖ And the ˋsort of °question we ˅ask them | is how ˅little they can ₒdo | and ˈstill produce °something inˋtelligible. ‖ — I'm aˈfraid I °don't ˋfollow ˌthat. ‖ — Well, the ˋsounds °made by a ˅human ₒvoice | are eˈnormously ˎcomplex. ‖ And a ˅lot of the ₒinforₒmation they conₒvey | is ˈpurely ˎpersonal. ‖ — You mean, like what ˋsex the ₒspeaker ₒis? ‖ What ˋage? ‖ Where ˋfrom? ‖ ˈThings like ˋthat? ‖ — ˋRight. ‖ And what ˅we'd like to ₒknow | is ˋwhether you can get ˅rid of these ₒpersonal ₒfeatures | and ˈstill conˋvey inforˋmation. ‖ — I ˋsee. ‖ And you ˈcan't ˋdo this | with a ˌhuman °voice. ‖ So you ˈuse the maˋchines. ‖ — ˈThat's ˌit. ‖ It's ˈso much °easier to conˋtrol them. ‖ — And ˈthat's why they °don't sound very ˋlifelike. ‖ — Eˋxactly. ‖ — I'd ˈlike to ˋlisten to ₒone of them, | ˌsometime. ‖ — ˅That's ₒnot ₒdifficult. ‖ ˈCome aˋlong ₒone ₒday, | and I'll ˈintroˋduce you. ‖

8   ˈFeel like a °trip up to ˌTown this °morning? ‖ — ˌTown? ‖ ˉThis ˌmorning? ‖ But how ˋcan we? ‖ ˈYou've got an ap°pointment with ˋJackson, | at his ˋoffice, | at eˌleven ˌthirty, °haven't you? ‖ — No, ˈnot ˌnow. ‖ I ˅did ₒhave. ‖ But a few ˅moments aₒgo | his ˈsecretary rang °up to ˋcancel it. ‖ ˈJackson's °down with ˋflu or ₒsomething, apₒparently. ‖ — ˌIs he? ‖ But ˌall the ˋsame, | ˌwhy the °sudden °urge to go to ˋLondon? ‖ — Well, I ˈthought it might °make a ˋchange. ‖ — Yes, but you were ˌsaying only ˌyesterday | ˌhow much you disˋlike the ₒbig ₒcity ₒnowadays. ‖ — ˋYes, | I ˋknow I ₒdid. ‖ But we're ˈboth ˋfree toₒday | ˌnow. ‖ And it oc˅curred to me | we ˈmight make a ˋstart | on the ˈChristmas ˎshopping. ‖ — ˈChristmas ˎshopping? ‖ ˈOh, ˌlord! ‖ ˌMust we? ‖ You ˋknow how I ˅hate ₒshopping, | at the ˋbest of ₒtimes. ‖ — I ˌdon't see °why you °make such a ˋfuss. ‖ You ˌhardly °ever ˋgo ₒshopping. ‖ — ˅Too often for ˅my ₒliking. ‖ And at

ˇChristmas ₒtime, | well, that's the 'absolute ˎend. ‖ 'Just
ˎthink | of 'all those °thousands of ˎpeople, | 'milling aˎbout |
in the 'Oxford Street ˎstores. ‖ And 'what are they ˎdoing? ‖ —
Well, what ˋare they ₒdoing? ‖ — Buying 'useless and ex-
°pensive ˎpresents. ‖ And 'who are they ˎfor, d'you supₒpose? ‖
— ˋAll right, | ˎScrooge. ‖ 'You ˎtell me ₒwho they're ₒfor. ‖ —
For un'grateful ˎrelatives | they're 'scarcely on ˎspeaking
terms ₒwith the ₒrest of the ₒyear! ‖ — To hear ˇyou ₒtalking, |
ˎanyone would °think you didn't ˋlike giving ₒChristmas
ₒpresents. ‖ ˎAnyway, | are you ˎcoming | or ˎnot? ‖ — But
ˎwhat's the ˋrush? ‖ We're ˎnot °out of Ocˋtober | ˎyet. ‖ And
'Christmas is °still a ˋlong way ₒoff, thank ₒgoodness. ‖ —
ˎWell! ‖ I 'like ˎthat! ‖ ˎLast °year, | when we ˎleft it till ₒearly
Deˎcember, | you comˎplained ˋbitterly. ‖ — ˎDid I? ‖ I
ˎdon't reˎmember. ‖ — You ˋknow you ₒdid. ‖ ˎWhat was it
you °said? ‖ 'Oh, ₒyes. ‖ 'Too many ˎpeople. ‖ 'Last minute
ˎrush. ‖ 'All the °best things ˎgone. ‖ And 'lord knows ˋwhat
ₒelse! ‖ — ˋAll °absoˋlutely ˇtrue, | you must aˋgree. ‖ — And
now ˎthis °year, | when I sugˎgest getting it ₒover ˎearly, |
ˋmore comₒplaints! ‖ ⁻I ˎmust ₒsay! ‖ There's 'no ˋpleasing
ˎsome °people! ‖ — Oh, ˎI'm not °difficult to °please. ‖ Just
'keep me °out of a ˋshop, | and I'm as 'happy as a ˎsandboy. ‖
Still, we'll ˋhave to get °down to it ˇsometime, I supₒpose. ‖
And ˋbetter °now than on °Christmas ˇEve, I ₒreckon. ‖ —
ˋJust as °well I don't °take you ˇseriously, | ˋisn't it? ‖ ˎAny-
way, | 'Christmas °shopping or ˎnot. ‖ I 'want to buy a °new
ˎcoat. ‖ — So ˋthat's why we're ₒgoing to ₒTown. ‖ I 'might
have ˎguessed. ‖ — ˎYes, ₒdear. ‖ ˋWhat time did you °say
you'd be °ready? ‖

9   'Isn't it exˎtraordinary | 'how sugˎgestible one ₒis? ‖ — No
^doubt! ‖ But 'what makes you °say so ˋnow? ‖ — Well, I was
re'cording a ˋtalk | this ˎmorning. ‖ For the 'B.B.ˋC. ‖ —
A'nother in your intoˋnation °series? ‖ — ˋYes. ‖ And we ˎhad
the ₒusual reˎhearsal | to ˎget the ˎtiming °right, and °so on. ‖
And 'that went ˋperfectly ₒwell. ‖ But as ˋsoon as I °knew it
was being reˇcorded, | I got as 'nervous as a ˎkitten. ‖ —

ˎYes. ‖ It's 'always the ˏsame. ‖ It 'isn't so ˎbad │ 'once you've got ˋstarted. ‖ What ˇI ˳hate │ is 'just beˋforehand. ‖ ˇYou ˳know. ‖ When the ˇchap in the °little °glass ˇbox ˳says . . . │ — '. . . We'll 'go aˎhead │ in 'ten ˎseconds │ from ˎnow.' ‖ 'I ˎknow! │ And it seems ˋhours │ before the ˏred ˏlight goes °on, │ ˋdoesn't it? ‖ — ^Hours! ‖ And 'does this °happen with ˏyou? ‖ I ˳always take a 'nice °deep ˏbreath, │ 'ready to ˏstart, │ 'much too ˋsoon. ‖ So I'm 'practically ˋsuffocating │ when the ˏtime ˏcomes. ‖ — ˋEither ˇthat │ or I 'hurriedly breathe ˏout │ at the 'very ˎmoment │ they 'put the ˋlight on. ‖ So I 'have to breathe ˋin aˏgain, │ 'just like a ˋsteamˏengine. ‖ — 'Oh, ˏlord! ‖ ˋTerrible! ‖ But at ˋleast they °do the re-°cordings on ˇtape ˏnowadays. ‖ — ˋYes, thank ˳goodness! ‖ 'I used to ˋhate it, │ in the ˏold °days, │ ˏwhen it was on ˏdisc. ‖ You'd get 'almost to the ˏend │ and 'then ˋfluff! ‖ — Or say e'xactly the °opposite of what you ˋshould. ‖ — ˋRight. ‖ And you ˳had to do the 'whole ˋdisc ˳over aˏgain. ‖ ˋNot just the ˇlast ˳bit. ‖ — 'I ˎknow! ‖ And the ˇmore °times it ˇhappened, │ the 'worse you ˋgot. ‖ — ˋYes. ‖ Until ˇfinally, │ you 'didn't know ˋwhat you were ˳reading. ‖ — Well, I sup'pose we °ought to be ˋgrateful for ˳tape, │ ˏreally. ‖

10 Hulˋlo, ˳George. ‖ 'Nice to ˋsee you aˏgain. ‖ 'Quite a ˋstranger, │ ˏthese °days, │ ˋaren't you? ‖ ‾Been aˏway or °something? ‖ — ˏNo. ‖ At ˋleast not ˇrecently. ‖ — ‾Well, ˏwhat have you been ˋup to, ˳then? ‖ We ˏhaven't °seen you °here for ˋages. ‖ — I ˋknow. ‖ But ˇsomehow, │ what with ˇone thing and aˇnother, ‖ I 'haven't had ˋtime for an ˳evening ˳out │ these ˏlast few ˏweeks. ‖ — ˏOh? ‖ ˏReally? ‖ How's ˋthat? ‖ — Well, to beˇgin ˳with, │ we're 'pretty °busy at the ˋoffice │ at the ˏmoment. ‖ — What, 'more than ˊusual? ‖ — Yes, we ˋare, │ ˏrather. ‖ ˇYou ˳know. ‖ 'All the °usual ˇyearly ˳business. ‖ — What, 'annual acˋcounts, │ ˋstockˏtaking, │ ˋthat sort of ˳thing? ‖ — ˋYes. ‖ And we've had a 'couple ot °rush ˋexport ˳orders to ˳cope with, │ as ˋwell. ‖ — So 'that's meant °working ˋlate ocˏcasionally, │ ˏhas it? ‖ — Oh, in-ˇvariably ˇtwo nights a ˳week. ‖ And ˇsome ˳weeks │ ^three

₀even. ‖ — But ‚what about the ˅other ₀evenings? ‖ ⁻You could have ‚spared us ₀one of ‚those, | ˅surely. ‖ — Well, as if ˅working °late at the ˅office weren't e₀nough, ‖ my ˅wife, | ‚bless her, | has 'taken it °into her ˃head | to 'do some in-°terior ‚decorating. ‖ 'Lounge and ‚dining₀room. ‖ 'Both at the °same ˅time! ‖ — And 'you've been °roped in to ^help! ‖ 'Poor °old ‚George! ‖ 'Rather over˅rated ₀pastimes, | ˅aren't they, | ‚painting and ‚wall°papering? ‖ — 'Very ^much ₀so. ‖ Though it 'wouldn't have °been so ˅bad | if it had °only been a °question of °paint and ˅paper. ‖ — Well, what ˅else have you ₀had to ₀do? ‖ — I've been 'stripping the ˅woodwork. ‖ With a ˅blowlamp! ‖ — ⁻With a ‚blowlamp? ‖ ˅That ₀can't have been ₀easy. ‖ — 'Under°statement of the ˅week, | ‚that is. ‖ The ˅times I've °scorched my ˅fingers, ‖ well, that's ˅nobody's ₀business. ‖ And just 'how I a˃voided | burning the ˅whole ˅house ₀down | I 'simply °can't ˅think! ‖ — ⁻But ‚why use a °blowlamp at ˅all? ‖ A ˅chemical ₀stripper | is 'just as ef₀ficient. ‖ And ‚much less ˅lethal. ‖ — 'That's what ˅I said. ‖ But my ˃wife | 'just °wouldn't ‚have it. ‖ — ⁻Why-‚ever ˅not? ‖ — Well, you see, her ˅favourite °do-it-your˅self ₀man | on the ˅radio ‖ is a 'devo°tee of the ‚lamp. ‖ So 'blow-lamp it °had to ‚be. ‖ — With 'you °cast as the ˅genie! ‖ — Yes, I never ˅did ₀fancy myself ₀much as A‚laddin! ‖

11 I 'really °don't see ˅why you're ₀so pessi₀mistic. ‖ — 'Don't you? ‖ ˅I ₀do. ‖ It was 'all very ˅well | in the ‚past. ‖ The tech˅niques of °mass per˅suasion | 'weren't so very °highly de˅veloped. ‖ But ˅nowadays, | what with 'moti°vational re-˃search | and ˅sub°liminal per˅ception, | 'men's °minds are so ˅vulnerable. ‖ — But they 'always ˅have been ₀vulnerable. ‖ There've ˅always been ₀mob ‚orators | and pro₀fessional per‚suaders. ‖ But they've ˅never been °able to ˅dominate | ˅all the °people ˅all the ₀time. ‖ — ⁻I a^gree with you. ‖ But the tech˅niques a°vailable ˅now | 'seem to °promise °just ˅that. ‖ — I 'think you °under˅estimate your ₀fellow ₀men. ‖ In ˅my ₀view, | they've got suf'ficient ˃sense | to see ˅through these ₀tricks. ‖ — ⁻But it ‚isn't a ˅matter of ₀sense. ‖ That's e‚xactly my ˋpoint. ‖ If ˋthings go °on as they ˅are | ‾we ‚shan't even °know we're ˋbeing per₀suaded. ‖ It ˋwon't be an ap°peal to ˅reason | or ˅sense. ‖ It'll be a di'rect °influencing of the subˋconscious ₀mind. ‖ — But that's e‚xactly what °mob °orators have ˋalways ₀done. ‖ They've ˋalways ap₀pealed to the sub₀conscious ₀mind. ‖ ˋNever to ˅reason. ‖ But 'even ˋso, | they ‚haven't been ₀able to ₀lead the ₀people by the ₀nose for ‚long. ‖ — ˋLong e˅nough. ‖ And it was 'only °intu'ition | ˅they were ₀working by. ‖ 'Now it's on a scien-ˋtific ₀basis. ‖ So 'goodness knows ˋwhat we can be per₀suaded to ac₀cept. ‖ And with'out even °knowing we're ˆbeing per-₀suaded. ‖ — 'So you °said beˋfore. ‖ But I ˋstill think you're ₀being ₀too pessi‚mistic. ‖ — But it's ˋhappening. ‖ In ˅ad-vertising, | eˋspecially. ‖ The ˅advertisers | are 'finding out our ˋreal ₀motives for pre₀ferring ₀one brand of ₀goods to a₀nother. ‖ And unˋless we've °studied the °advertisers' ˅methods, | we're 'quite unaˋware of ₀these ₀motives. ‖ — So in ˅your o₀pinion, | we ˅buy what₀ever it is | with'out having °made a ˅conscious ₀choice | at ˋall. ‖ — ˋYes, | I'm ˋsure we ₀do. ‖ And apˋply those °methods to ˅politics | and you can 'see the ˋdanger. ‖ ˋNow d'you ₀wonder I'm ₀pessi₀mistic? ‖

Glossary of Technical Terms

Accent: the means whereby a word is made to stand out in an utterance. Accent always entails the occurrence of a strong stress on the appropriate syllable of the accented word; and when this word contains the nucleus of the word group, accent is also shown by a change in pitch or by a sustention of pitch. See pp. 5 and 31.

Attitude: the feeling or sentiment which, with respect to the situation in which he finds himself, the speaker expresses by intonation rather than by words.

Compound Tune: a tune containing more than one nuclear tone.

Head: *either* that part of a word group which begins with the stressed syllable of the first accented word, not being the nucleus, and which ends with the syllable immediately preceding the nucleus; *or* the pitch pattern associated with that part of a word group. With the latter significance, a head can be one of four types: **Low, High** (when emphatic, called *Stepping*), **Falling** (when emphatic, called *Sliding*) and **Rising** (when emphatic, called *Climbing*). See pp. 17–22 and 37–38.

Nuclear Tone: the pitch treatment of the nucleus. There are seven types of nuclear tone: **Low Fall, High Fall, Rise-Fall, Low Rise, High Rise, Fall-Rise** and **Mid-Level.** See pp. 7–17.

Nucleus: the stressed syllable of the last accented word in a word group.

Pre-head: *either* the syllable(s) occurring before the stressed syllable of the first accented word in a word group; *or* the pitch pattern associated with these syllables. In the latter sense there are two types of pre-head: **Low** and **High.** See pp. 22–28.

Pre-nuclear Pattern: the pitch treatment of all words and syllables occurring before the nucleus.

Question Tag: for example, *won't she?, didn't they?, can't I?*

Rhythm: in English speech, shown by the tendency of stressed syllables in a word group to occur at approximately even intervals of time.

Simple Tune: a tune containing only one nuclear tone.

Stress: in a word group a syllable is stressed if it is said with markedly greater effort than some other syllables whether in the same or adjoining word group; stressed syllables often appear louder than unstressed ones, and they tend to occur at approximately equal intervals of time in a word group.

Tail: *either* all the syllables, stressed and unstressed, following the nucleus; *or* the pitch pattern associated with these syllables.

Tone Group: a group of tunes which, though intonationally not identical, all have one or more pitch features in common and all convey the same attitude on the part of the speaker. See pp. 39–45.

Tune: the complete pitch pattern of a word group.

Wh-Question: a question which needs a full answer, that is, which cannot sensibly be answered by *Yes* or *No* or their equivalent. This kind of question often begins with an interrogative word, such as *which, what, how.*

Word Group: a grammatically close-knit group of words which is coterminous with and unified by an intonation tune; it is often separated from a preceding or following word group by a pause of some kind. See p. 2.

Yes-No Question: a question which can be answered by *Yes* or *No* or their equivalent and which often begins with a special finite such as *can, will, did.*

PITCH FEATURES OF TONE GROUP (UNEMPHATIC)

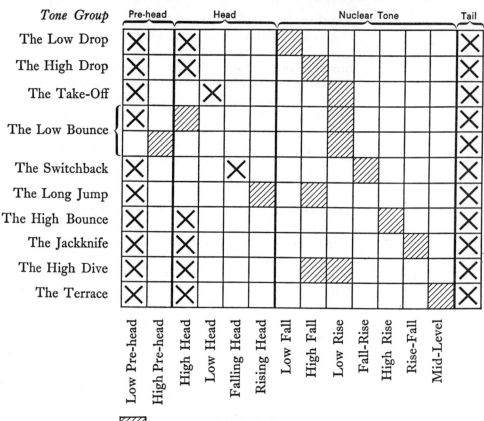

▨ an essential pitch feature of a tone group.

☒ a pitch feature that may occur in a tone group.

N.B. In all tone groups except the Take-Off and the Low Bounce the High Pre-head can be used instead of the Low Pre-head; its effect is to add emphasis to the utterance. In the Take-Off the high pre-head can be used for emphasis only when the tune also includes a Low Head. In the Low Bounce the High Pre-head can be used for emphasis only when the tune also includes a High Head.

288

Table of

Position in tune		Pitch	Diagram on page
[˅]	last syllable	Medium falling to very low.	15
	otherwise	Medium falling to very low; *or* medium level with following tail syllable(s) very low level.	15
[ˋ]	last syllable	High falling to very low.	15
	otherwise	High falling to very low; *or* high level with following tail syllable(s) very low level.	15
[ˆ]	last syllable	Medium rising to high, then falling to very low.	15
	last syllable but one	Medium rising to high with following tail syllable very low level; *or* medium level with following tail syllable falling from high to very low.	9
	otherwise	Medium rising to high with following tail syllables very low level; *or* medium level with first tail syllable high level and remaining tail syllable(s) very low level.	11
[˰]	last syllable	Very low rising to medium.	15
	otherwise	Very low level with following tail syllable(s) in an ascending pitch scale ending on medium pitch.	15
[ˊ]	last syllable	Medium rising to high.	16
	otherwise	Medium level with following tail syllable(s) in an ascending pitch scale ending on high pitch.	16
[˯]	last syllable	Moderately high falling to low, then rising to medium.	16
	otherwise	Moderately high falling to low with the following tail syllable(s) carrying rise to medium; *or* moderately high level with first tail syllable low level and remaining tail syllable(s) carrying rise to medium.	16, 17
			16
[ˀ]	all positions	Medium level with any following tail syllable(s) on same level.	16
[ˈ]	all positions	Relatively high level with any following pre-nuclear syllable(s) on same pitch.	19
[ˌ]	all positions	Very low level with any following pre-nuclear syllable(s) on same pitch.	19

Tone Marks

Position in tune	Pitch	Diagram on page
['] all positions	Relatively high level with any following pre-nuclear syllable(s) forming pitch scale descending to medium-low.	20
[,] all positions	Very low level with any following pre-nuclear syllable(s) forming pitch scale rising to pitch slightly lower than beginning of following ['].	21
[°] after [']	Relatively high level, same pitch as preceding ['].	• 20
after ['] [,]	Level, varying from relatively high to quite low and forming part of descending pitch scale indicated by ['] or of ascending pitch scale indicated by [,].	20, 21
after [,]	Level, varying from quite low to medium and always higher than [,] or [°] immediately preceding.	17
after [']	Level, varying from medium high to very high and always higher than ['] or [°] immediately preceding.	17
otherwise	Relatively high level.	27
[₀] last syllable after [ˇ]	Very low rising to medium.	17
before ['] [']	Level, varying from low to medium.	24
otherwise	Very low level.	16, 24
[‾]	All syllables following this tone-mark and preceding a head or, in its absence, a nuclear tone, have the same high level pitch.	
[	]	Indicates the end of a word group and its accompanying tune, after which there is little or no pause.	.
[‖]	Indicates the end of a word group and its accompanying tune, after which there is an appreciable pause.	

Except for [‾], [|] and [‖], all tone marks indicate a stressed syllable.

Except for [‾], [|], [‖], and for [°] and [₀] when occurring in pre-heads and tails, all tone marks indicate an accented word.

For the pitch of ['], ['] and [,] in emphatic word groups, see Chapter I, pp. 36–38.